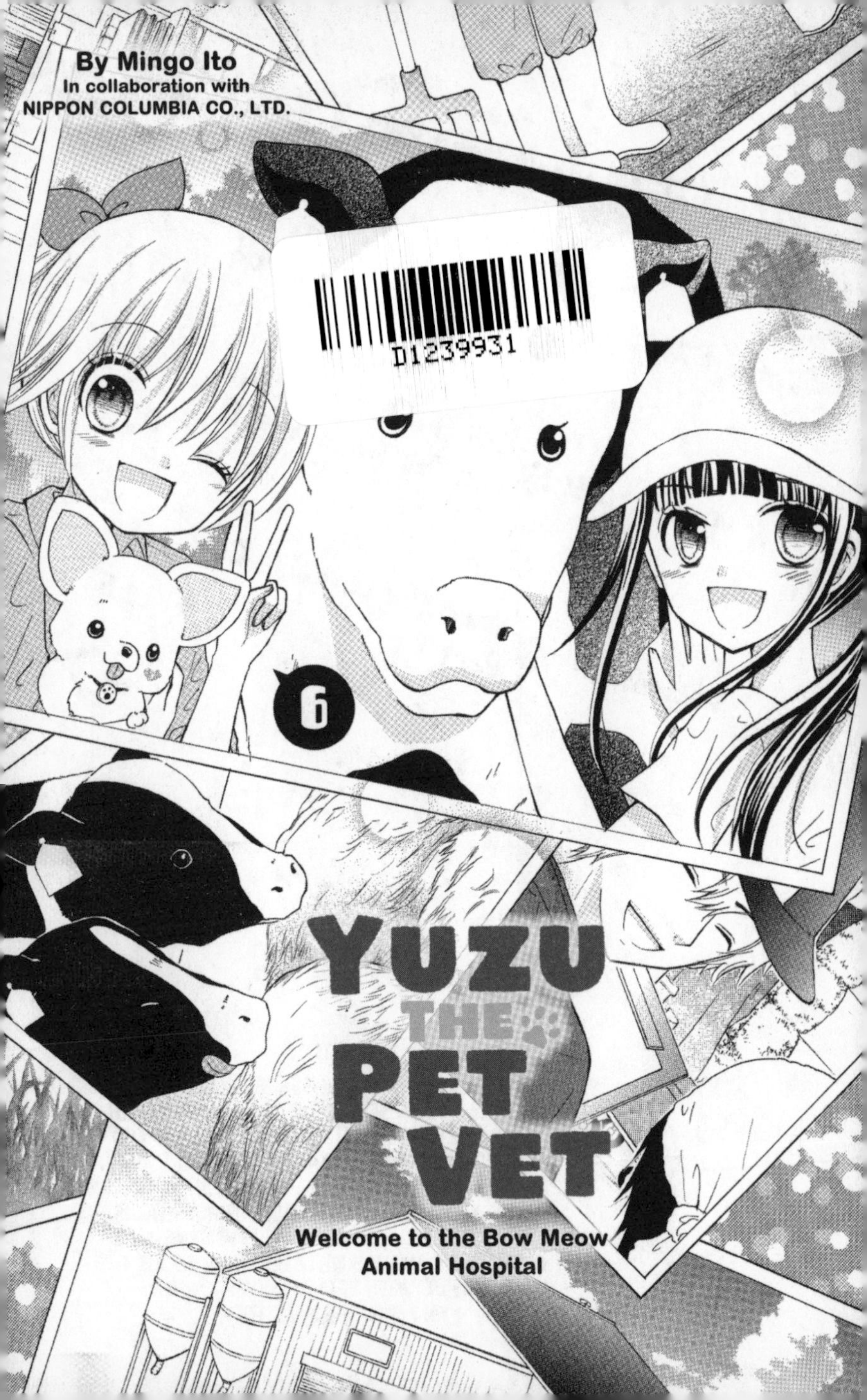
By Mingo Ito
In collaboration with
NIPPON COLUMBIA CO., LTD.
6
YUZU THE PET VET
Welcome to the Bow Meow
Animal Hospital

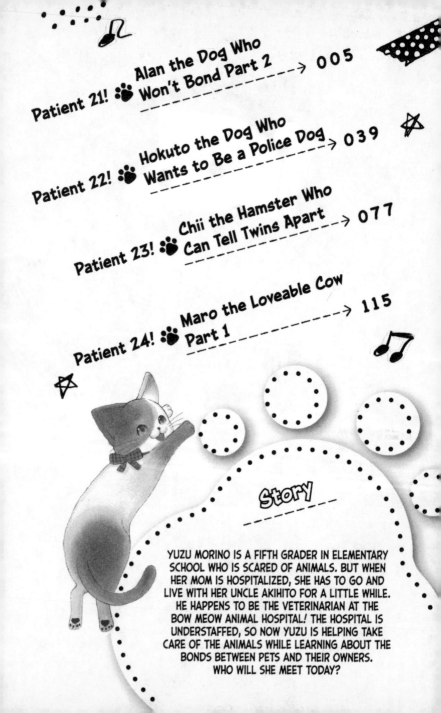

Story

YUZU MORINO IS A FIFTH GRADER IN ELEMENTARY SCHOOL WHO IS SCARED OF ANIMALS. BUT WHEN HER MOM IS HOSPITALIZED, SHE HAS TO GO AND LIVE WITH HER UNCLE AKIHITO FOR A LITTLE WHILE. HE HAPPENS TO BE THE VETERINARIAN AT THE BOW MEOW ANIMAL HOSPITAL! THE HOSPITAL IS UNDERSTAFFED, SO NOW YUZU IS HELPING TAKE CARE OF THE ANIMALS WHILE LEARNING ABOUT THE BONDS BETWEEN PETS AND THEIR OWNERS. WHO WILL SHE MEET TODAY?

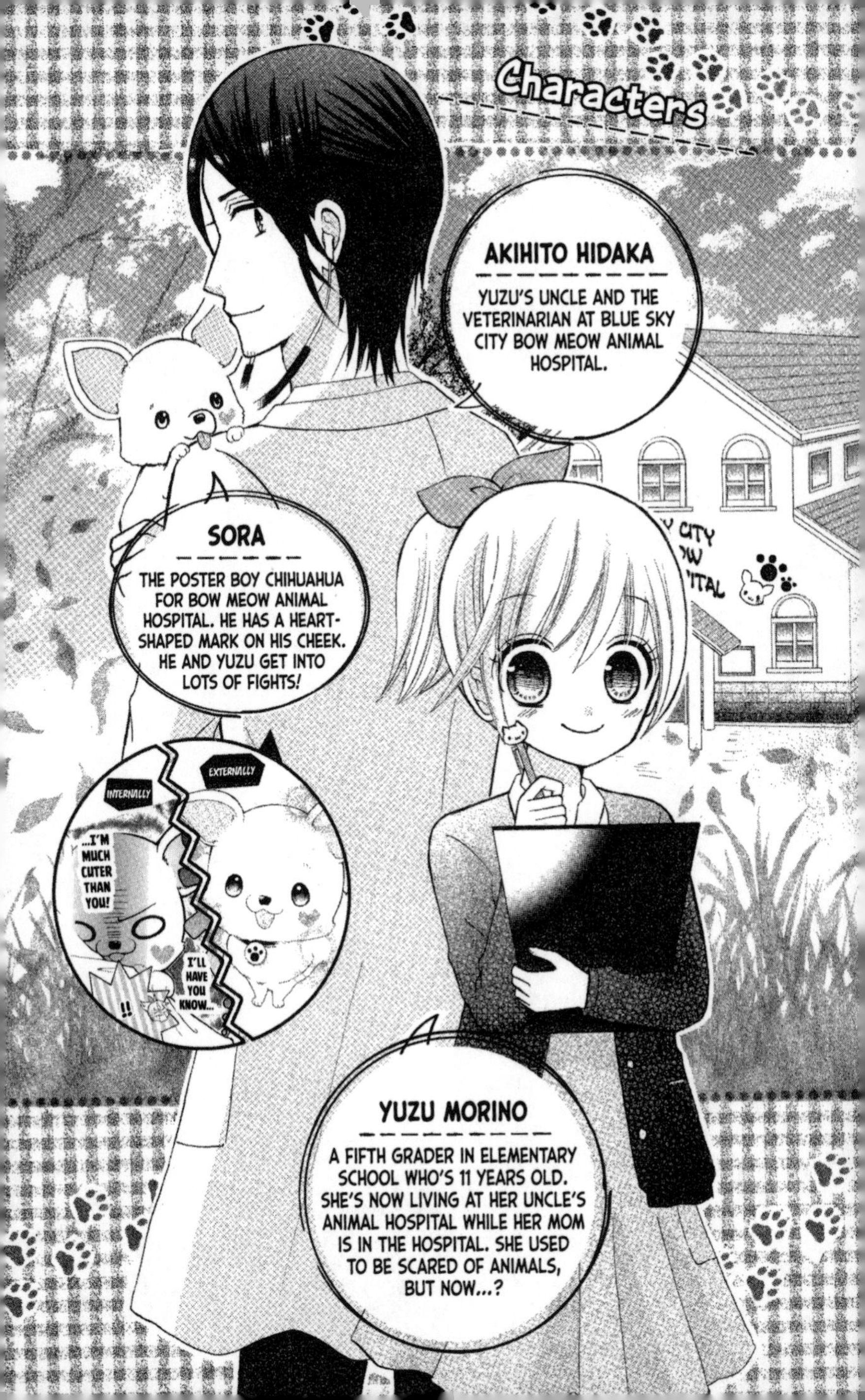
Characters
AKIHITO HIDAKA
YUZU'S UNCLE AND THE VETERINARIAN AT BLUE SKY CITY BOW MEOW ANIMAL HOSPITAL.
SORA
THE POSTER BOY CHIHUAHUA FOR BOW MEOW ANIMAL HOSPITAL. HE HAS A HEART-SHAPED MARK ON HIS CHEEK. HE AND YUZU GET INTO LOTS OF FIGHTS!
EXTERNALLY
I'LL HAVE YOU KNOW...
INTERNALLY
...I'M MUCH CUTER THAN YOU!
!!
YUZU MORINO
A FIFTH GRADER IN ELEMENTARY SCHOOL WHO'S 11 YEARS OLD. SHE'S NOW LIVING AT HER UNCLE'S ANIMAL HOSPITAL WHILE HER MOM IS IN THE HOSPITAL. SHE USED TO BE SCARED OF ANIMALS, BUT NOW...?

YUZU THE PET VET

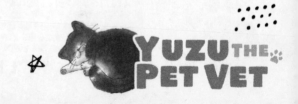

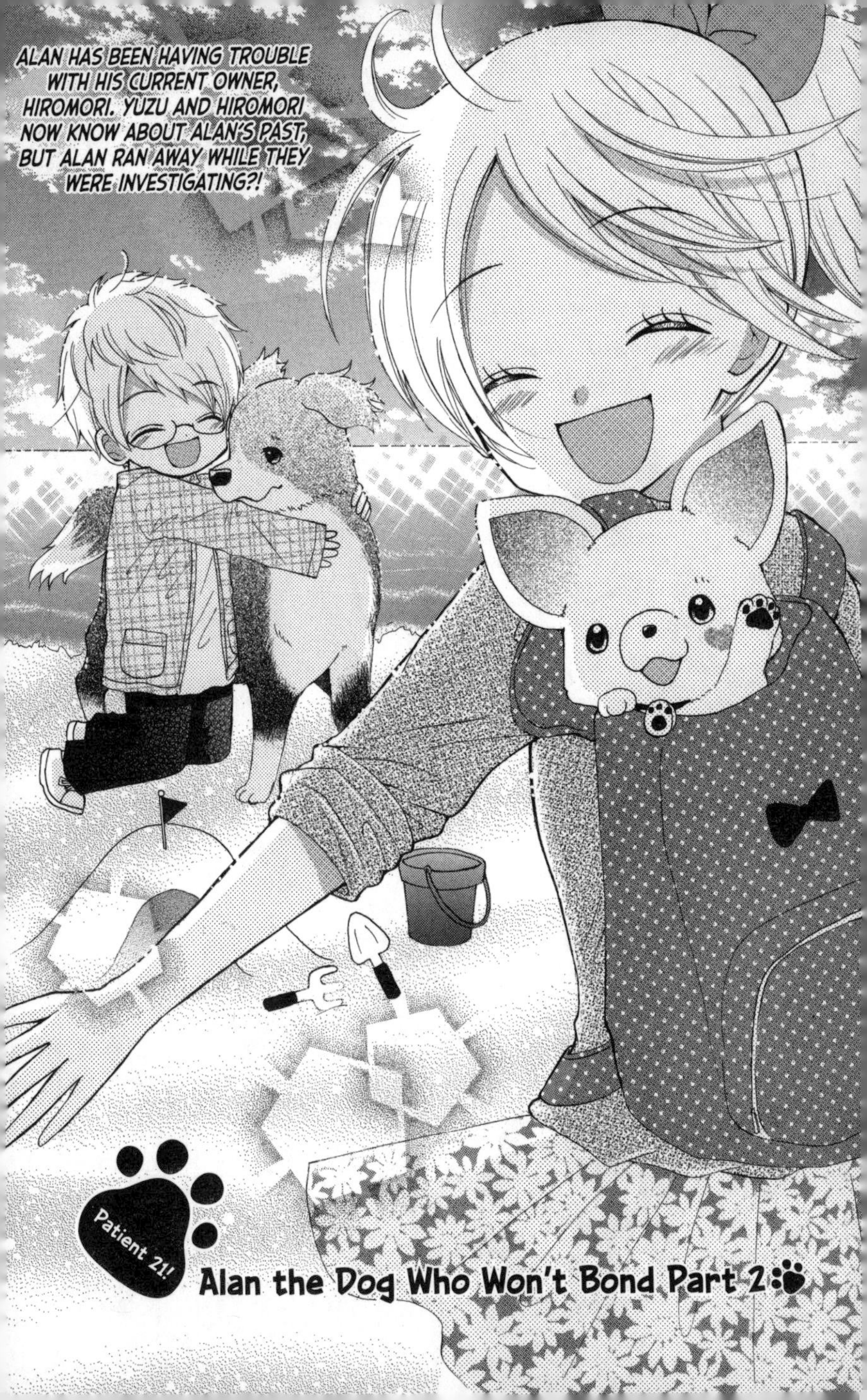
ALAN HAS BEEN HAVING TROUBLE WITH HIS CURRENT OWNER, HIROMORI. YUZU AND HIROMORI NOW KNOW ABOUT ALAN'S PAST, BUT ALAN RAN AWAY WHILE THEY WERE INVESTIGATING?!
Patient 21!
Alan the Dog Who Won't Bond Part 2

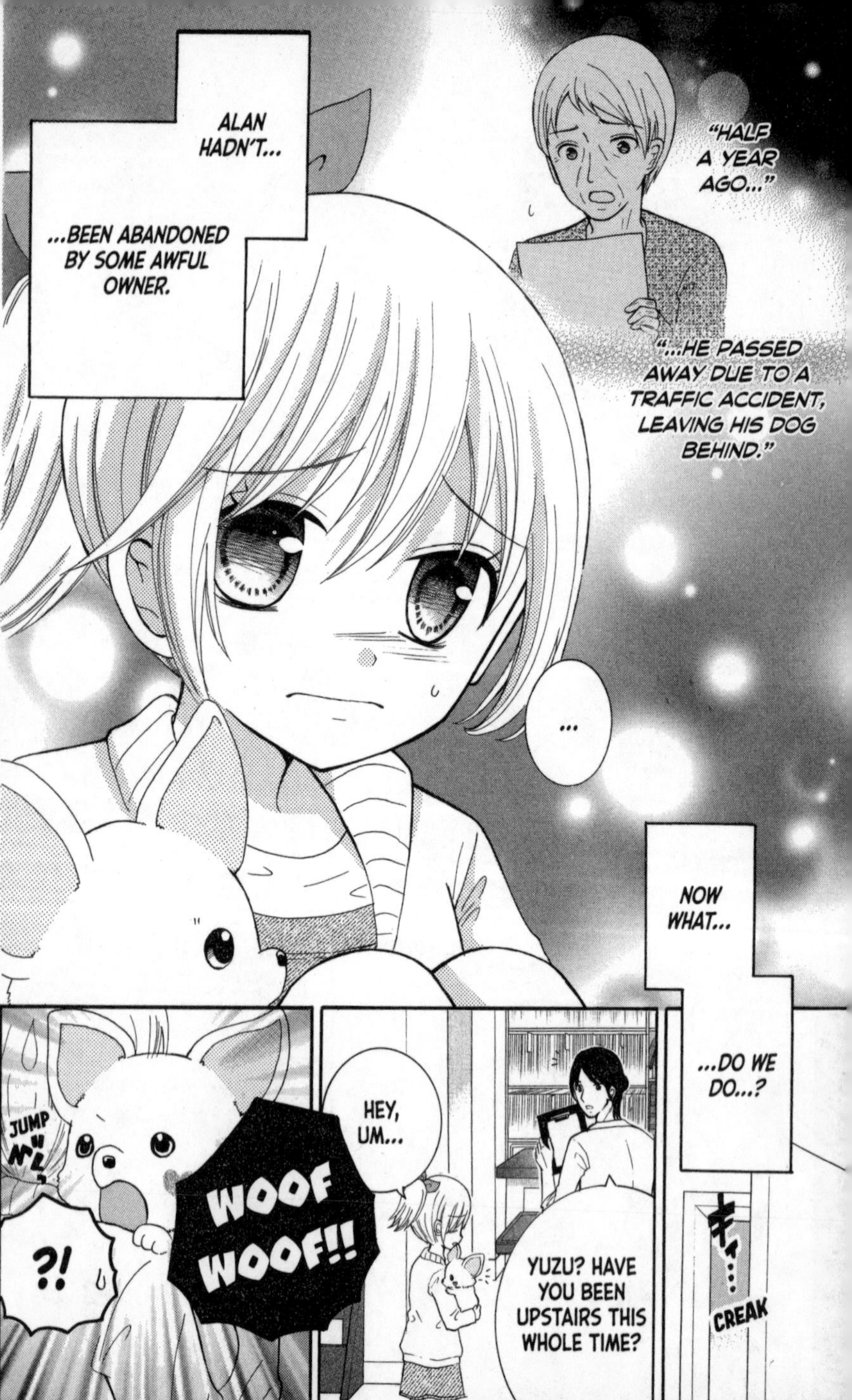
"HALF A YEAR AGO..."
"...HE PASSED AWAY DUE TO A TRAFFIC ACCIDENT, LEAVING HIS DOG BEHIND."
ALAN HADN'T...
...BEEN ABANDONED BY SOME AWFUL OWNER.
...
NOW WHAT...
...DO WE DO...?
CREAK
YUZU? HAVE YOU BEEN UPSTAIRS THIS WHOLE TIME?
HEY, UM...
WOOF WOOF!!
JUMP
?!

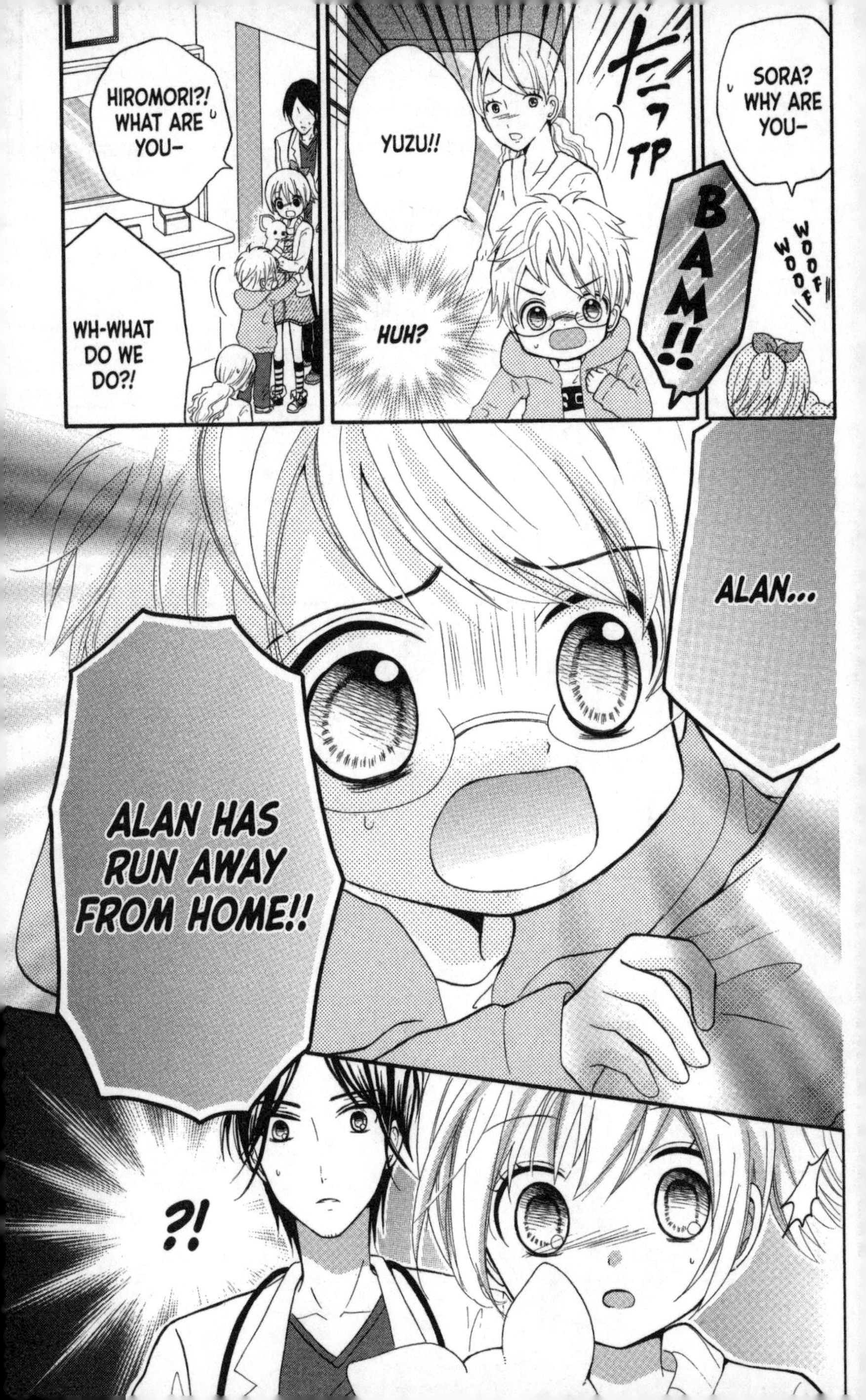
SORA? WHY ARE YOU–
WOOF WOOF
BAM!!
TP
YUZU!!
HUH?
HIROMORI?! WHAT ARE YOU–
WH-WHAT DO WE DO?!
ALAN...
ALAN HAS RUN AWAY FROM HOME!!
?!

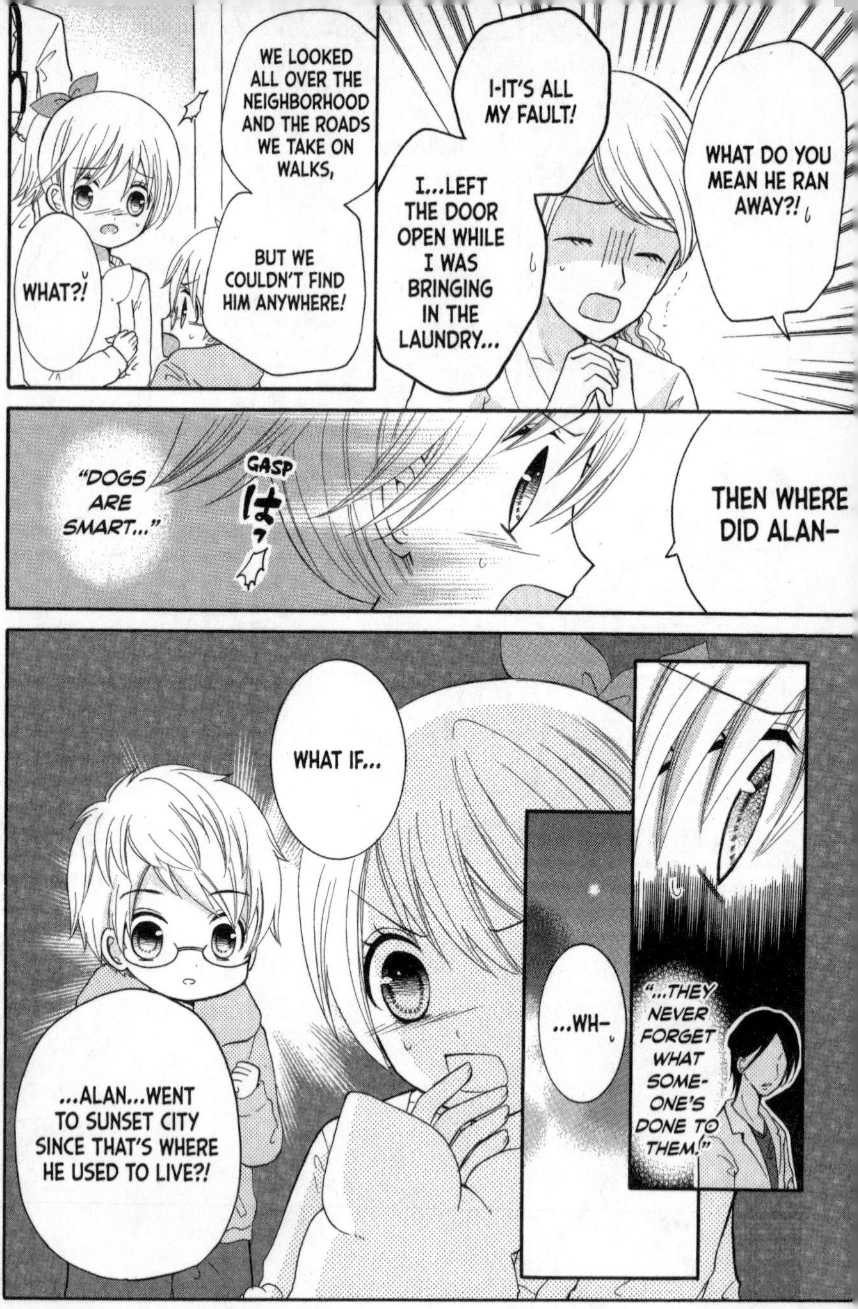
WHAT DO YOU MEAN HE RAN AWAY?!
I-IT'S ALL MY FAULT!
I...LEFT THE DOOR OPEN WHILE I WAS BRINGING IN THE LAUNDRY...
WE LOOKED ALL OVER THE NEIGHBORHOOD AND THE ROADS WE TAKE ON WALKS,
BUT WE COULDN'T FIND HIM ANYWHERE!
WHAT?!
THEN WHERE DID ALAN-
GASP
はっ
"DOGS ARE SMART..."
"...THEY NEVER FORGET WHAT SOME-ONE'S DONE TO THEM!"
...WH-
WHAT IF...
...ALAN...WENT TO SUNSET CITY SINCE THAT'S WHERE HE USED TO LIVE?!

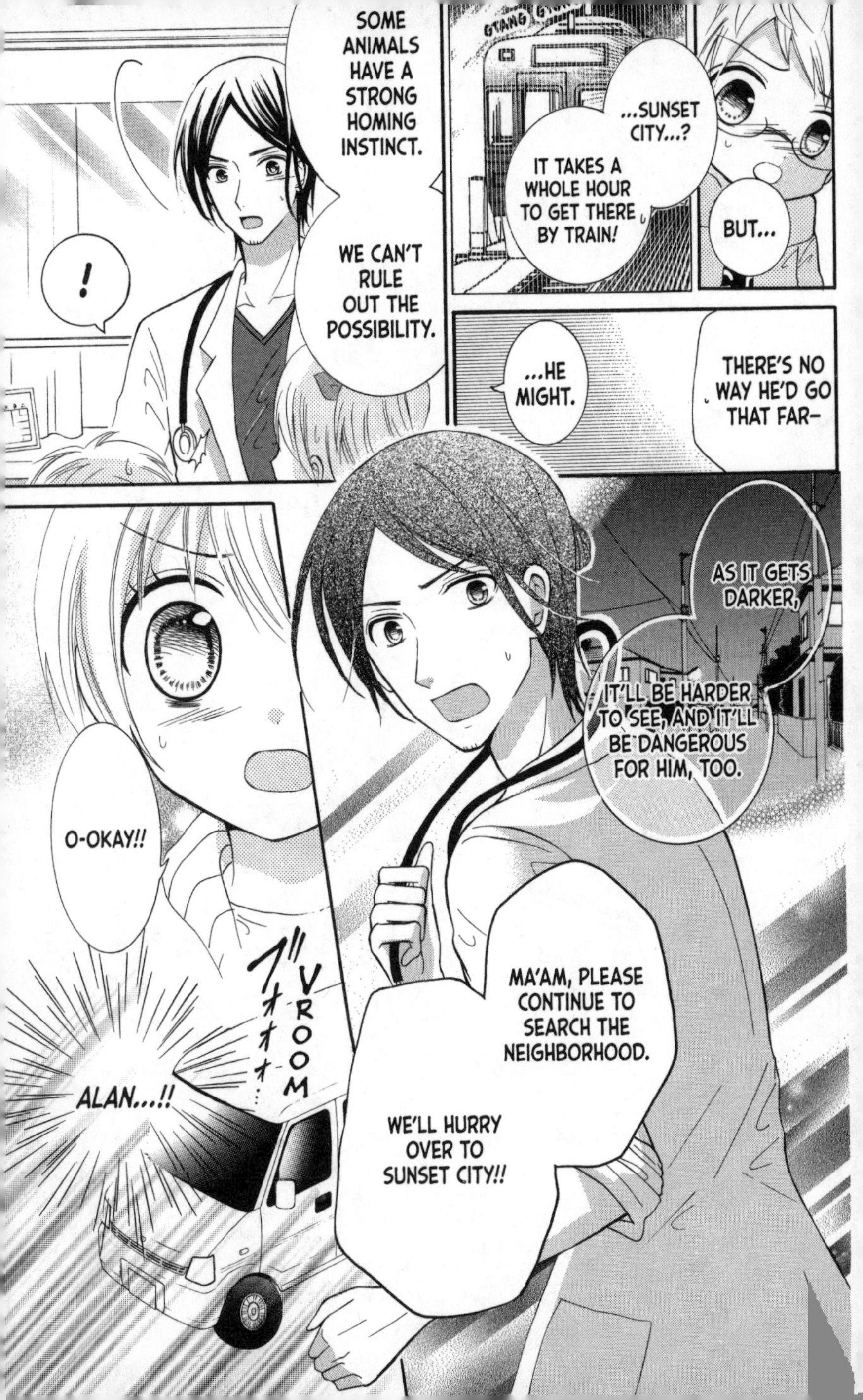
...SUNSET CITY...?
BUT...
IT TAKES A WHOLE HOUR TO GET THERE BY TRAIN!
THERE'S NO WAY HE'D GO THAT FAR—
...HE MIGHT.
SOME ANIMALS HAVE A STRONG HOMING INSTINCT.
WE CAN'T RULE OUT THE POSSIBILITY.
!
AS IT GETS DARKER,
IT'LL BE HARDER TO SEE, AND IT'LL BE DANGEROUS FOR HIM, TOO.
MA'AM, PLEASE CONTINUE TO SEARCH THE NEIGHBORHOOD.
WE'LL HURRY OVER TO SUNSET CITY!!
O-OKAY!!
VROOM
ALAN...!!

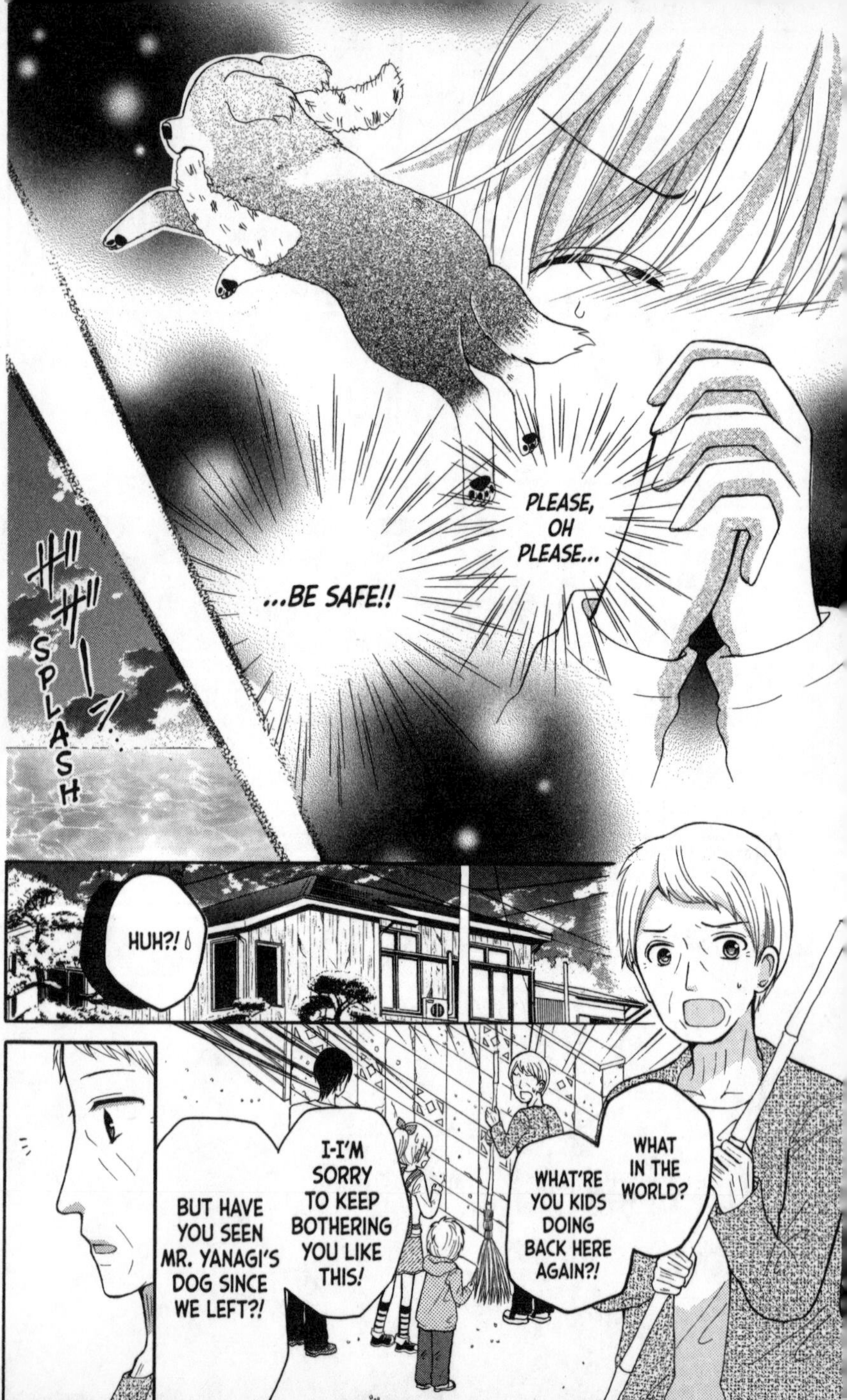
PLEASE, OH PLEASE...
...BE SAFE!!
ザザーン
SPLASH
HUH?!
WHAT IN THE WORLD?
WHAT'RE YOU KIDS DOING BACK HERE AGAIN?!
I-I'M SORRY TO KEEP BOTHERING YOU LIKE THIS!
BUT HAVE YOU SEEN MR. YANAGI'S DOG SINCE WE LEFT?!

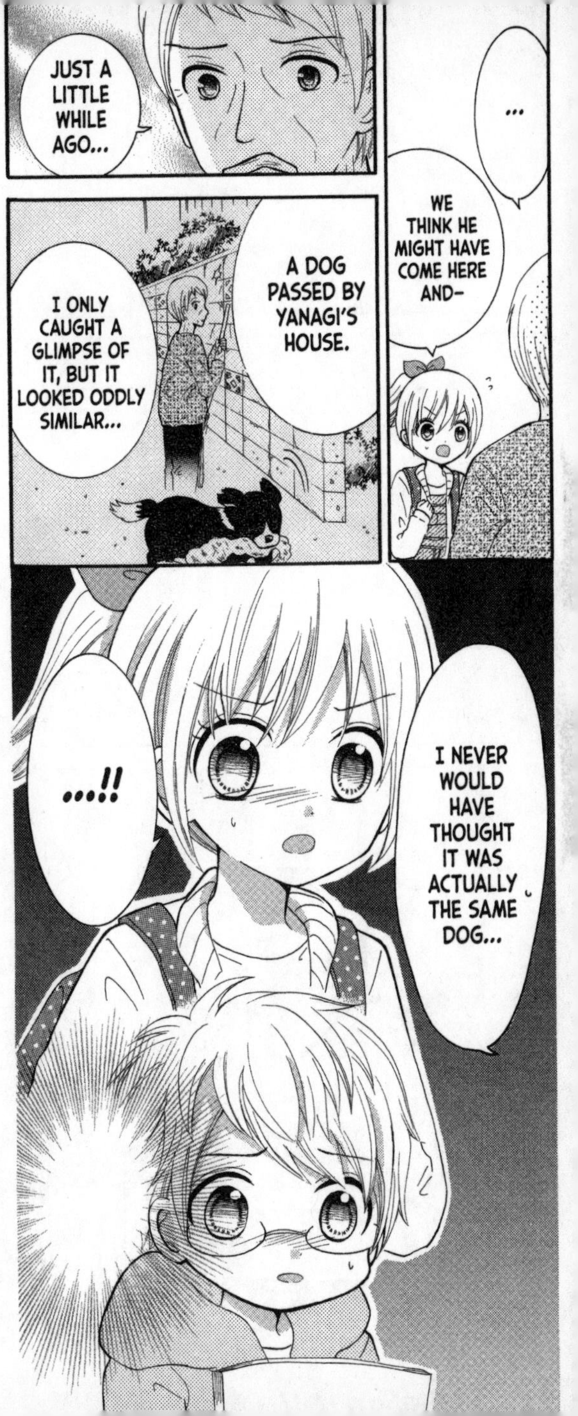
...
WE THINK HE MIGHT HAVE COME HERE AND-
JUST A LITTLE WHILE AGO...
A DOG PASSED BY YANAGI'S HOUSE.
I ONLY CAUGHT A GLIMPSE OF IT, BUT IT LOOKED ODDLY SIMILAR...
I NEVER WOULD HAVE THOUGHT IT WAS ACTUALLY THE SAME DOG...
...!!

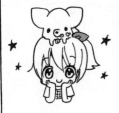

GREETINGS.

THANK YOU SO MUCH FOR BUYING YUZU THE PET VET VOLUME 6!

IT'S BEEN A WHILE SINCE I DREW SORA SO BIG ON THE COVER. I FEEL LIKE I HAVEN'T DONE A FULL-SIZE PORTRAIT OF HIM SINCE VOLUME 1 (LOL). ISN'T THAT NICE, SORA?

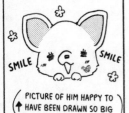

SMILE SMILE

(↑ PICTURE OF HIM HAPPY TO HAVE BEEN DRAWN SO BIG AND IN COLOR.)

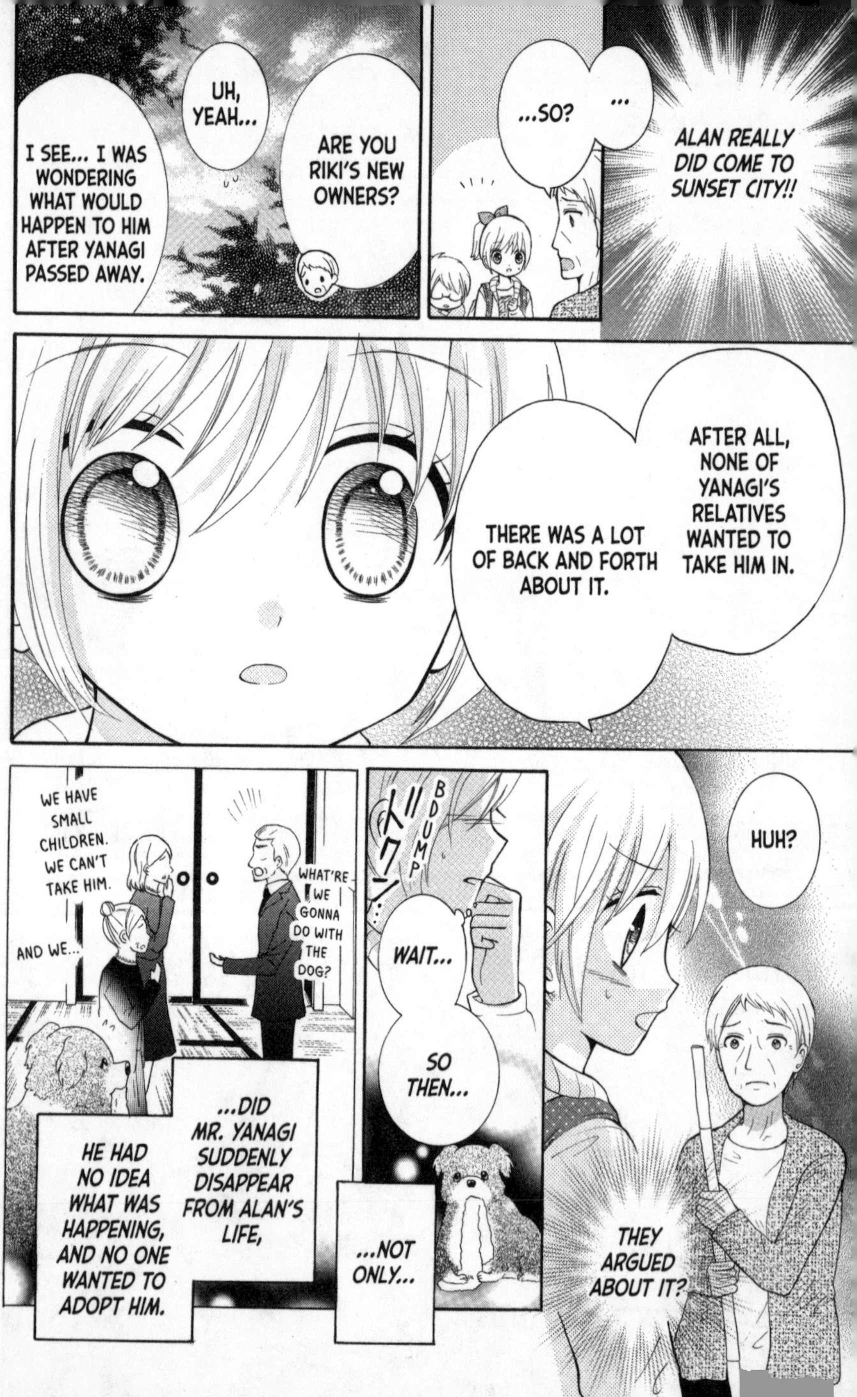
ALAN REALLY DID COME TO SUNSET CITY!!
...
...SO?
ARE YOU RIKI'S NEW OWNERS?
UH, YEAH...
I SEE... I WAS WONDERING WHAT WOULD HAPPEN TO HIM AFTER YANAGI PASSED AWAY.
AFTER ALL, NONE OF YANAGI'S RELATIVES WANTED TO TAKE HIM IN.
THERE WAS A LOT OF BACK AND FORTH ABOUT IT.
HUH?
THEY ARGUED ABOUT IT?
BDUMP
WAIT...
SO THEN...
...NOT ONLY...
WHAT'RE WE GONNA DO WITH THE DOG?
WE HAVE SMALL CHILDREN. WE CAN'T TAKE HIM.
AND WE...
...DID MR. YANAGI SUDDENLY DISAPPEAR FROM ALAN'S LIFE,
HE HAD NO IDEA WHAT WAS HAPPENING, AND NO ONE WANTED TO ADOPT HIM.

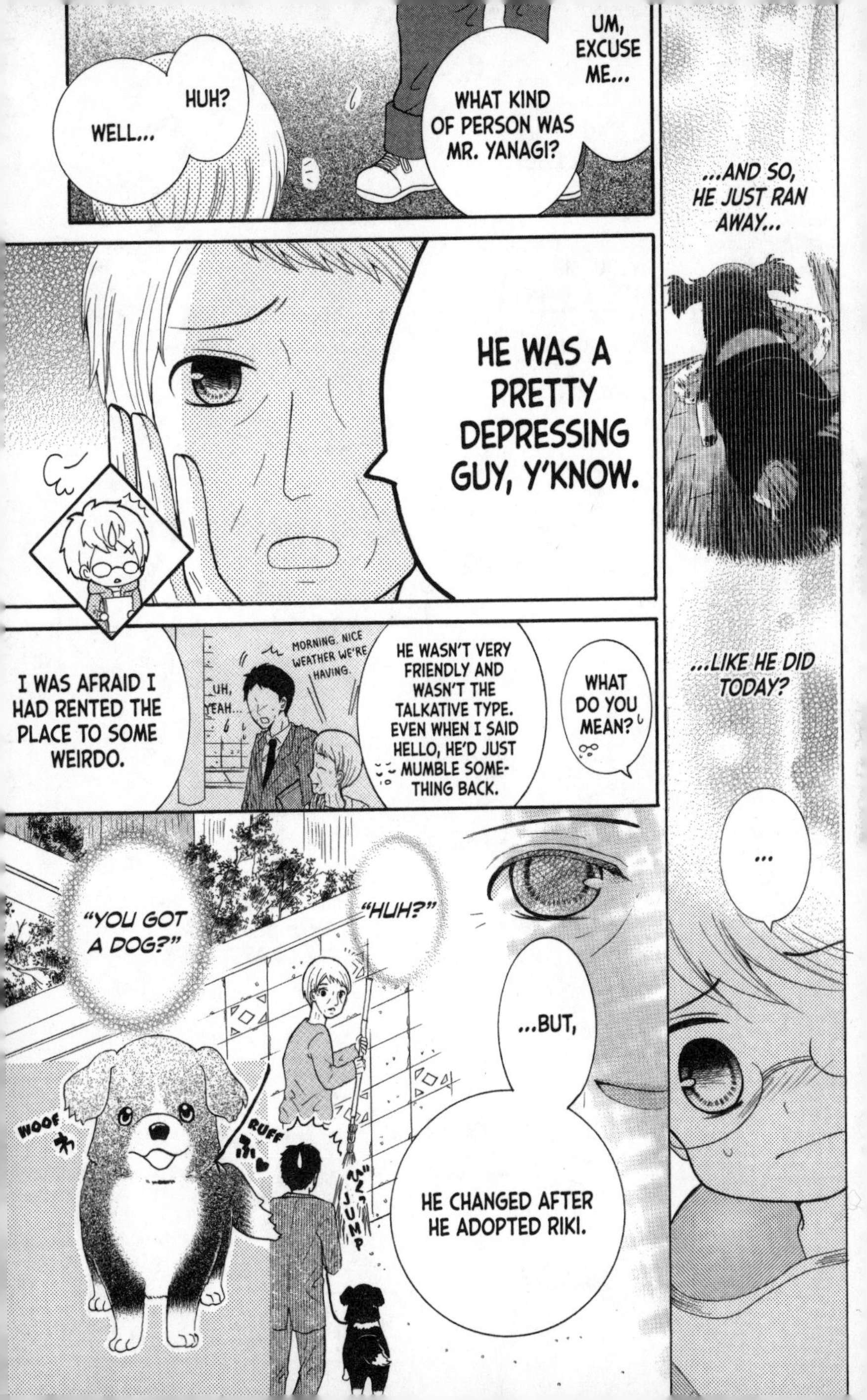
...AND SO, HE JUST RAN AWAY...
...LIKE HE DID TODAY?
...
UM, EXCUSE ME...
WHAT KIND OF PERSON WAS MR. YANAGI?
HUH?
WELL...
HE WAS A PRETTY DEPRESSING GUY, Y'KNOW.
WHAT DO YOU MEAN?
HE WASN'T VERY FRIENDLY AND WASN'T THE TALKATIVE TYPE. EVEN WHEN I SAID HELLO, HE'D JUST MUMBLE SOMETHING BACK.
MORNING. NICE WEATHER WE'RE HAVING.
UH, YEAH...
I WAS AFRAID I HAD RENTED THE PLACE TO SOME WEIRDO.
...BUT,
HE CHANGED AFTER HE ADOPTED RIKI.
“HUH?”
“YOU GOT A DOG?”
WOOF
RUFF
JUMP

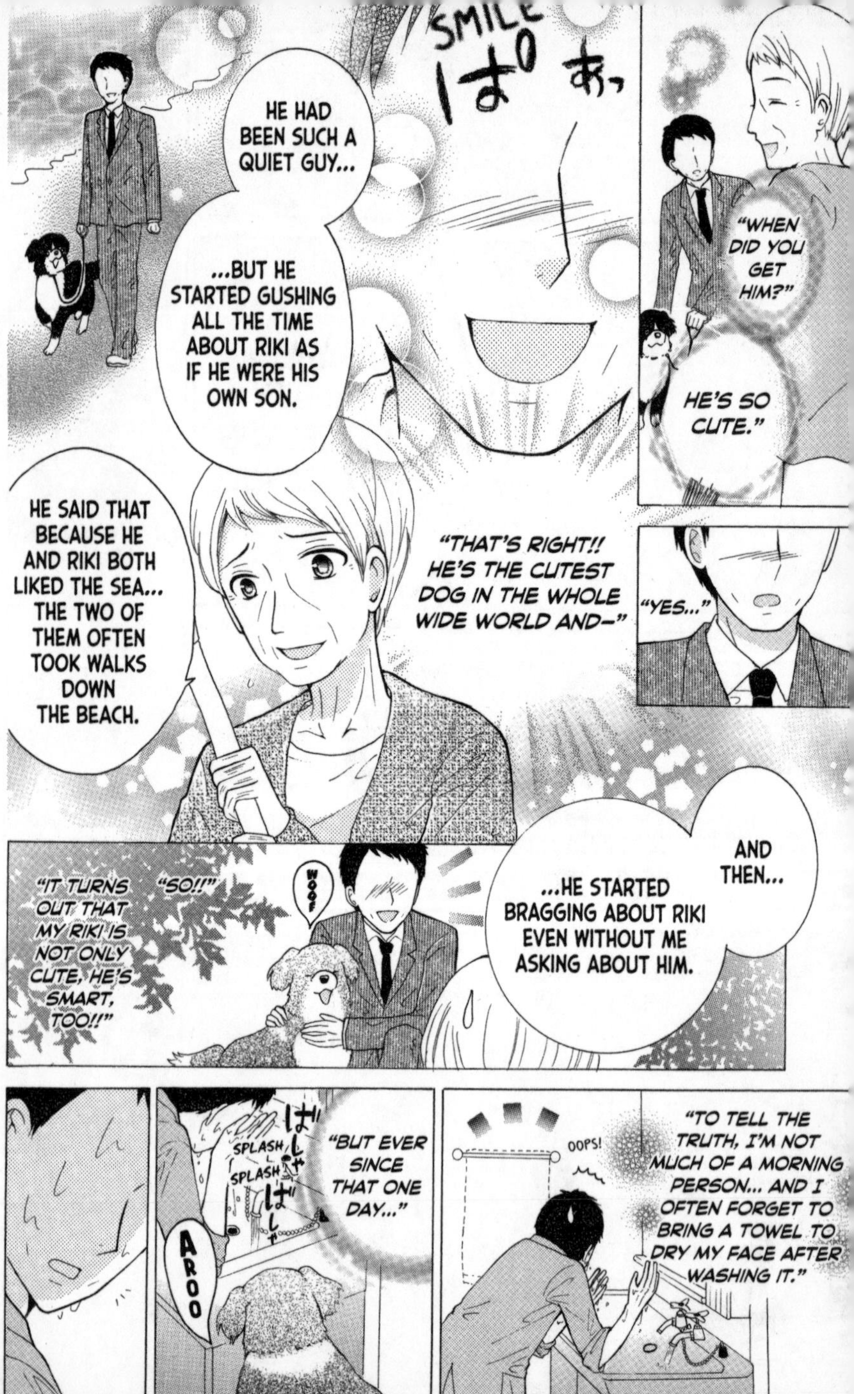
"WHEN DID YOU GET HIM?
HE'S SO CUTE."
"YES..."
SMILE ぱあっ
HE HAD BEEN SUCH A QUIET GUY...
...BUT HE STARTED GUSHING ALL THE TIME ABOUT RIKI AS IF HE WERE HIS OWN SON.
"THAT'S RIGHT!! HE'S THE CUTEST DOG IN THE WHOLE WIDE WORLD AND—"
HE SAID THAT BECAUSE HE AND RIKI BOTH LIKED THE SEA... THE TWO OF THEM OFTEN TOOK WALKS DOWN THE BEACH.
AND THEN...
...HE STARTED BRAGGING ABOUT RIKI EVEN WITHOUT ME ASKING ABOUT HIM.
WOOF
"SO!!"
"IT TURNS OUT THAT MY RIKI IS NOT ONLY CUTE, HE'S SMART, TOO!!"
"TO TELL THE TRUTH, I'M NOT MUCH OF A MORNING PERSON... AND I OFTEN FORGET TO BRING A TOWEL TO DRY MY FACE AFTER WASHING IT."
OOPS!
"BUT EVER SINCE THAT ONE DAY..."
SPLASH ばしゃ
SPLASH ばしゃ
AROO

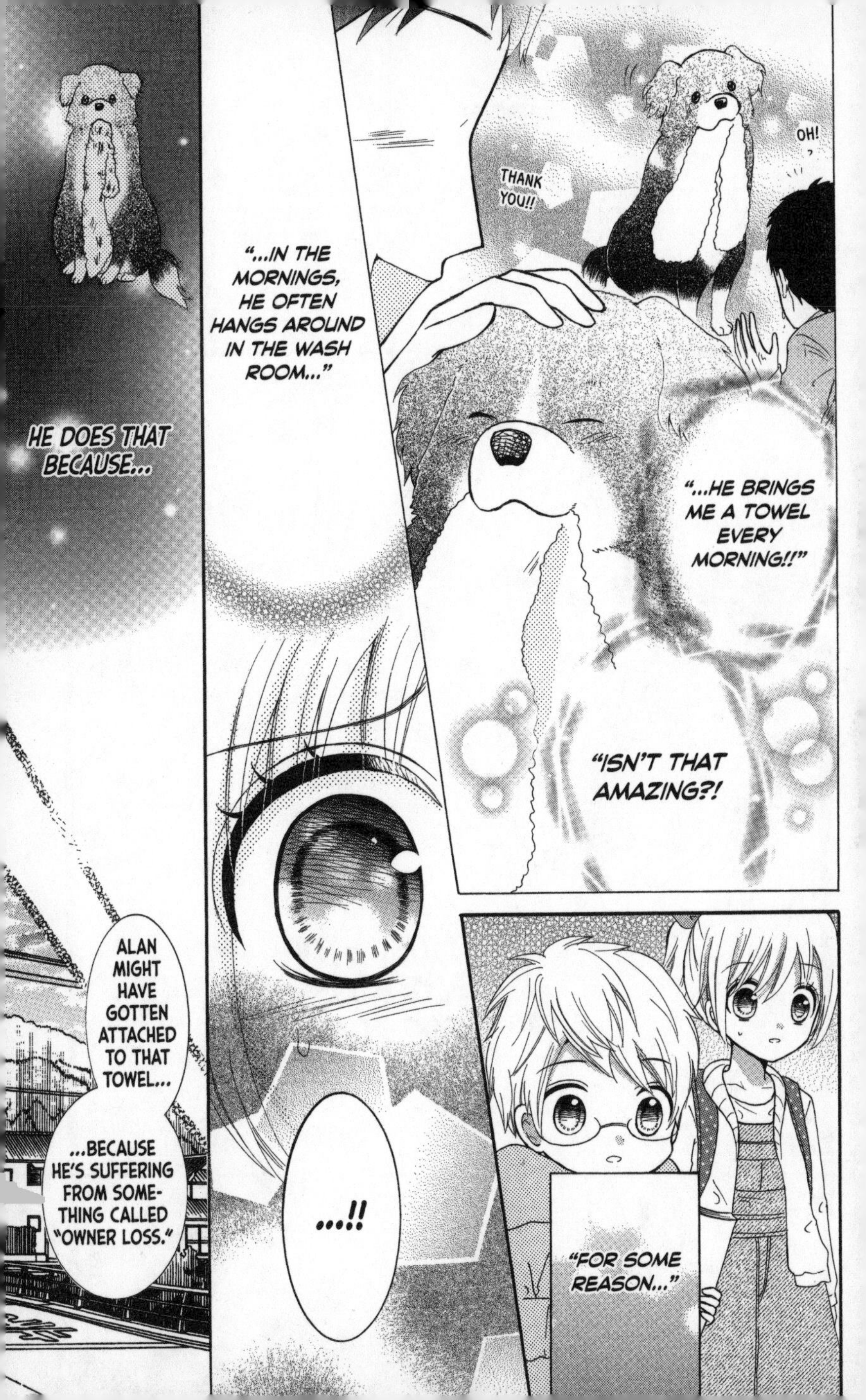
OH!
THANK YOU!!
"...HE BRINGS ME A TOWEL EVERY MORNING!!"
"ISN'T THAT AMAZING?!
"FOR SOME REASON..."
"...IN THE MORNINGS, HE OFTEN HANGS AROUND IN THE WASH ROOM..."
...!!
HE DOES THAT BECAUSE...
ALAN MIGHT HAVE GOTTEN ATTACHED TO THAT TOWEL...
...BECAUSE HE'S SUFFERING FROM SOME-THING CALLED "OWNER LOSS."

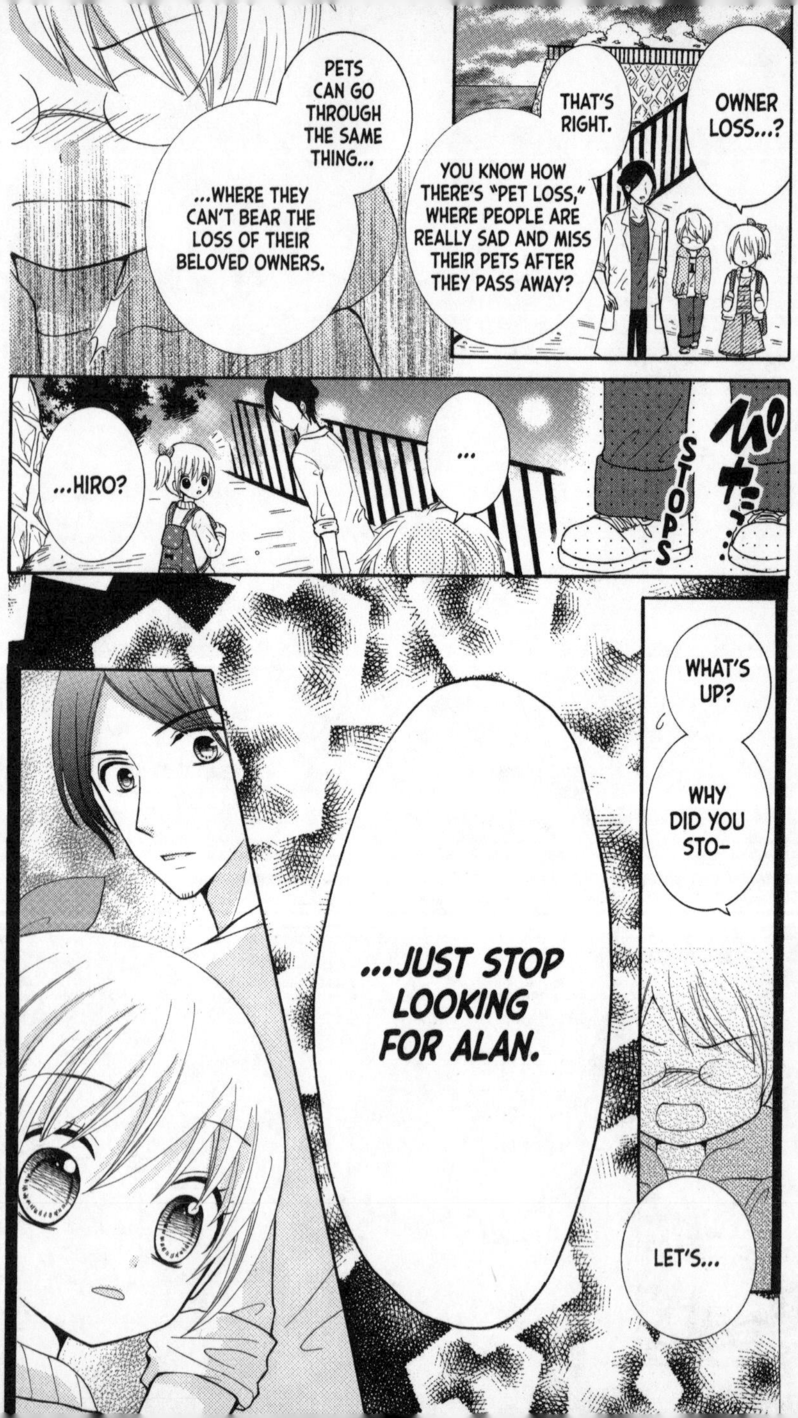
OWNER LOSS...?
THAT'S RIGHT.
YOU KNOW HOW THERE'S "PET LOSS," WHERE PEOPLE ARE REALLY SAD AND MISS THEIR PETS AFTER THEY PASS AWAY?
PETS CAN GO THROUGH THE SAME THING...
...WHERE THEY CAN'T BEAR THE LOSS OF THEIR BELOVED OWNERS.
STOPS
...
...HIRO?
WHAT'S UP?
WHY DID YOU STO-
LET'S...
...JUST STOP LOOKING FOR ALAN.

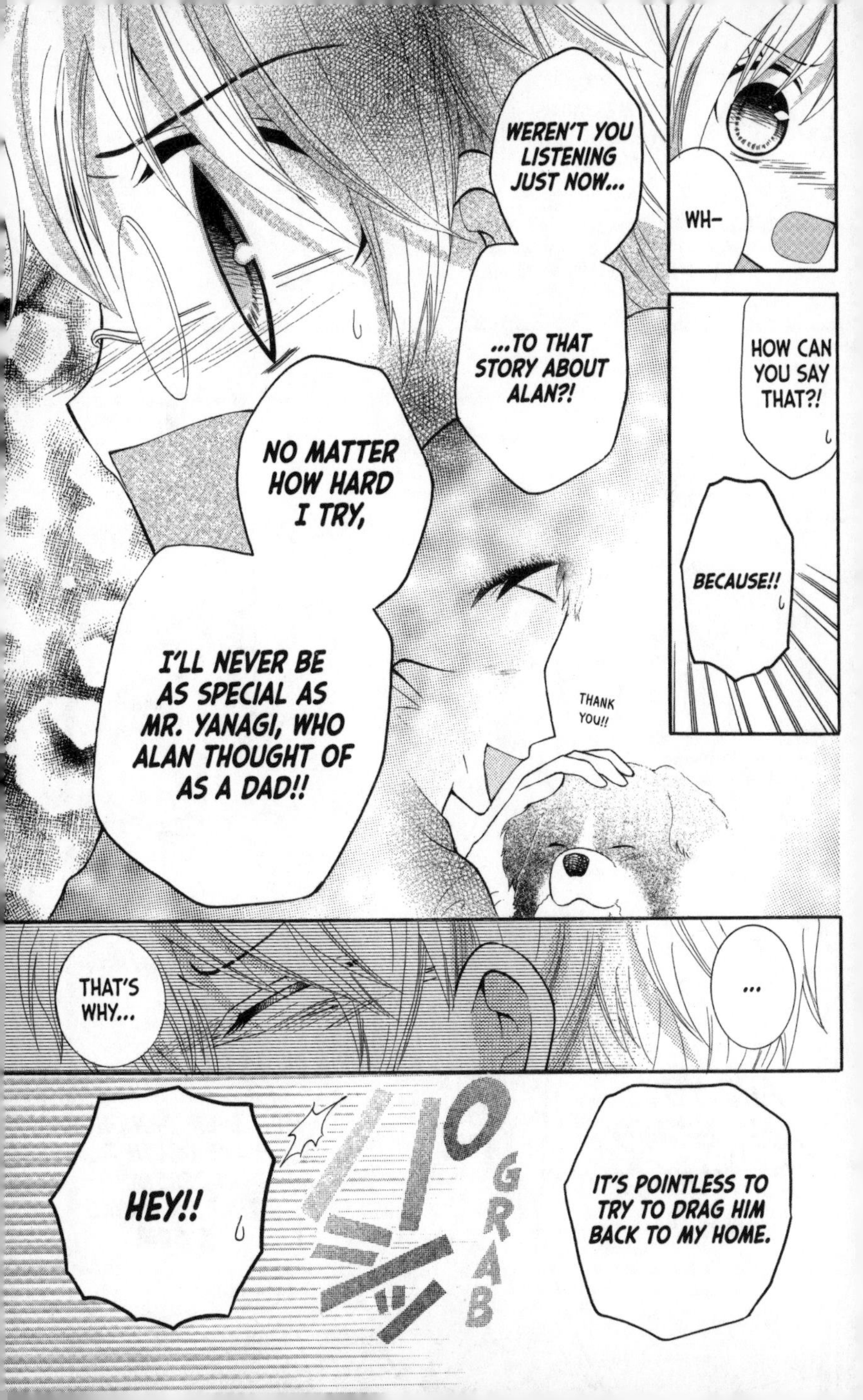
WH-
HOW CAN YOU SAY THAT?!
BECAUSE!!
WEREN'T YOU LISTENING JUST NOW...
...TO THAT STORY ABOUT ALAN?!
NO MATTER HOW HARD I TRY,
I'LL NEVER BE AS SPECIAL AS MR. YANAGI, WHO ALAN THOUGHT OF AS A DAD!!
THANK YOU!!
...
THAT'S WHY...
IT'S POINTLESS TO TRY TO DRAG HIM BACK TO MY HOME.
GRAB
HEY!!

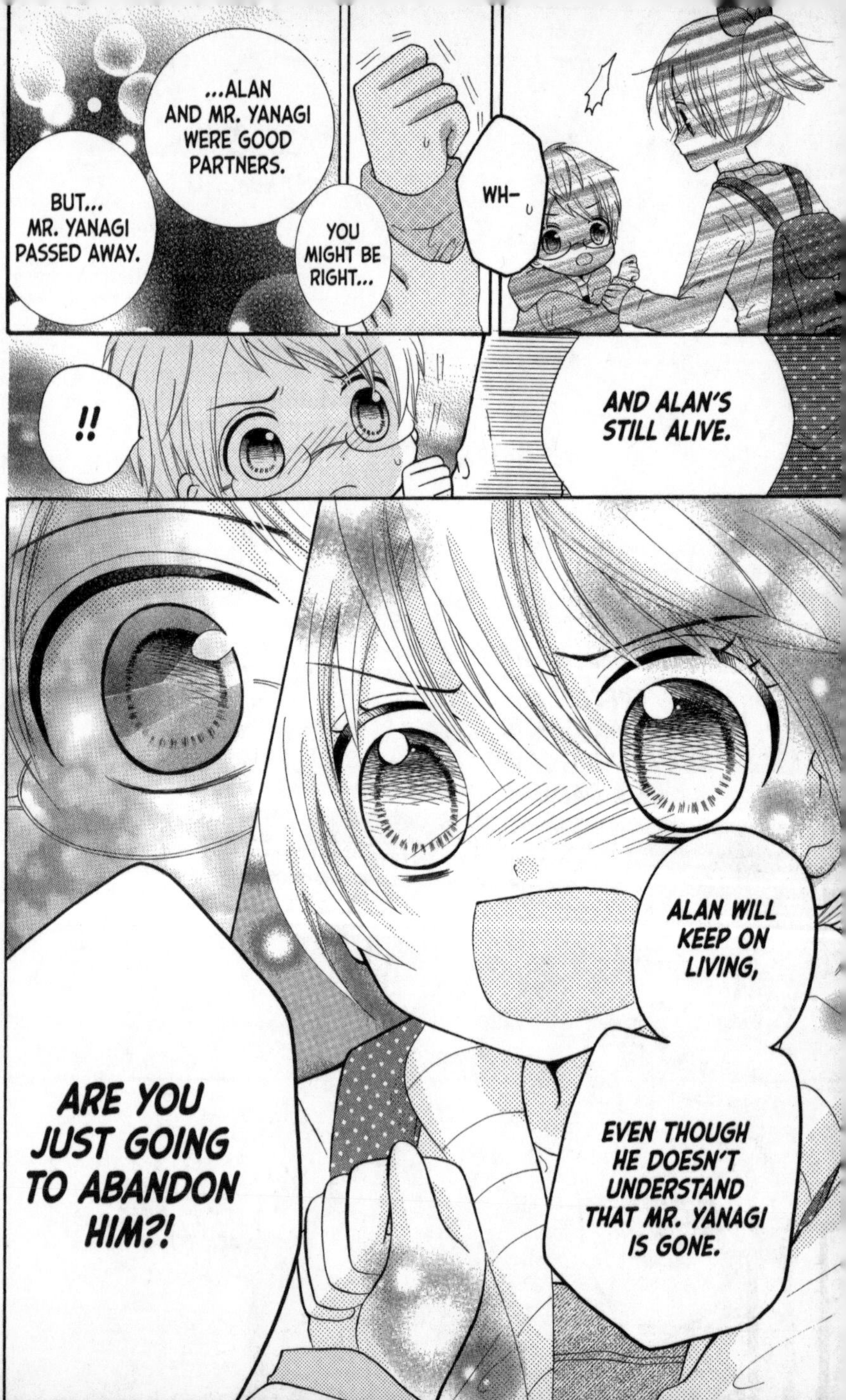
WH-
YOU MIGHT BE RIGHT...
...ALAN AND MR. YANAGI WERE GOOD PARTNERS.
BUT... MR. YANAGI PASSED AWAY.
AND ALAN'S STILL ALIVE.
!!
ALAN WILL KEEP ON LIVING,
EVEN THOUGH HE DOESN'T UNDERSTAND THAT MR. YANAGI IS GONE.
ARE YOU JUST GOING TO ABANDON HIM?!

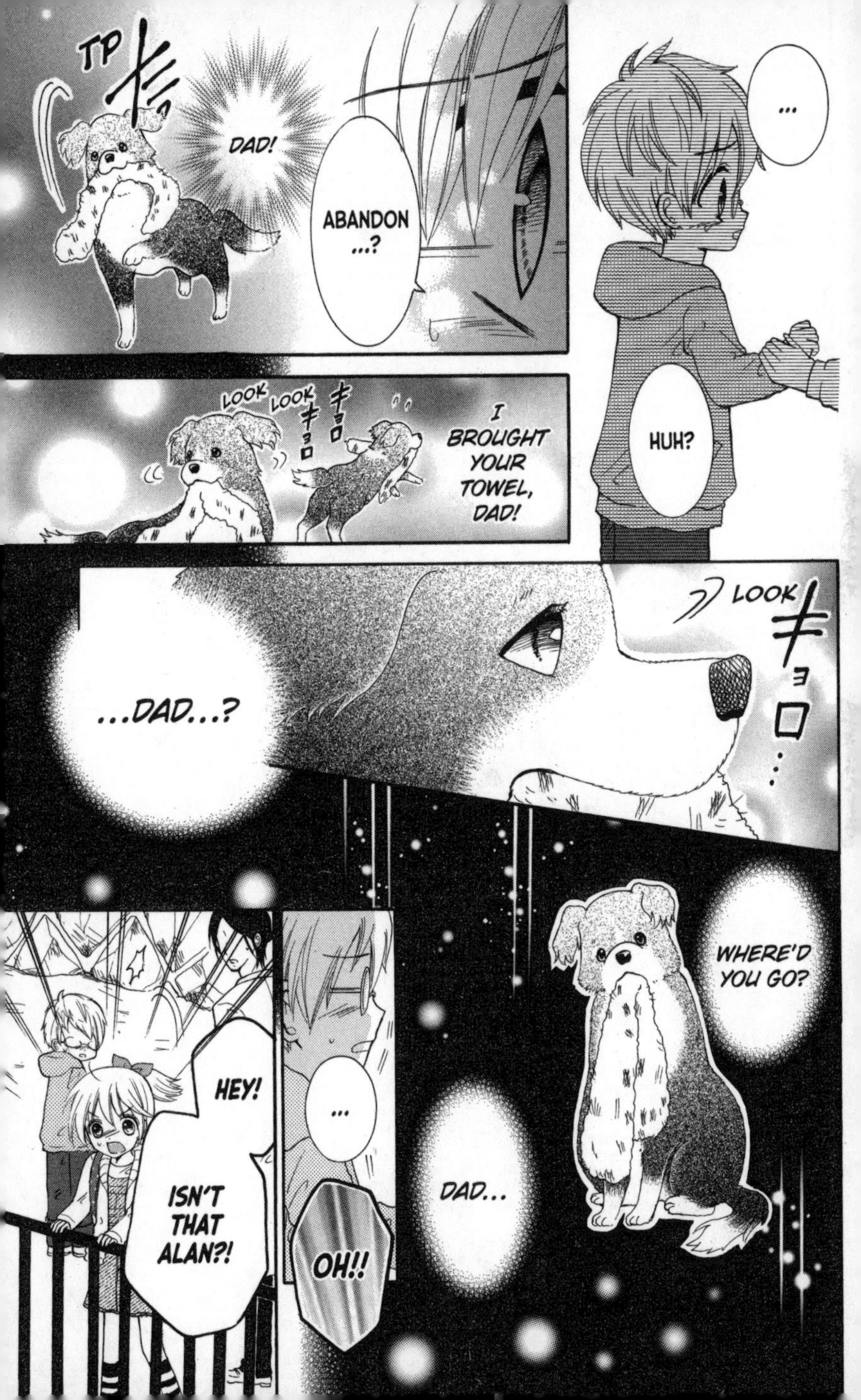
...
HUH?
ABANDON ...?
TP
DAD!
I BROUGHT YOUR TOWEL, DAD!
LOOK キョ
LOOK キョロ
LOOK キョロ...
...DAD...?
WHERE'D YOU GO?
DAD...
...
OH!!
HEY!
ISN'T THAT ALAN?!

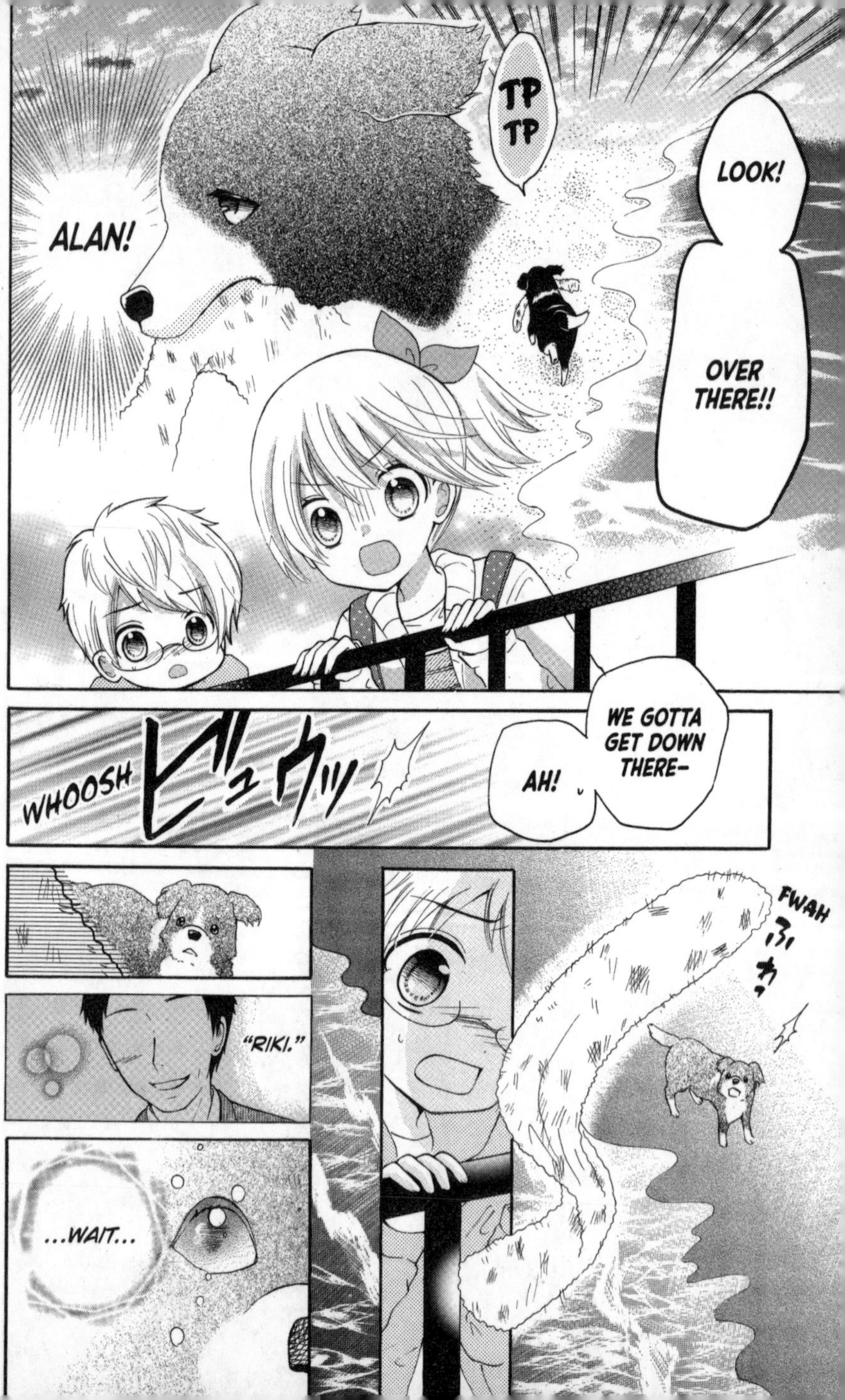
LOOK!
OVER THERE!!
TP TP
ALAN!
WE GOTTA GET DOWN THERE–
AH!
WHOOSH ビュウッ
FWAH ふわっ
"RIKI."
...WAIT...

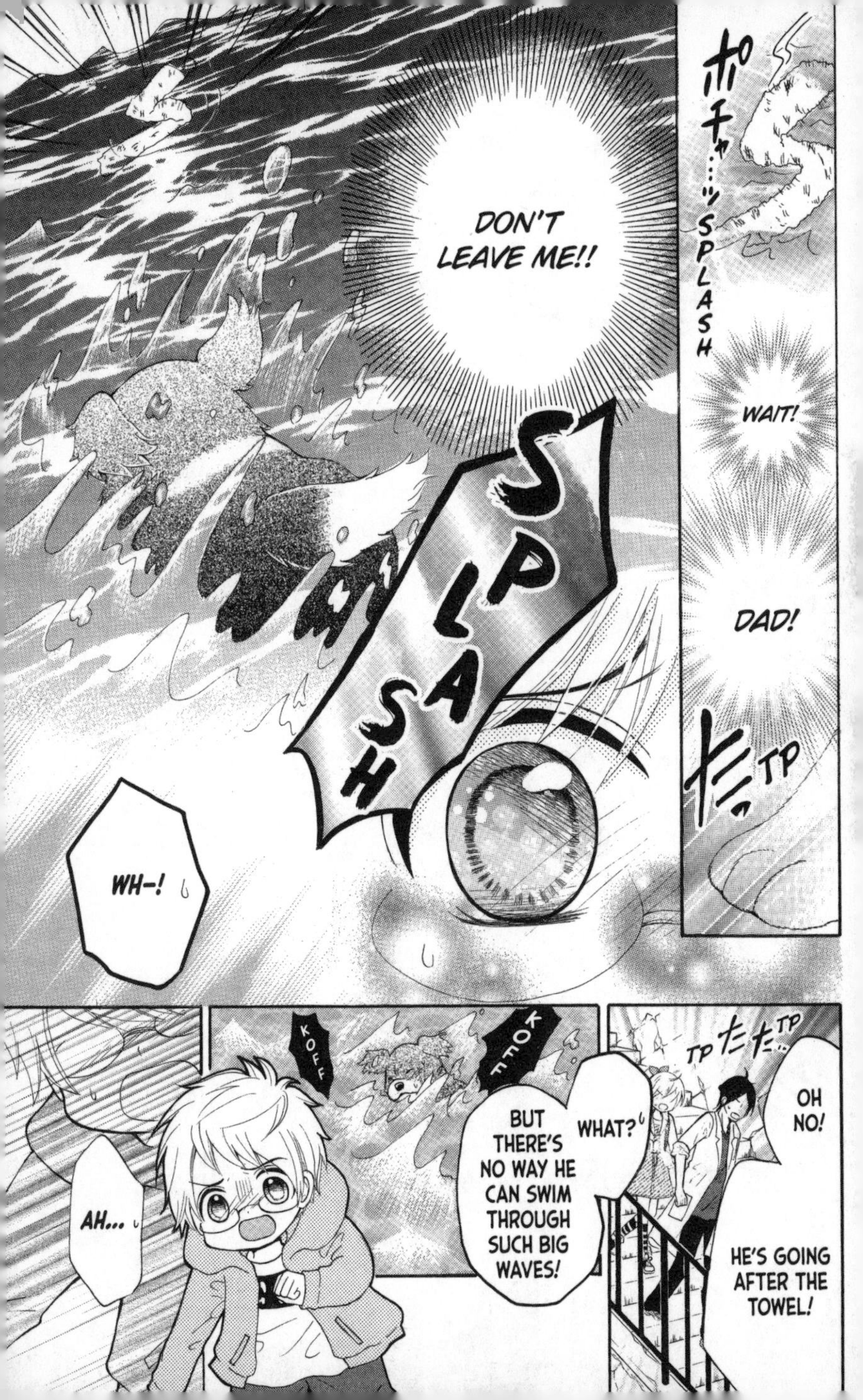
ポチャ…ッ
SPLASH
WAIT!
DAD!
たっ
TP
DON'T LEAVE ME!!
SPLASH
WH-!
TP たた TP..
OH NO!
HE'S GOING AFTER THE TOWEL!
WHAT?
KOFF
KOFF
BUT THERE'S NO WAY HE CAN SWIM THROUGH SUCH BIG WAVES!
AH...

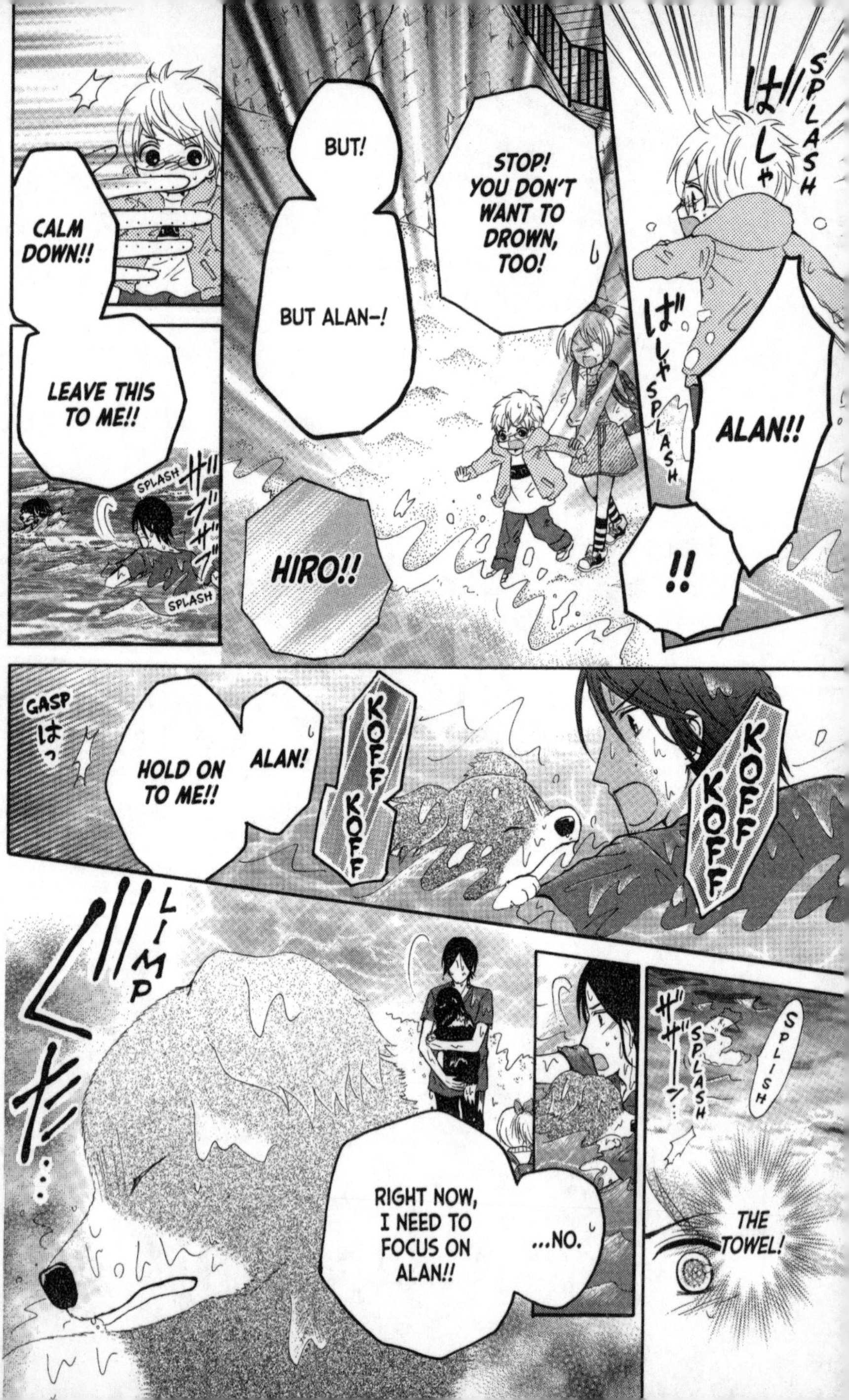
SPLASH
はしゃ
ALAN!!
ばしゃ
SPLASH
!!
STOP! YOU DON'T WANT TO DROWN, TOO!
BUT!
BUT ALAN–!
HIRO!!
CALM DOWN!!
LEAVE THIS TO ME!!
SPLASH
SPLASH
KOFF KOFF KOFF
KOFF KOFF
ALAN!
HOLD ON TO ME!!
GASP
はっ
SPLASH
SPLASH
THE TOWEL!
...NO.
RIGHT NOW, I NEED TO FOCUS ON ALAN!!
LIMP
くた…

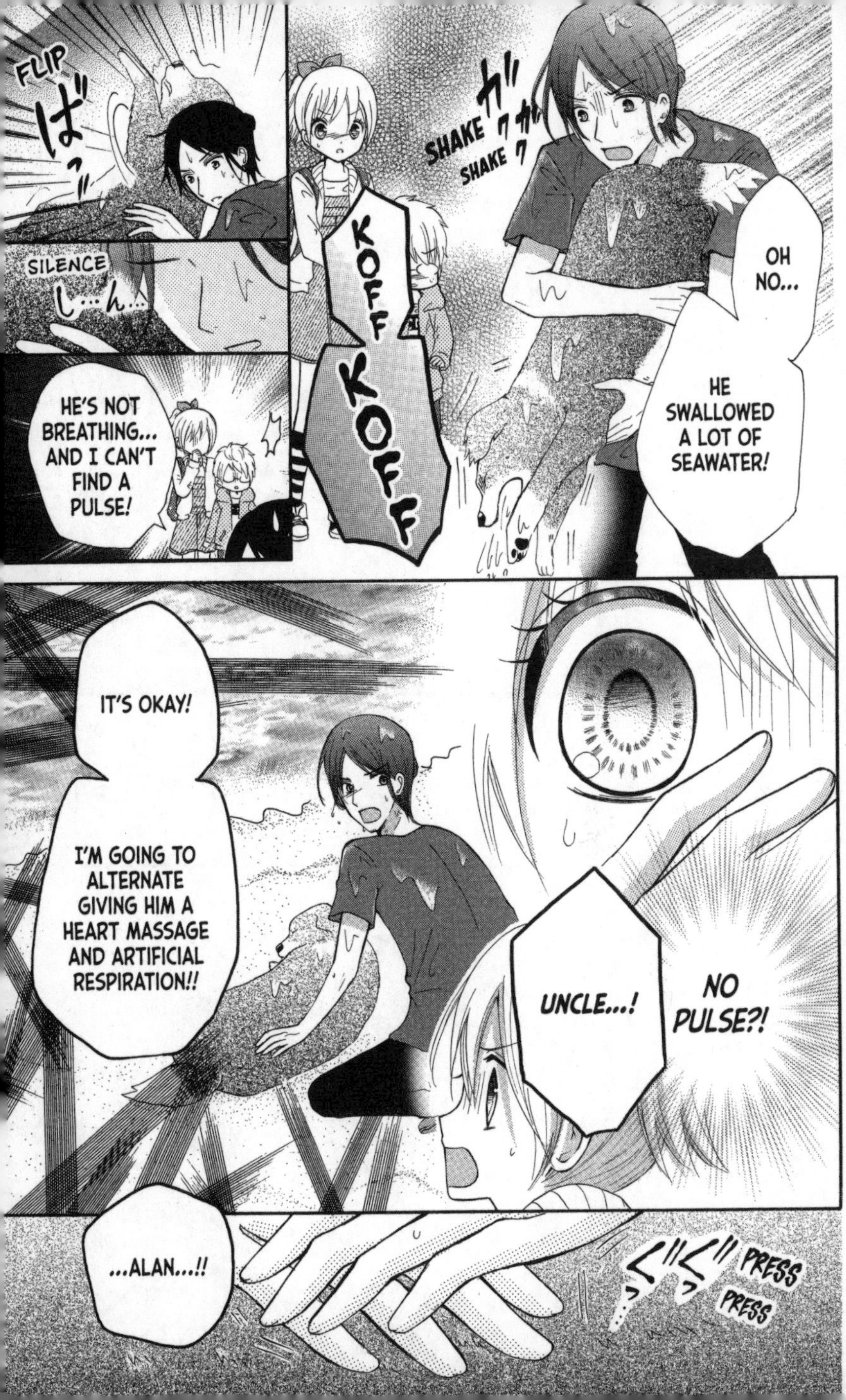

SHAKE SHAKE
ガクガク
OH NO...
HE SWALLOWED A LOT OF SEAWATER!
KOFF KOFF KOFF
FLIP
ばっ
SILENCE
し…ん…
HE'S NOT BREATHING... AND I CAN'T FIND A PULSE!
NO PULSE?!
UNCLE...!
IT'S OKAY!
I'M GOING TO ALTERNATE GIVING HIM A HEART MASSAGE AND ARTIFICIAL RESPIRATION!!
PRESS PRESS
...ALAN...!!

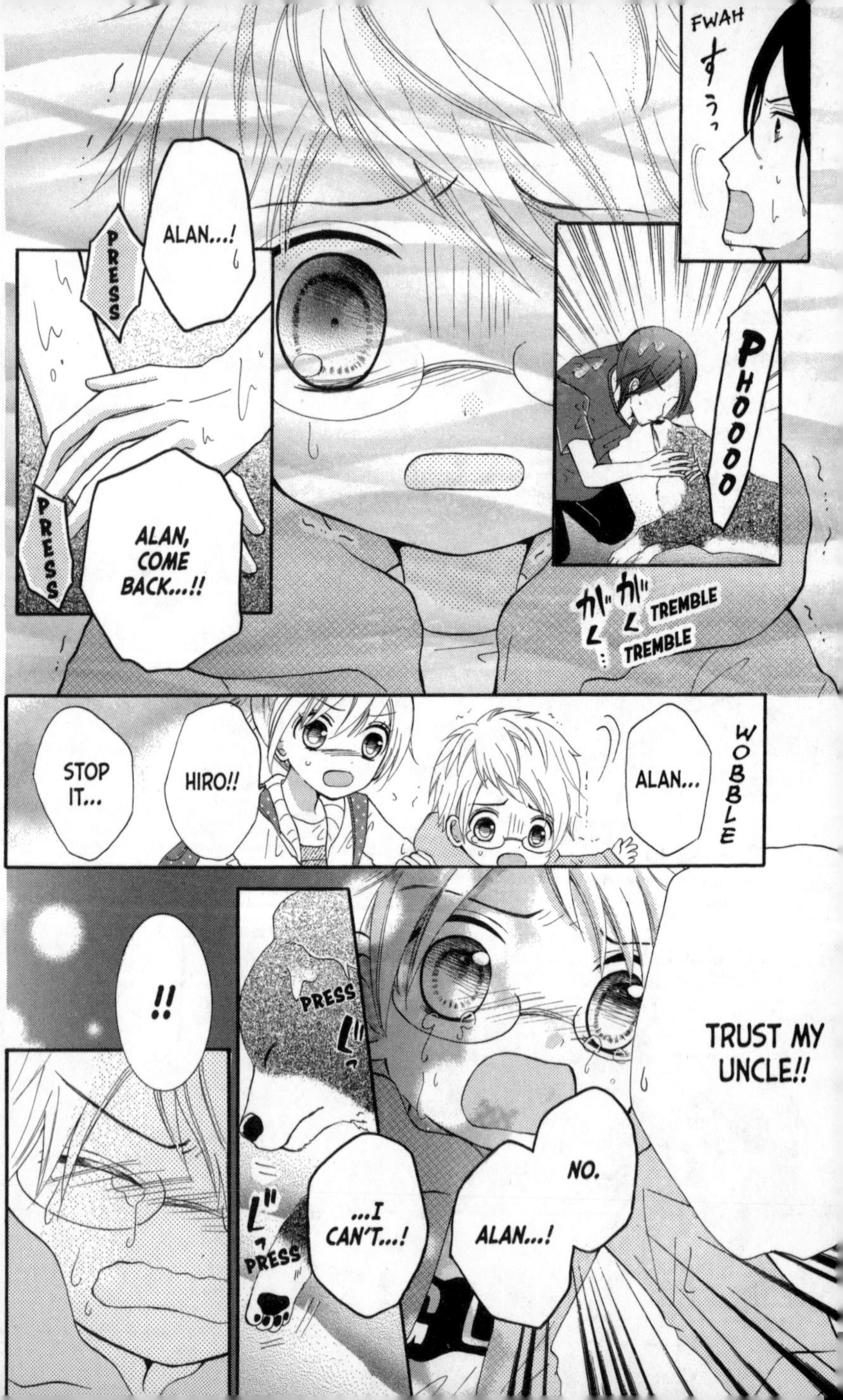
FWAH
すぅっ
PHOOOOO
ALAN...!
PRESS
PRESS
ALAN, COME BACK...!!
がくがく…
TREMBLE TREMBLE
WOBBLE
ALAN...
HIRO!!
STOP IT...
TRUST MY UNCLE!!
NO. ALAN...!
...I CAN'T...!
PRESS
PRESS
!!

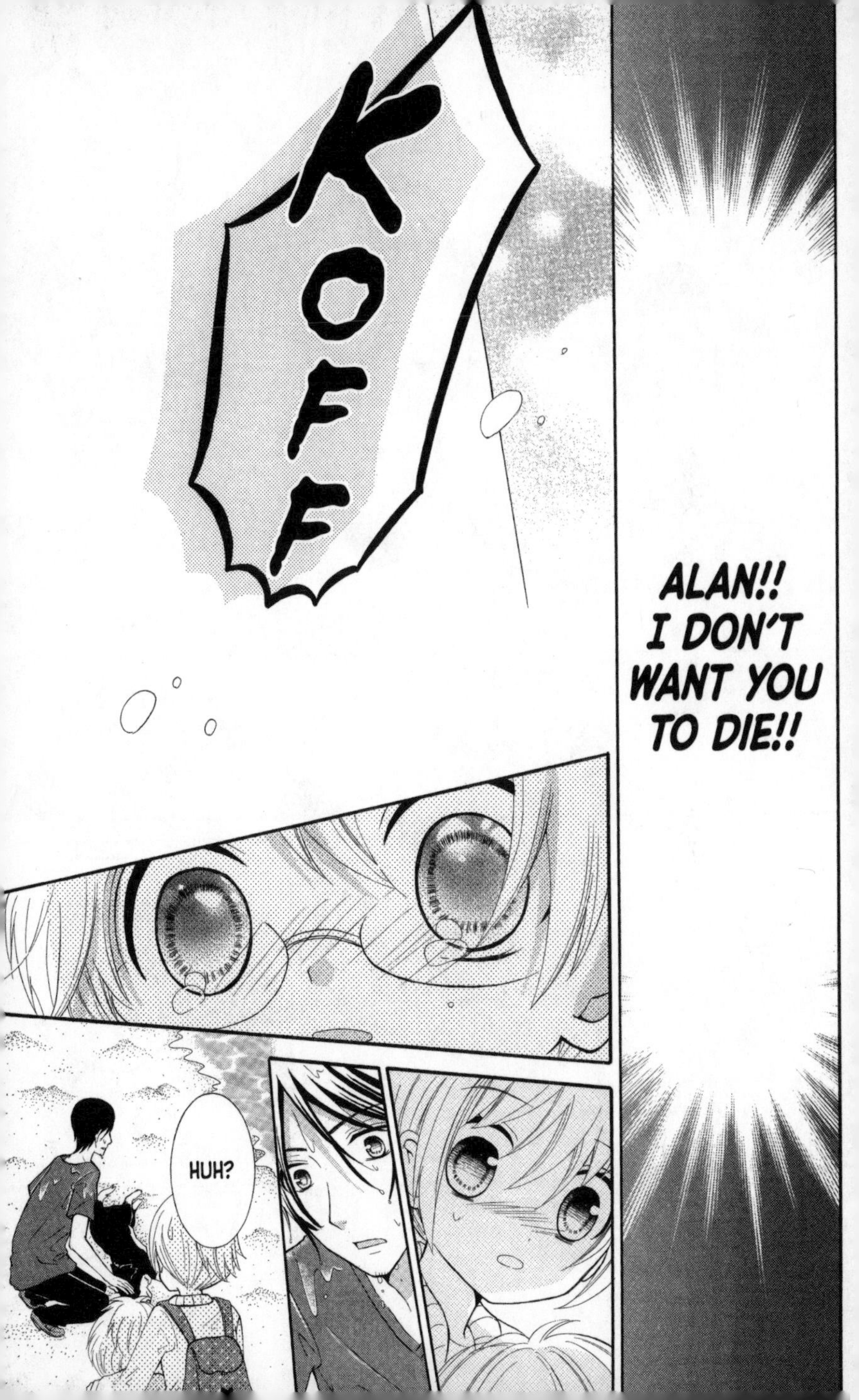
ALAN!! I DON'T WANT YOU TO DIE!!
KOFF
HUH?

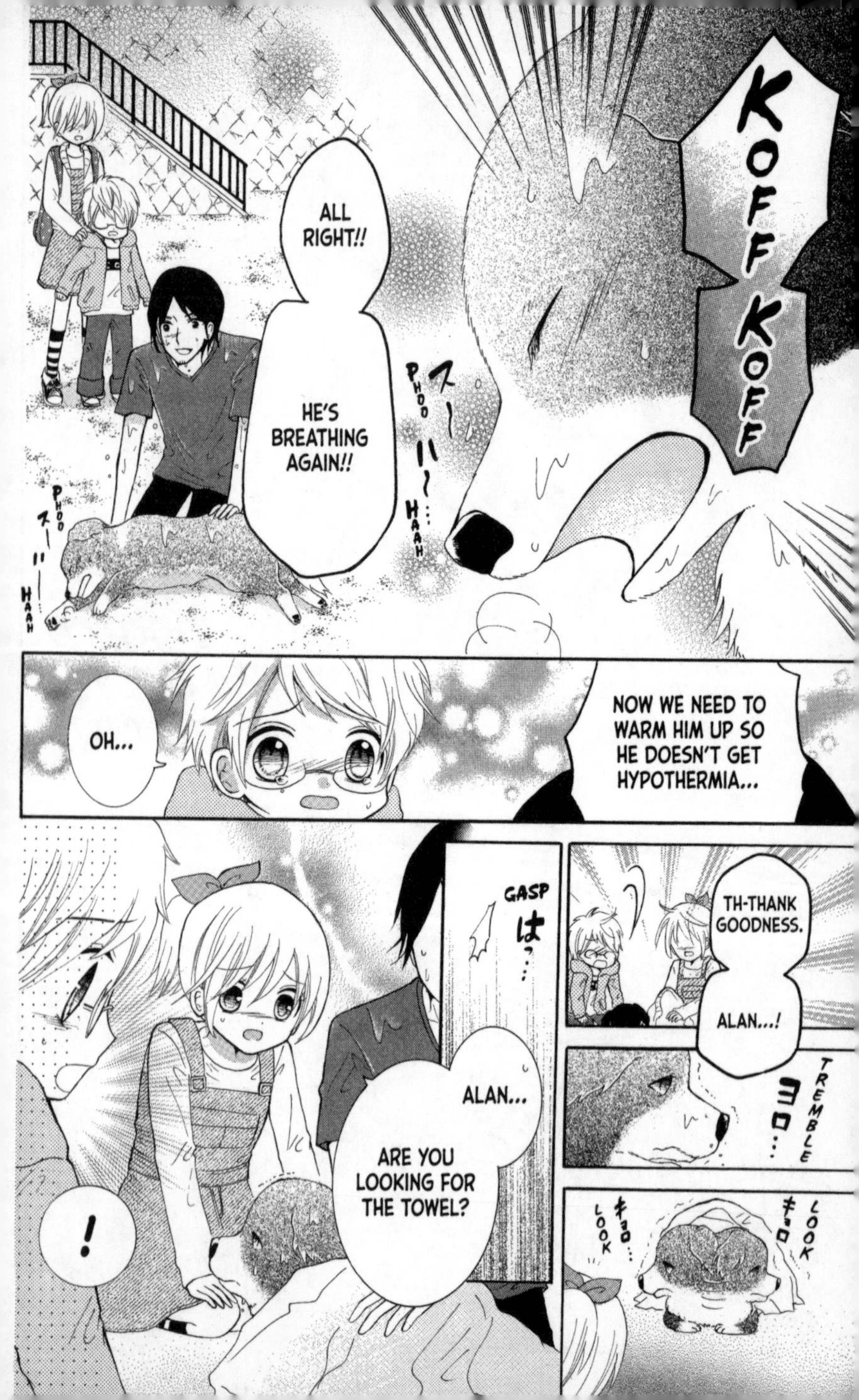
KOFF KOFF
PHOO HAAH
ALL RIGHT!!
HE'S BREATHING AGAIN!!
PHOO HAAH
NOW WE NEED TO WARM HIM UP SO HE DOESN'T GET HYPOTHERMIA...
OH...
TH-THANK GOODNESS.
ALAN...!
TREMBLE
LOOK
LOOK
GASP
ALAN...
ARE YOU LOOKING FOR THE TOWEL?
!

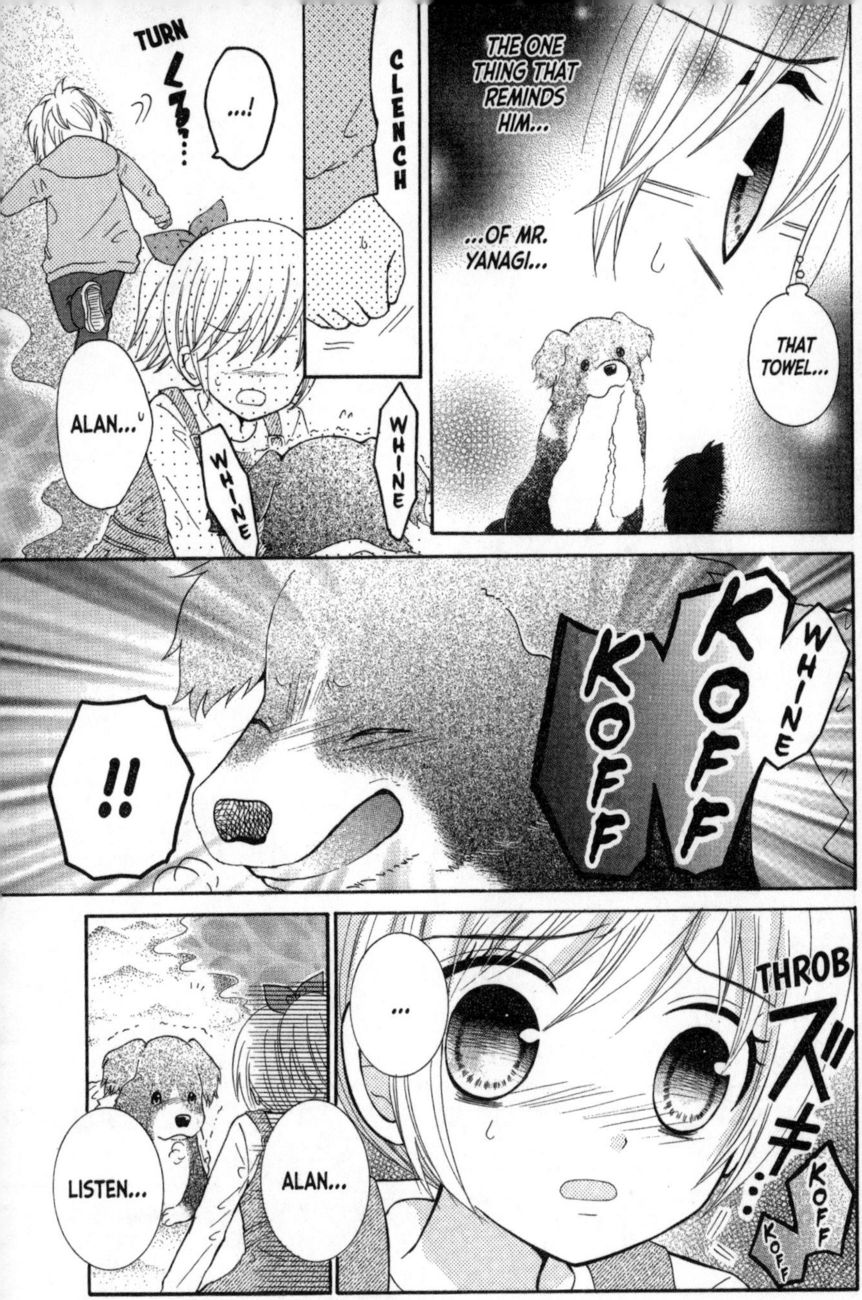
THE ONE THING THAT REMINDS HIM...
...OF MR. YANAGI...
THAT TOWEL...
CLENCH
TURN
...!
ALAN...
WHINE
WHINE
KOFF
KOFF
WHINE
!!
THROB
KOFF
KOFF
...
ALAN...
LISTEN...

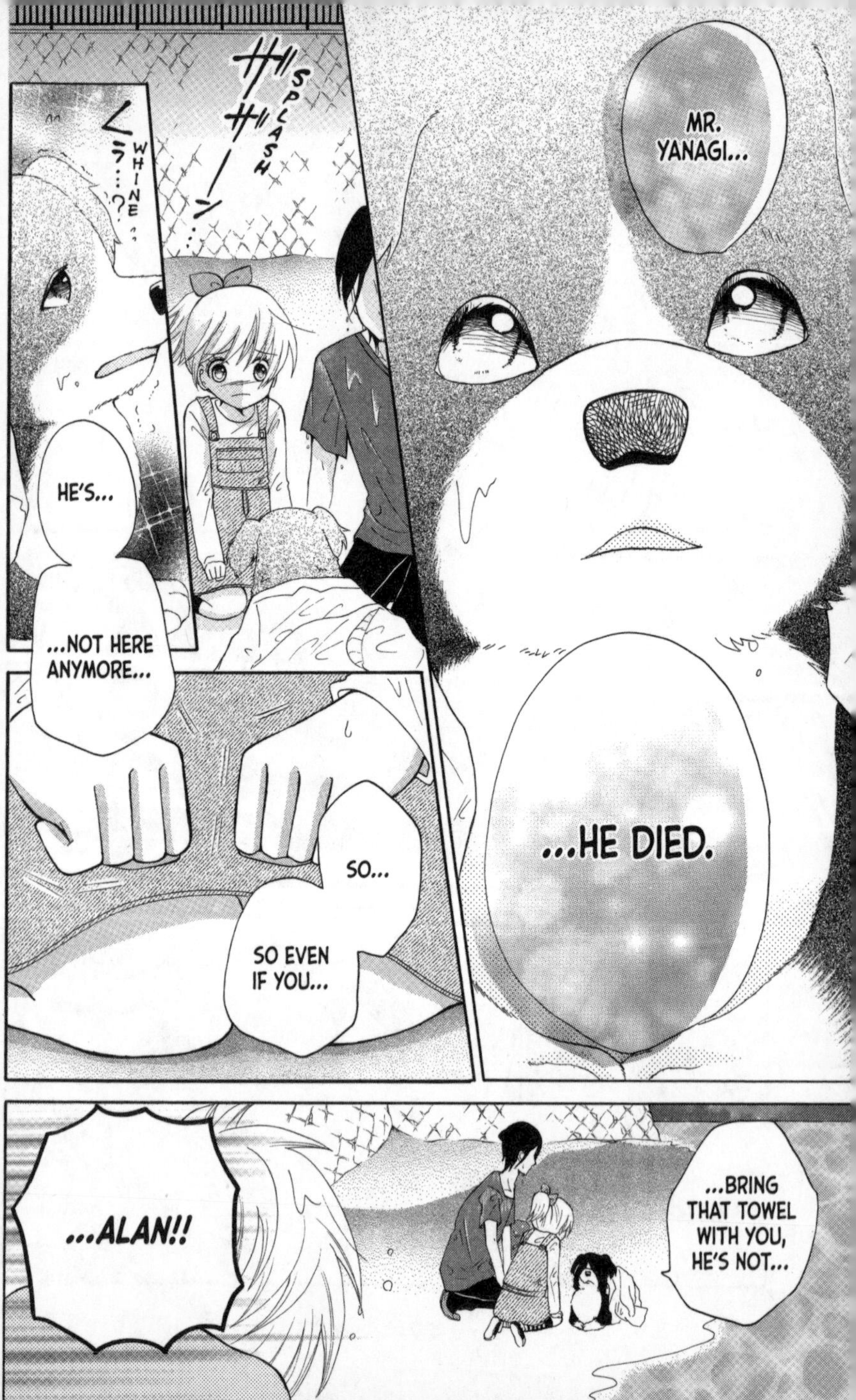
MR. YANAGI...
...HE DIED.
ザザーン
SPLASH
くぅ…?
WHINE...?
HE'S...
...NOT HERE ANYMORE...
SO...
SO EVEN IF YOU...
...BRING THAT TOWEL WITH YOU, HE'S NOT...
...ALAN!!

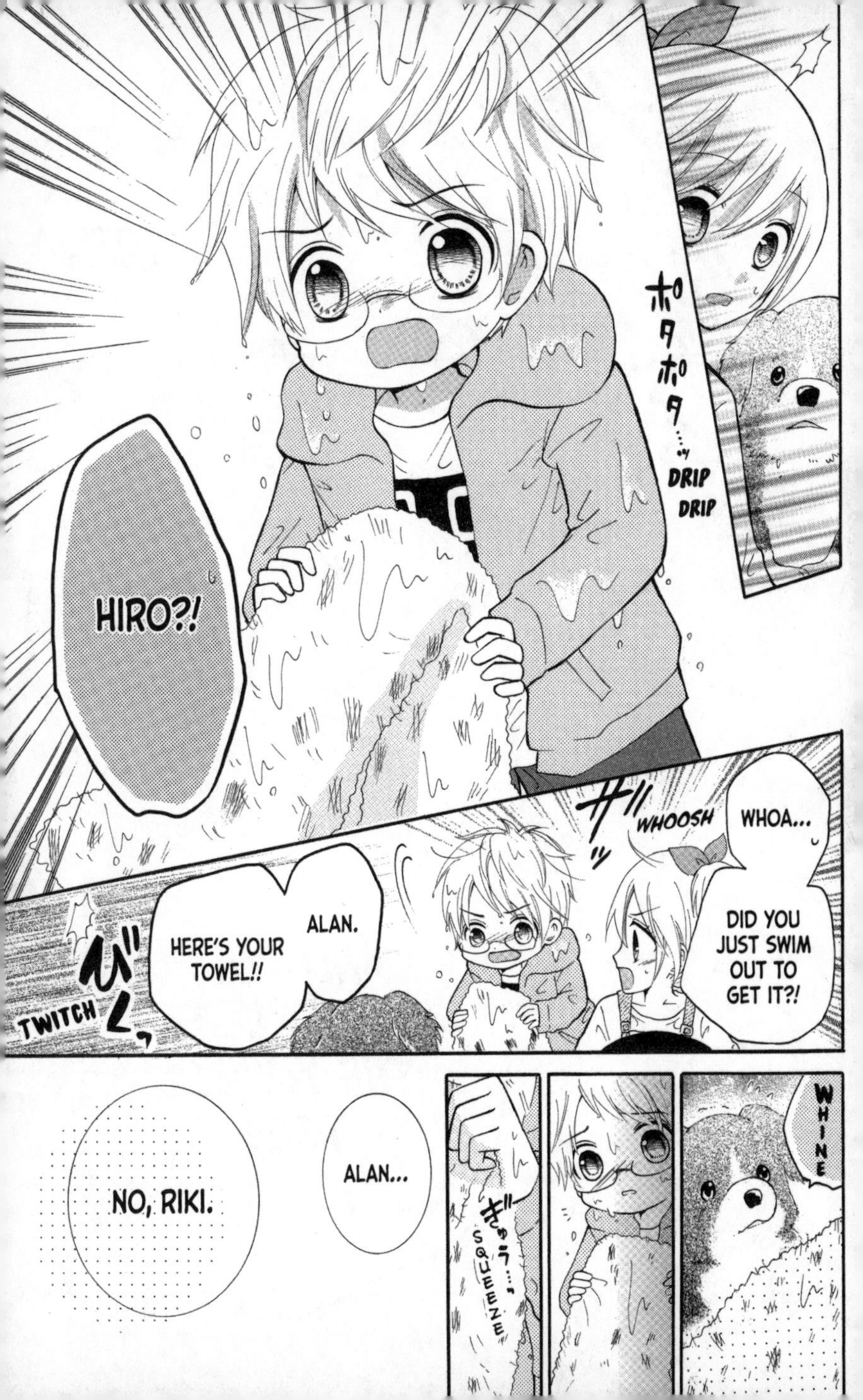
ポタポタ……
DRIP DRIP
HIRO?!
ザッ
WHOOSH
WHOA...
DID YOU JUST SWIM OUT TO GET IT?!
ALAN.
HERE'S YOUR TOWEL!!
びくっ
TWITCH
WHINE
ぎゅう…
SQUEEZE
ALAN...
NO, RIKI.

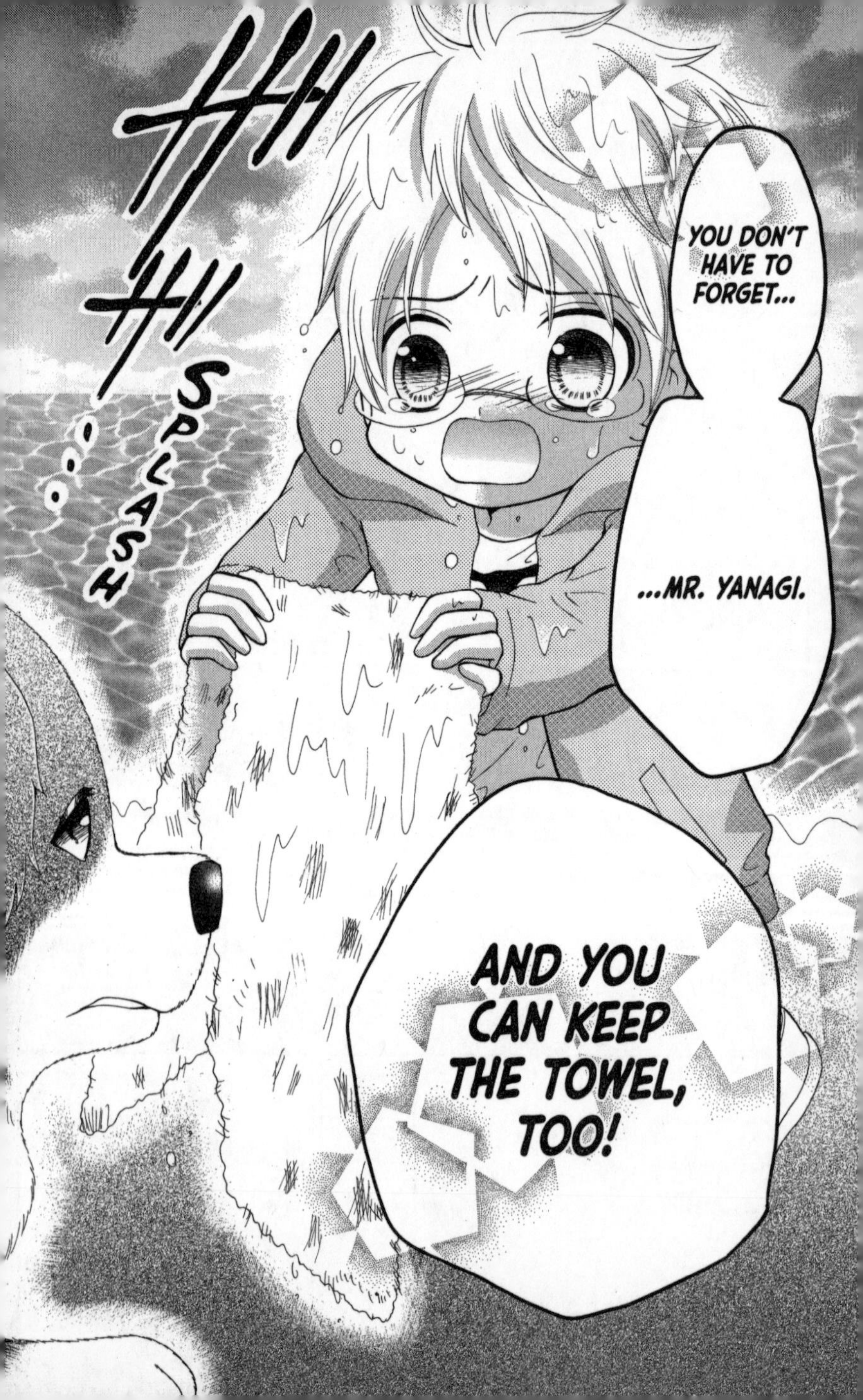
YOU DON'T HAVE TO FORGET...
...MR. YANAGI.
AND YOU CAN KEEP THE TOWEL, TOO!
SPLASH...

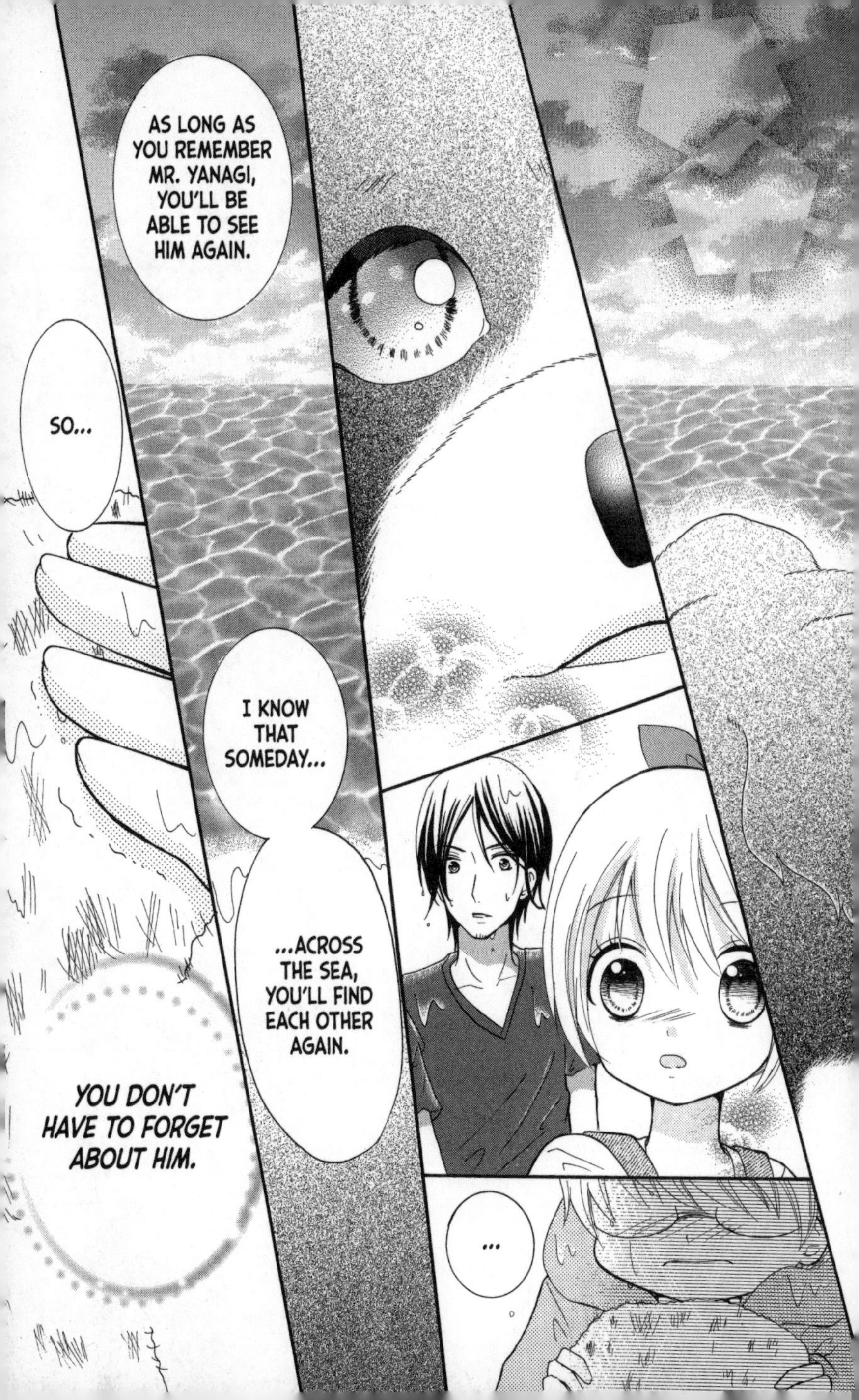
AS LONG AS YOU REMEMBER MR. YANAGI, YOU'LL BE ABLE TO SEE HIM AGAIN.
I KNOW THAT SOMEDAY...
...ACROSS THE SEA, YOU'LL FIND EACH OTHER AGAIN.
SO...
YOU DON'T HAVE TO FORGET ABOUT HIM.
...

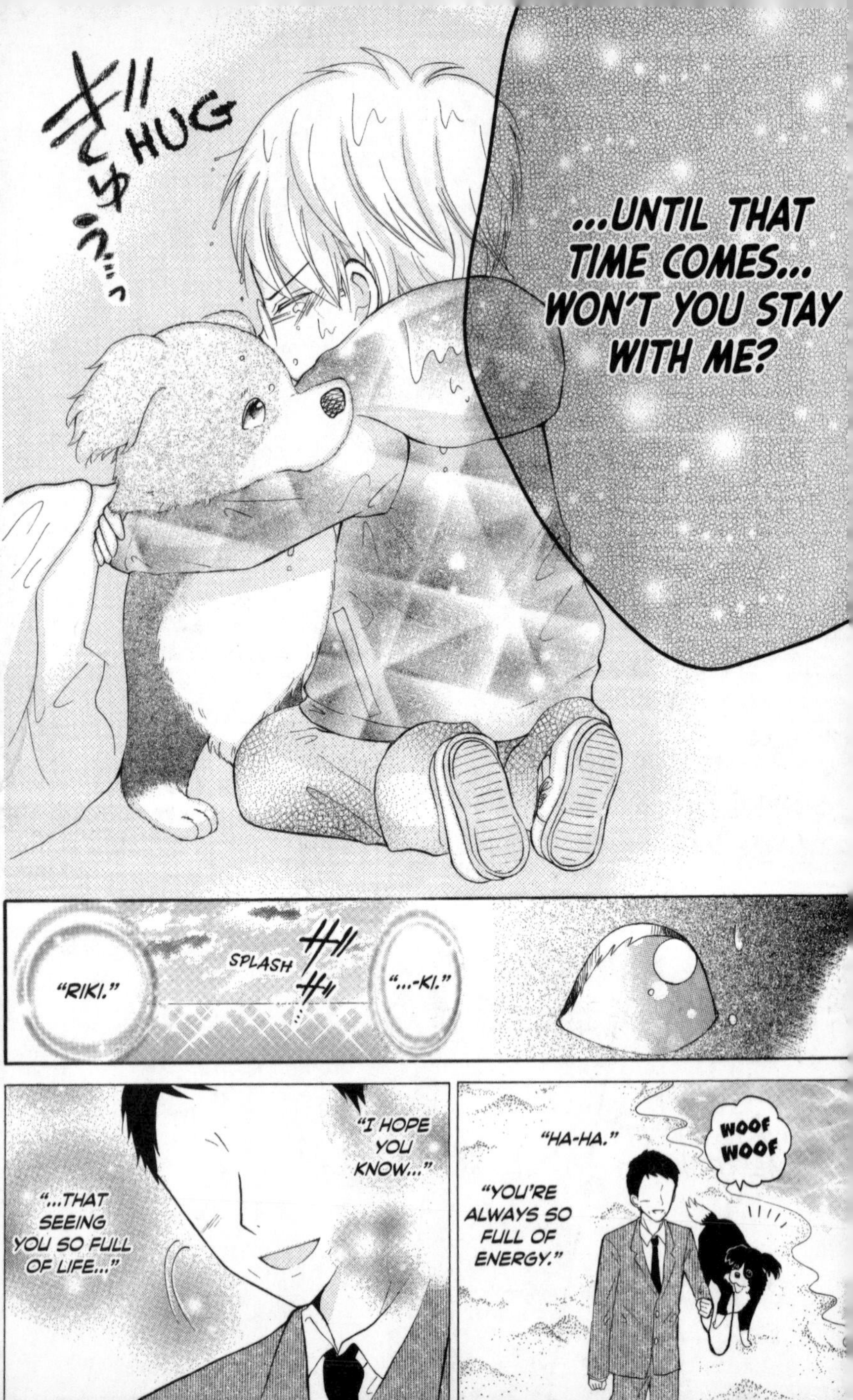
...UNTIL THAT TIME COMES... WON'T YOU STAY WITH ME?
HUG
"...-KI."
SPLASH
"RIKI."
WOOF WOOF
"HA-HA."
"YOU'RE ALWAYS SO FULL OF ENERGY."
"I HOPE YOU KNOW..."
"...THAT SEEING YOU SO FULL OF LIFE..."

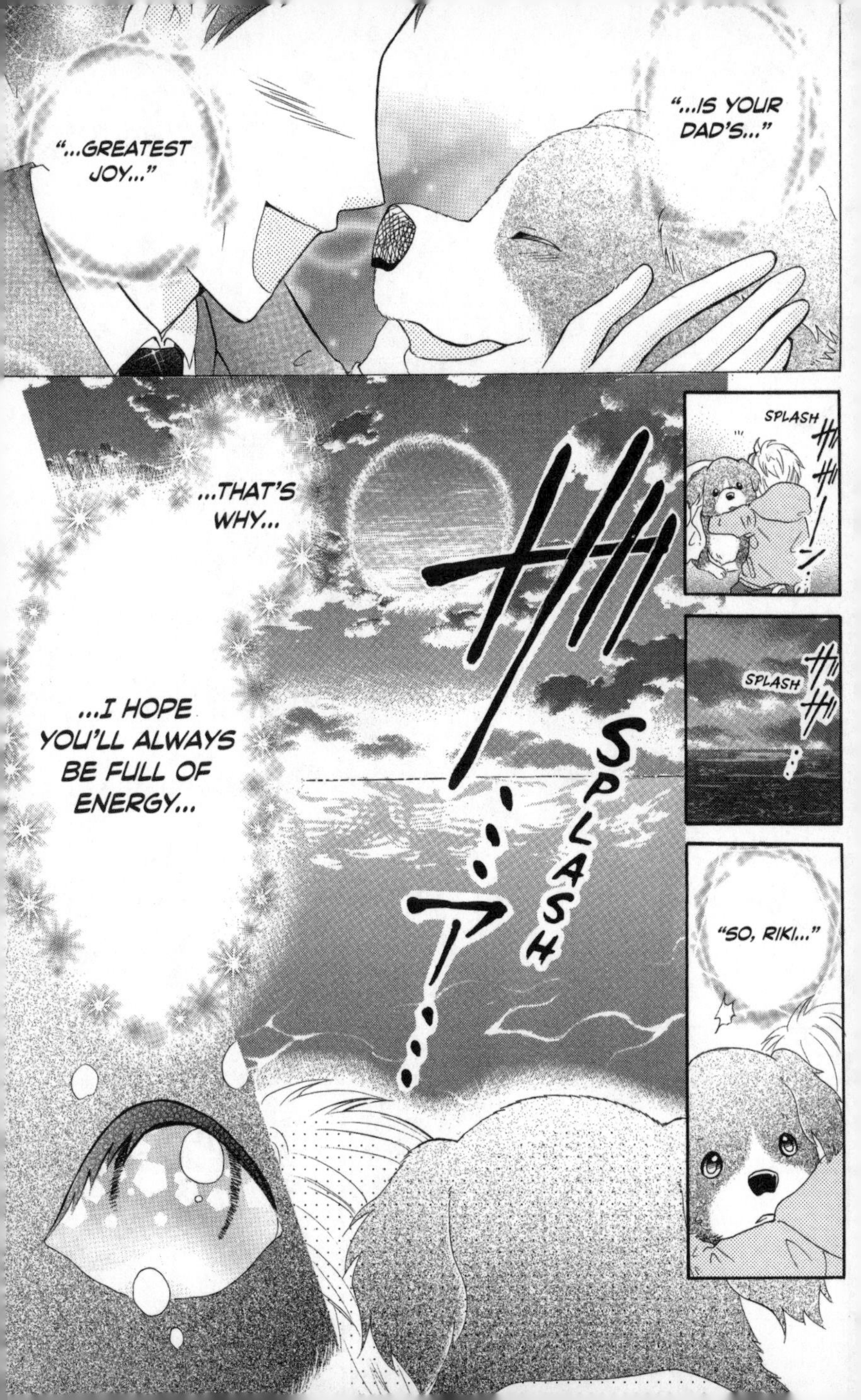
"...IS YOUR DAD'S..."
"...GREATEST JOY..."
SPLASH
SPLASH
"SO, RIKI..."
SPLASH
...THAT'S WHY...
...I HOPE YOU'LL ALWAYS BE FULL OF ENERGY...

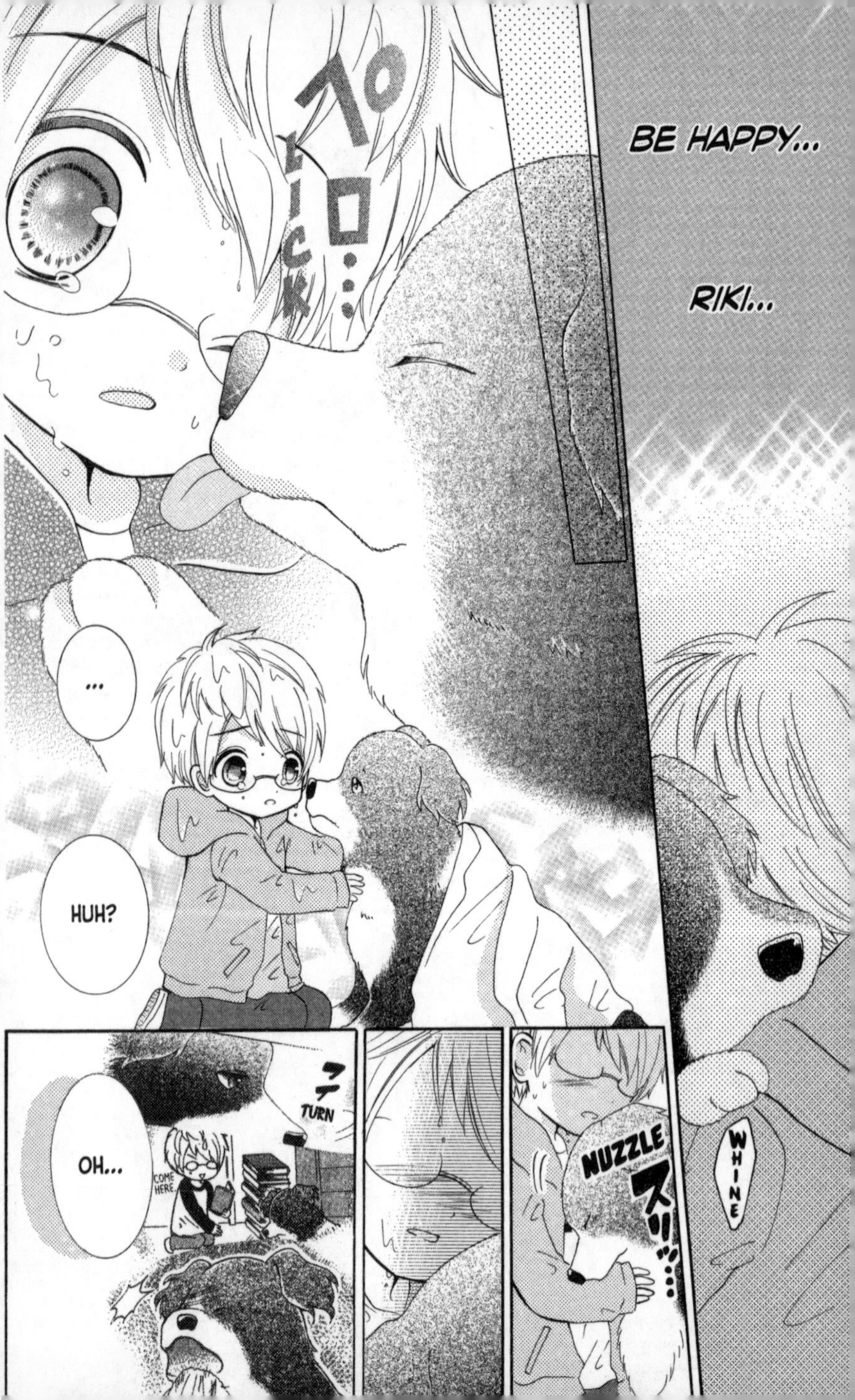
BE HAPPY...
RIKI...
WHINE
ペロ…
LICK
...
HUH?
NUZZLE
スリッ…
TURN
OH...
COME HERE.

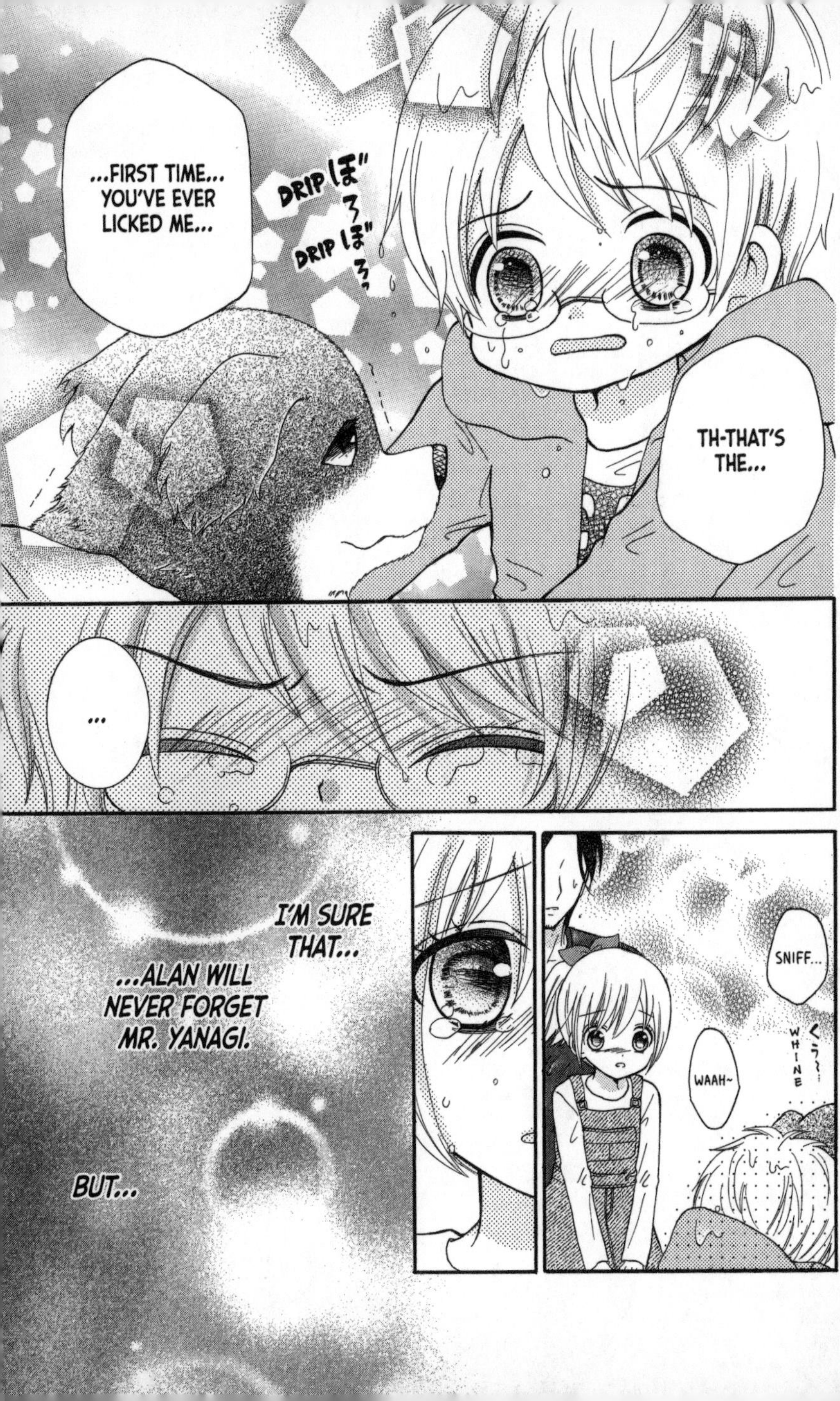
TH-THAT'S THE...
DRIP ぼ"ろ
DRIP ぼ"ろっ
...FIRST TIME... YOU'VE EVER LICKED ME...
...
SNIFF...
WHINE くぅ~
WAAH~
I'M SURE THAT...
...ALAN WILL NEVER FORGET MR. YANAGI.
BUT...

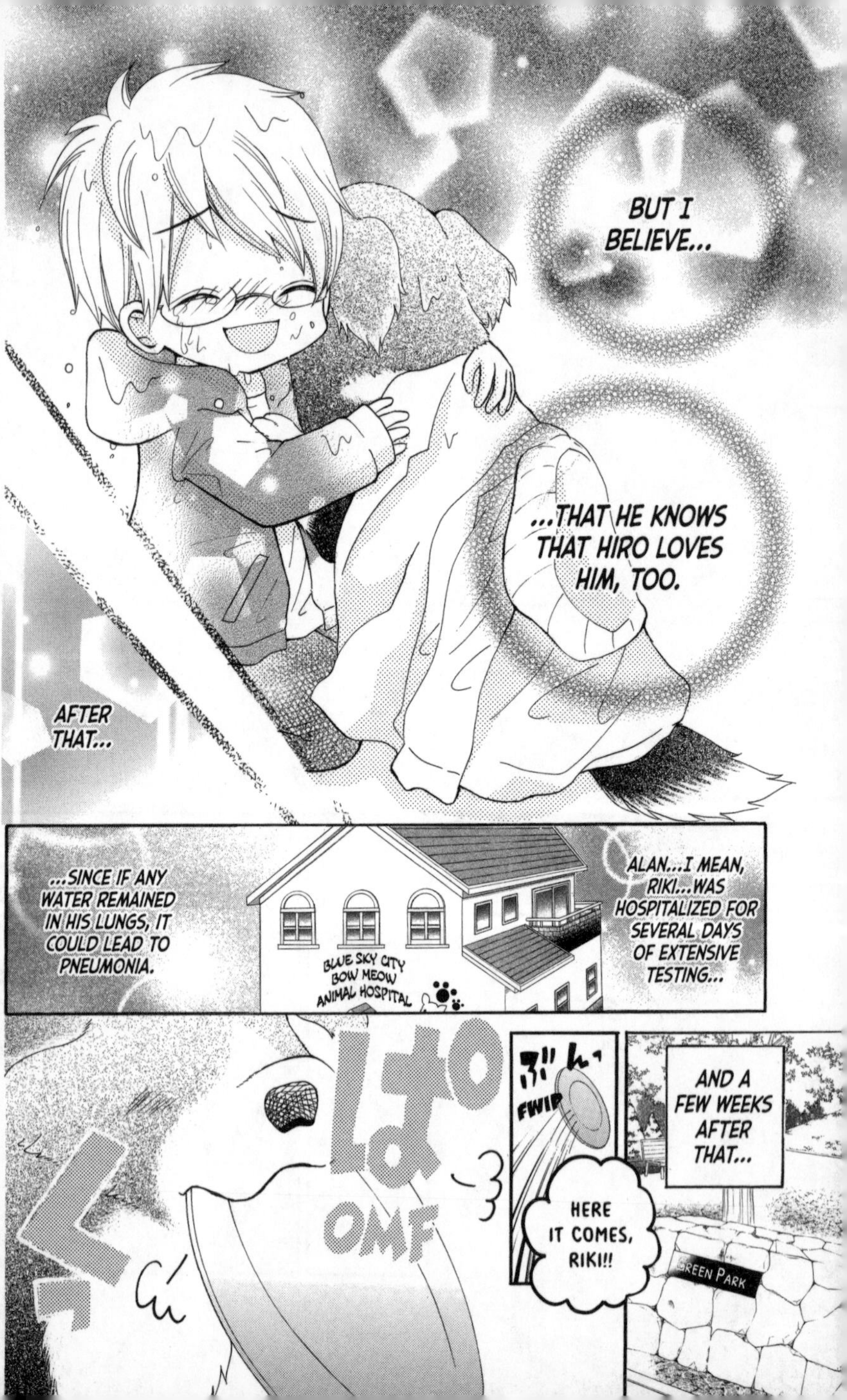
BUT I BELIEVE...
...THAT HE KNOWS THAT HIRO LOVES HIM, TOO.
AFTER THAT...
ALAN...I MEAN, RIKI...WAS HOSPITALIZED FOR SEVERAL DAYS OF EXTENSIVE TESTING...
...SINCE IF ANY WATER REMAINED IN HIS LUNGS, IT COULD LEAD TO PNEUMONIA.
BLUE SKY CITY BOW MEOW ANIMAL HOSPITAL
AND A FEW WEEKS AFTER THAT...
GREEN PARK
HERE IT COMES, RIKI!!
ぶん
FWIP
OMF

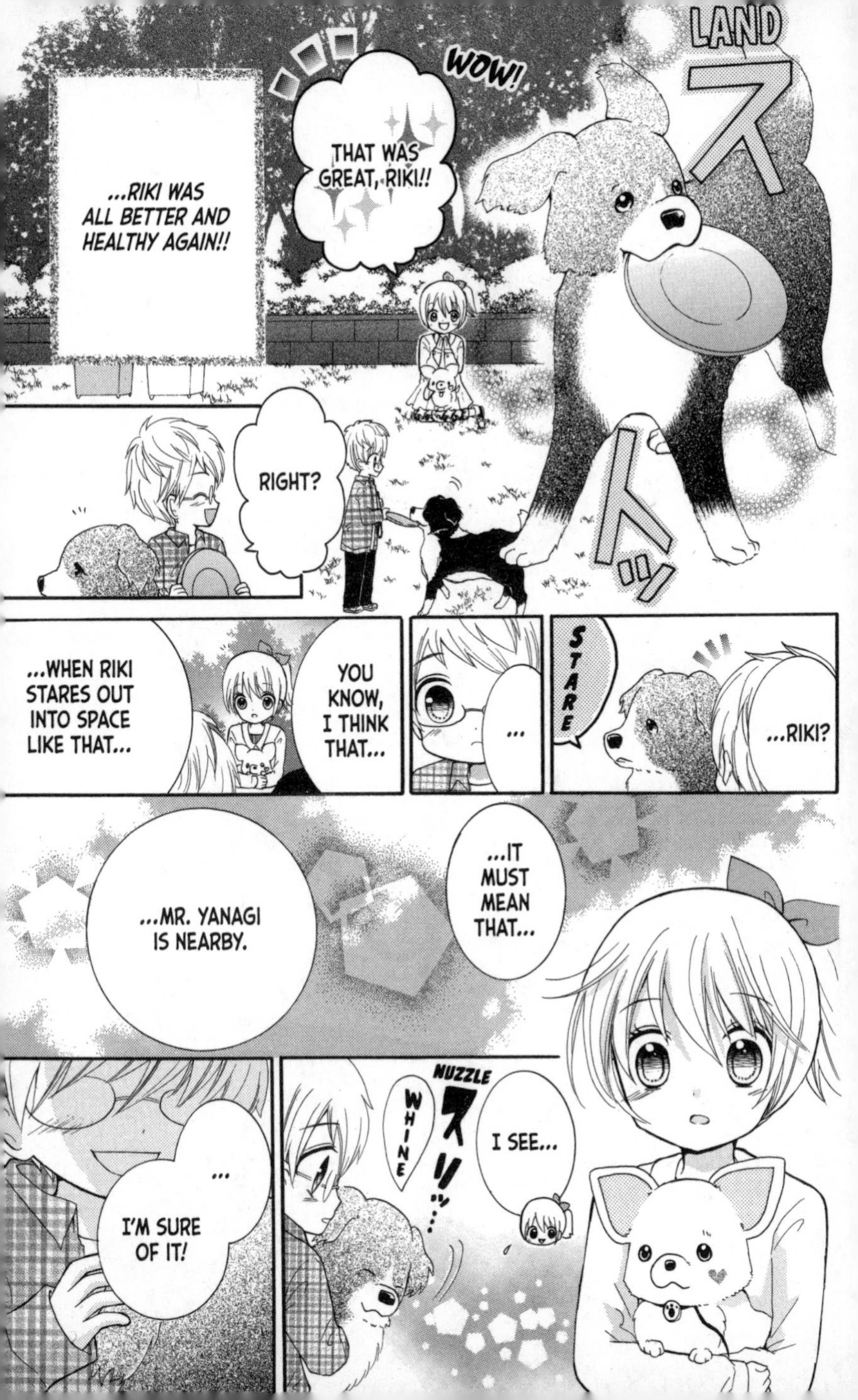
LAND
WOW!
THAT WAS GREAT, RIKI!!
...RIKI WAS ALL BETTER AND HEALTHY AGAIN!!
RIGHT?
...RIKI?
STARE
...
YOU KNOW, I THINK THAT...
...WHEN RIKI STARES OUT INTO SPACE LIKE THAT...
...IT MUST MEAN THAT...
...MR. YANAGI IS NEARBY.
I SEE...
NUZZLE
WHINE
...
I'M SURE OF IT!

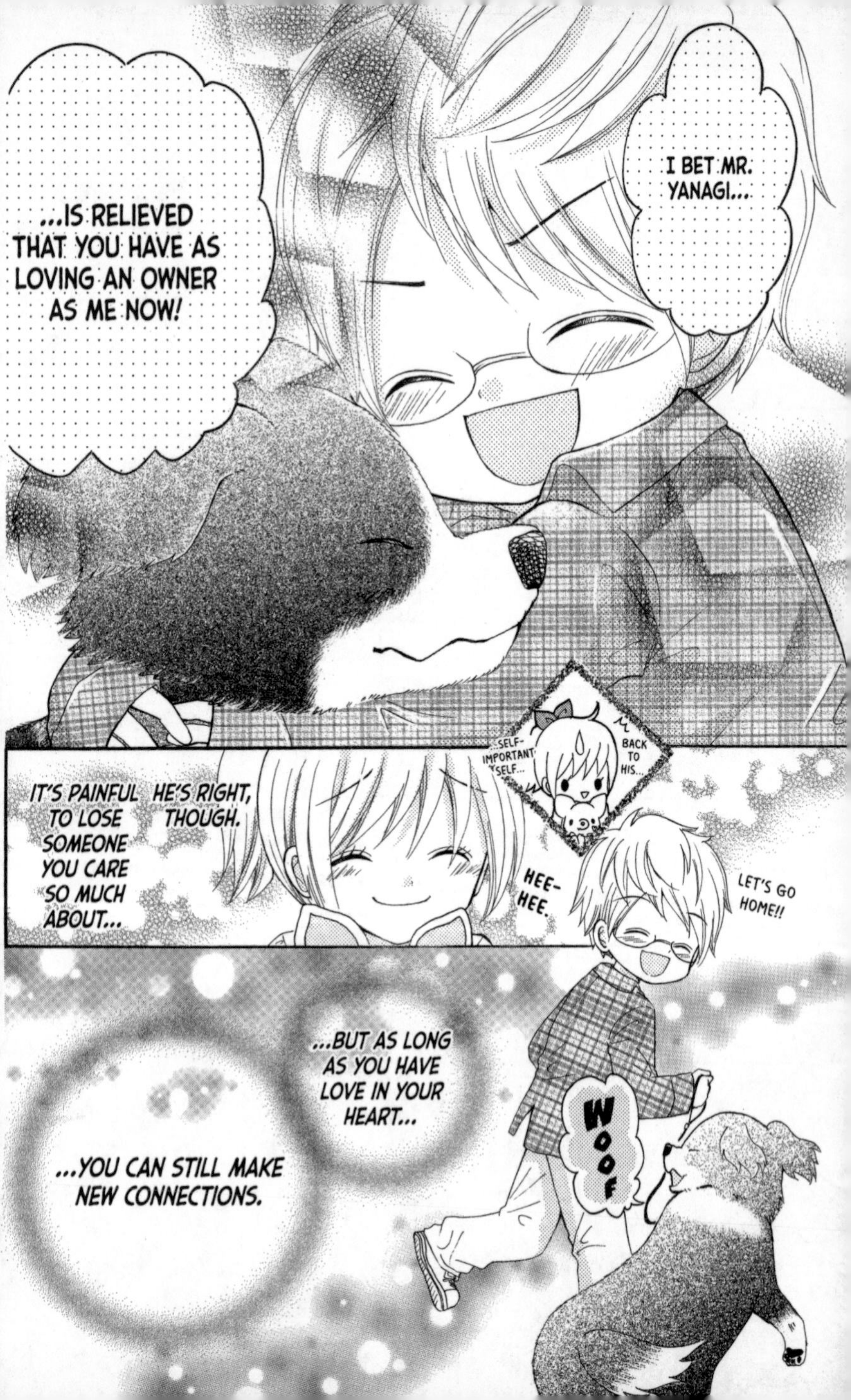
I BET MR. YANAGI...
...IS RELIEVED THAT YOU HAVE AS LOVING AN OWNER AS ME NOW!
LET'S GO HOME!!
HEE-HEE.
BACK TO HIS...
...SELF-IMPORTANT SELF...
HE'S RIGHT, THOUGH.
IT'S PAINFUL TO LOSE SOMEONE YOU CARE SO MUCH ABOUT...
WOOF
...BUT AS LONG AS YOU HAVE LOVE IN YOUR HEART...
...YOU CAN STILL MAKE NEW CONNECTIONS.

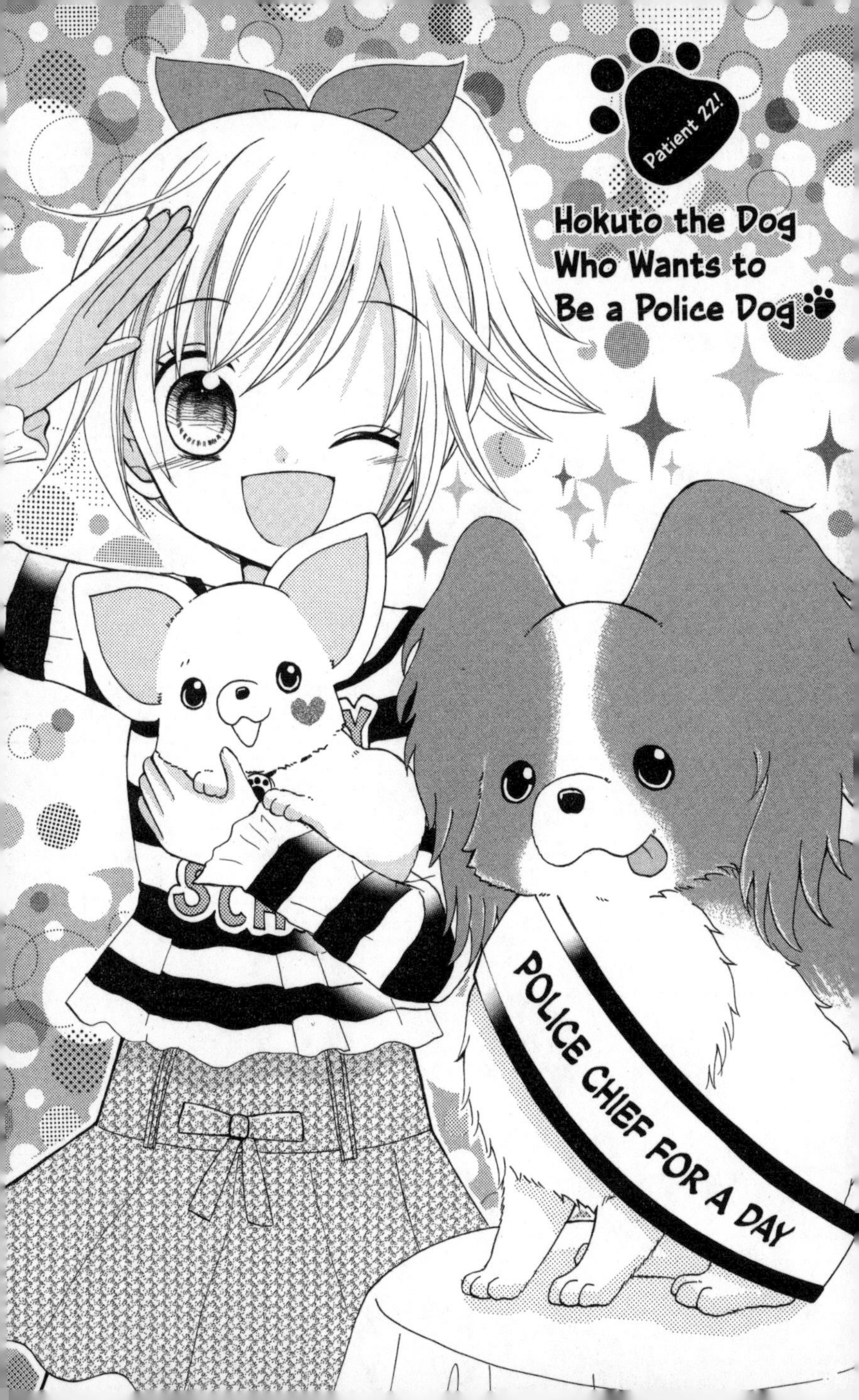
Patient 22!
Hokuto the Dog Who Wants to Be a Police Dog
POLICE CHIEF FOR A DAY

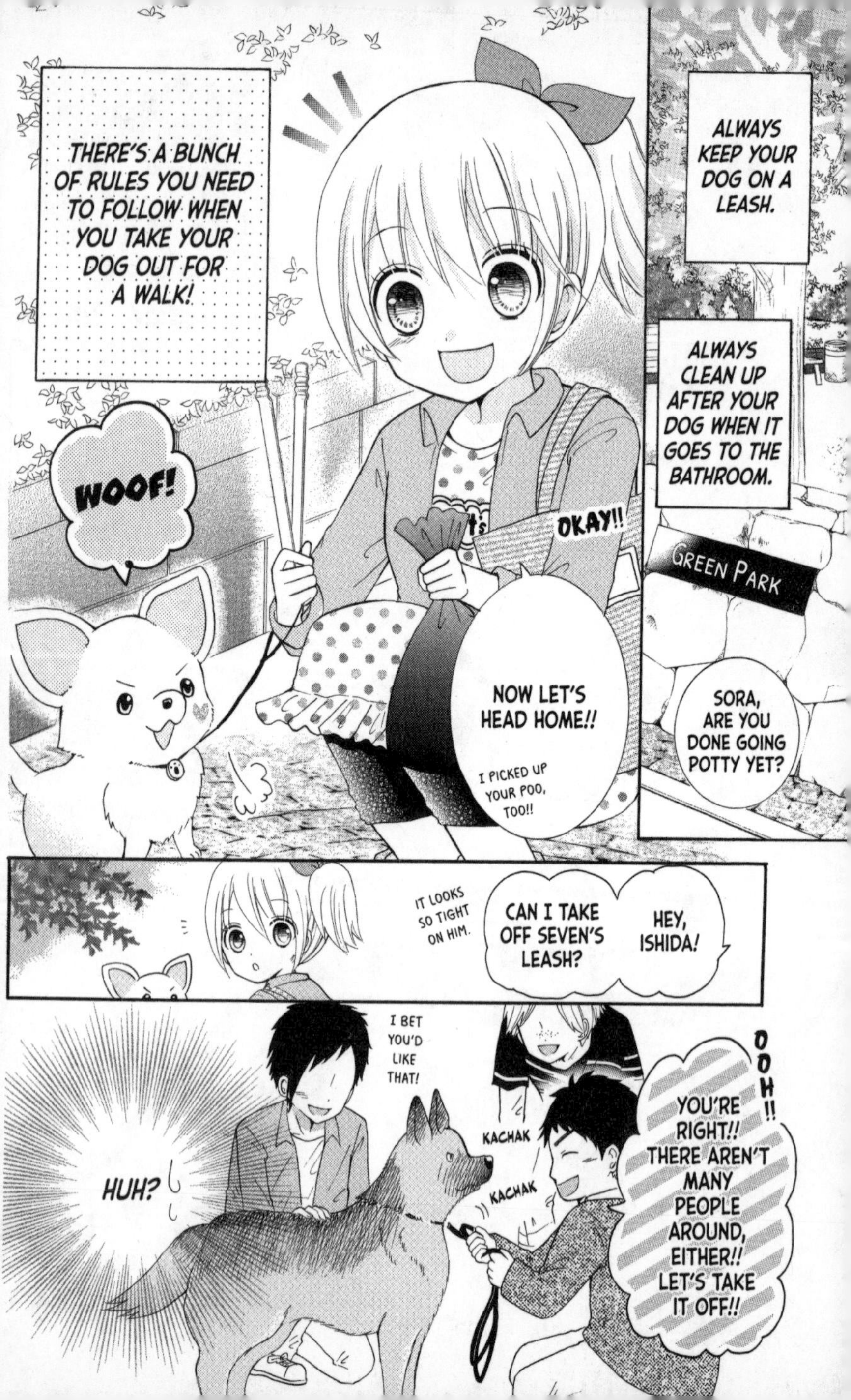
ALWAYS KEEP YOUR DOG ON A LEASH.
ALWAYS CLEAN UP AFTER YOUR DOG WHEN IT GOES TO THE BATHROOM.
GREEN PARK
SORA, ARE YOU DONE GOING POTTY YET?
THERE'S A BUNCH OF RULES YOU NEED TO FOLLOW WHEN YOU TAKE YOUR DOG OUT FOR A WALK!
OKAY!!
NOW LET'S HEAD HOME!!
I PICKED UP YOUR POO, TOO!!
WOOF!
HEY, ISHIDA!
CAN I TAKE OFF SEVEN'S LEASH?
IT LOOKS SO TIGHT ON HIM.
OOH!!
YOU'RE RIGHT!! THERE AREN'T MANY PEOPLE AROUND, EITHER!! LET'S TAKE IT OFF!!
KACHAK
KACHAK
I BET YOU'D LIKE THAT!
HUH?

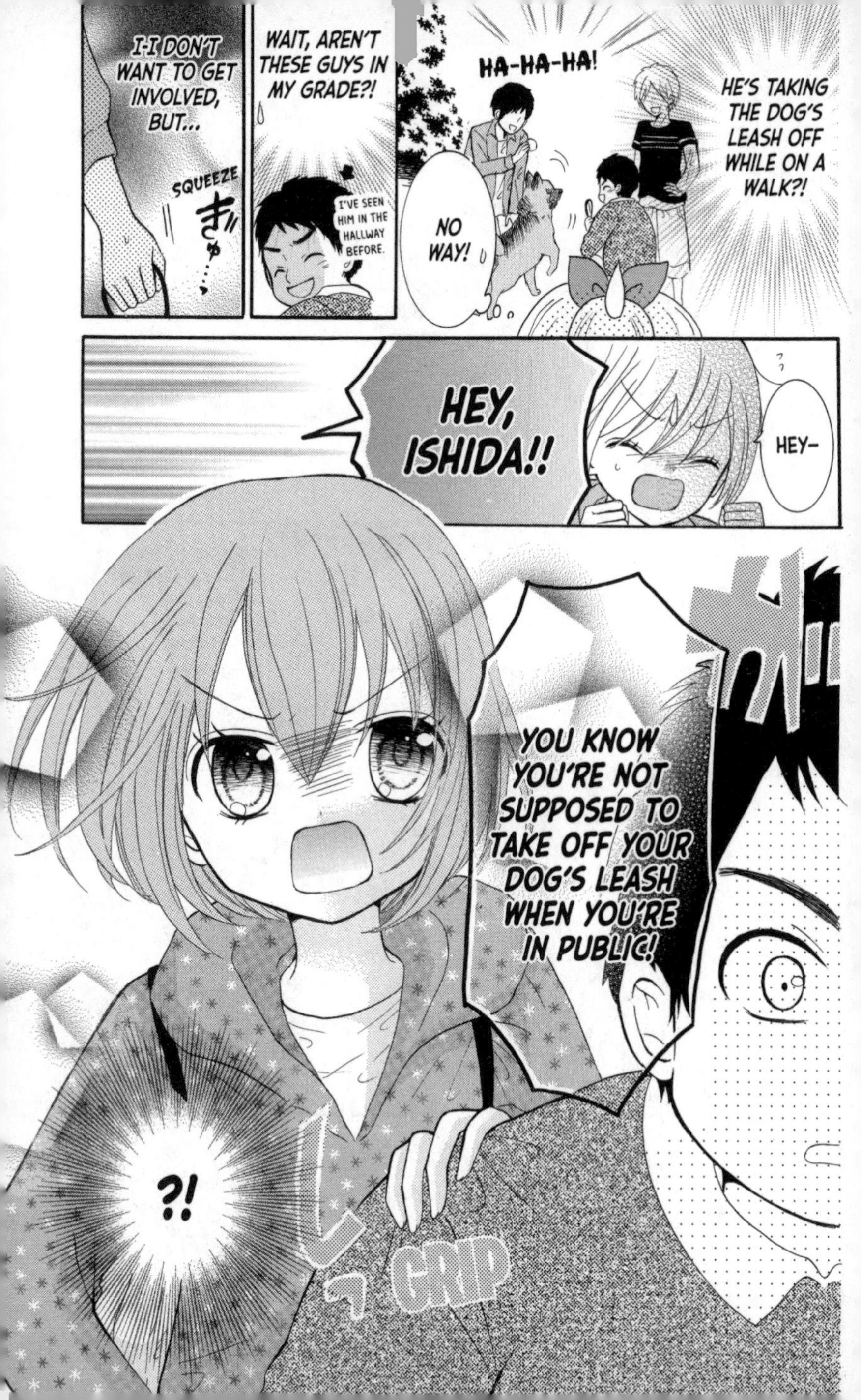
HE'S TAKING THE DOG'S LEASH OFF WHILE ON A WALK?!
HA-HA-HA!
NO WAY!
WAIT, AREN'T THESE GUYS IN MY GRADE?!
I'VE SEEN HIM IN THE HALLWAY BEFORE.
I-I DON'T WANT TO GET INVOLVED, BUT...
SQUEEZE
ぎゅ…
HEY–
HEY, ISHIDA!!
YOU KNOW YOU'RE NOT SUPPOSED TO TAKE OFF YOUR DOG'S LEASH WHEN YOU'RE IN PUBLIC!
?!
GRIP

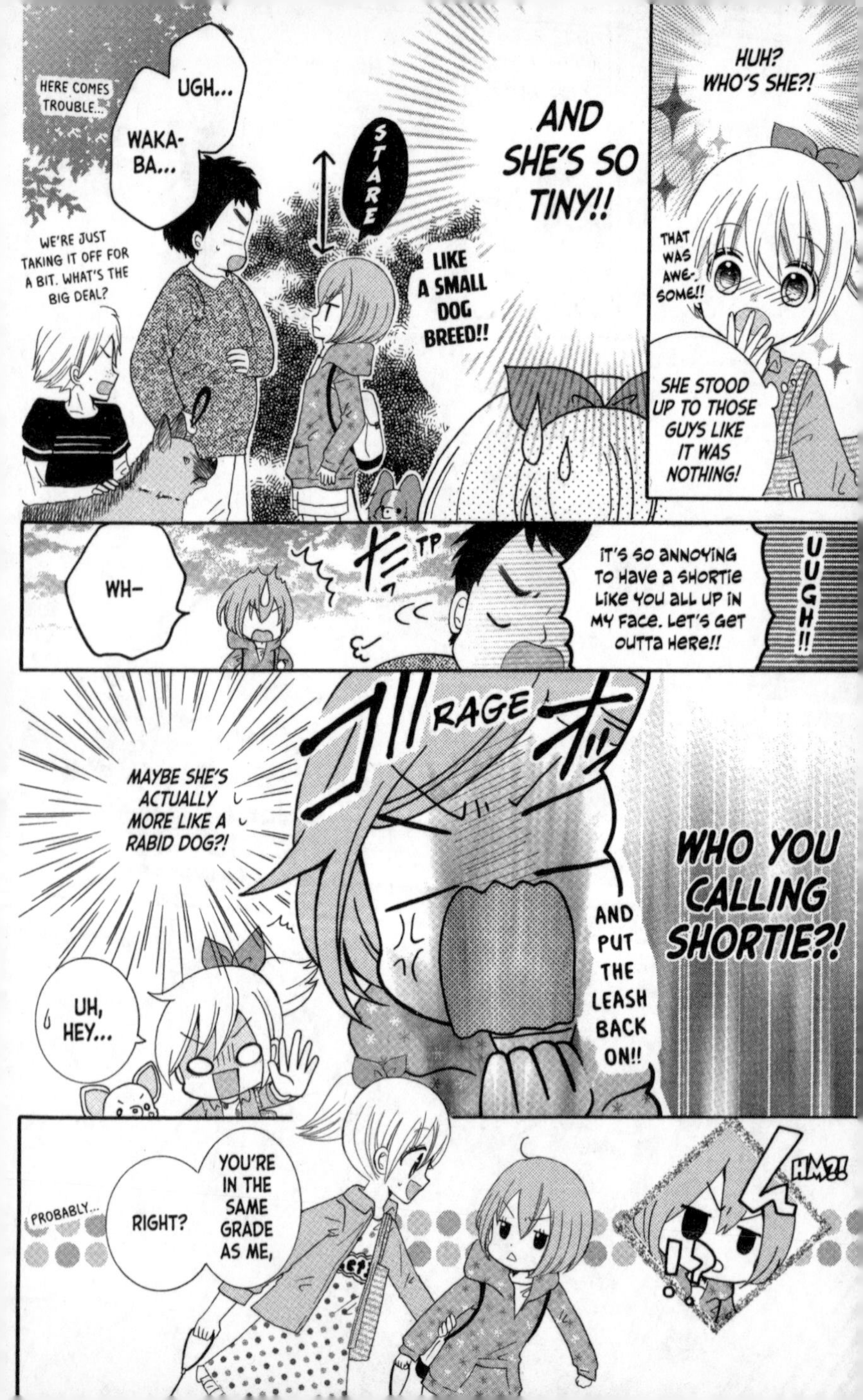
HUH? WHO'S SHE?!
THAT WAS AWE-SOME!!
SHE STOOD UP TO THOSE GUYS LIKE IT WAS NOTHING!
AND SHE'S SO TINY!!
STARE
LIKE A SMALL DOG BREED!!
UGH...
WAKA-BA...
HERE COMES TROUBLE...
WE'RE JUST TAKING IT OFF FOR A BIT. WHAT'S THE BIG DEAL?
UUGH!!
IT'S SO ANNOYING TO HAVE A SHORTIE LIKE YOU ALL UP IN MY FACE. LET'S GET OUTTA HERE!!
TP
WH–
WHO YOU CALLING SHORTIE?!
AND PUT THE LEASH BACK ON!!
RAGE
MAYBE SHE'S ACTUALLY MORE LIKE A RABID DOG?!
UH, HEY...
HM?!
YOU'RE IN THE SAME GRADE AS ME,
RIGHT?
PROBABLY...

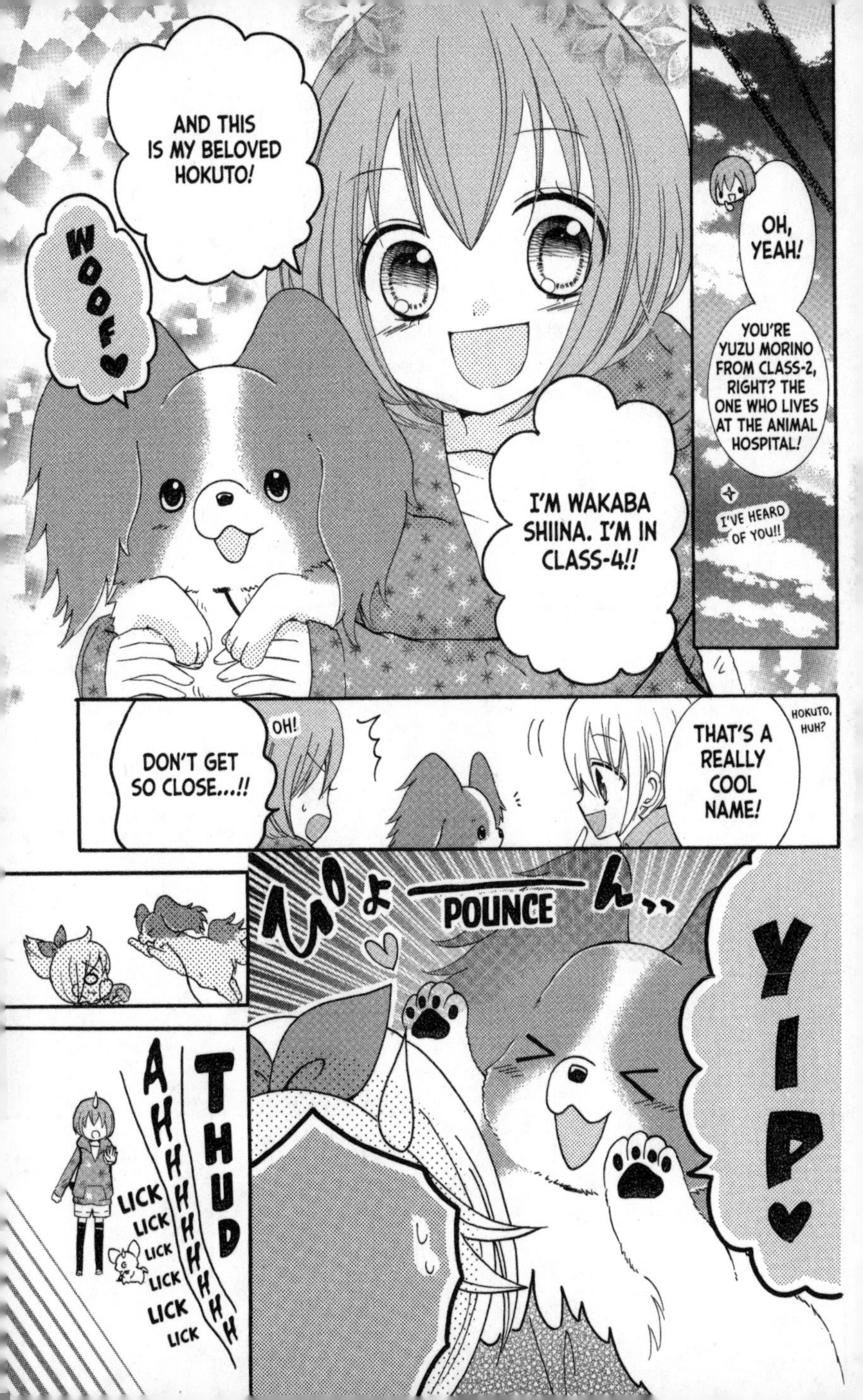

OH, YEAH!
YOU'RE YUZU MORINO FROM CLASS-2, RIGHT? THE ONE WHO LIVES AT THE ANIMAL HOSPITAL!
I'VE HEARD OF YOU!!
I'M WAKABA SHIINA. I'M IN CLASS-4!!
AND THIS IS MY BELOVED HOKUTO!
WOOF♥
HOKUTO, HUH?
THAT'S A REALLY COOL NAME!
OH!
DON'T GET SO CLOSE...!!
YIP♥
ぴょ——ん
POUNCE
THUD
AHHHHHHHHHH
LICK LICK LICK LICK LICK LICK LICK

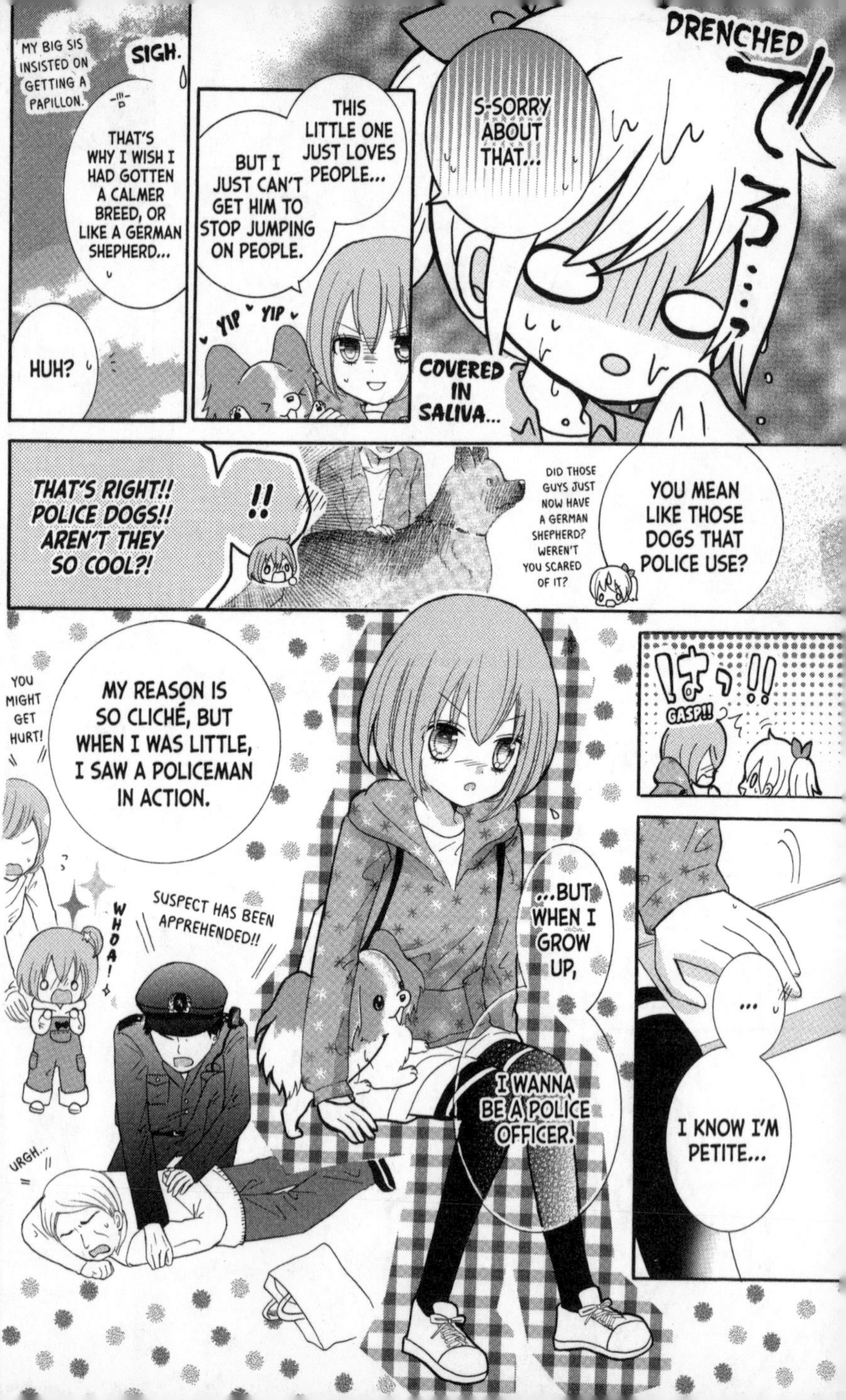

DRENCHED
でろ…
S-SORRY ABOUT THAT...
COVERED IN SALIVA...
THIS LITTLE ONE JUST LOVES PEOPLE...
BUT I JUST CAN'T GET HIM TO STOP JUMPING ON PEOPLE.
YIP YIP
MY BIG SIS INSISTED ON GETTING A PAPILLON.
SIGH.
THAT'S WHY I WISH I HAD GOTTEN A CALMER BREED, OR LIKE A GERMAN SHEPHERD...
HUH?
YOU MEAN LIKE THOSE DOGS THAT POLICE USE?
DID THOSE GUYS JUST NOW HAVE A GERMAN SHEPHERD? WEREN'T YOU SCARED OF IT?
!!
THAT'S RIGHT!! POLICE DOGS!! AREN'T THEY SO COOL?!
!はっ!!
GASP!!
...
I KNOW I'M PETITE...
...BUT WHEN I GROW UP,
I WANNA BE A POLICE OFFICER!
MY REASON IS SO CLICHÉ, BUT WHEN I WAS LITTLE, I SAW A POLICEMAN IN ACTION.
YOU MIGHT GET HURT!
SUSPECT HAS BEEN APPREHENDED!!
WHOA!
URGH...

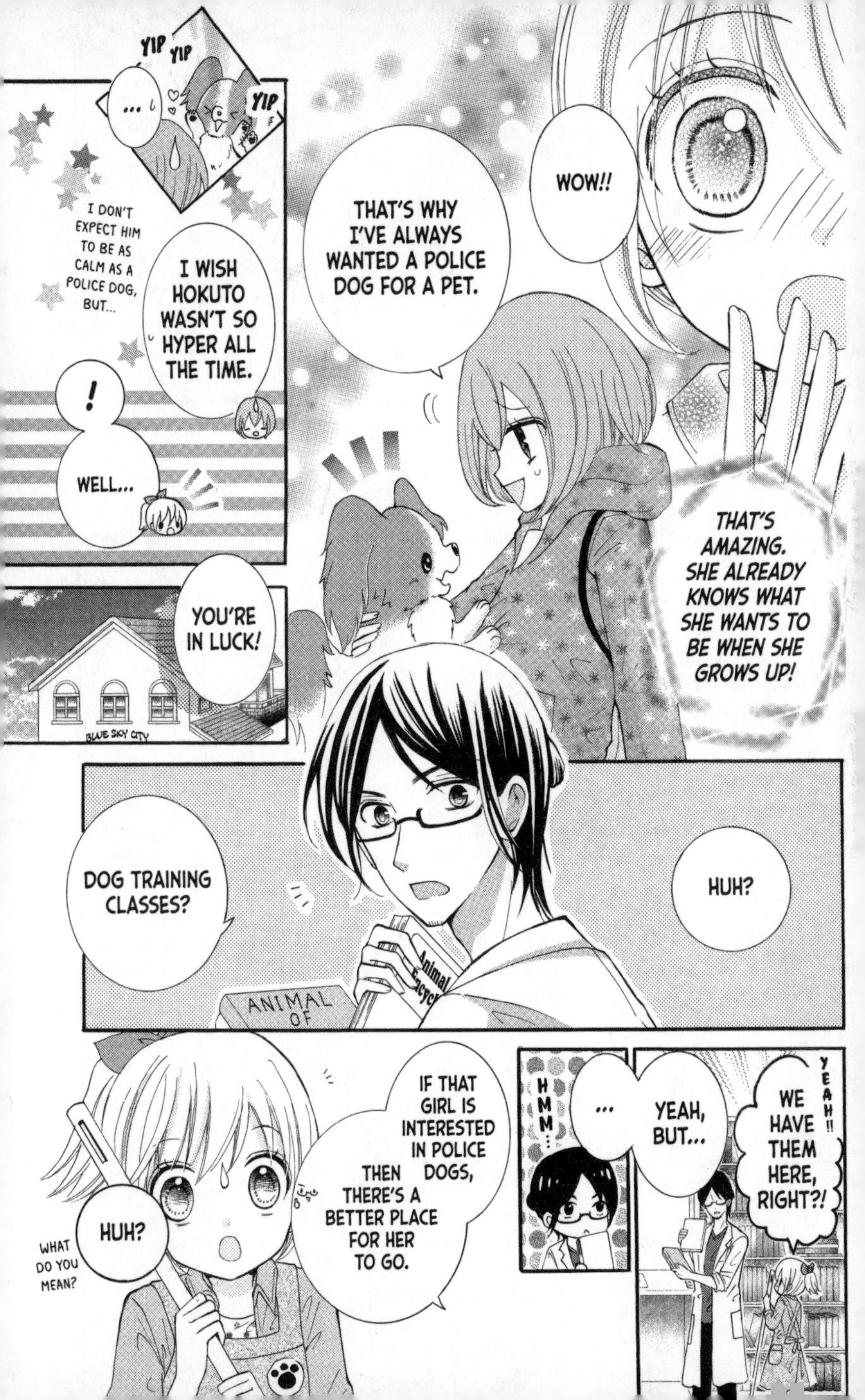
WOW!!
THAT'S WHY I'VE ALWAYS WANTED A POLICE DOG FOR A PET.
THAT'S AMAZING. SHE ALREADY KNOWS WHAT SHE WANTS TO BE WHEN SHE GROWS UP!
YIP YIP
YIP
...
I WISH HOKUTO WASN'T SO HYPER ALL THE TIME.
I DON'T EXPECT HIM TO BE AS CALM AS A POLICE DOG, BUT...
!
WELL...
YOU'RE IN LUCK!
BLUE SKY CITY
HUH?
DOG TRAINING CLASSES?
ANIMAL OF
Animal Encyc
YEAH!!
WE HAVE THEM HERE, RIGHT?!
YEAH, BUT...
...
HMM...
IF THAT GIRL IS INTERESTED IN POLICE DOGS, THEN THERE'S A BETTER PLACE FOR HER TO GO.
HUH?
WHAT DO YOU MEAN?

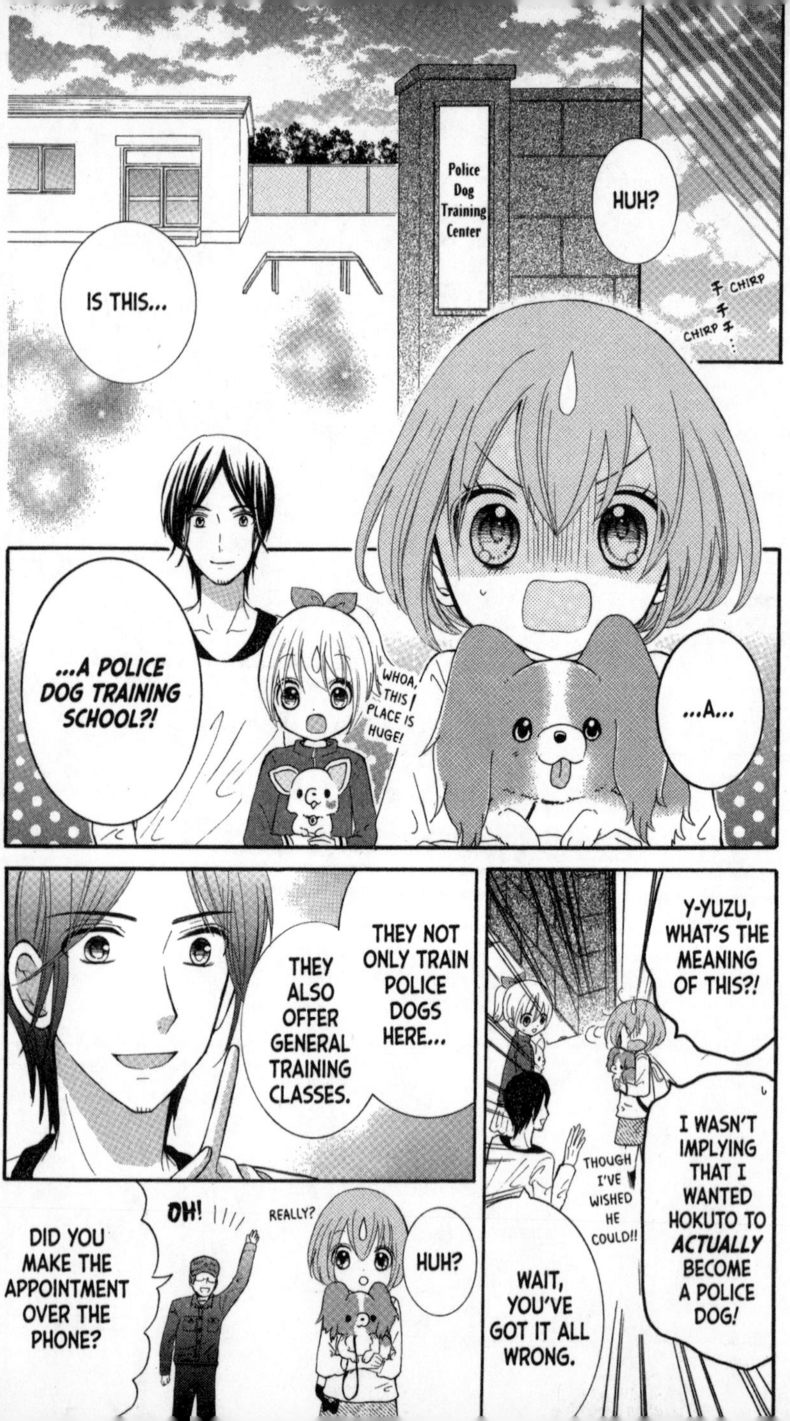
Police Dog Training Center
HUH?
チ CHIRP
チ
CHIRP チ...
IS THIS...
...A...
WHOA, THIS PLACE IS HUGE!
...A POLICE DOG TRAINING SCHOOL?!
Y-YUZU, WHAT'S THE MEANING OF THIS?!
I WASN'T IMPLYING THAT I WANTED HOKUTO TO ACTUALLY BECOME A POLICE DOG!
THOUGH I'VE WISHED HE COULD!!
WAIT, YOU'VE GOT IT ALL WRONG.
THEY NOT ONLY TRAIN POLICE DOGS HERE...
THEY ALSO OFFER GENERAL TRAINING CLASSES.
HUH?
REALLY?
OH!
DID YOU MAKE THE APPOINTMENT OVER THE PHONE?

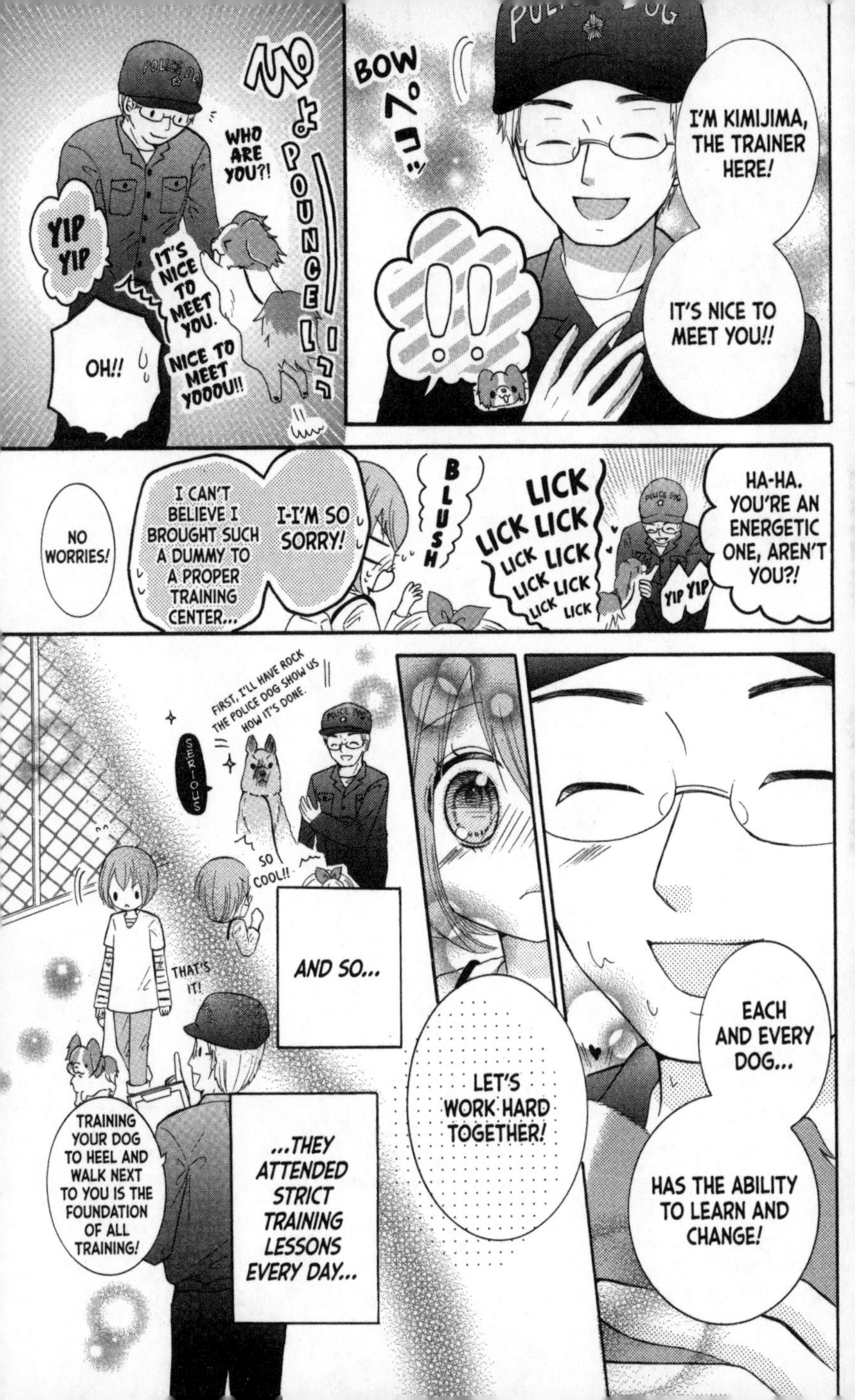
I'M KIMIJIMA, THE TRAINER HERE!
IT'S NICE TO MEET YOU!!
BOW
ペコッ
POUNCE
WHO ARE YOU?!
IT'S NICE TO MEET YOU.
NICE TO MEET YOOOU!!
YIP YIP
OH!!
HA-HA. YOU'RE AN ENERGETIC ONE, AREN'T YOU?!
YIP YIP
LICK LICK LICK LICK LICK LICK LICK LICK LICK
BLUSH
I-I'M SO SORRY!
I CAN'T BELIEVE I BROUGHT SUCH A DUMMY TO A PROPER TRAINING CENTER...
NO WORRIES!
EACH AND EVERY DOG...
HAS THE ABILITY TO LEARN AND CHANGE!
LET'S WORK HARD TOGETHER!
AND SO...
FIRST, I'LL HAVE ROCK THE POLICE DOG SHOW US HOW IT'S DONE.
SERIOUS
SO COOL!!
THAT'S IT!
...THEY ATTENDED STRICT TRAINING LESSONS EVERY DAY...
TRAINING YOUR DOG TO HEEL AND WALK NEXT TO YOU IS THE FOUNDATION OF ALL TRAINING!

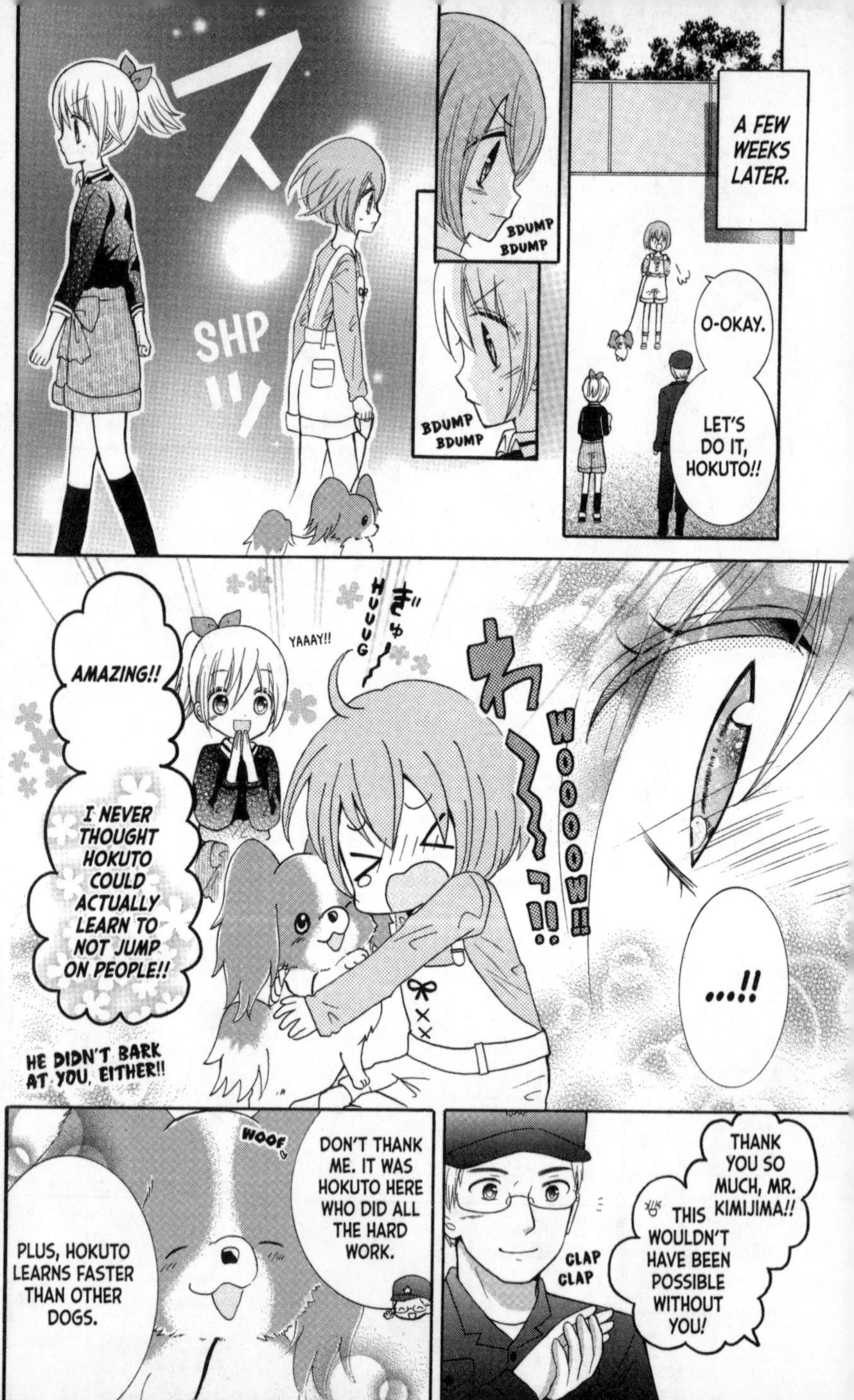
A FEW WEEKS LATER.
O-OKAY.
LET'S DO IT, HOKUTO!!
BDUMP BDUMP
BDUMP BDUMP
SHP
...!!
WOOOOOW!!
HUUUG
YAAAY!!
AMAZING!!
I NEVER THOUGHT HOKUTO COULD ACTUALLY LEARN TO NOT JUMP ON PEOPLE!!
HE DIDN'T BARK AT YOU, EITHER!!
THANK YOU SO MUCH, MR. KIMIJIMA!!
THIS WOULDN'T HAVE BEEN POSSIBLE WITHOUT YOU!
CLAP CLAP
WOOF
DON'T THANK ME. IT WAS HOKUTO HERE WHO DID ALL THE HARD WORK.
PLUS, HOKUTO LEARNS FASTER THAN OTHER DOGS.

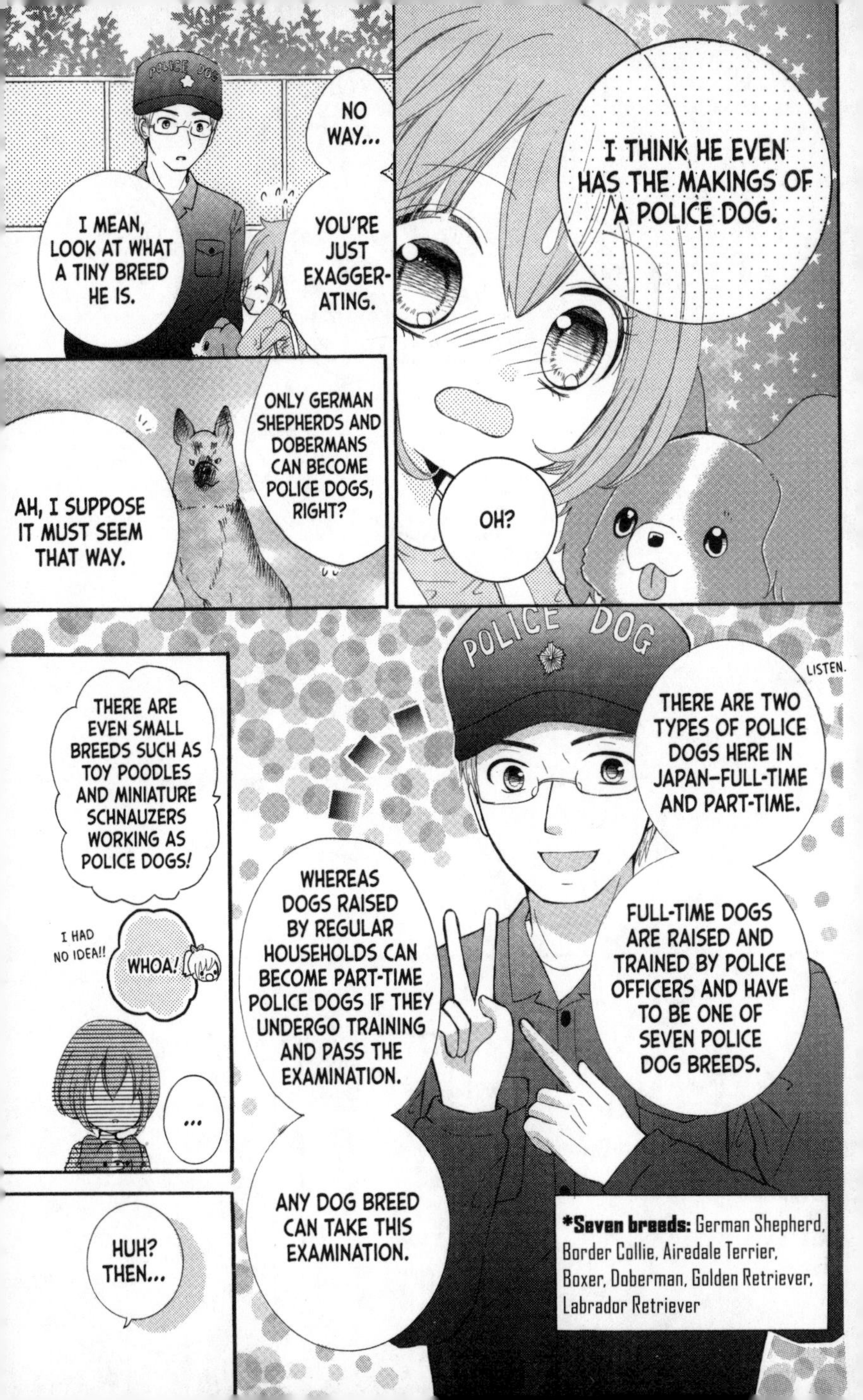
I THINK HE EVEN HAS THE MAKINGS OF A POLICE DOG.
OH?
NO WAY...
YOU'RE JUST EXAGGER-ATING.
I MEAN, LOOK AT WHAT A TINY BREED HE IS.
ONLY GERMAN SHEPHERDS AND DOBERMANS CAN BECOME POLICE DOGS, RIGHT?
AH, I SUPPOSE IT MUST SEEM THAT WAY.
POLICE DOG
LISTEN.
THERE ARE TWO TYPES OF POLICE DOGS HERE IN JAPAN—FULL-TIME AND PART-TIME.
FULL-TIME DOGS ARE RAISED AND TRAINED BY POLICE OFFICERS AND HAVE TO BE ONE OF SEVEN POLICE DOG BREEDS.
WHEREAS DOGS RAISED BY REGULAR HOUSEHOLDS CAN BECOME PART-TIME POLICE DOGS IF THEY UNDERGO TRAINING AND PASS THE EXAMINATION.
ANY DOG BREED CAN TAKE THIS EXAMINATION.
*Seven breeds: German Shepherd, Border Collie, Airedale Terrier, Boxer, Doberman, Golden Retriever, Labrador Retriever
THERE ARE EVEN SMALL BREEDS SUCH AS TOY POODLES AND MINIATURE SCHNAUZERS WORKING AS POLICE DOGS!
WHOA!
I HAD NO IDEA!!
...
HUH? THEN...

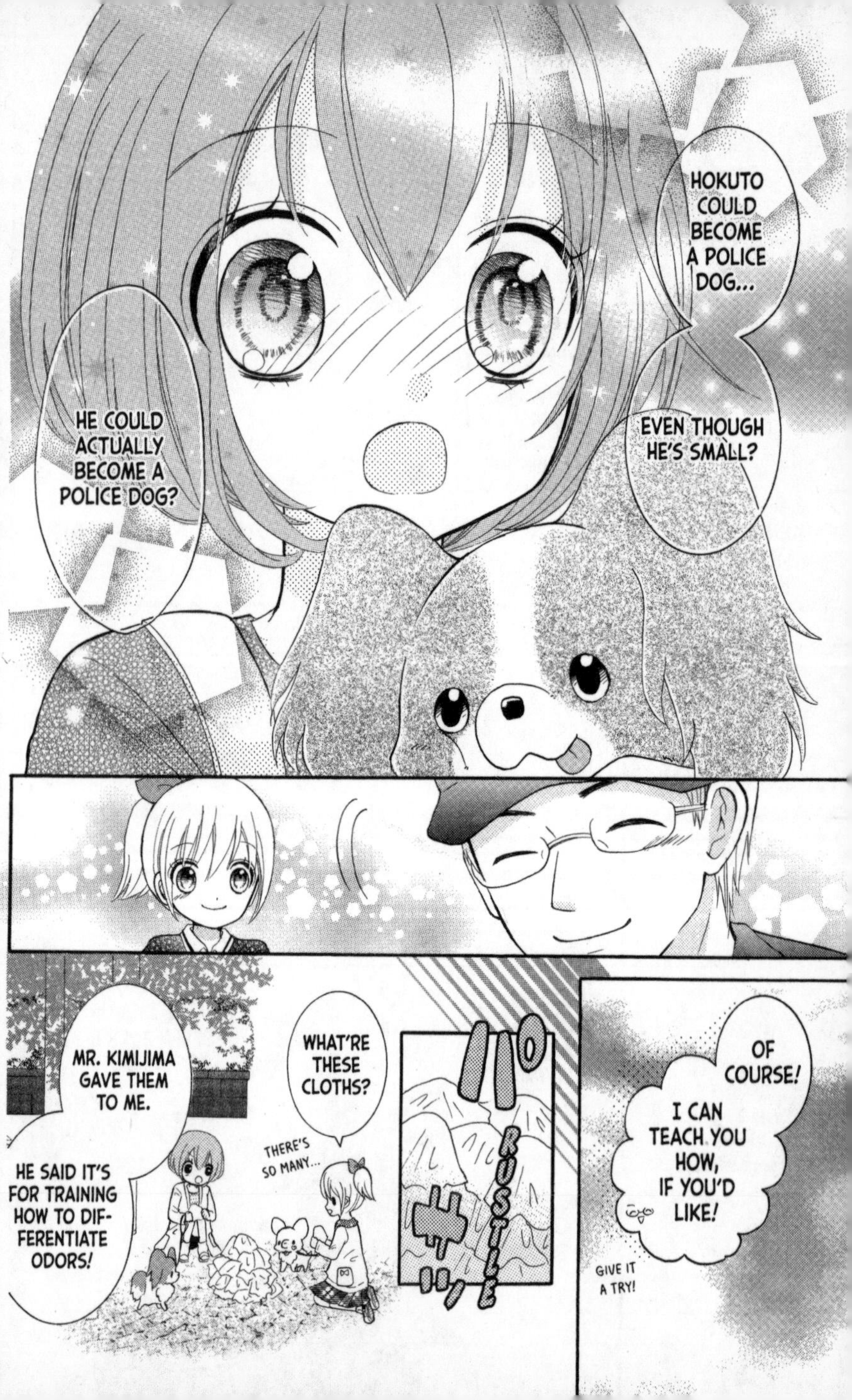
HOKUTO COULD BECOME A POLICE DOG...
EVEN THOUGH HE'S SMALL?
HE COULD ACTUALLY BECOME A POLICE DOG?
OF COURSE!
I CAN TEACH YOU HOW, IF YOU'D LIKE!
GIVE IT A TRY!
RUSTLE
WHAT'RE THESE CLOTHS?
THERE'S SO MANY...
MR. KIMIJIMA GAVE THEM TO ME.
HE SAID IT'S FOR TRAINING HOW TO DIF-FERENTIATE ODORS!

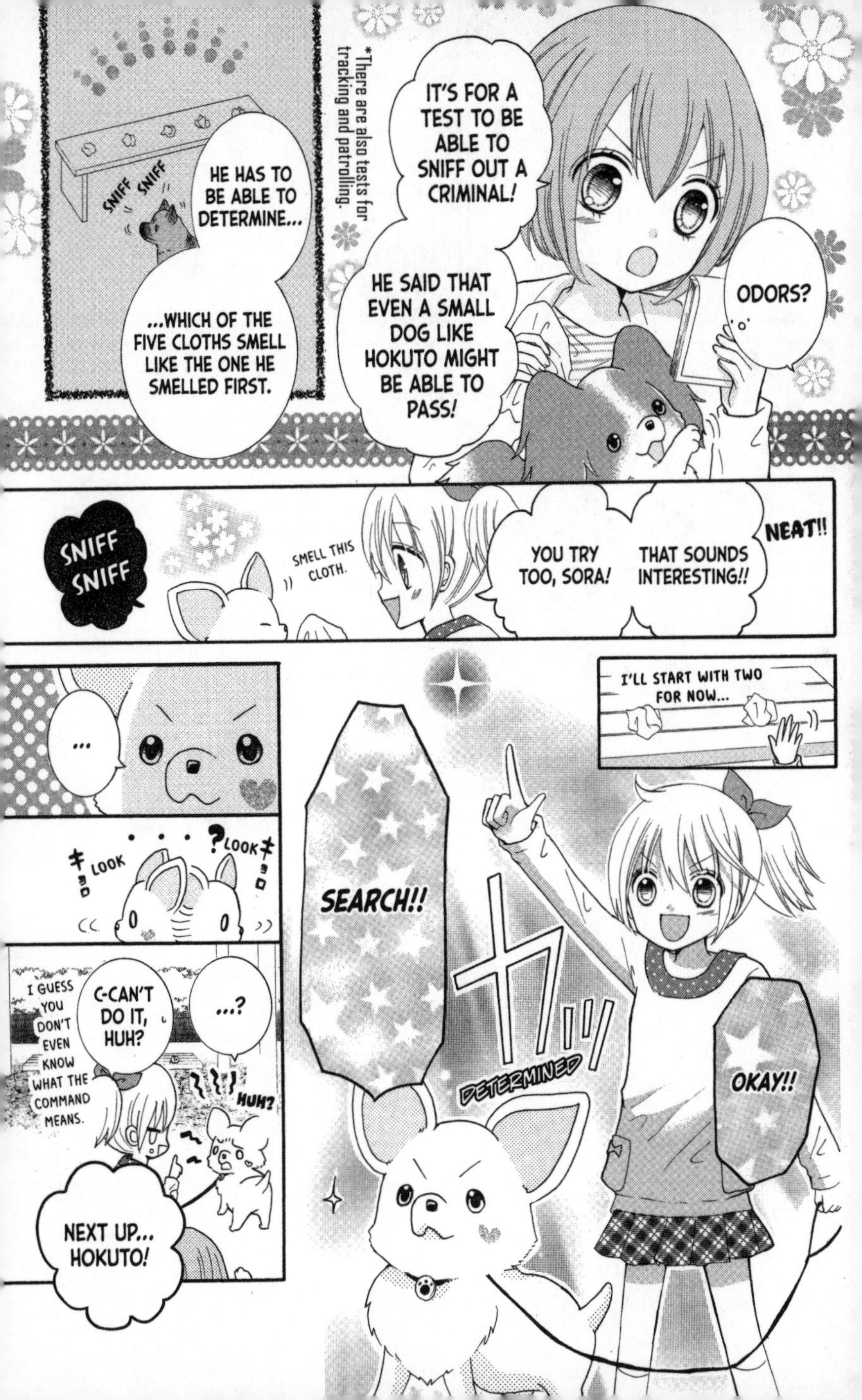

IT'S FOR A TEST TO BE ABLE TO SNIFF OUT A CRIMINAL!
ODORS?
HE SAID THAT EVEN A SMALL DOG LIKE HOKUTO MIGHT BE ABLE TO PASS!
*There are also tests for tracking and patrolling.
HE HAS TO BE ABLE TO DETERMINE...
SNIFF SNIFF
...WHICH OF THE FIVE CLOTHS SMELL LIKE THE ONE HE SMELLED FIRST.
NEAT!!
THAT SOUNDS INTERESTING!!
YOU TRY TOO, SORA!
SMELL THIS CLOTH.
SNIFF SNIFF
I'LL START WITH TWO FOR NOW...
OKAY!!
DETERMINED
SEARCH!!
...
LOOK
?
LOOK
...?
HUH?
C-CAN'T DO IT, HUH?
I GUESS YOU DON'T EVEN KNOW WHAT THE COMMAND MEANS.
NEXT UP... HOKUTO!

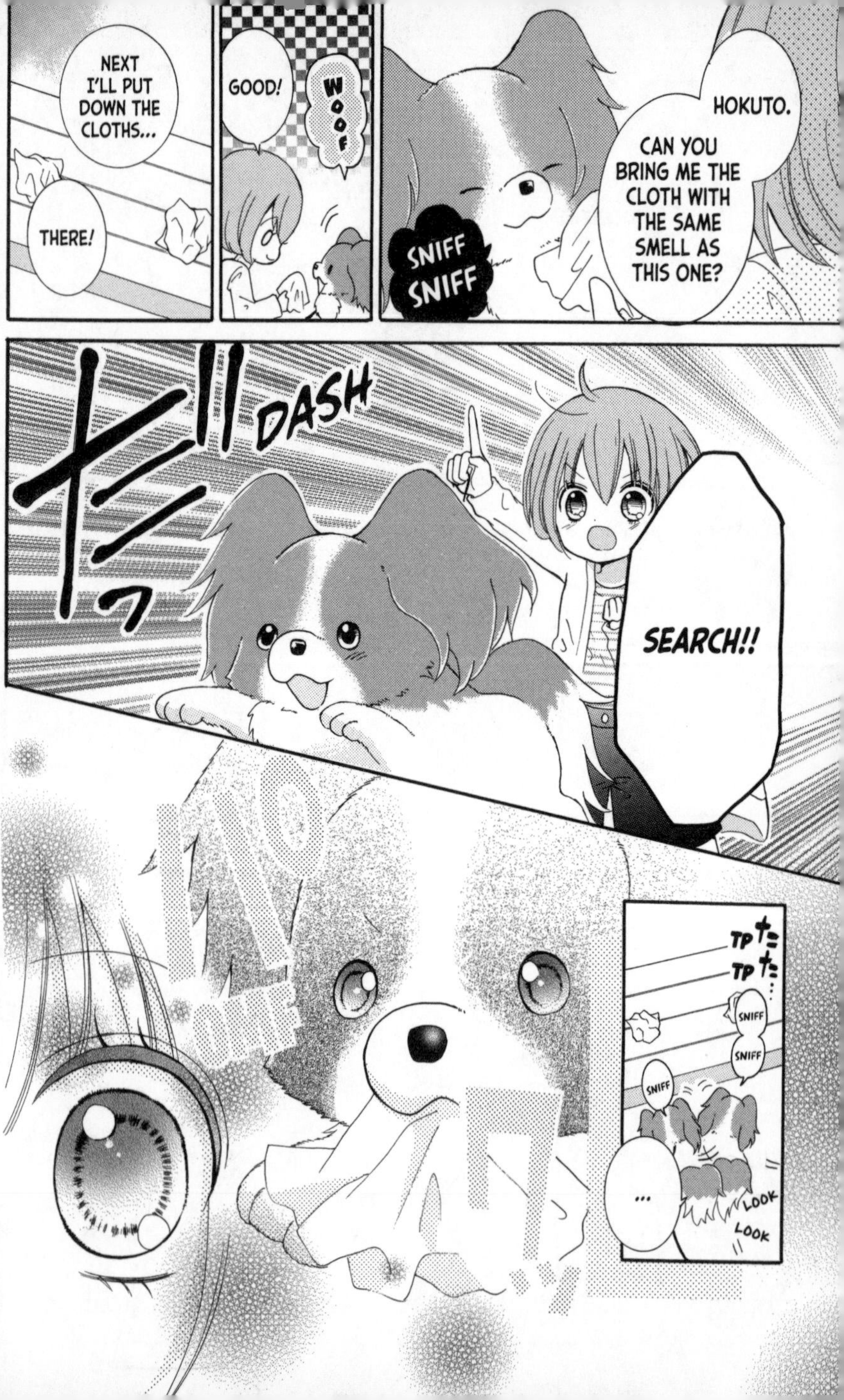
HOKUTO.
CAN YOU BRING ME THE CLOTH WITH THE SAME SMELL AS THIS ONE?
SNIFF SNIFF
WOOF
GOOD!
NEXT I'LL PUT DOWN THE CLOTHS...
THERE!
SEARCH!!
DASH
TP
TP...
SNIFF
SNIFF
SNIFF
...
LOOK
LOOK

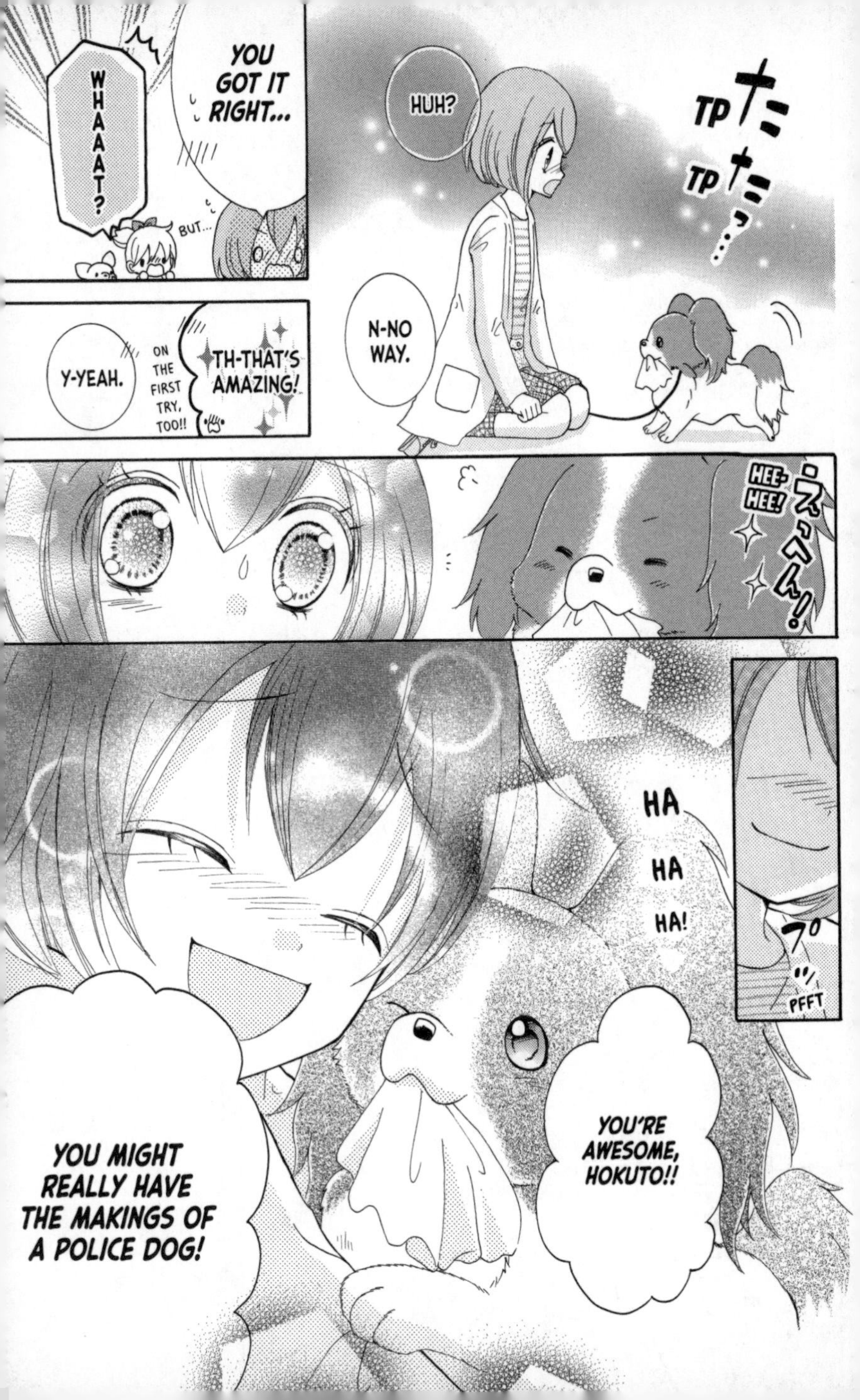
TP TP
HUH?
N-NO WAY.
YOU GOT IT RIGHT...
BUT...
WHAAAAT?
TH-THAT'S AMAZING!
ON THE FIRST TRY, TOO!!
Y-YEAH.
HEE-HEE!
PFFT
HA HA HA!
YOU'RE AWESOME, HOKUTO!!
YOU MIGHT REALLY HAVE THE MAKINGS OF A POLICE DOG!

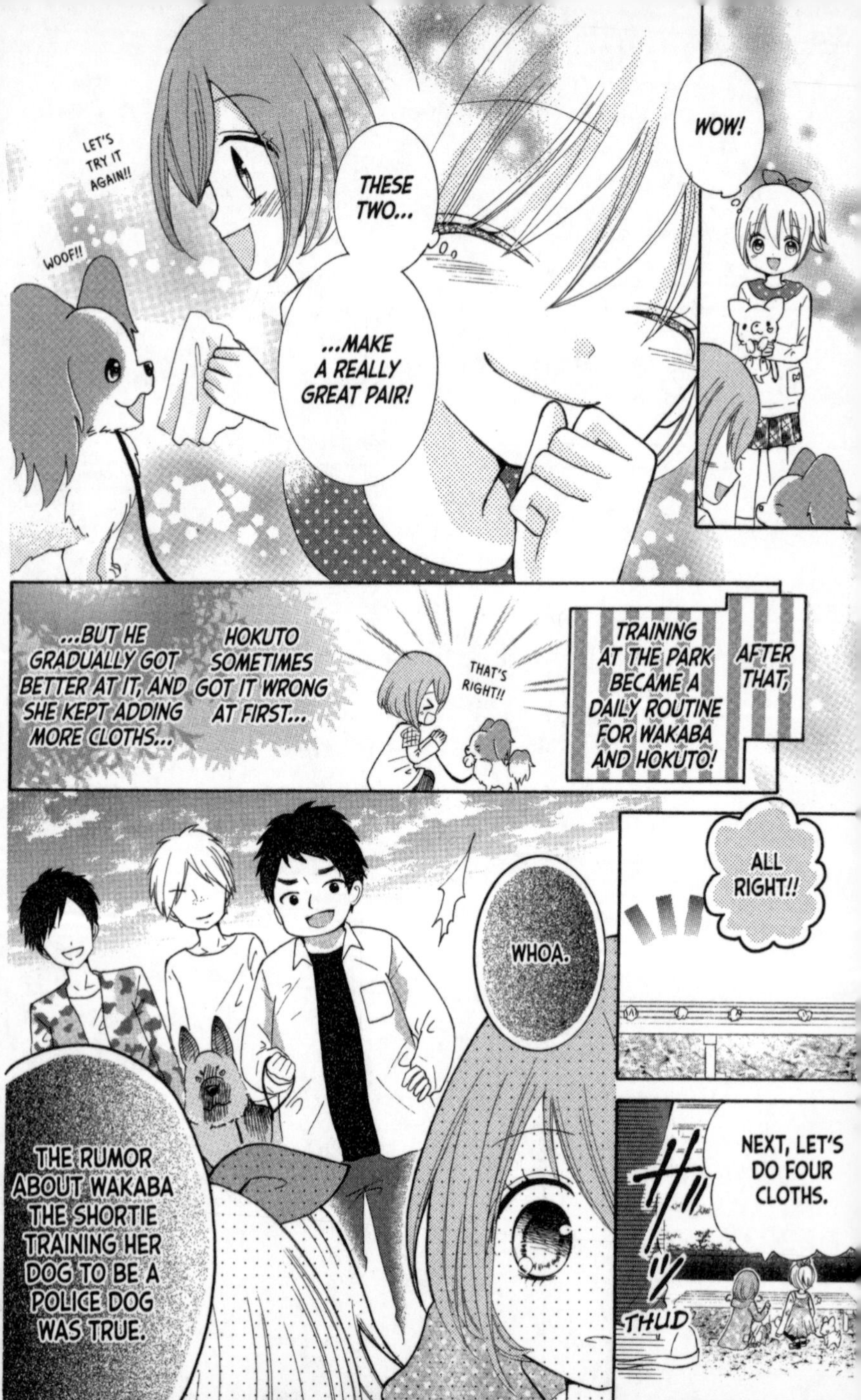
WOW!
THESE TWO...
...MAKE A REALLY GREAT PAIR!
LET'S TRY IT AGAIN!!
WOOF!!
AFTER THAT,
TRAINING AT THE PARK BECAME A DAILY ROUTINE FOR WAKABA AND HOKUTO!
THAT'S RIGHT!!
HOKUTO SOMETIMES GOT IT WRONG AT FIRST...
...BUT HE GRADUALLY GOT BETTER AT IT, AND SHE KEPT ADDING MORE CLOTHS...
ALL RIGHT!!
NEXT, LET'S DO FOUR CLOTHS.
THUD
WHOA.
THE RUMOR ABOUT WAKABA THE SHORTIE TRAINING HER DOG TO BE A POLICE DOG WAS TRUE.

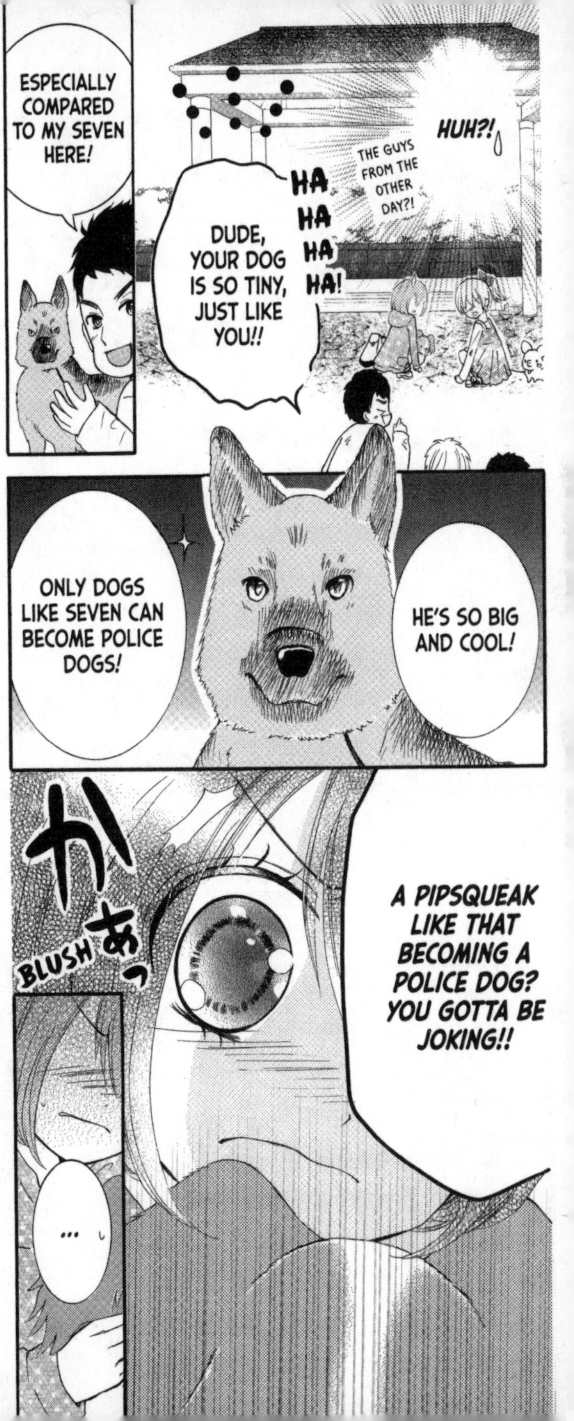
HUH?!
THE GUYS FROM THE OTHER DAY?!
DUDE, YOUR DOG IS SO TINY, JUST LIKE YOU!!
HA HA HA HA!
ESPECIALLY COMPARED TO MY SEVEN HERE!
HE'S SO BIG AND COOL!
ONLY DOGS LIKE SEVEN CAN BECOME POLICE DOGS!
A PIPSQUEAK LIKE THAT BECOMING A POLICE DOG? YOU GOTTA BE JOKING!!
かあっ
BLUSH
...

HAMSTERS

THERE'S A STORY ABOUT A HAMSTER IN THIS VOLUME. WHEN I WAS IN ELEMENTARY SCHOOL, I ACTUALLY HAD A PET WINTER WHITE DWARF HAMSTER!

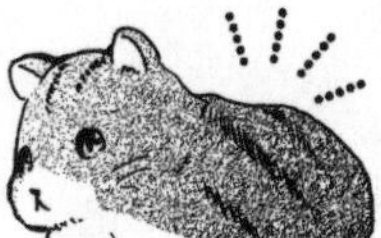

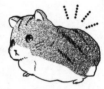

HIS NAME WAS CHIPPIE. HE WAS REALLY ENERGETIC AND SCURRIED AROUND A LOT. IT WAS SO CUTE, BUT HE WAS QUITE SCARY—HE BIT MY FINGER EVERY CHANCE HE GOT (LOL).

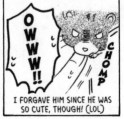

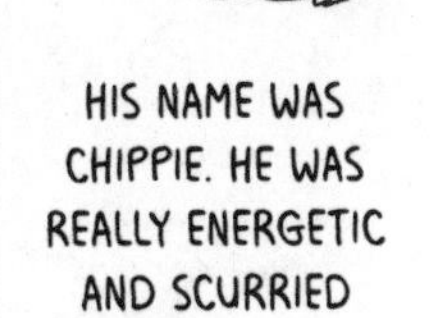
OWWW!!
CHOMP

I FORGAVE HIM SINCE HE WAS SO CUTE, THOUGH! (LOL)

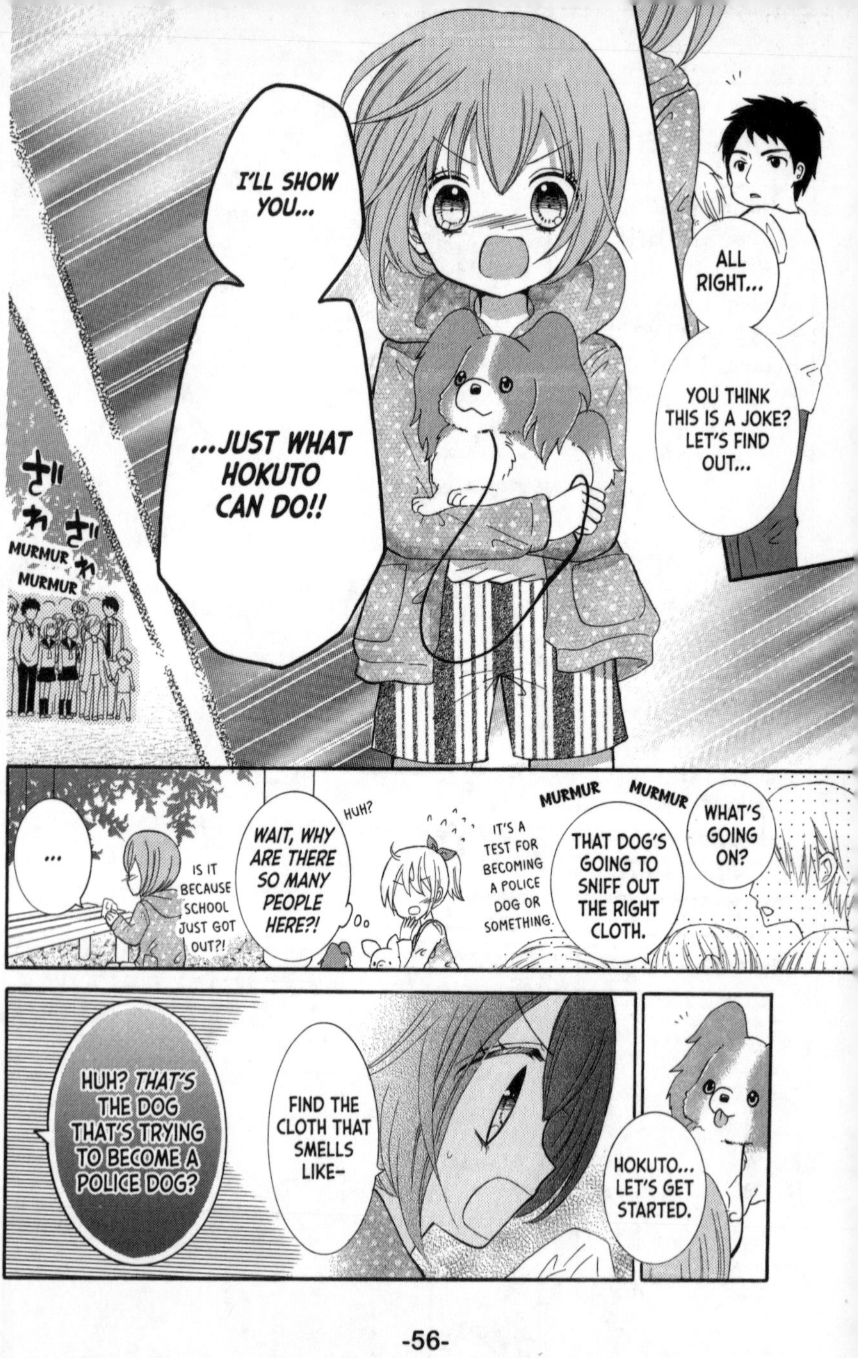
ALL RIGHT...
YOU THINK THIS IS A JOKE? LET'S FIND OUT...
I'LL SHOW YOU...
...JUST WHAT HOKUTO CAN DO!!
ざわざわ
MURMUR MURMUR
WHAT'S GOING ON?
MURMUR MURMUR
THAT DOG'S GOING TO SNIFF OUT THE RIGHT CLOTH.
IT'S A TEST FOR BECOMING A POLICE DOG OR SOMETHING.
HUH?
WAIT, WHY ARE THERE SO MANY PEOPLE HERE?!
IS IT BECAUSE SCHOOL JUST GOT OUT?!
...
HOKUTO... LET'S GET STARTED.
FIND THE CLOTH THAT SMELLS LIKE–
HUH? *THAT'S* THE DOG THAT'S TRYING TO BECOME A POLICE DOG?

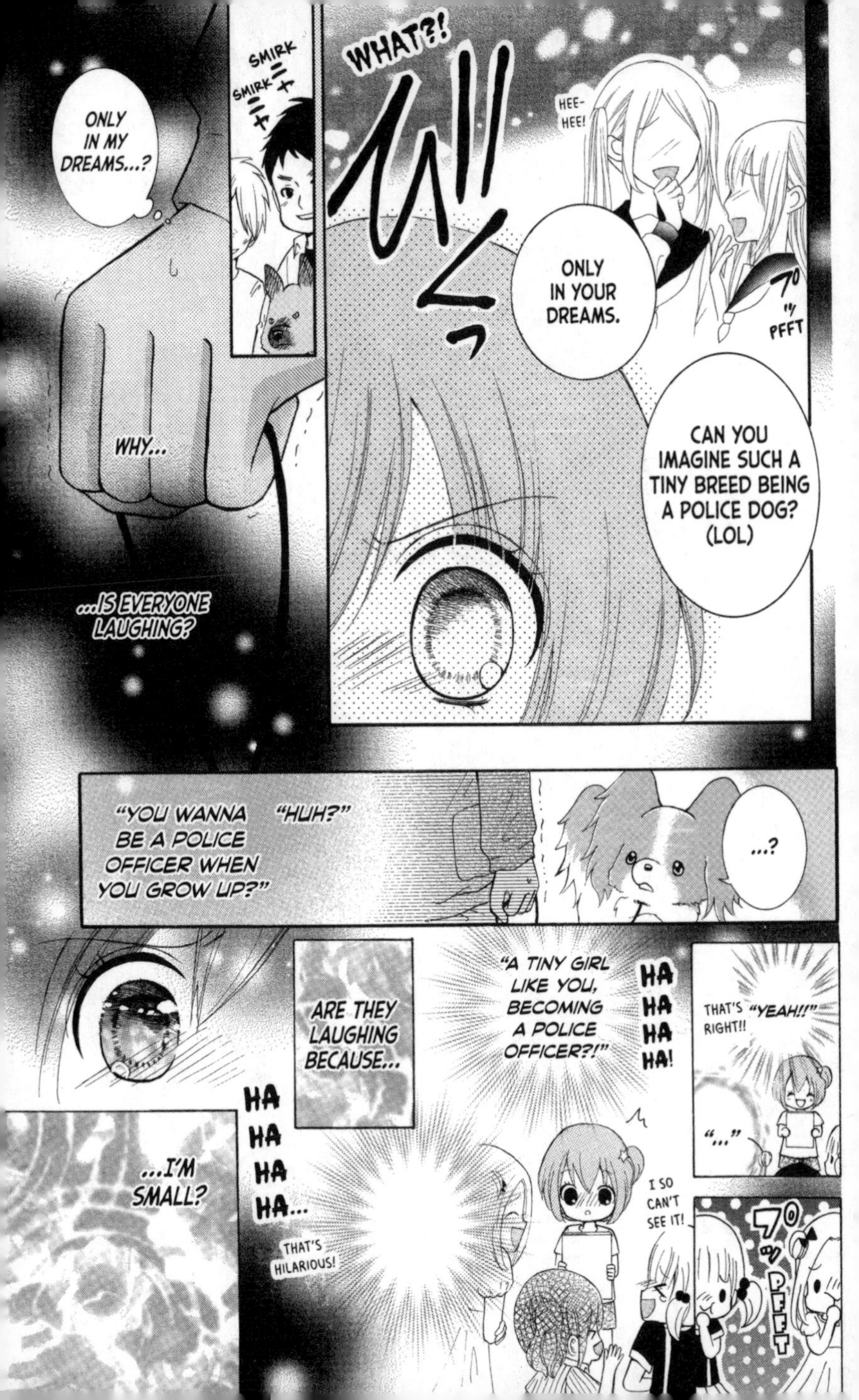
WHAT?!
HEE-HEE!
ONLY IN YOUR DREAMS.
PFFT
CAN YOU IMAGINE SUCH A TINY BREED BEING A POLICE DOG? (LOL)
SMIRK SMIRK
ONLY IN MY DREAMS...?
WHY...
...IS EVERYONE LAUGHING?
...?
“HUH?”
“YOU WANNA BE A POLICE OFFICER WHEN YOU GROW UP?”
“YEAH!!”
THAT'S RIGHT!!
“...”
HA HA HA HA!
“A TINY GIRL LIKE YOU, BECOMING A POLICE OFFICER?!”
ARE THEY LAUGHING BECAUSE...
PFFT
I SO CAN'T SEE IT!
HA HA HA HA...
THAT'S HILARIOUS!
...I'M SMALL?

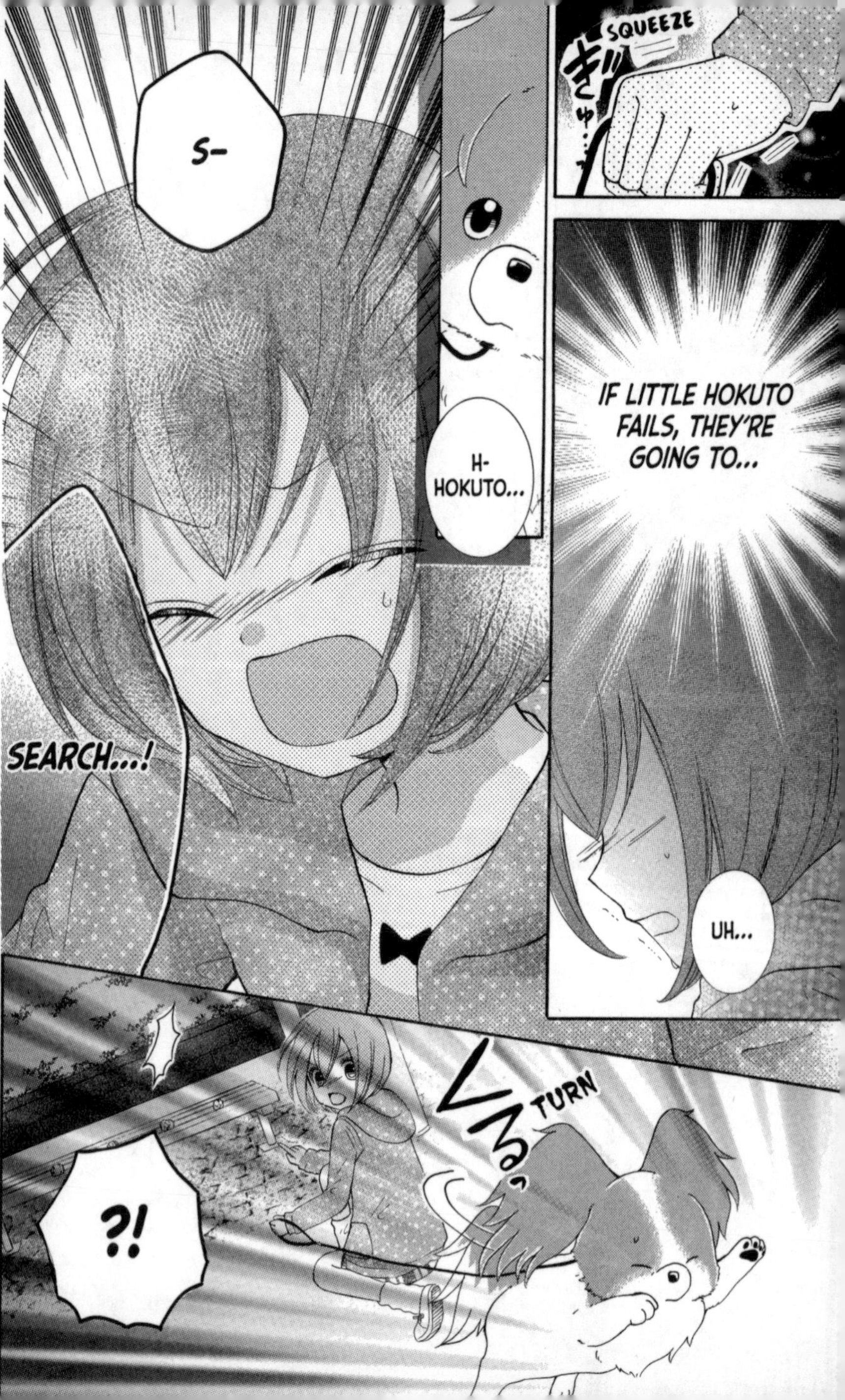
SQUEEZE
ぎゅ…
IF LITTLE HOKUTO FAILS, THEY'RE GOING TO...
UH...
H-HOKUTO...
S-
SEARCH...!
くるっ
TURN
?!

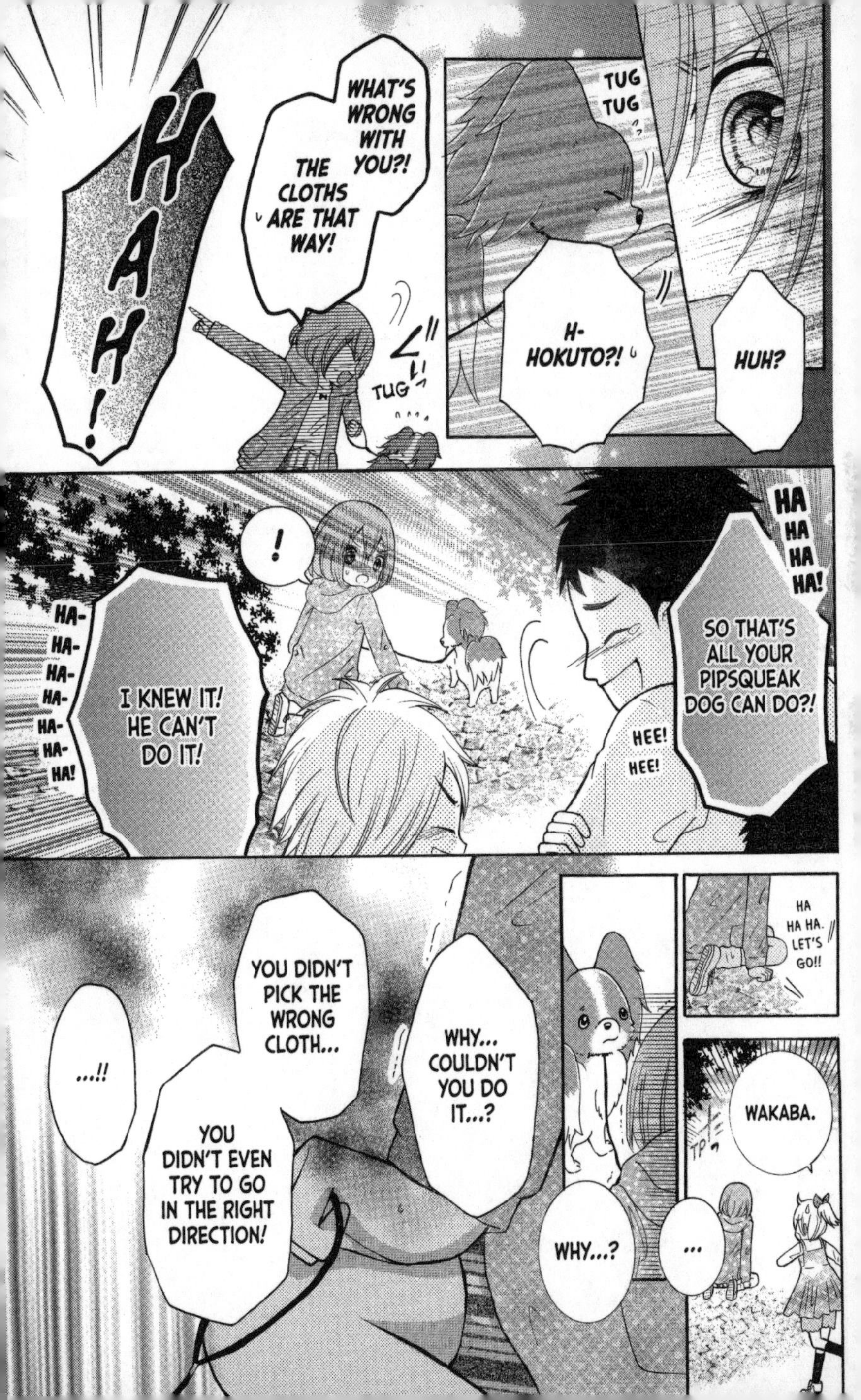
HUH?
TUG TUG
H-HOKUTO?!
WHAT'S WRONG WITH YOU?!
THE CLOTHS ARE THAT WAY!
TUG!
HAH!
HA HA HA HA!
SO THAT'S ALL YOUR PIPSQUEAK DOG CAN DO?!
HEE! HEE!
!
I KNEW IT! HE CAN'T DO IT!
HA-HA-HA-HA-HA-HA-HA!
HA HA HA. LET'S GO!!
WAKABA.
TP
...
WHY...?
WHY... COULDN'T YOU DO IT...?
YOU DIDN'T PICK THE WRONG CLOTH...
YOU DIDN'T EVEN TRY TO GO IN THE RIGHT DIRECTION!
...!!

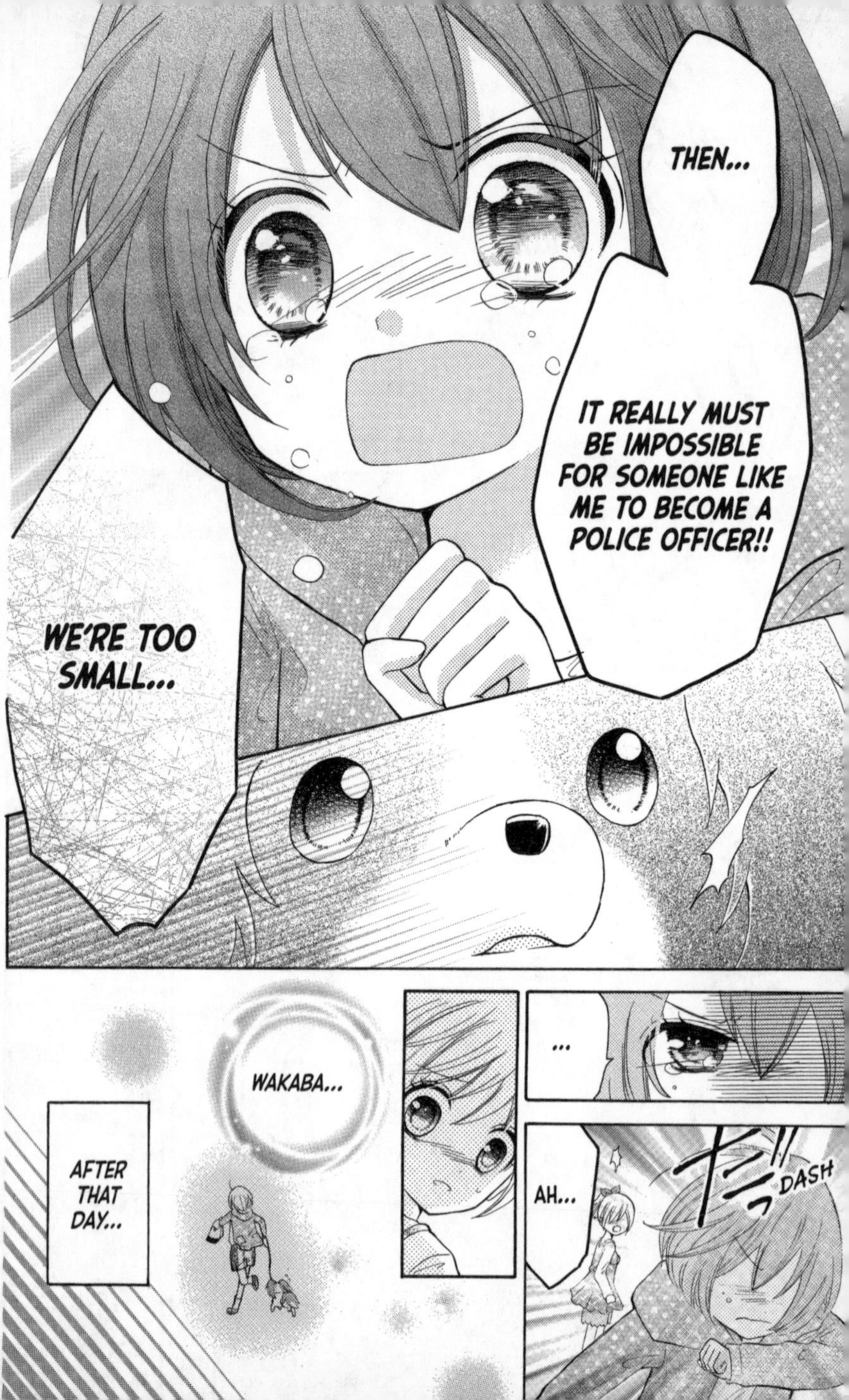
THEN...
IT REALLY MUST BE IMPOSSIBLE FOR SOMEONE LIKE ME TO BECOME A POLICE OFFICER!!
WE'RE TOO SMALL...
...
DASH
AH...
WAKABA...
AFTER THAT DAY...

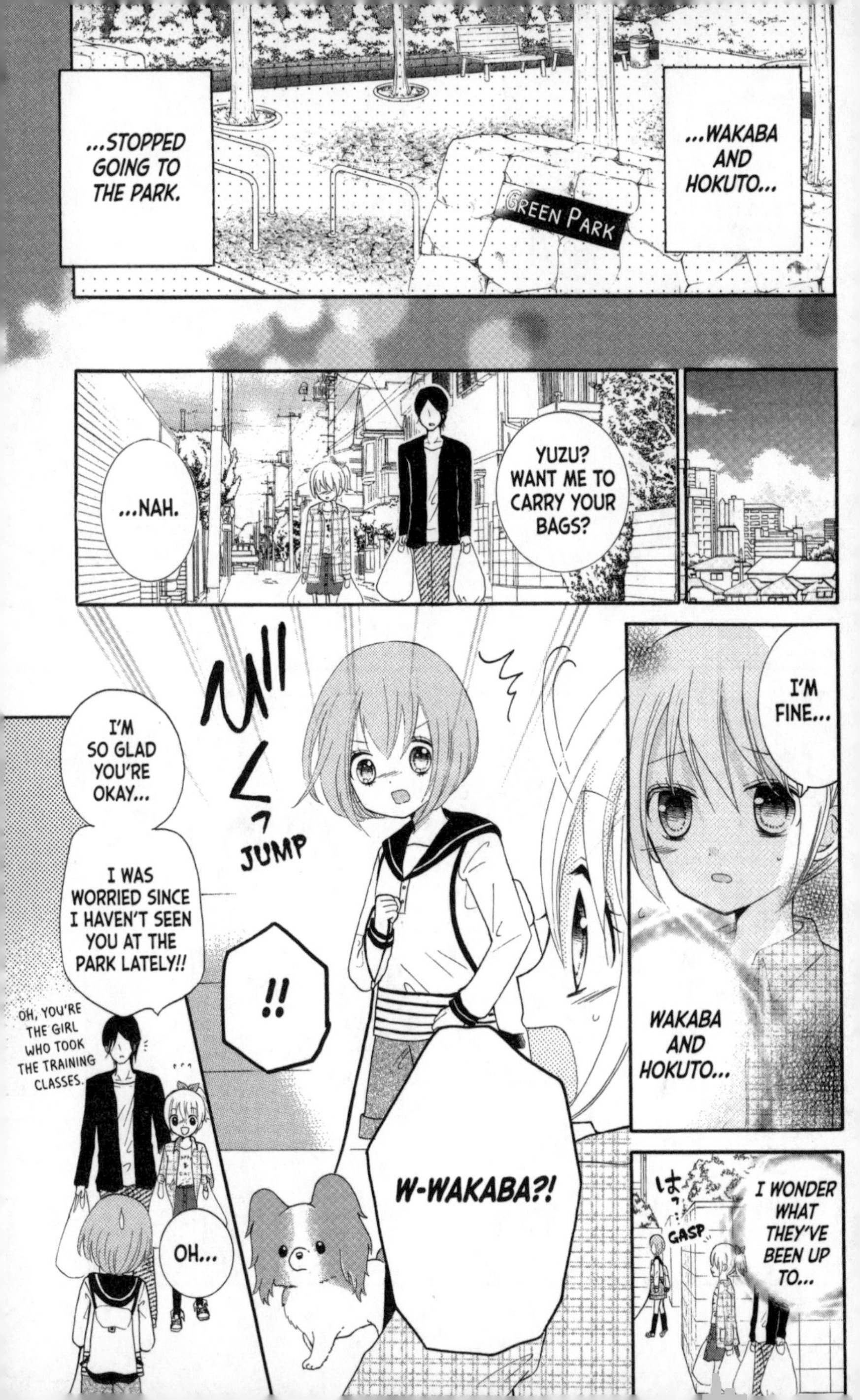
...WAKABA AND HOKUTO...
...STOPPED GOING TO THE PARK.
GREEN PARK
YUZU? WANT ME TO CARRY YOUR BAGS?
...NAH.
I'M FINE...
WAKABA AND HOKUTO...
はっ
GASP
I WONDER WHAT THEY'VE BEEN UP TO...
JUMP
W-WAKABA?!
!!
I'M SO GLAD YOU'RE OKAY...
I WAS WORRIED SINCE I HAVEN'T SEEN YOU AT THE PARK LATELY!!
OH, YOU'RE THE GIRL WHO TOOK THE TRAINING CLASSES.
OH...

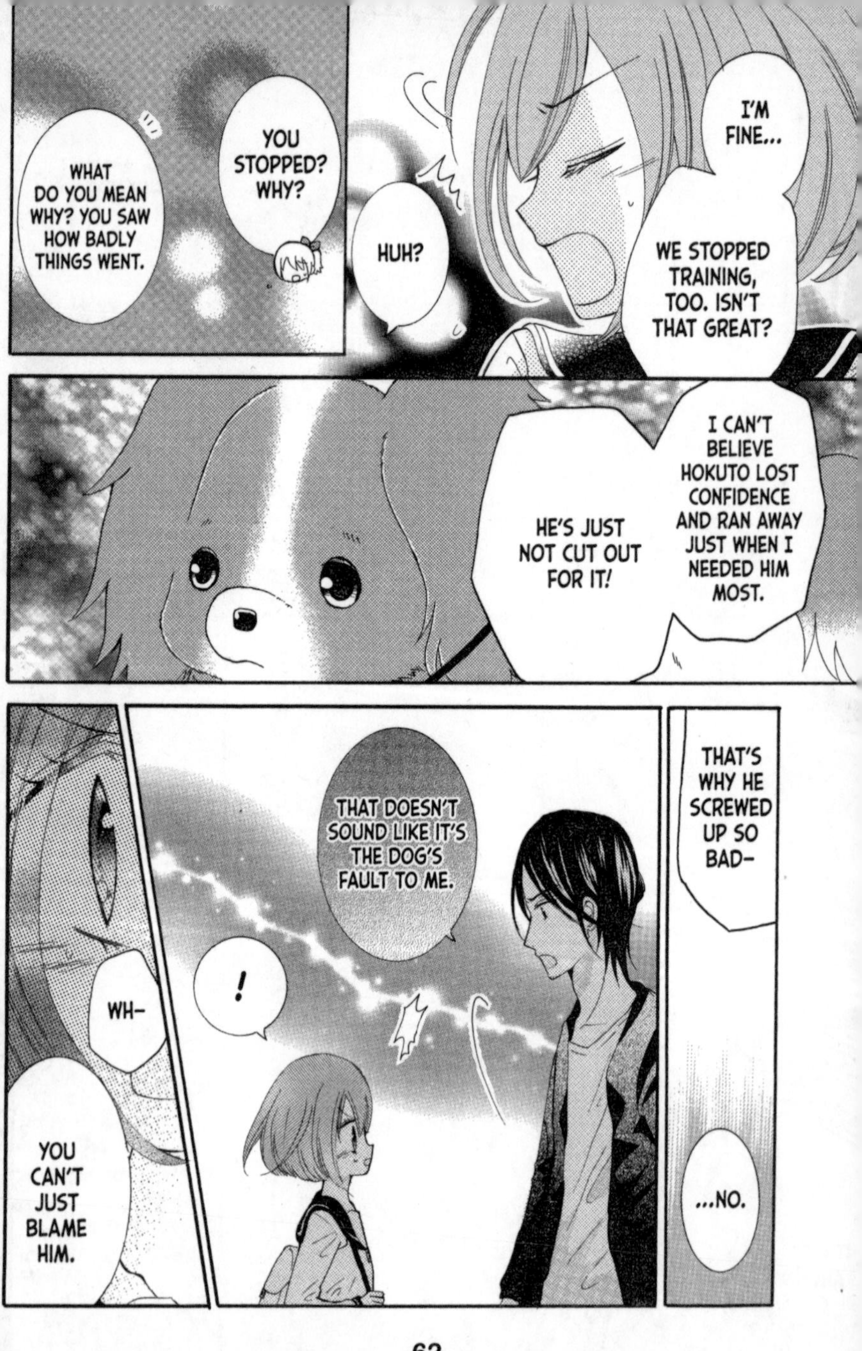
I'M FINE...
WE STOPPED TRAINING, TOO. ISN'T THAT GREAT?
HUH?
YOU STOPPED? WHY?
WHAT DO YOU MEAN WHY? YOU SAW HOW BADLY THINGS WENT.
I CAN'T BELIEVE HOKUTO LOST CONFIDENCE AND RAN AWAY JUST WHEN I NEEDED HIM MOST.
HE'S JUST NOT CUT OUT FOR IT!
THAT'S WHY HE SCREWED UP SO BAD–
...NO.
THAT DOESN'T SOUND LIKE IT'S THE DOG'S FAULT TO ME.
!
WH–
YOU CAN'T JUST BLAME HIM.

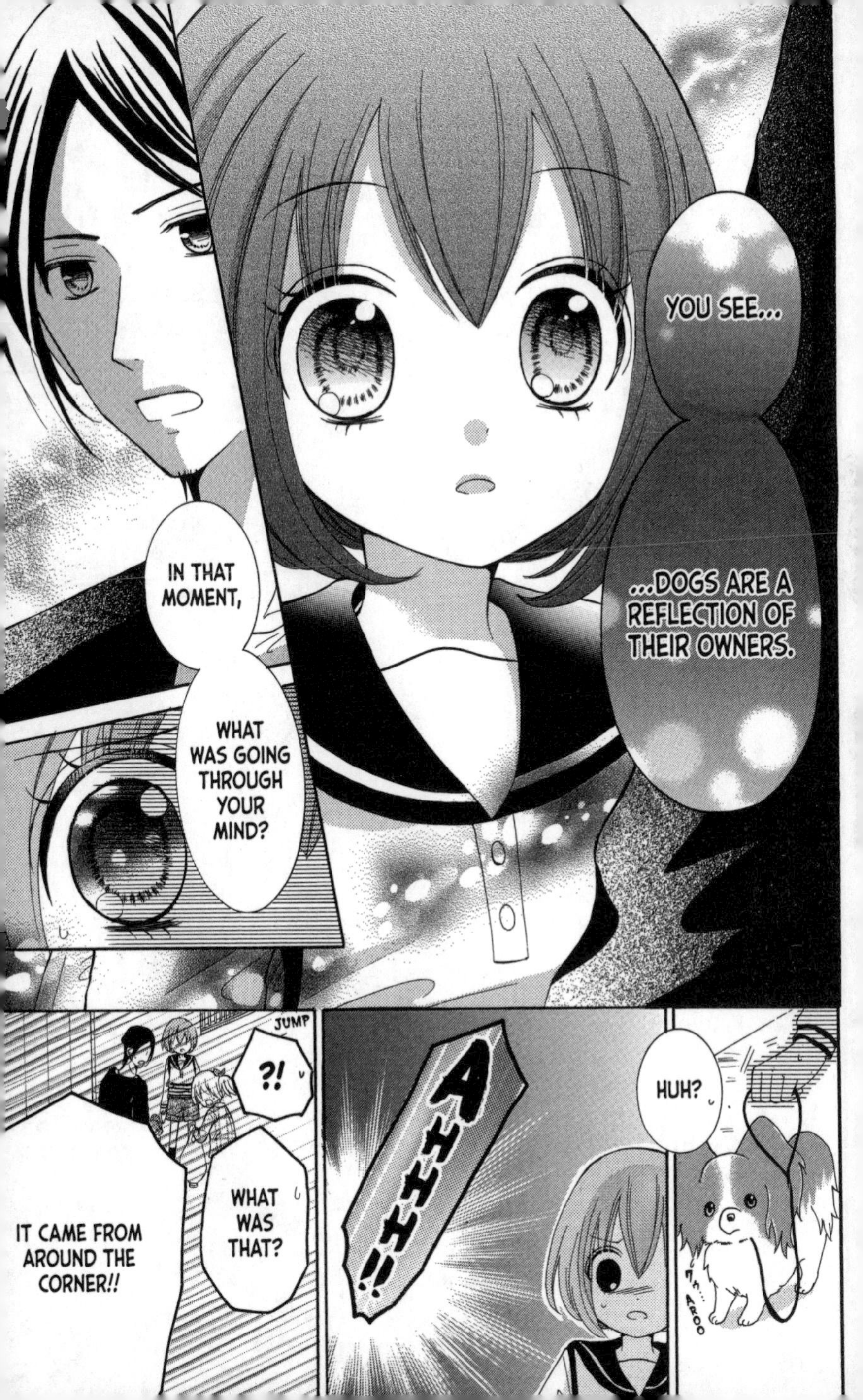

YOU SEE...
...DOGS ARE A REFLECTION OF THEIR OWNERS.
IN THAT MOMENT,
WHAT WAS GOING THROUGH YOUR MIND?
HUH?
AROO
A
JUMP
?!
WHAT WAS THAT?
IT CAME FROM AROUND THE CORNER!!

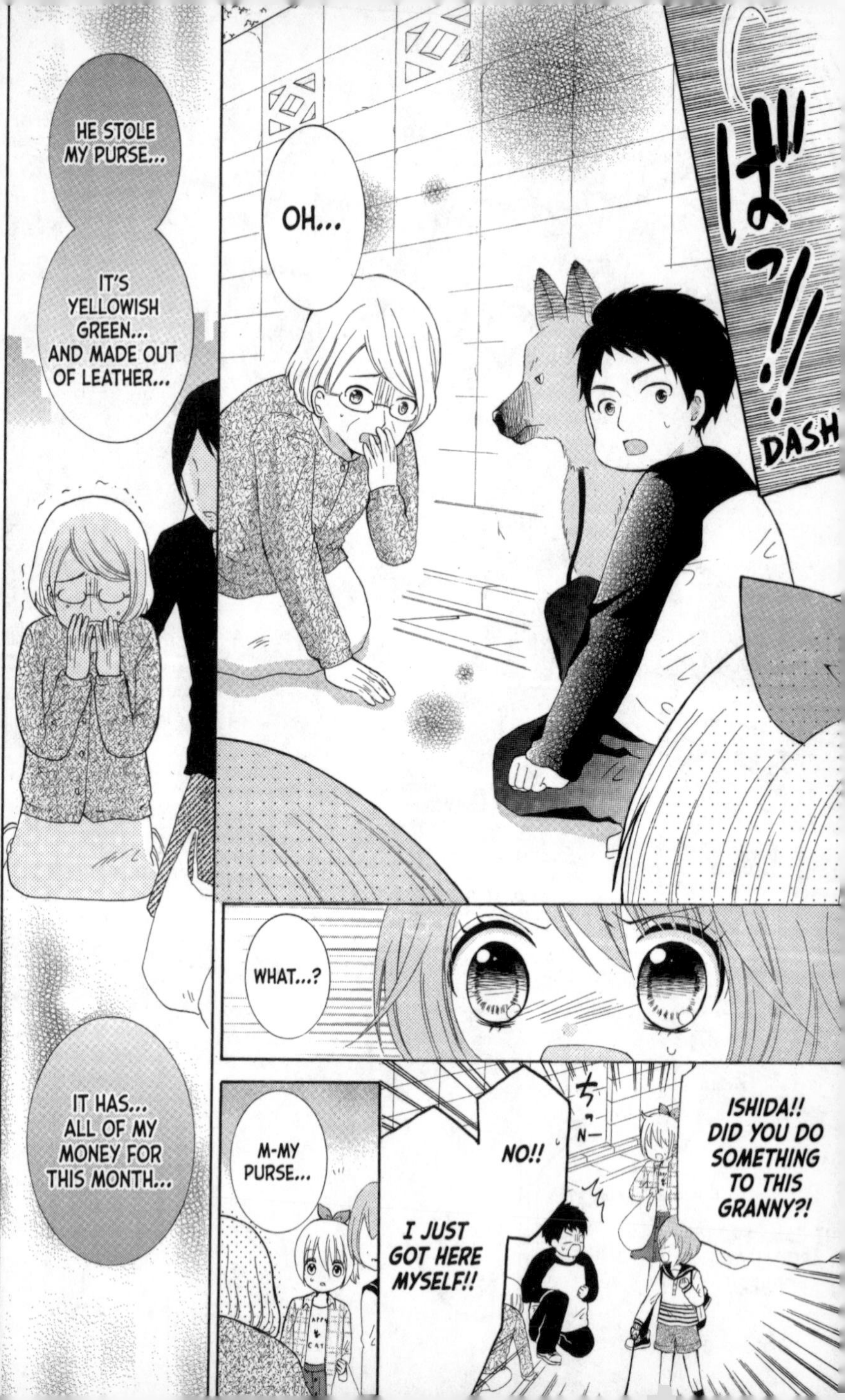
ばっ!!
DASH
OH...
WHAT...?
ISHIDA!! DID YOU DO SOMETHING TO THIS GRANNY?!
NO!!
I JUST GOT HERE MYSELF!!
M-MY PURSE...
HE STOLE MY PURSE...
IT'S YELLOWISH GREEN... AND MADE OUT OF LEATHER...
IT HAS... ALL OF MY MONEY FOR THIS MONTH...

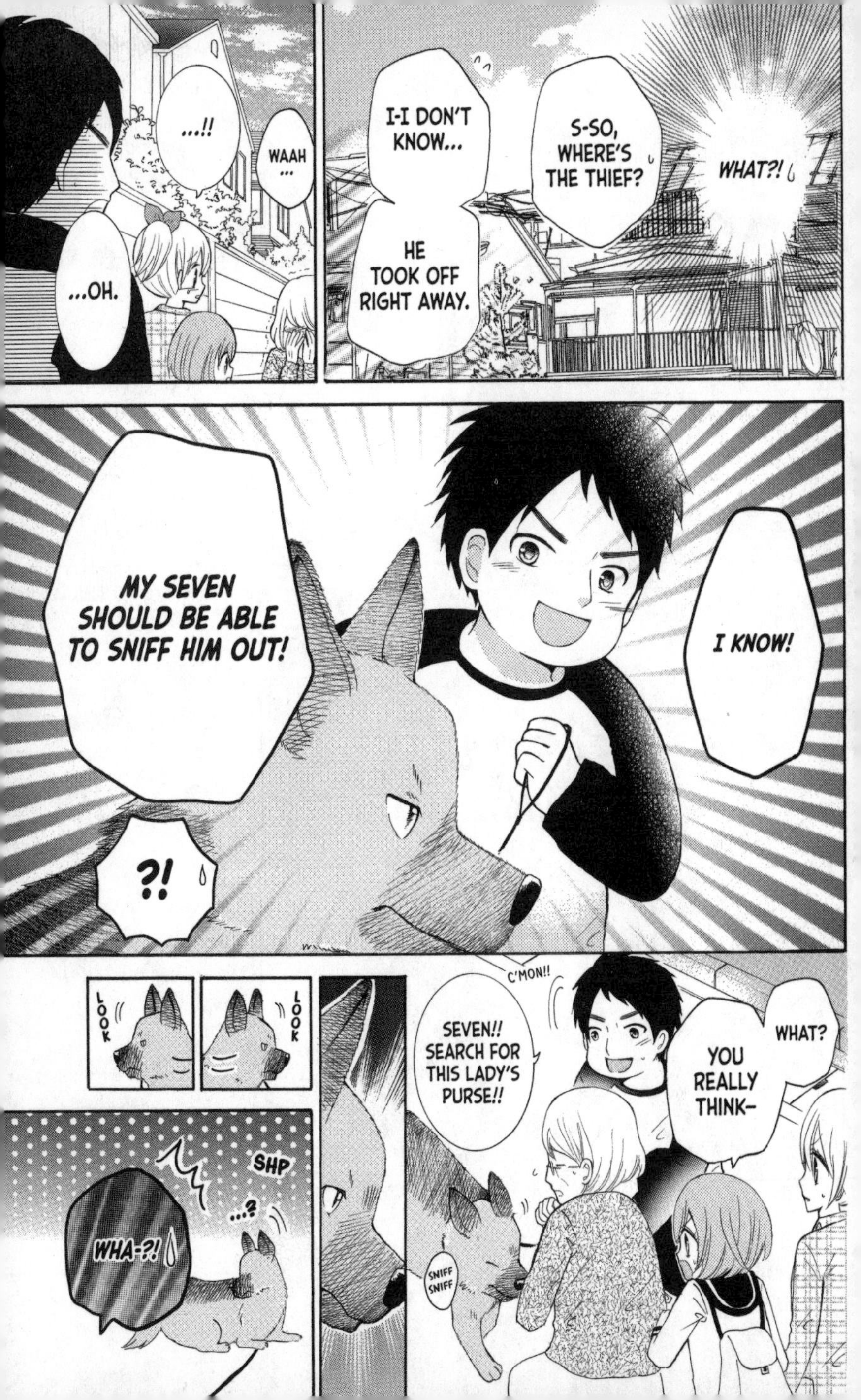
WHAT?!
S-SO, WHERE'S THE THIEF?
I-I DON'T KNOW...
HE TOOK OFF RIGHT AWAY.
WAAH...
...!!
...OH.
I KNOW!
MY SEVEN SHOULD BE ABLE TO SNIFF HIM OUT!
?!
WHAT?
YOU REALLY THINK–
C'MON!!
SEVEN!! SEARCH FOR THIS LADY'S PURSE!!
SNIFF SNIFF
LOOK
LOOK
SHP
...?
WHA-?!

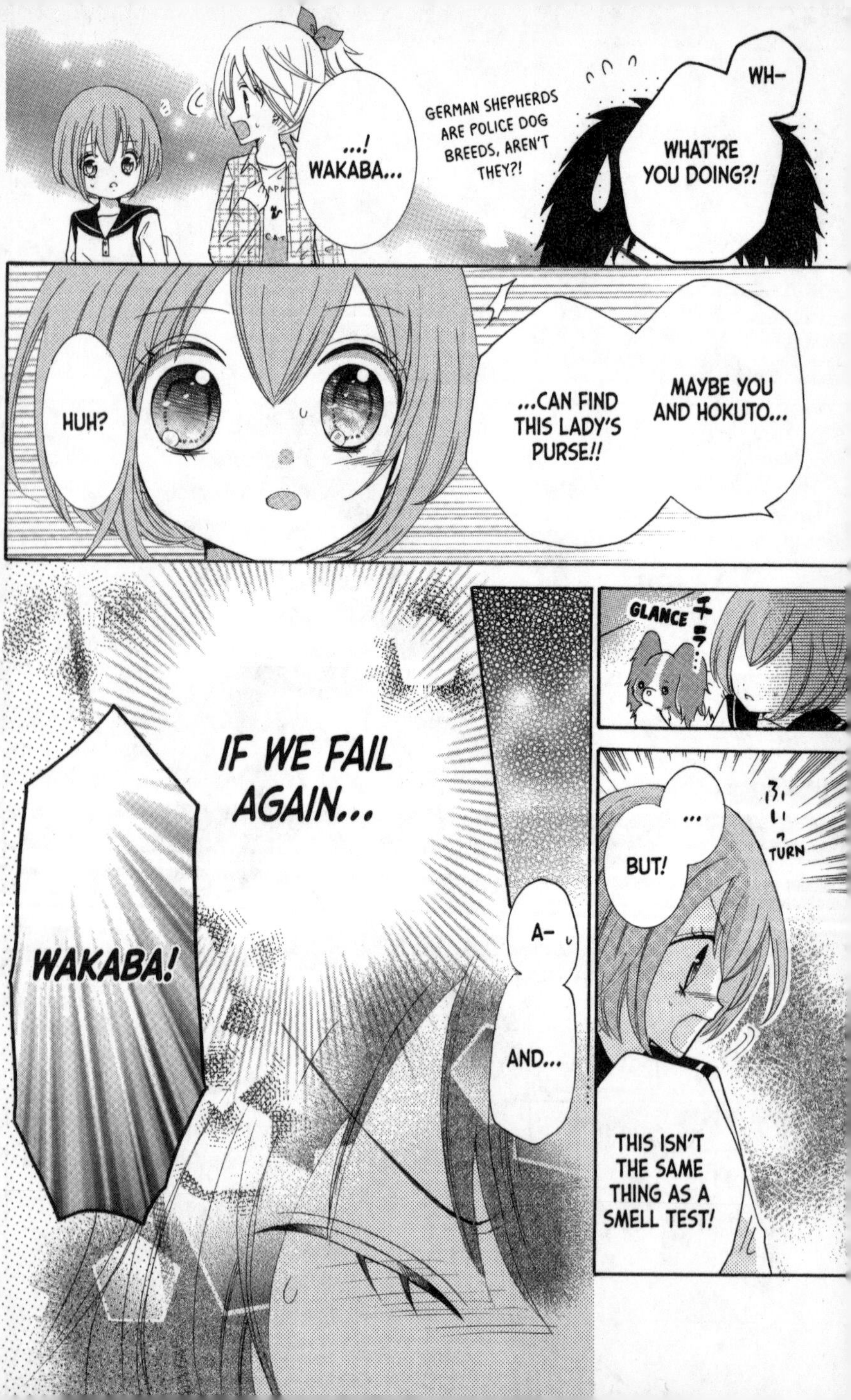
WH–
WHAT'RE YOU DOING?!
GERMAN SHEPHERDS ARE POLICE DOG BREEDS, AREN'T THEY?!
...! WAKABA...
MAYBE YOU AND HOKUTO...
...CAN FIND THIS LADY'S PURSE!!
HUH?
GLANCE
...
BUT!
TURN
THIS ISN'T THE SAME THING AS A SMELL TEST!
A–
AND...
IF WE FAIL AGAIN...
WAKABA!

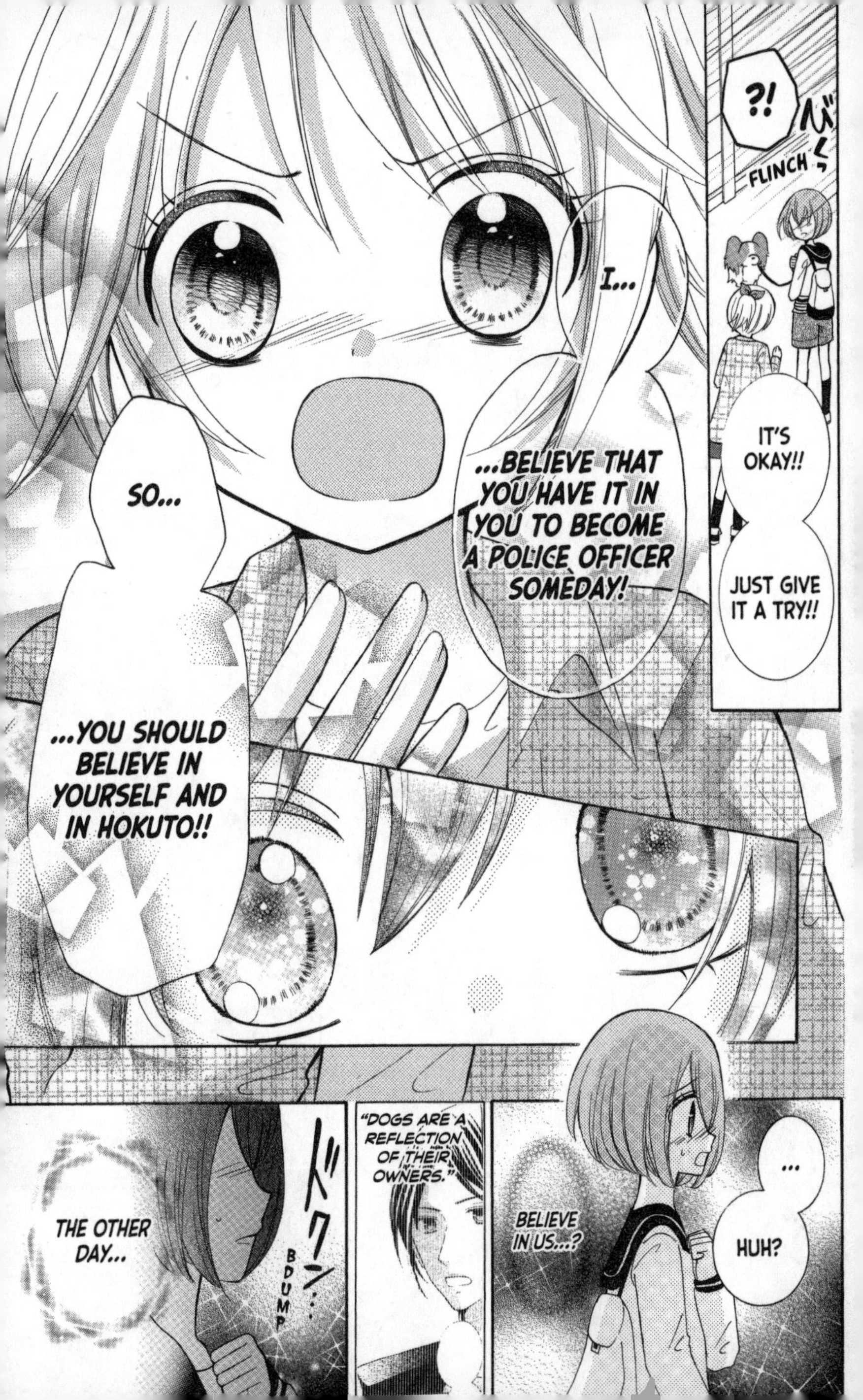
?!
びくっ
FLINCH
IT'S OKAY!!
JUST GIVE IT A TRY!!
I...
...BELIEVE THAT YOU HAVE IT IN YOU TO BECOME A POLICE OFFICER SOMEDAY!
SO...
...YOU SHOULD BELIEVE IN YOURSELF AND IN HOKUTO!!
...
HUH?
BELIEVE IN US...?
"DOGS ARE A REFLECTION OF THEIR OWNERS."
ドクン
BDUMP
THE OTHER DAY...

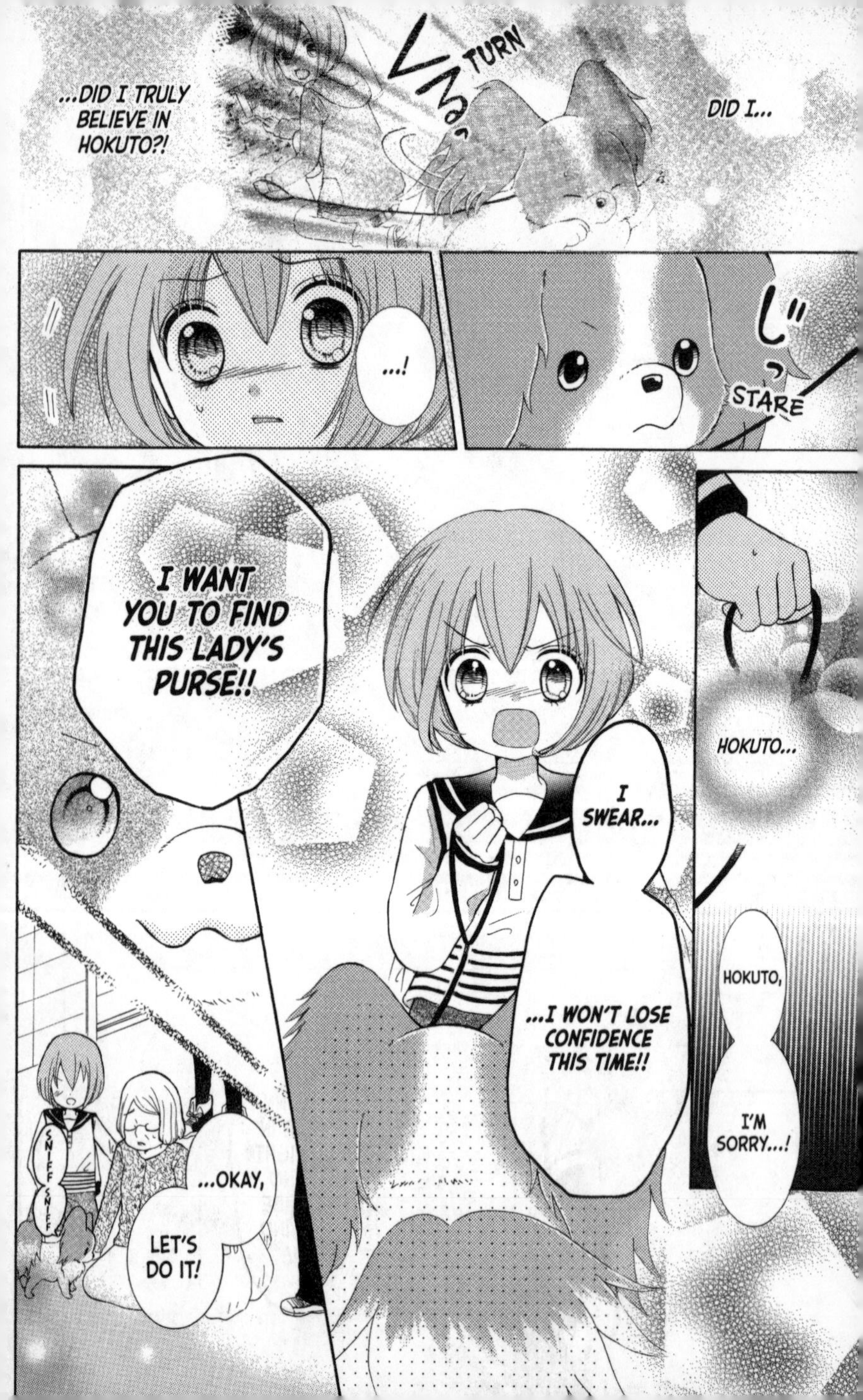
TURN
DID I...
...DID I TRULY BELIEVE IN HOKUTO?!
STARE
...!
HOKUTO...
HOKUTO,
I'M SORRY...!
I SWEAR...
...I WON'T LOSE CONFIDENCE THIS TIME!!
I WANT YOU TO FIND THIS LADY'S PURSE!!
SNIFF SNIFF
...OKAY,
LET'S DO IT!

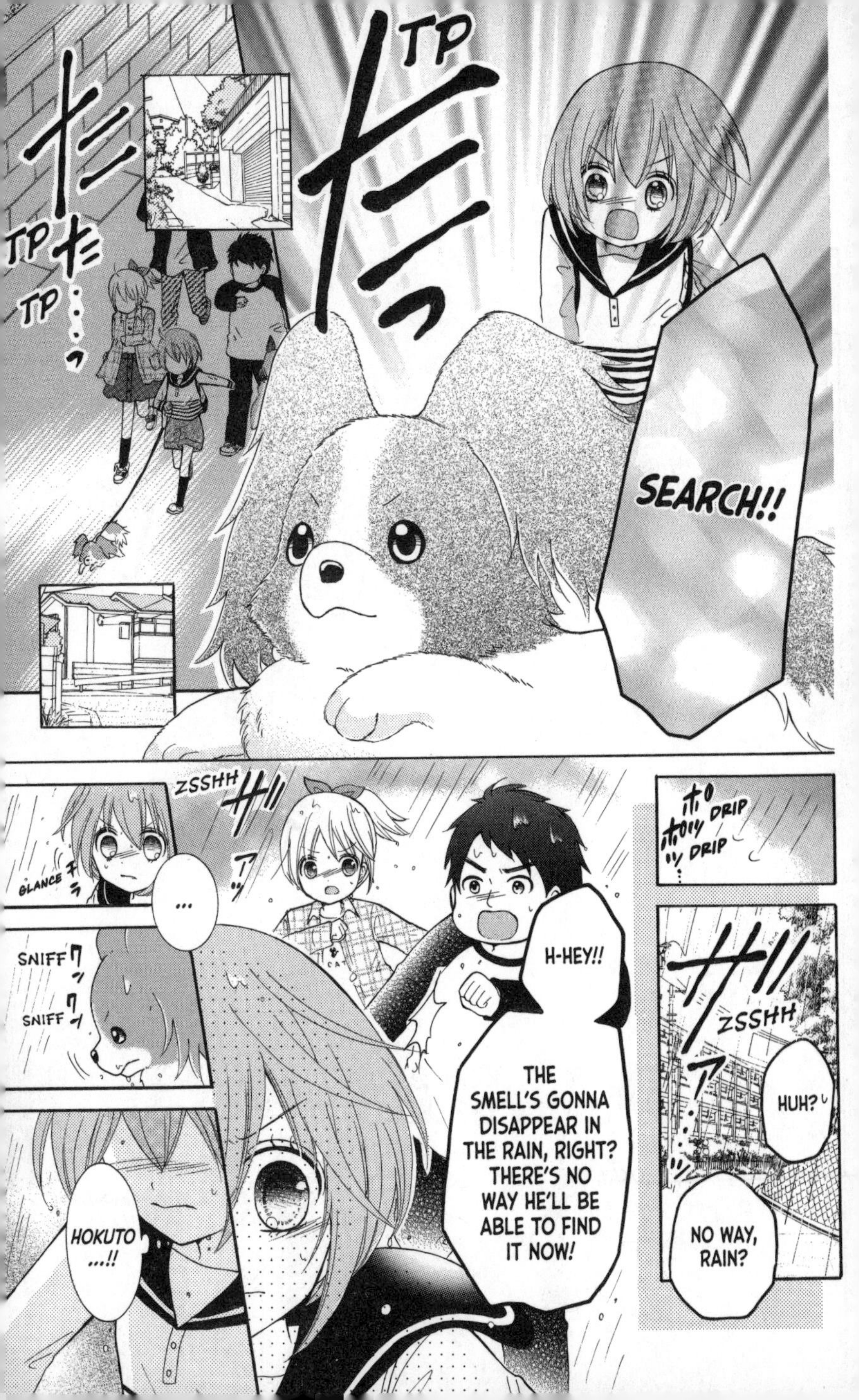
TP
SEARCH!!
TP
TP
TP
DRIP
DRIP
ZSSHH
HUH?
NO WAY, RAIN?
ZSSHH
H-HEY!!
THE SMELL'S GONNA DISAPPEAR IN THE RAIN, RIGHT? THERE'S NO WAY HE'LL BE ABLE TO FIND IT NOW!
GLANCE
...
SNIFF
SNIFF
HOKUTO ...!!

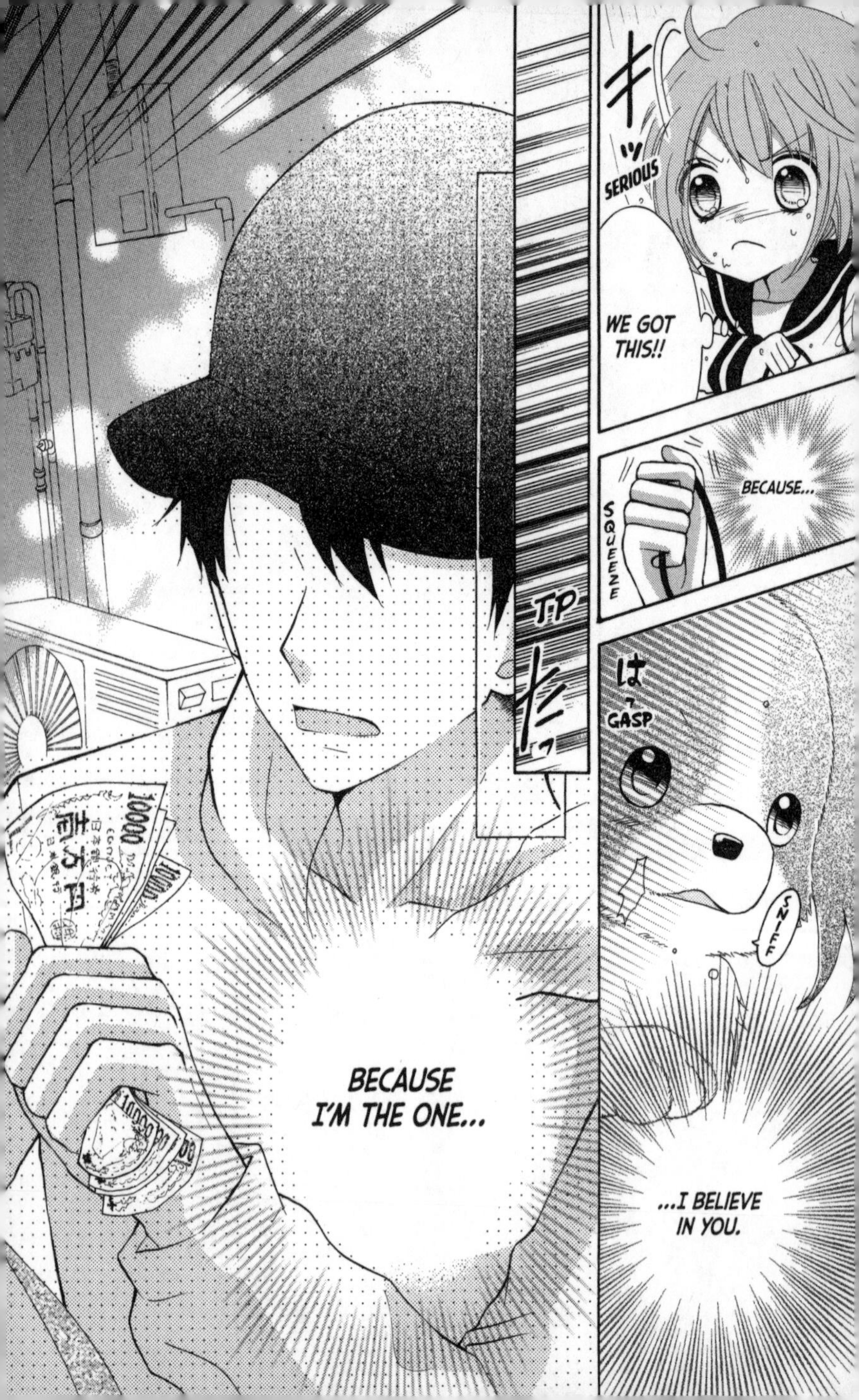
キッ
SERIOUS
WE GOT THIS!!
SQUEEZE
BECAUSE...
はっ
GASP
SNIFF
...I BELIEVE IN YOU.
TP
たっ
BECAUSE I'M THE ONE...

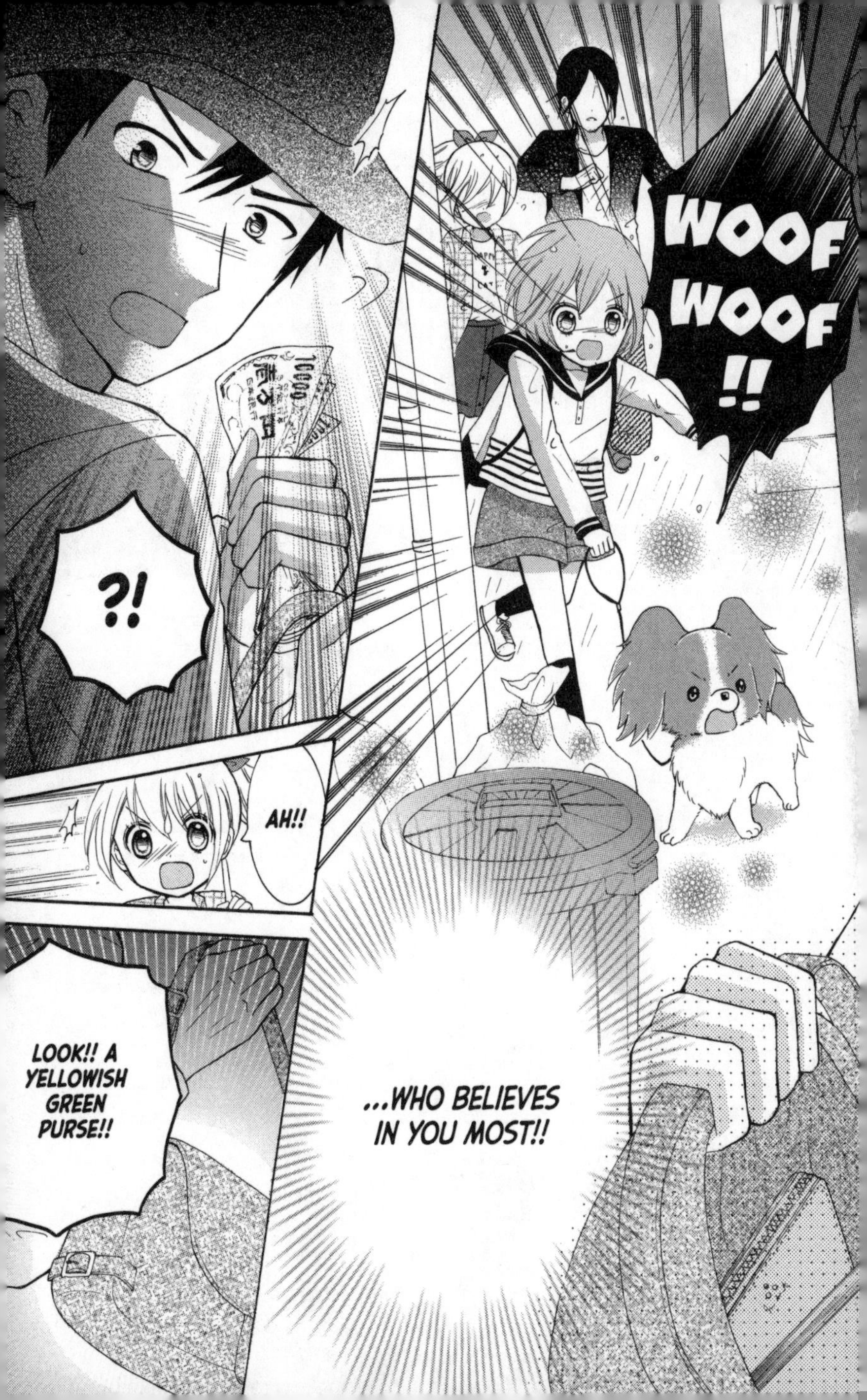
WOOF WOOF!!
?!
AH!!
...WHO BELIEVES IN YOU MOST!!
LOOK!! A YELLOWISH GREEN PURSE!!

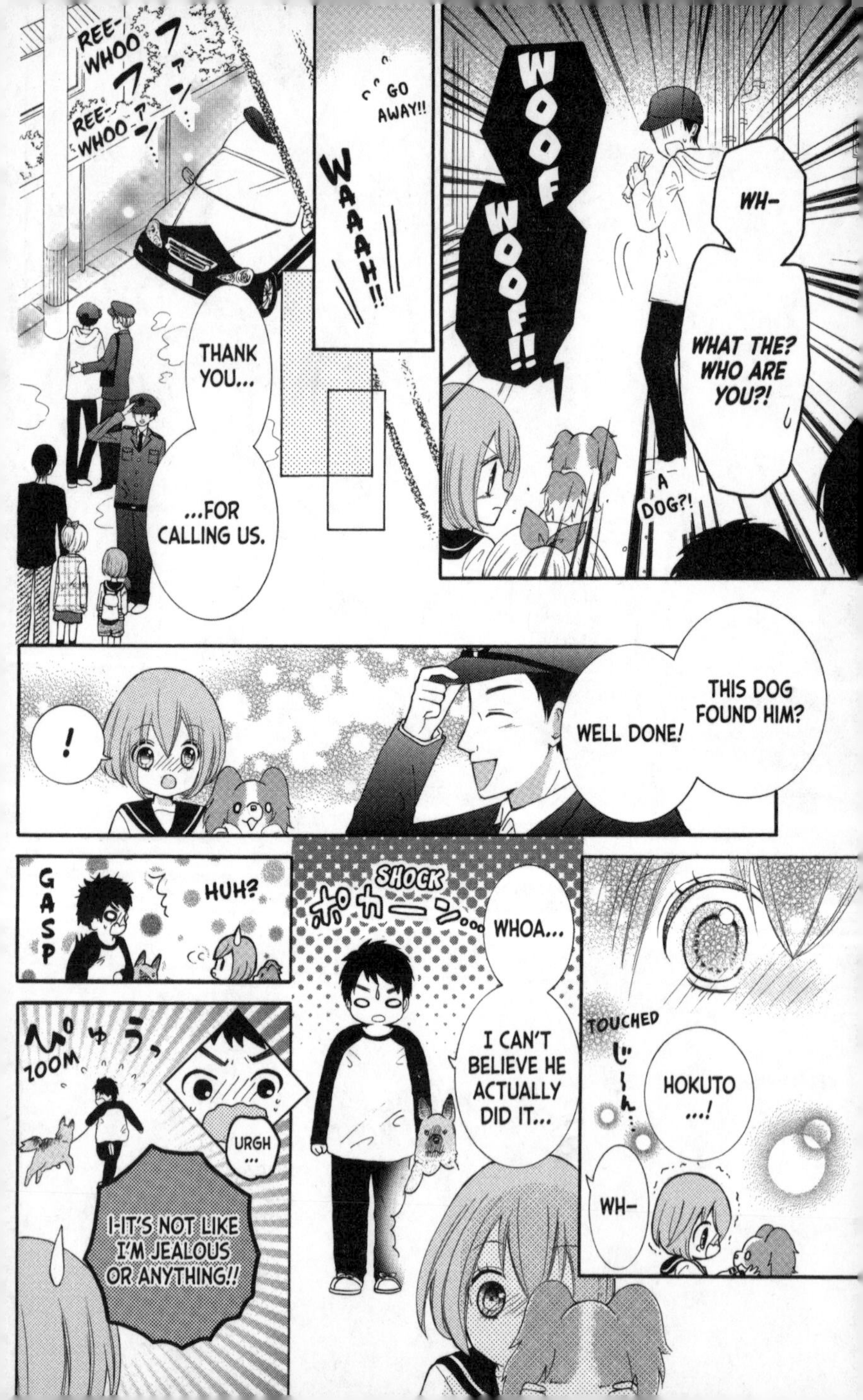
WOOF WOOF WOOF!!
WH-
WHAT THE? WHO ARE YOU?!
A DOG?!
GO AWAY!!
WAAAAH!!
REE-WHOO
REE-WHOO
THANK YOU...
...FOR CALLING US.
THIS DOG FOUND HIM?
WELL DONE!
!
TOUCHED
HOKUTO...!
WH-
SHOCK
ポカーン...
WHOA...
I CAN'T BELIEVE HE ACTUALLY DID IT...
GASP
HUH?
ZOOM
URGH...
I-IT'S NOT LIKE I'M JEALOUS OR ANYTHING!!

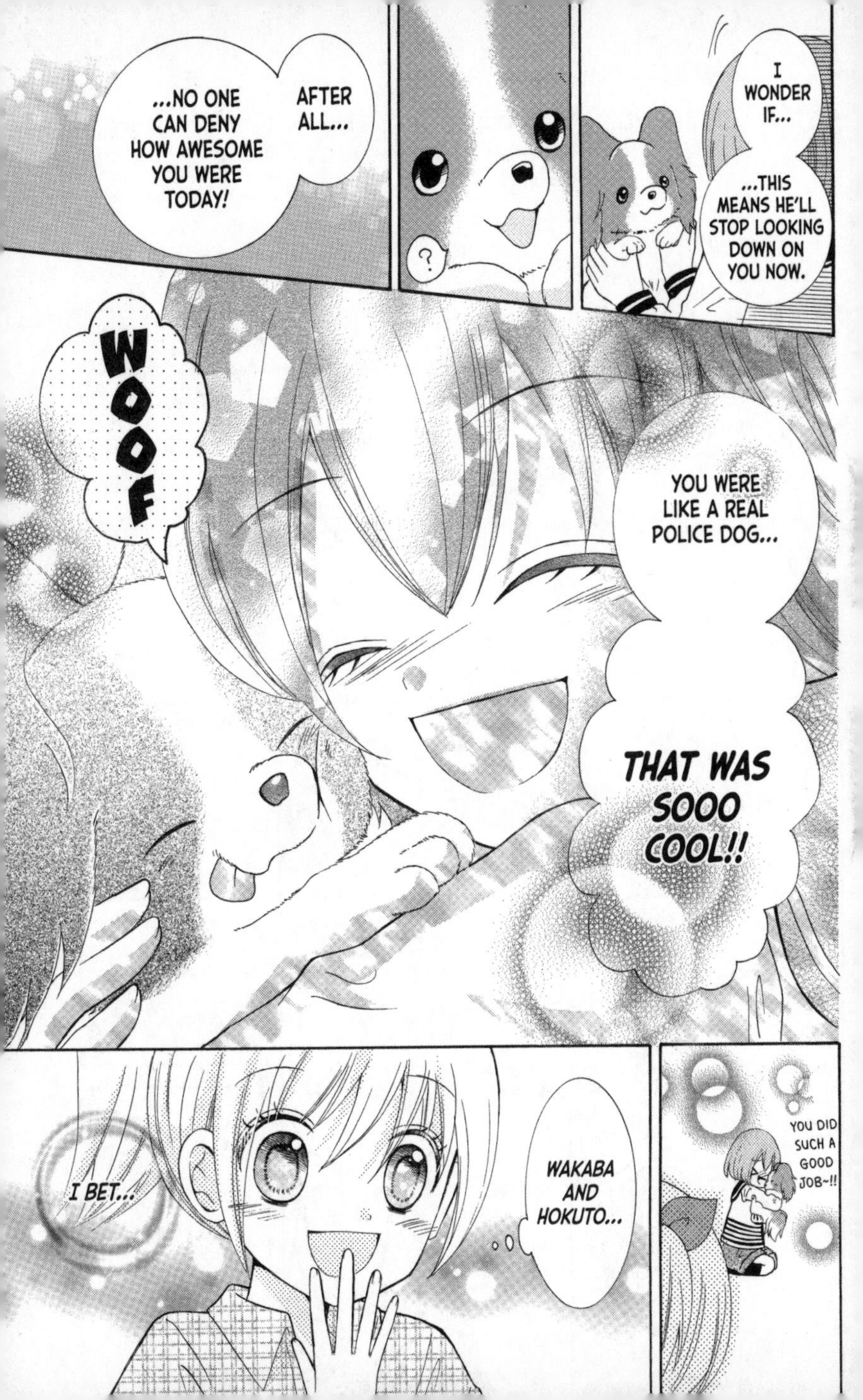
I WONDER IF...
...THIS MEANS HE'LL STOP LOOKING DOWN ON YOU NOW.
?
AFTER ALL...
...NO ONE CAN DENY HOW AWESOME YOU WERE TODAY!
YOU WERE LIKE A REAL POLICE DOG...
THAT WAS SOOO COOL!!
WOOF
YOU DID SUCH A GOOD JOB~!!
WAKABA AND HOKUTO...
I BET...

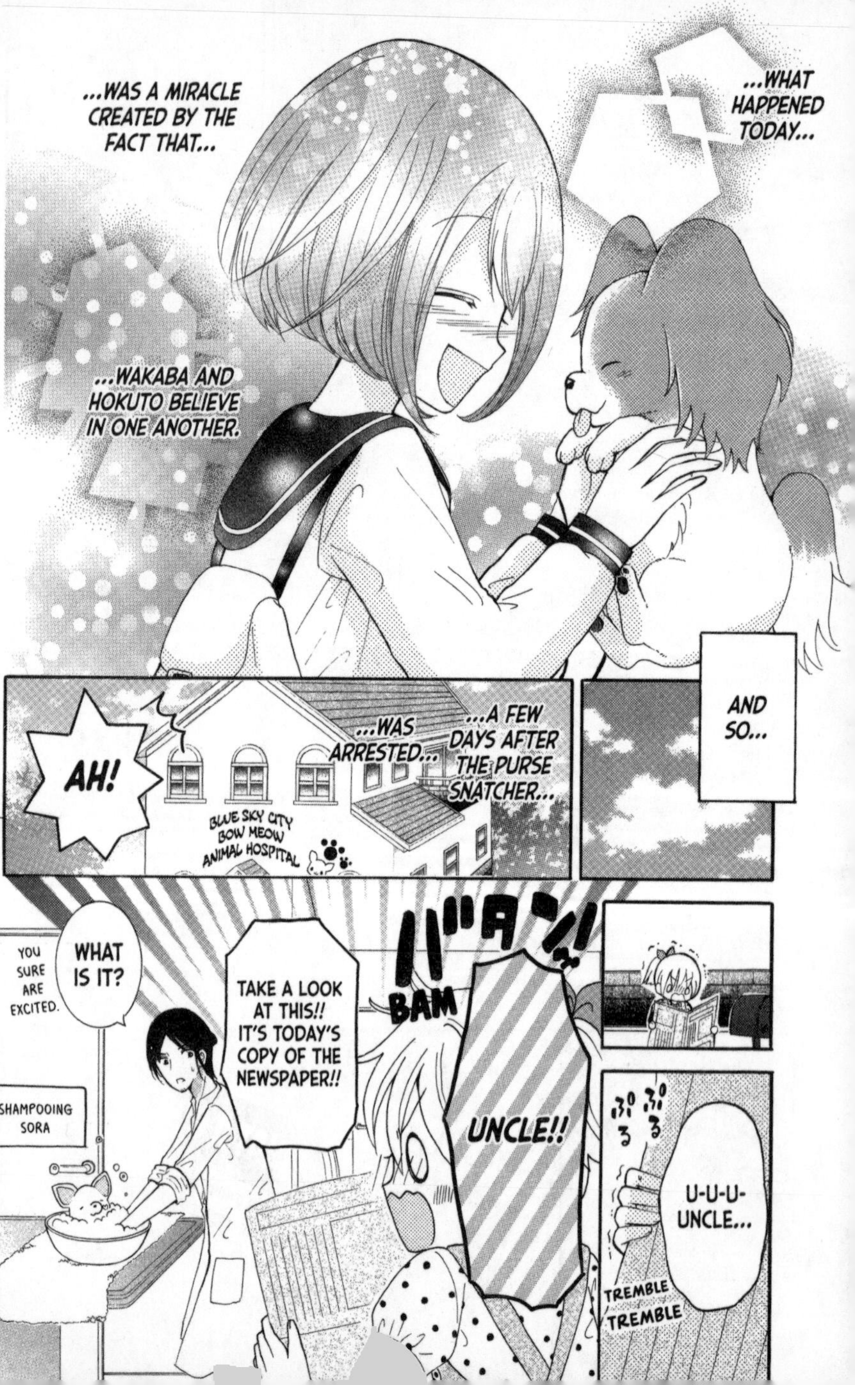
...WHAT HAPPENED TODAY...
...WAS A MIRACLE CREATED BY THE FACT THAT...
...WAKABA AND HOKUTO BELIEVE IN ONE ANOTHER.
AND SO...
...A FEW DAYS AFTER THE PURSE SNATCHER...
...WAS ARRESTED...
AH!
BLUE SKY CITY BOW MEOW ANIMAL HOSPITAL
ぶる ぶる
U-U-U-UNCLE...
TREMBLE TREMBLE
バタン!!
BAM
UNCLE!!
TAKE A LOOK AT THIS!! IT'S TODAY'S COPY OF THE NEWSPAPER!!
WHAT IS IT?
YOU SURE ARE EXCITED.
SHAMPOOING SORA

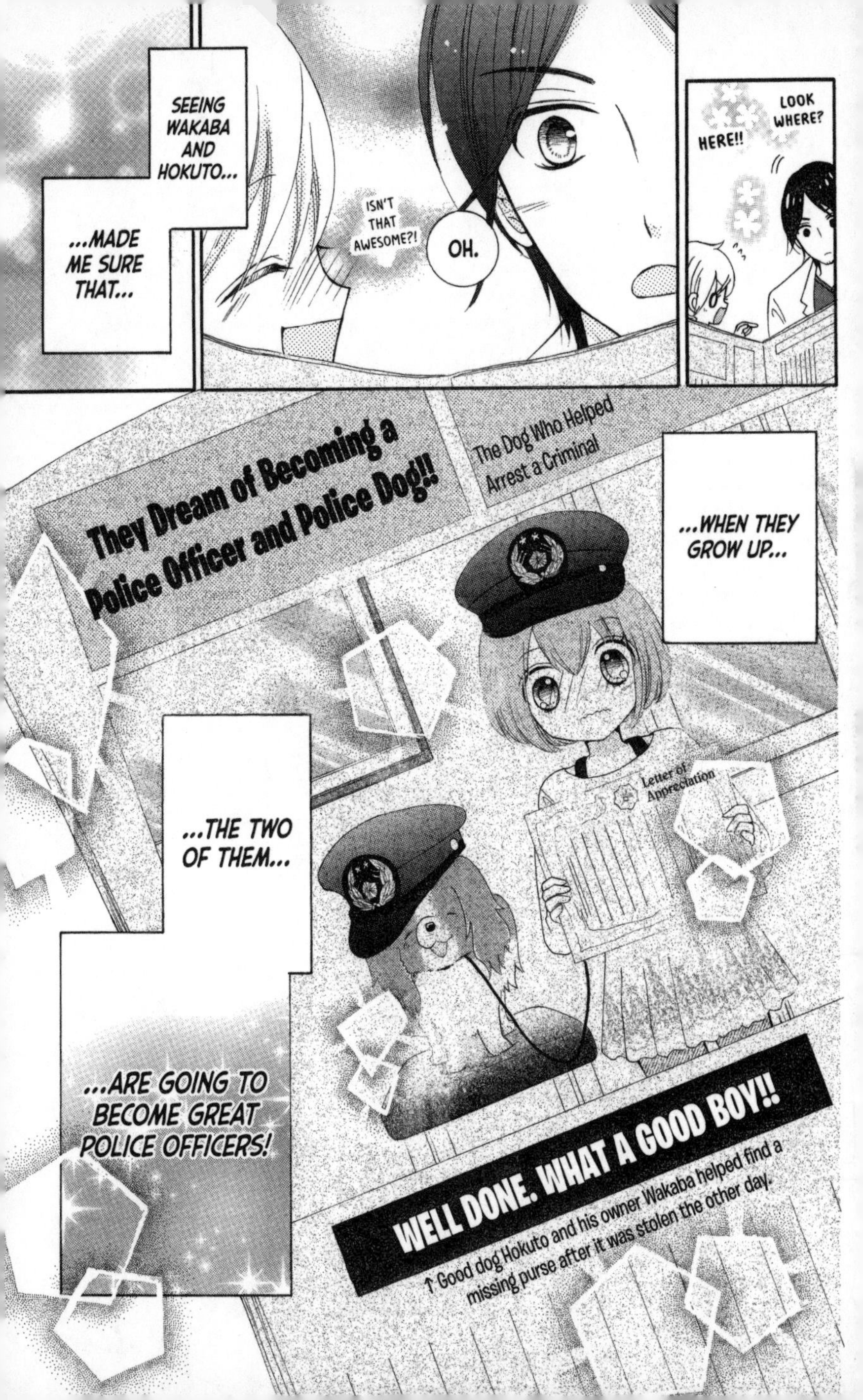
LOOK WHERE?
HERE!!
OH.
ISN'T THAT AWESOME?!
SEEING WAKABA AND HOKUTO...
...MADE ME SURE THAT...
The Dog Who Helped Arrest a Criminal
They Dream of Becoming a Police Officer and Police Dog!!
...WHEN THEY GROW UP...
Letter of Appreciation
...THE TWO OF THEM...
WELL DONE. WHAT A GOOD BOY!!
↑ Good dog Hokuto and his owner Wakaba helped find a missing purse after it was stolen the other day.
...ARE GOING TO BECOME GREAT POLICE OFFICERS!

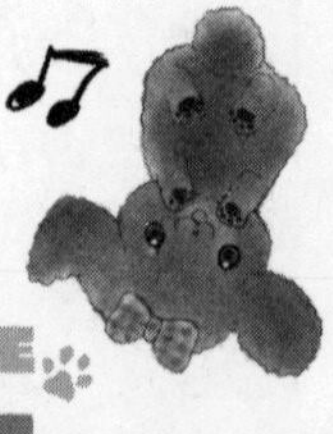

YUZU THE PET VET

ii

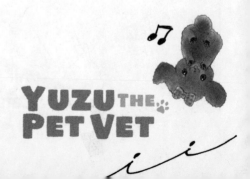

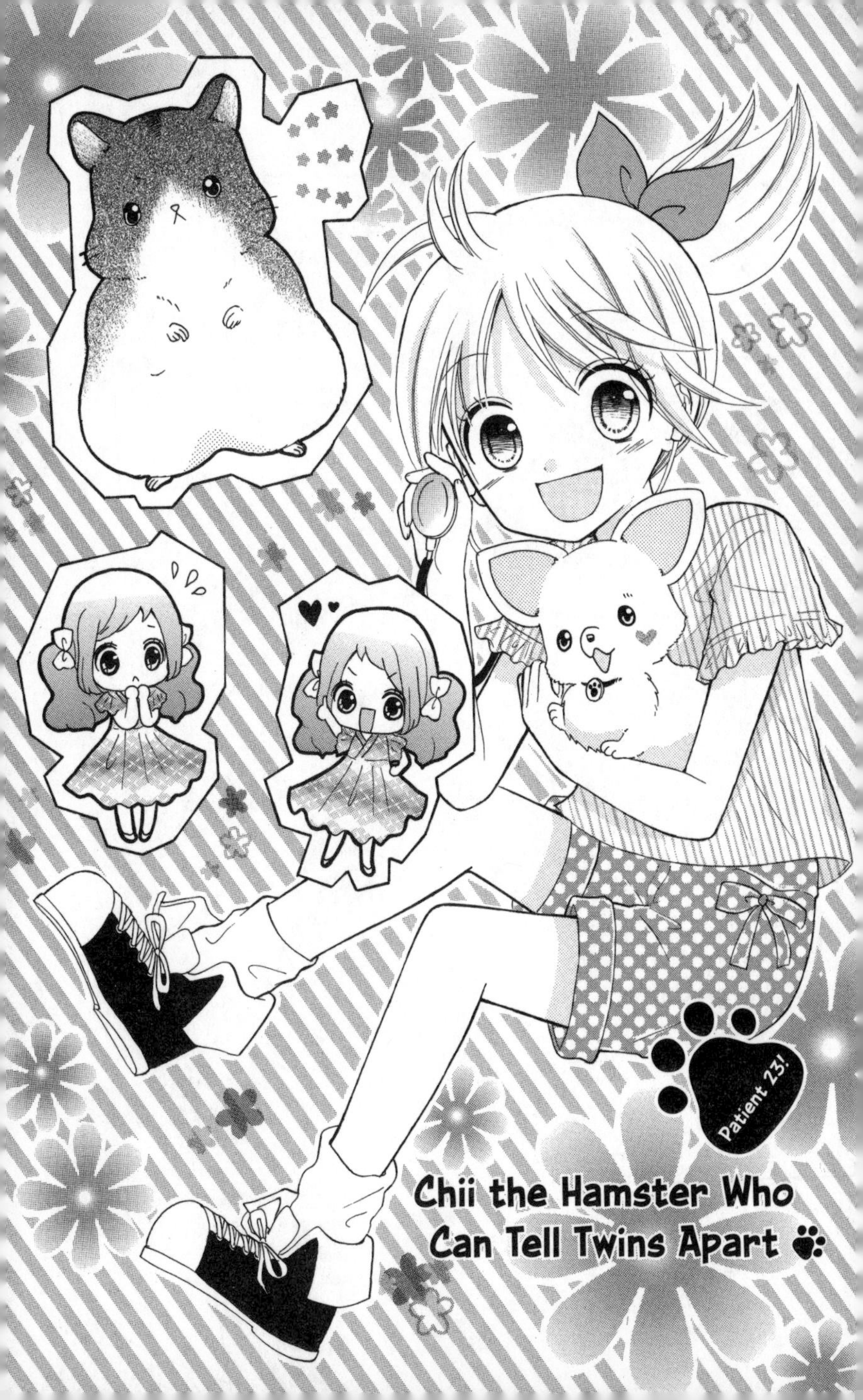
Patient 23!
Chii the Hamster Who
Can Tell Twins Apart

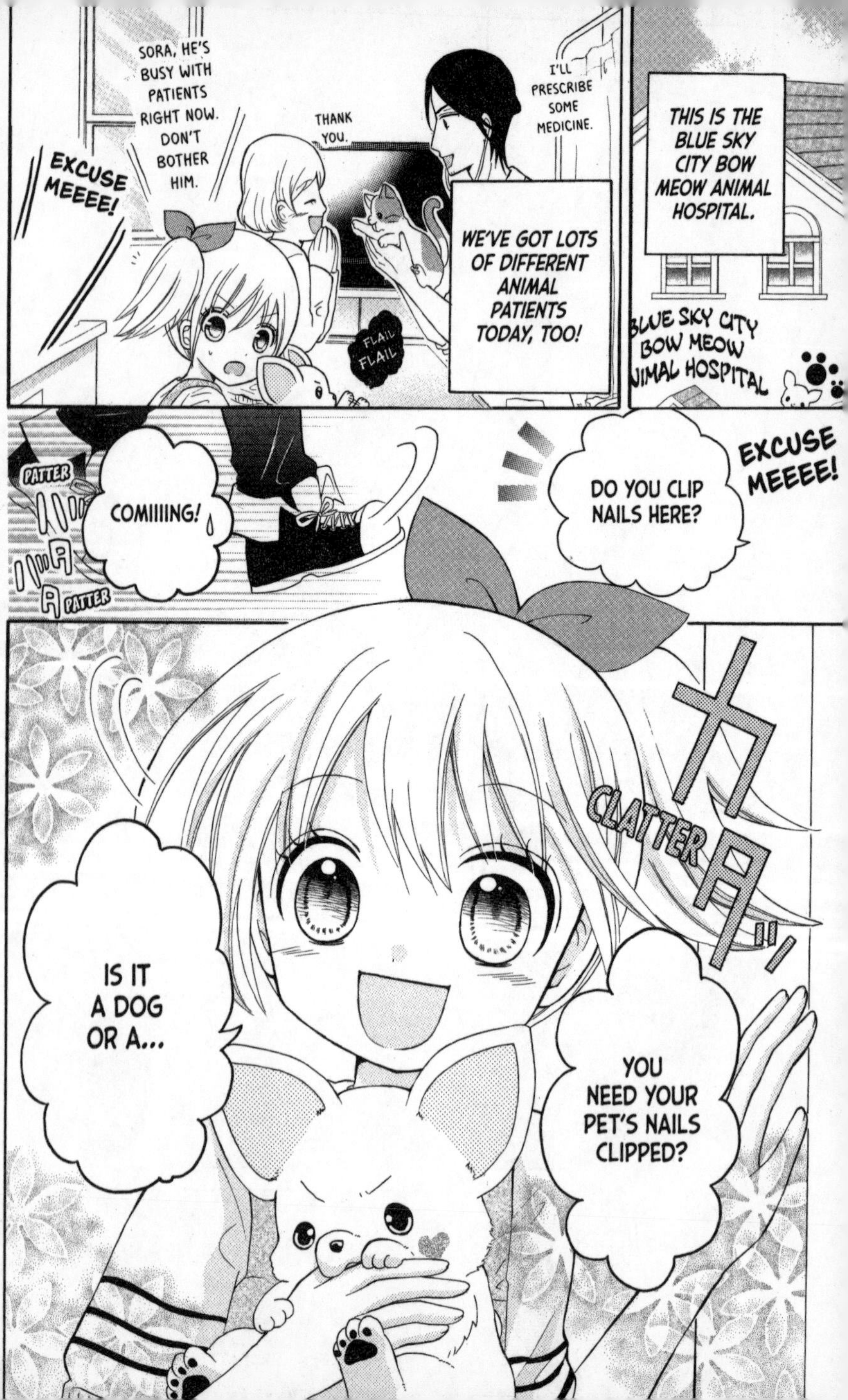
THIS IS THE BLUE SKY CITY BOW MEOW ANIMAL HOSPITAL.
BLUE SKY CITY BOW MEOW NIMAL HOSPITAL
WE'VE GOT LOTS OF DIFFERENT ANIMAL PATIENTS TODAY, TOO!
I'LL PRESCRIBE SOME MEDICINE.
THANK YOU.
SORA, HE'S BUSY WITH PATIENTS RIGHT NOW. DON'T BOTHER HIM.
EXCUSE MEEEE!
FLAIL FLAIL
EXCUSE MEEEE!
DO YOU CLIP NAILS HERE?
COMIIIING!
PATTER
PATTER
CLATTER
YOU NEED YOUR PET'S NAILS CLIPPED?
IS IT A DOG OR A...

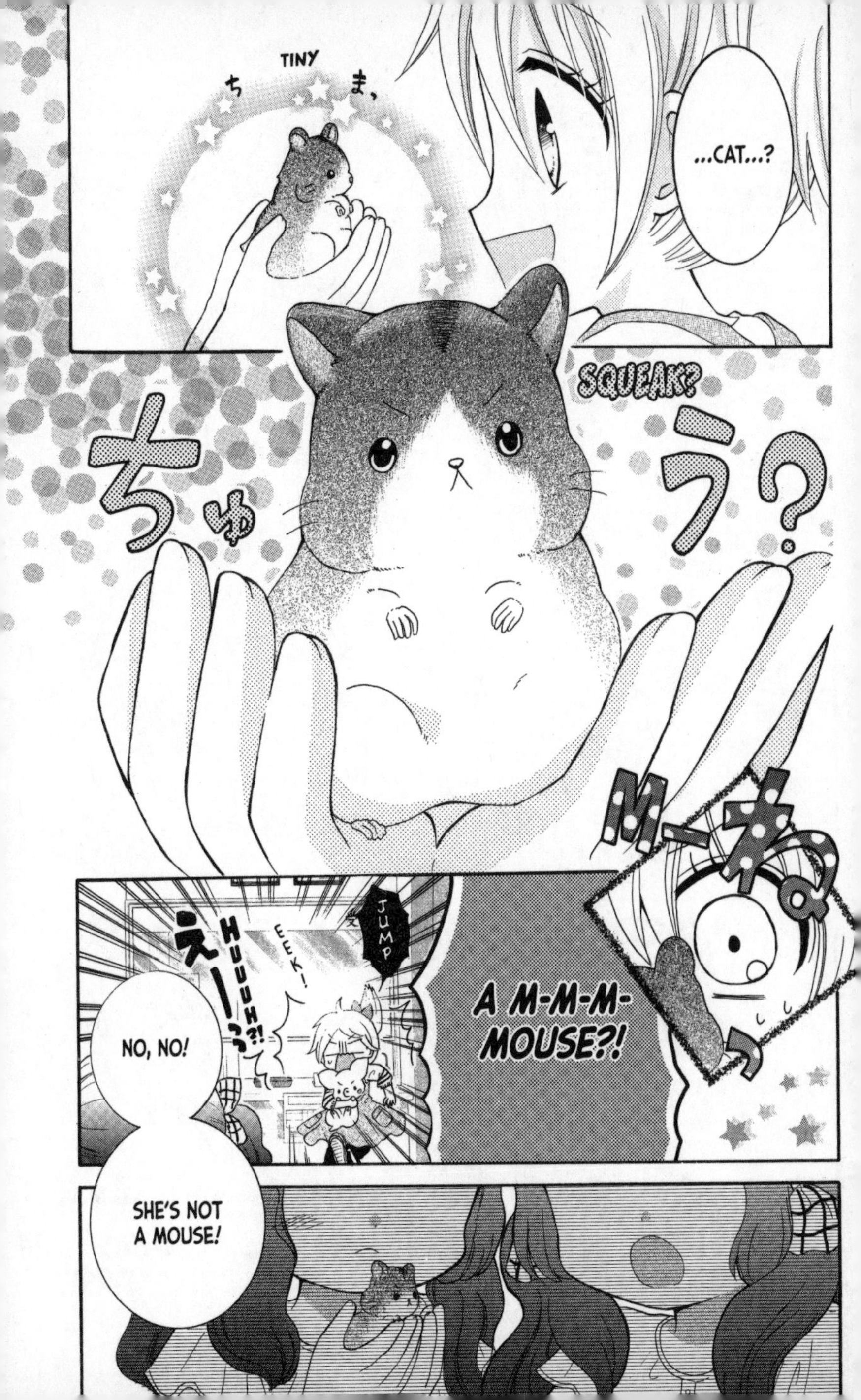
...CAT...?
TINY
ちま、
SQUEAK?
ちゅう?
A M-M-M-MOUSE?!
JUMP
EEK!
HUUUUH?!
NO, NO!
SHE'S NOT A MOUSE!

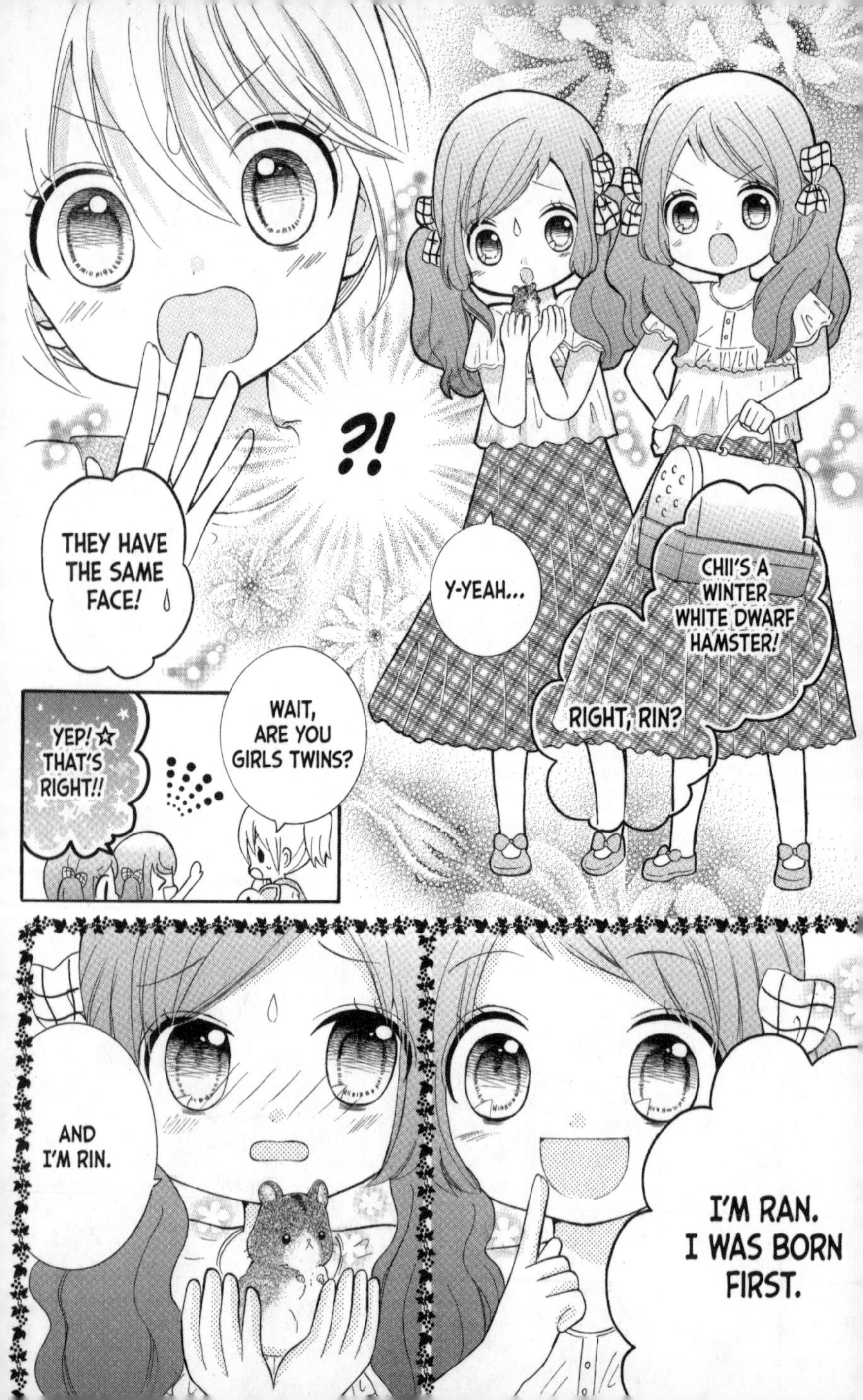
CHII'S A WINTER WHITE DWARF HAMSTER!
RIGHT, RIN?
Y-YEAH...
?!
THEY HAVE THE SAME FACE!
WAIT, ARE YOU GIRLS TWINS?
YEP! ☆ THAT'S RIGHT!!
I'M RAN. I WAS BORN FIRST.
AND I'M RIN.

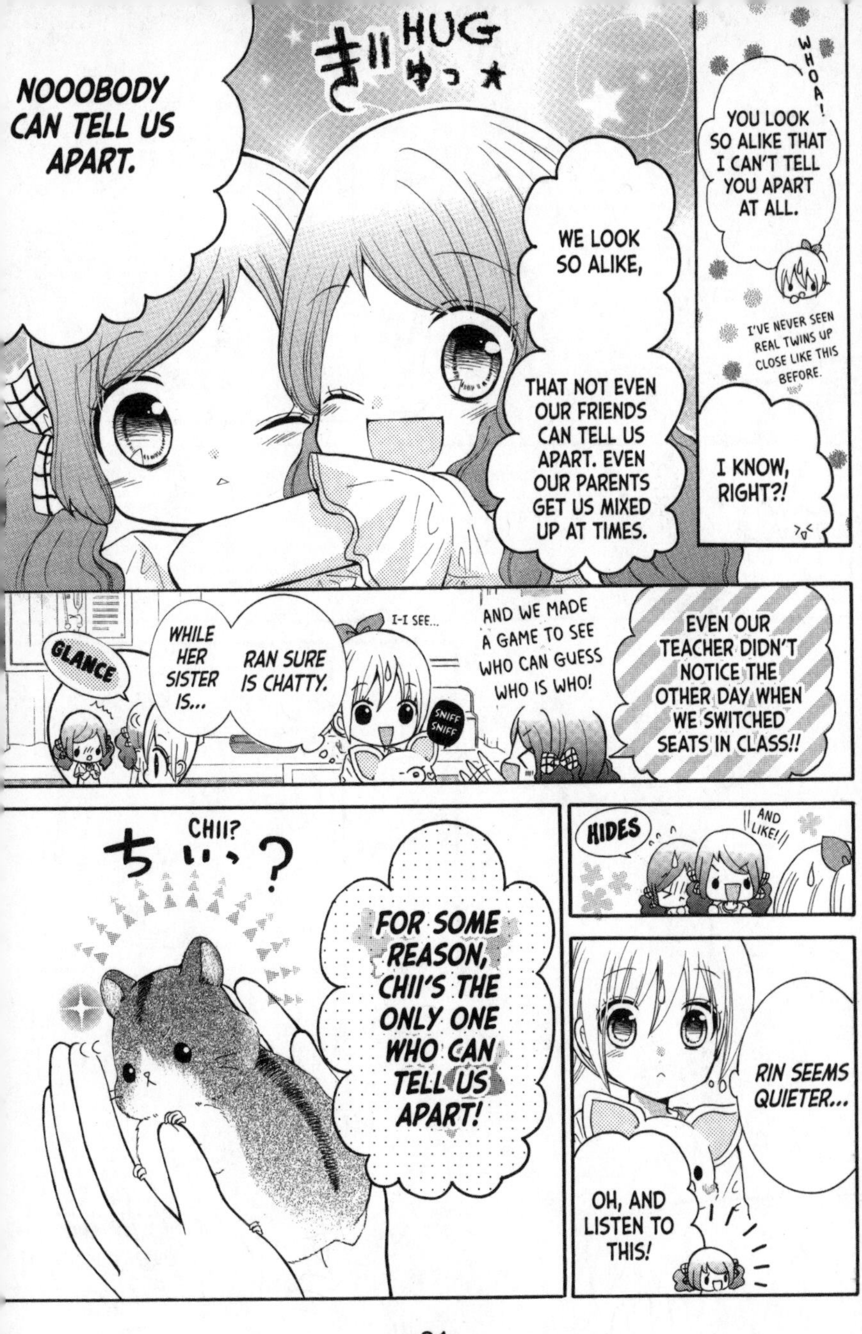
WHOA!
YOU LOOK SO ALIKE THAT I CAN'T TELL YOU APART AT ALL.
I'VE NEVER SEEN REAL TWINS UP CLOSE LIKE THIS BEFORE.
I KNOW, RIGHT?!
HUG
ぎゅっ★
WE LOOK SO ALIKE,
THAT NOT EVEN OUR FRIENDS CAN TELL US APART. EVEN OUR PARENTS GET US MIXED UP AT TIMES.
NOOOBODY CAN TELL US APART.
EVEN OUR TEACHER DIDN'T NOTICE THE OTHER DAY WHEN WE SWITCHED SEATS IN CLASS!!
AND WE MADE A GAME TO SEE WHO CAN GUESS WHO IS WHO!
I-I SEE...
SNIFF SNIFF
RAN SURE IS CHATTY.
WHILE HER SISTER IS...
GLANCE
AND LIKE!!
HIDES
RIN SEEMS QUIETER...
OH, AND LISTEN TO THIS!
CHII?
ちぃっ？
FOR SOME REASON, CHII'S THE ONLY ONE WHO CAN TELL US APART!

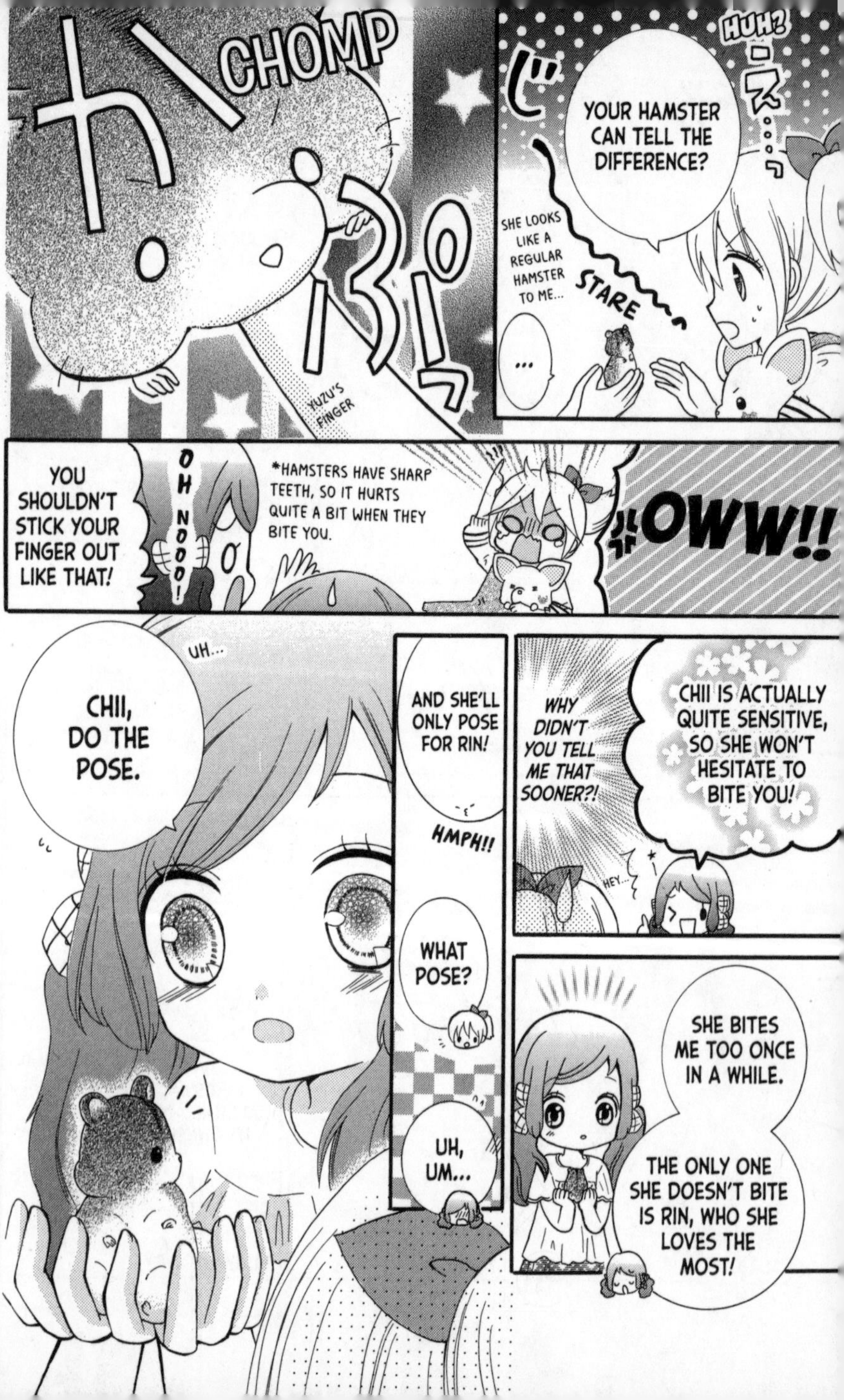
HUH?
YOUR HAMSTER CAN TELL THE DIFFERENCE?
STARE
SHE LOOKS LIKE A REGULAR HAMSTER TO ME...
...
CHOMP
YUZU'S FINGER
OWW!!
*HAMSTERS HAVE SHARP TEETH, SO IT HURTS QUITE A BIT WHEN THEY BITE YOU.
OH NOOOO!
YOU SHOULDN'T STICK YOUR FINGER OUT LIKE THAT!
CHII IS ACTUALLY QUITE SENSITIVE, SO SHE WON'T HESITATE TO BITE YOU!
HEY...
WHY DIDN'T YOU TELL ME THAT SOONER?!
SHE BITES ME TOO ONCE IN A WHILE.
THE ONLY ONE SHE DOESN'T BITE IS RIN, WHO SHE LOVES THE MOST!
AND SHE'LL ONLY POSE FOR RIN!
HMPH!!
WHAT POSE?
UH, UM...
UH...
CHII, DO THE POSE.

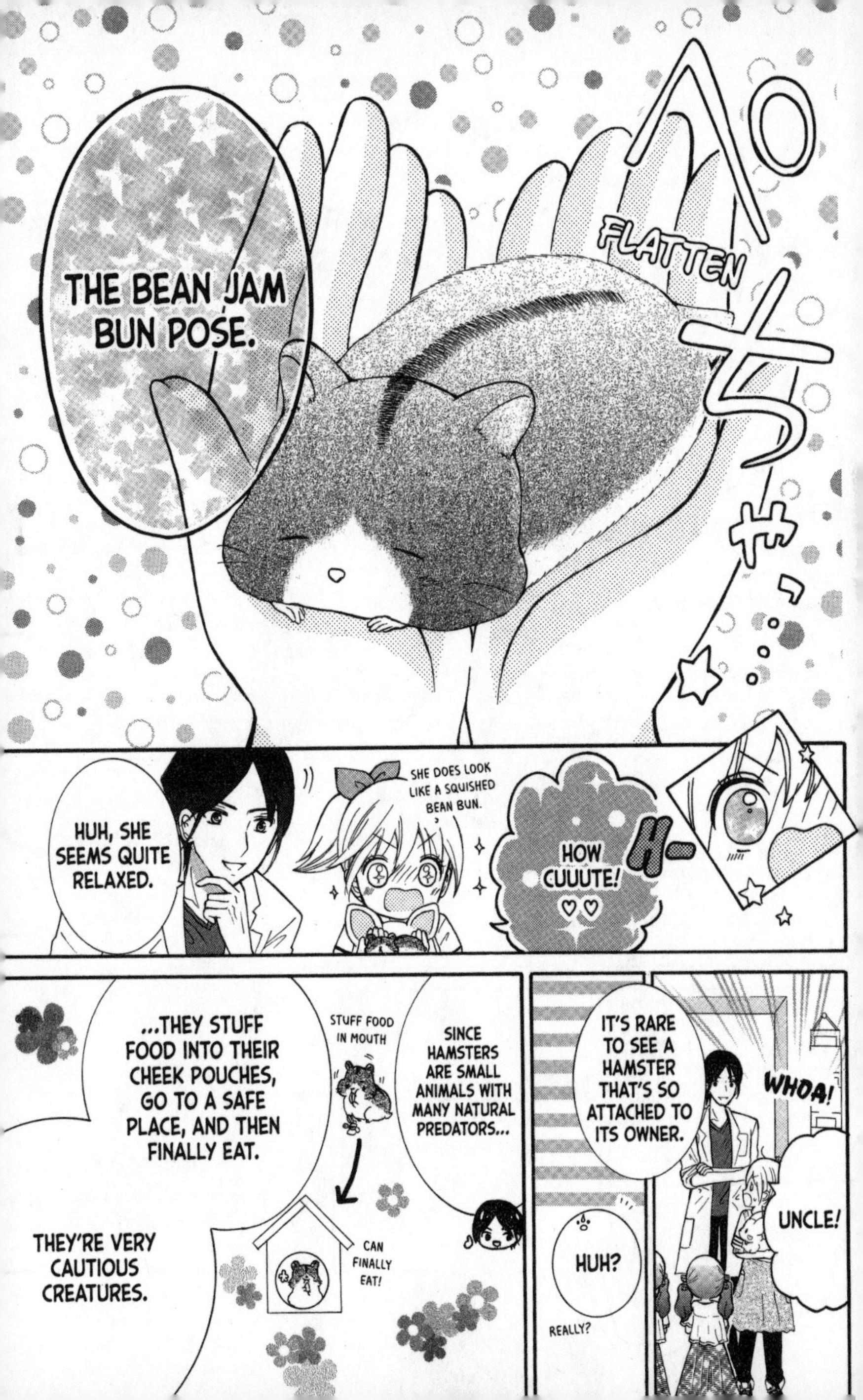
FLATTEN
THE BEAN JAM BUN POSE.
H-
HOW CUUUTE! ♡♡
SHE DOES LOOK LIKE A SQUISHED BEAN BUN.
HUH, SHE SEEMS QUITE RELAXED.
IT'S RARE TO SEE A HAMSTER THAT'S SO ATTACHED TO ITS OWNER.
WHOA!
UNCLE!
HUH?
REALLY?
SINCE HAMSTERS ARE SMALL ANIMALS WITH MANY NATURAL PREDATORS...
STUFF FOOD IN MOUTH
...THEY STUFF FOOD INTO THEIR CHEEK POUCHES, GO TO A SAFE PLACE, AND THEN FINALLY EAT.
CAN FINALLY EAT!
THEY'RE VERY CAUTIOUS CREATURES.

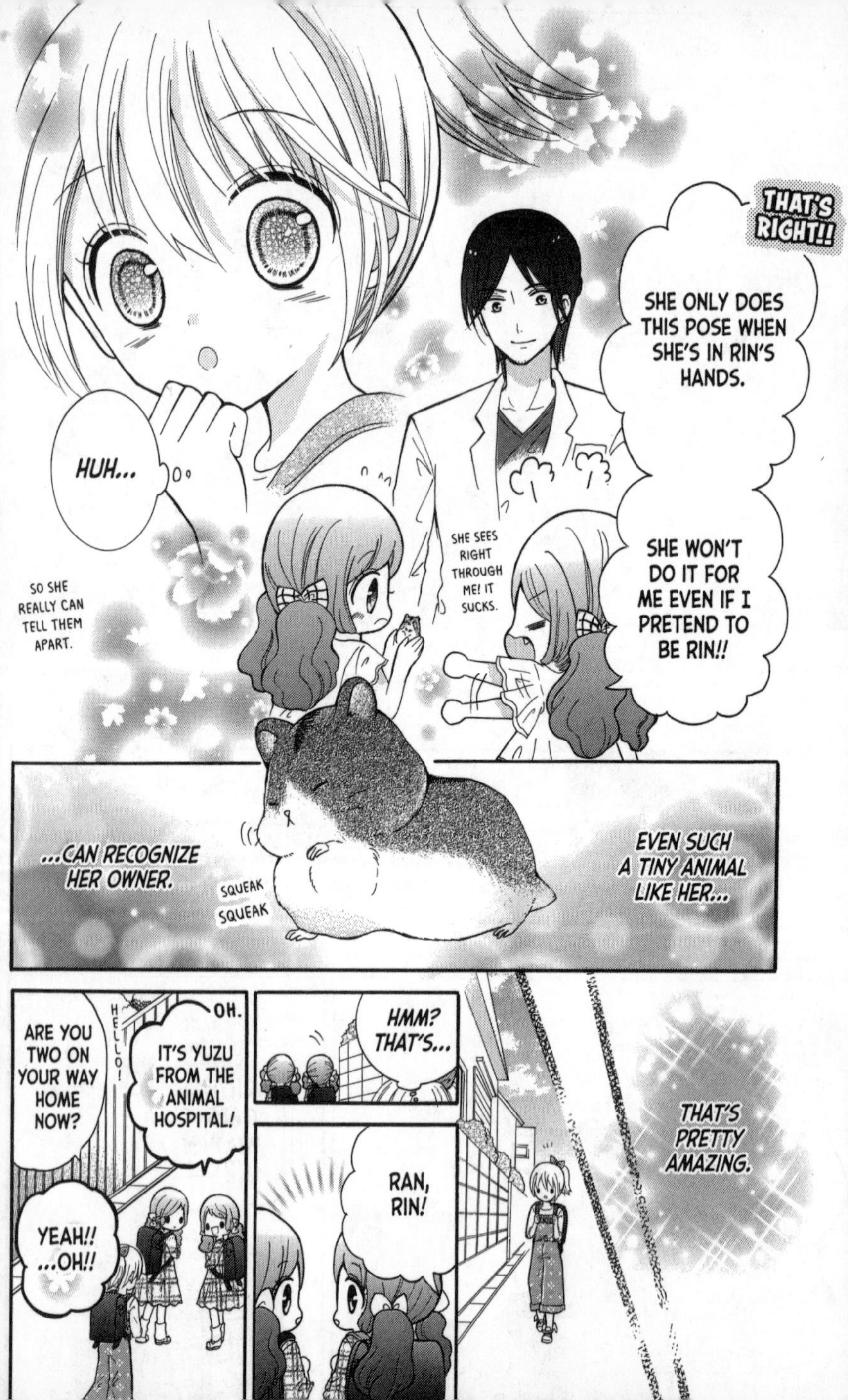
THAT'S RIGHT!!
SHE ONLY DOES THIS POSE WHEN SHE'S IN RIN'S HANDS.
SHE WON'T DO IT FOR ME EVEN IF I PRETEND TO BE RIN!!
SHE SEES RIGHT THROUGH ME! IT SUCKS.
HUH...
SO SHE REALLY CAN TELL THEM APART.
EVEN SUCH A TINY ANIMAL LIKE HER...
SQUEAK
SQUEAK
...CAN RECOGNIZE HER OWNER.
THAT'S PRETTY AMAZING.
HMM? THAT'S...
RAN, RIN!
OH.
IT'S YUZU FROM THE ANIMAL HOSPITAL!
HELLO!
ARE YOU TWO ON YOUR WAY HOME NOW?
YEAH!! ...OH!!

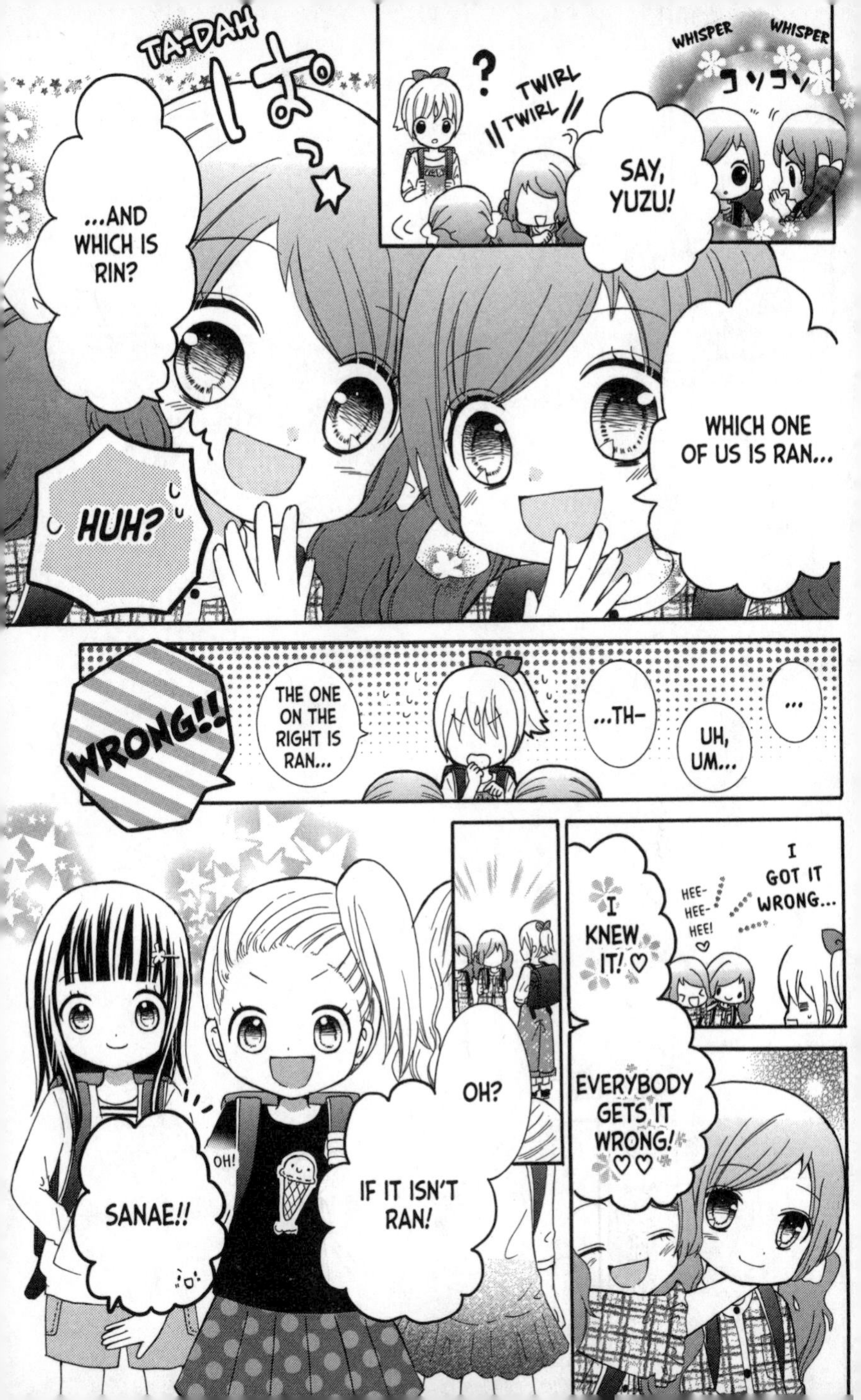
WHISPER WHISPER
コソコソ
?
TWIRL TWIRL
SAY, YUZU!
TA-DAH
ぱっ
WHICH ONE OF US IS RAN...
...AND WHICH IS RIN?
HUH?
...
UH, UM...
...TH-
THE ONE ON THE RIGHT IS RAN...
WRONG!!
I GOT IT WRONG...
HEE-HEE-HEE!
I KNEW IT! ♡
EVERYBODY GETS IT WRONG! ♡♡
OH?
IF IT ISN'T RAN!
OH!
SANAE!!

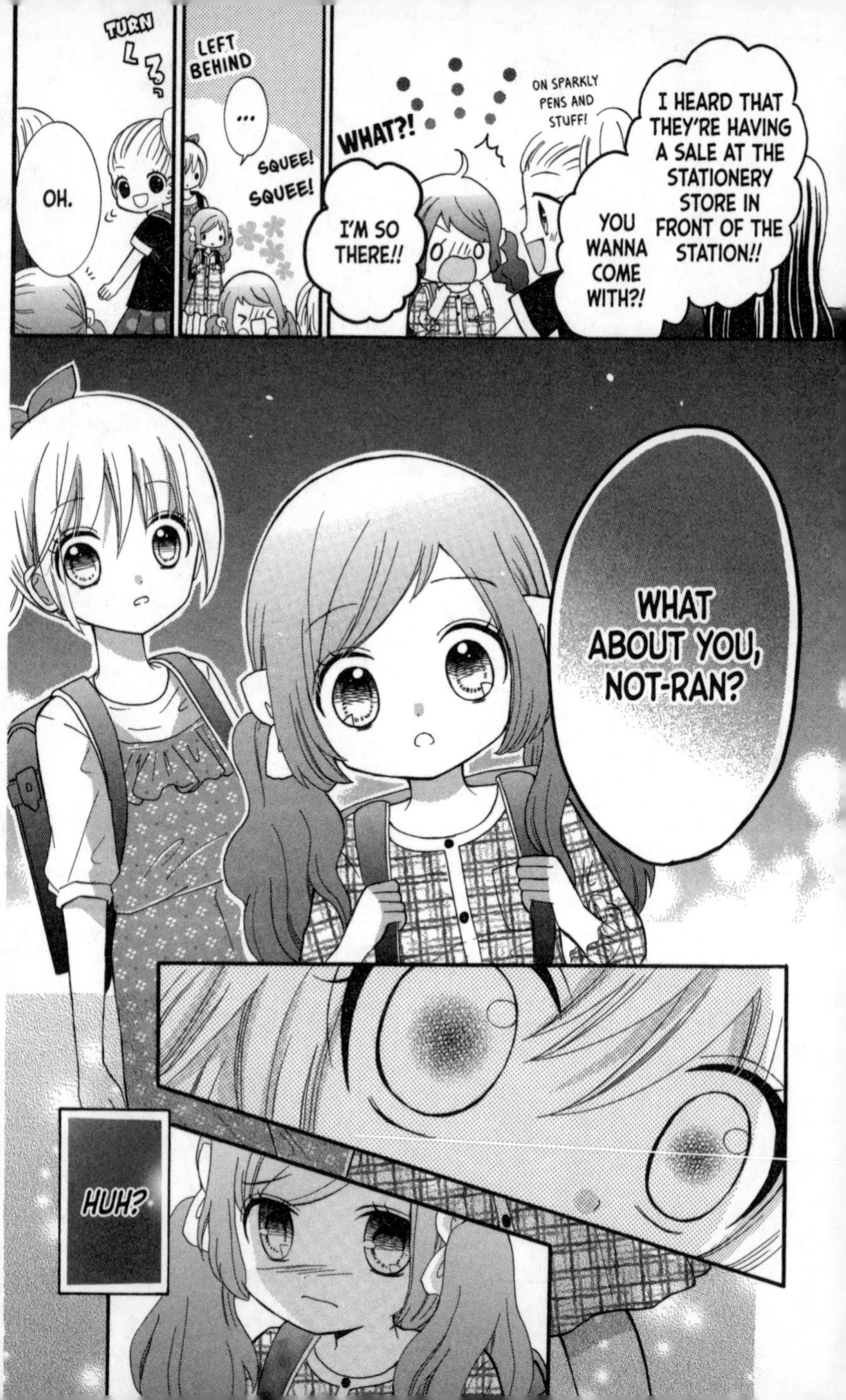
I HEARD THAT THEY'RE HAVING A SALE AT THE STATIONERY STORE IN FRONT OF THE STATION!!
ON SPARKLY PENS AND STUFF!
YOU WANNA COME WITH?!
WHAT?!
I'M SO THERE!!
LEFT BEHIND
...
SQUEE! SQUEE!
TURN
OH.
WHAT ABOUT YOU, NOT-RAN?
HUH?

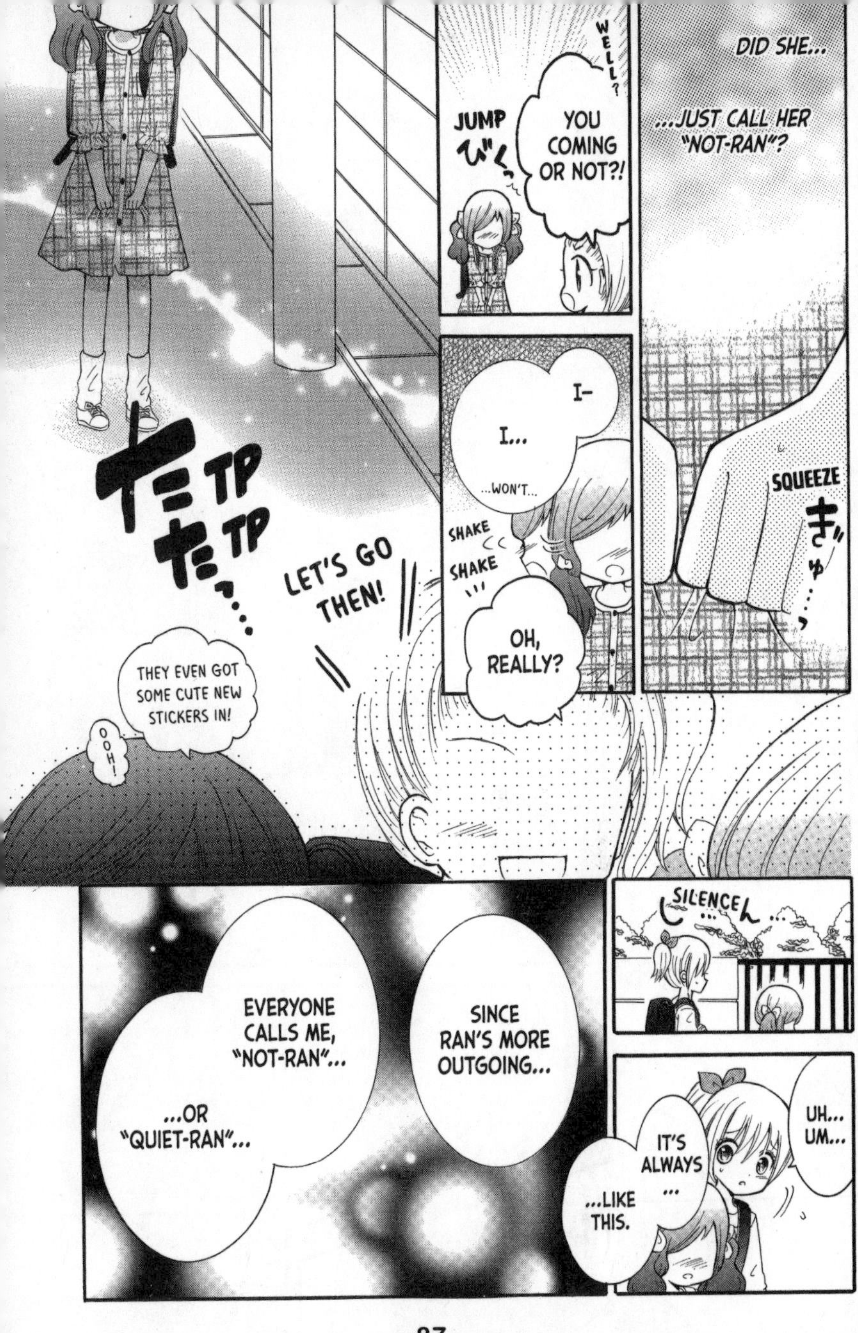
DID SHE...
...JUST CALL HER "NOT-RAN"?
SQUEEZE
WELL?
YOU COMING OR NOT?!
JUMP
I-
I...
...WON'T...
SHAKE
SHAKE
OH, REALLY?
LET'S GO THEN!
TP TP
THEY EVEN GOT SOME CUTE NEW STICKERS IN!
OOH!
SILENCE...
UH... UM...
IT'S ALWAYS...
...LIKE THIS.
SINCE RAN'S MORE OUTGOING...
EVERYONE CALLS ME, "NOT-RAN"...
...OR "QUIET-RAN"...

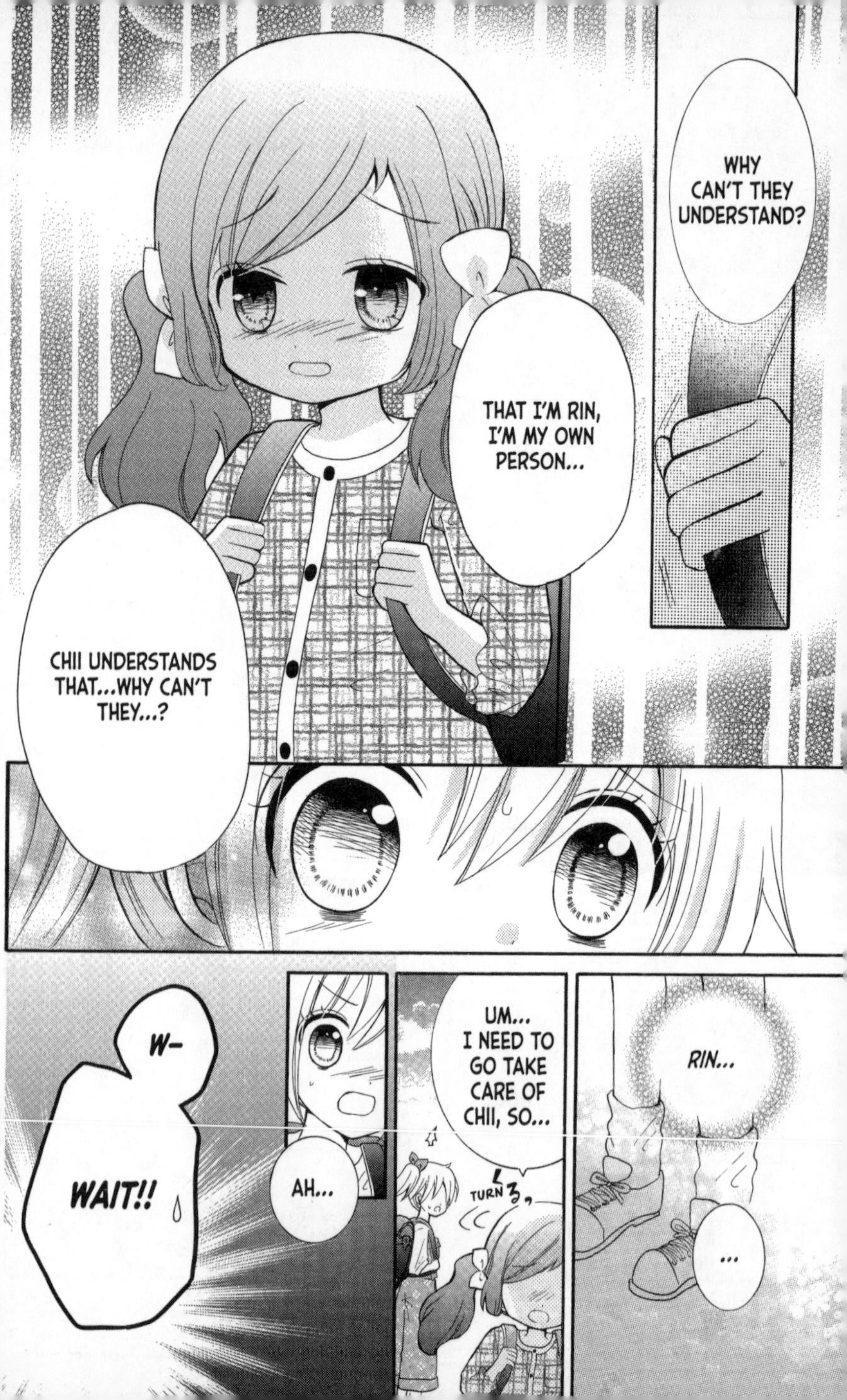
WHY CAN'T THEY UNDERSTAND?
THAT I'M RIN, I'M MY OWN PERSON...
CHII UNDERSTANDS THAT...WHY CAN'T THEY...?
RIN...
...
UM... I NEED TO GO TAKE CARE OF CHII, SO...
TURN
AH...
W-
WAIT!!

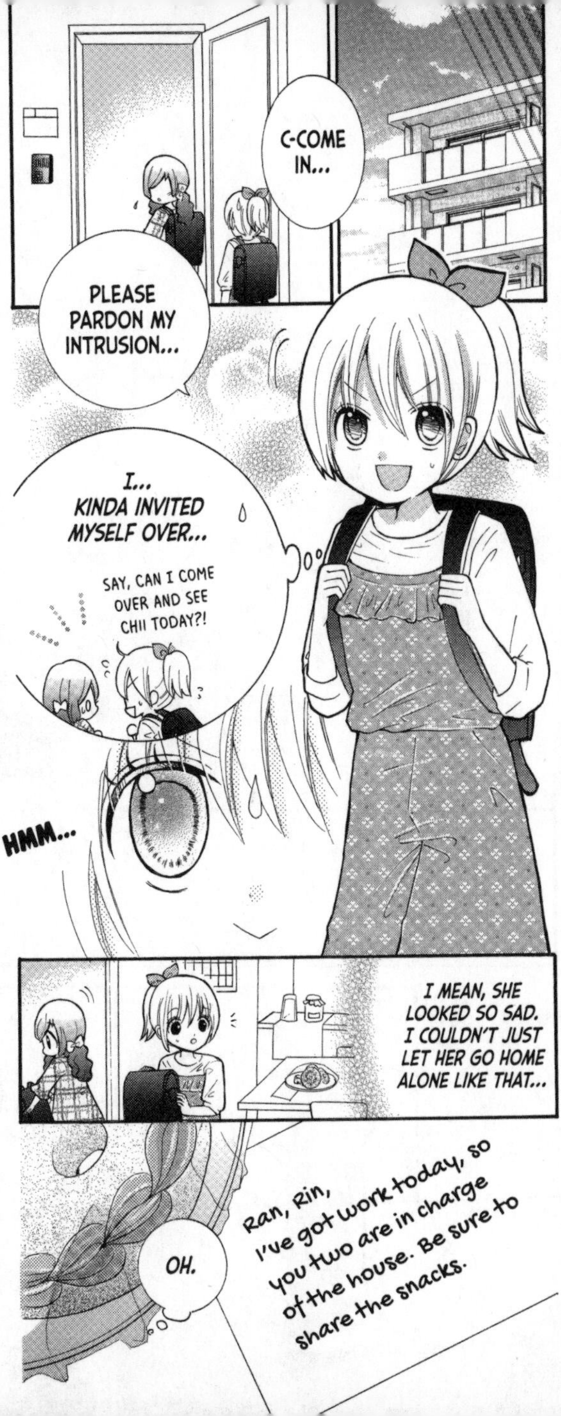
C-COME IN...
PLEASE PARDON MY INTRUSION...
I... KINDA INVITED MYSELF OVER...
SAY, CAN I COME OVER AND SEE CHII TODAY?!
HMM...
I MEAN, SHE LOOKED SO SAD. I COULDN'T JUST LET HER GO HOME ALONE LIKE THAT...
Ran, Rin, I've got work today, so you two are in charge of the house. Be sure to share the snacks.
OH.

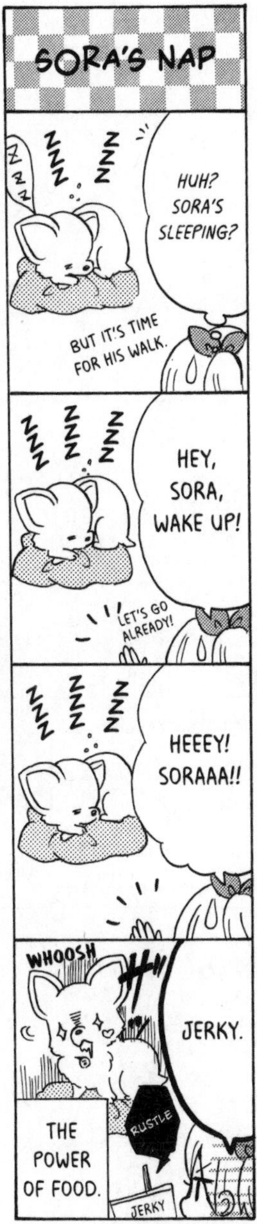
SORA'S NAP
ZZZ
ZZZ
ZZZ
HUH? SORA'S SLEEPING?
BUT IT'S TIME FOR HIS WALK.
ZZZ
ZZZ
ZZZ
HEY, SORA, WAKE UP!
LET'S GO ALREADY!
ZZZ
ZZZ
ZZZ
HEEEY! SORAAA!!
WHOOSH
JERKY.
RUSTLE
JERKY
THE POWER OF FOOD.

SLEEPINESS < HUNGER

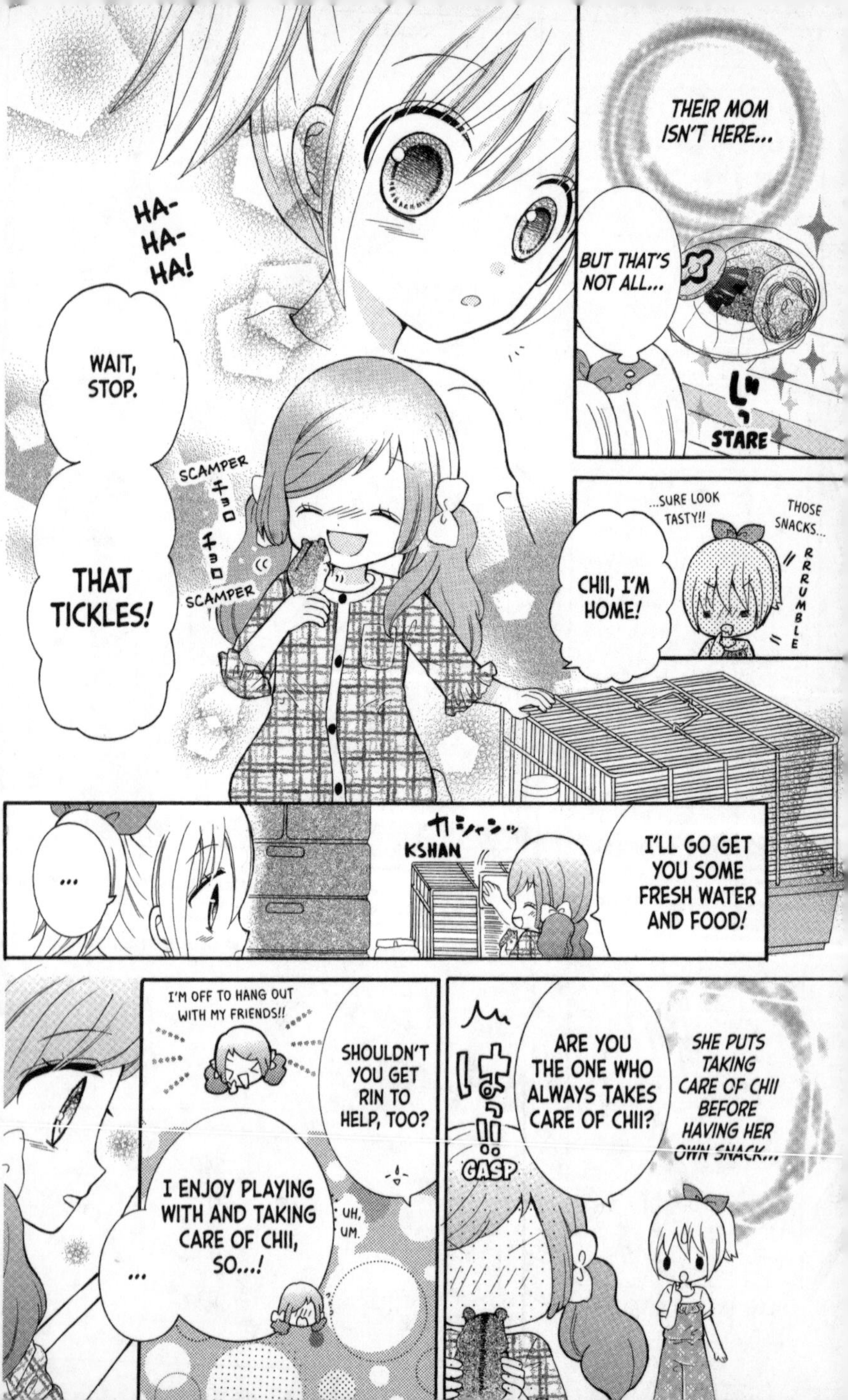
THEIR MOM ISN'T HERE...
BUT THAT'S NOT ALL...
じぃっ
STARE
THOSE SNACKS...
...SURE LOOK TASTY!!
RRRUMBLE
CHII, I'M HOME!
HA-HA-HA!
SCAMPER
チョロ
チョロ
SCAMPER
WAIT, STOP.
THAT TICKLES!
I'LL GO GET YOU SOME FRESH WATER AND FOOD!
カシャンッ
KSHAN
...
SHE PUTS TAKING CARE OF CHII BEFORE HAVING HER OWN SNACK...
ARE YOU THE ONE WHO ALWAYS TAKES CARE OF CHII?
はっ!!
GASP
SHOULDN'T YOU GET RIN TO HELP, TOO?
I'M OFF TO HANG OUT WITH MY FRIENDS!!
UH, UM.
I ENJOY PLAYING WITH AND TAKING CARE OF CHII, SO...!
...

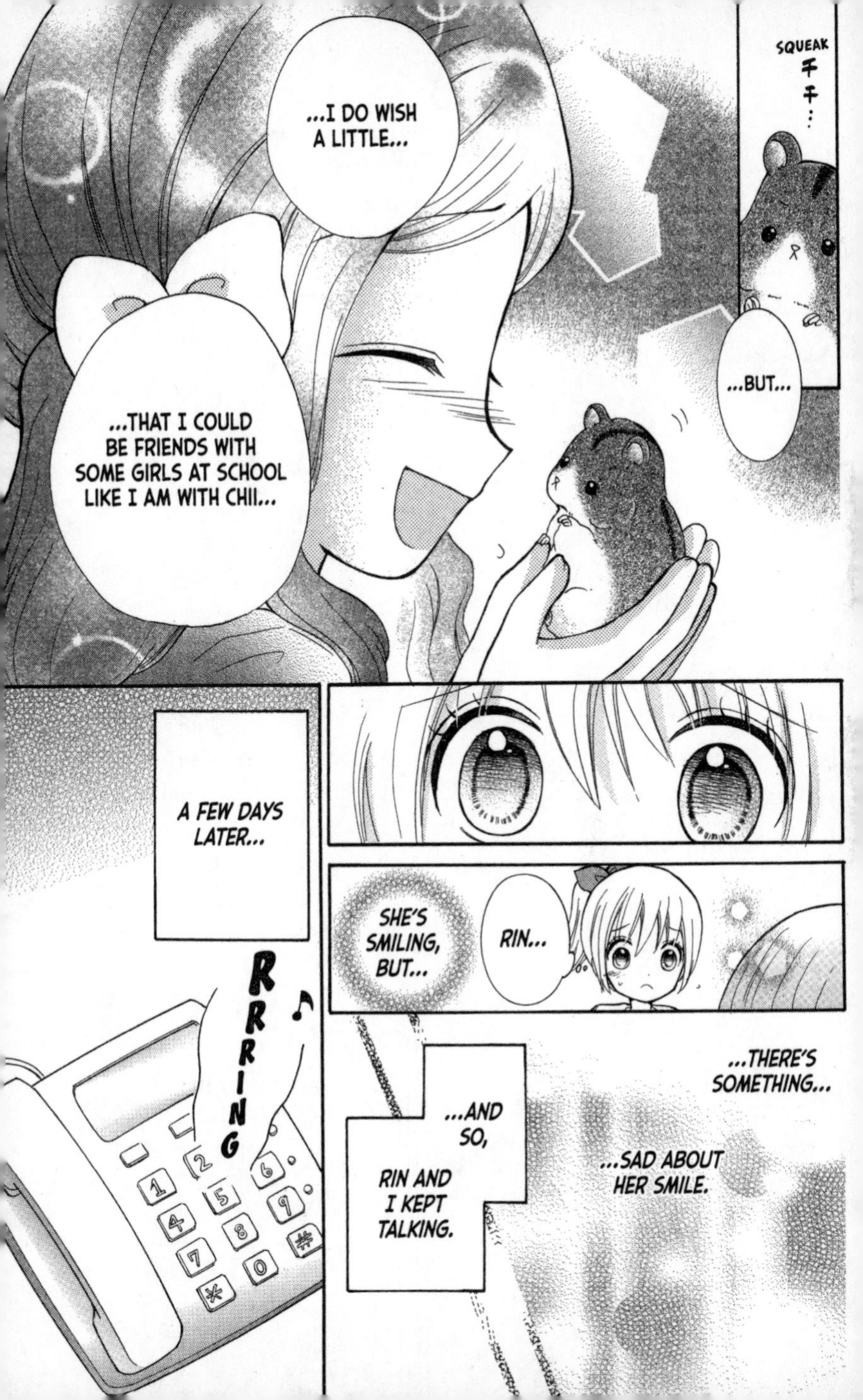
SQUEAK
チチ…
...BUT...
...I DO WISH A LITTLE...
...THAT I COULD BE FRIENDS WITH SOME GIRLS AT SCHOOL LIKE I AM WITH CHII...
RIN...
SHE'S SMILING, BUT...
...THERE'S SOMETHING...
...SAD ABOUT HER SMILE.
...AND SO, RIN AND I KEPT TALKING.
A FEW DAYS LATER...
RRRING

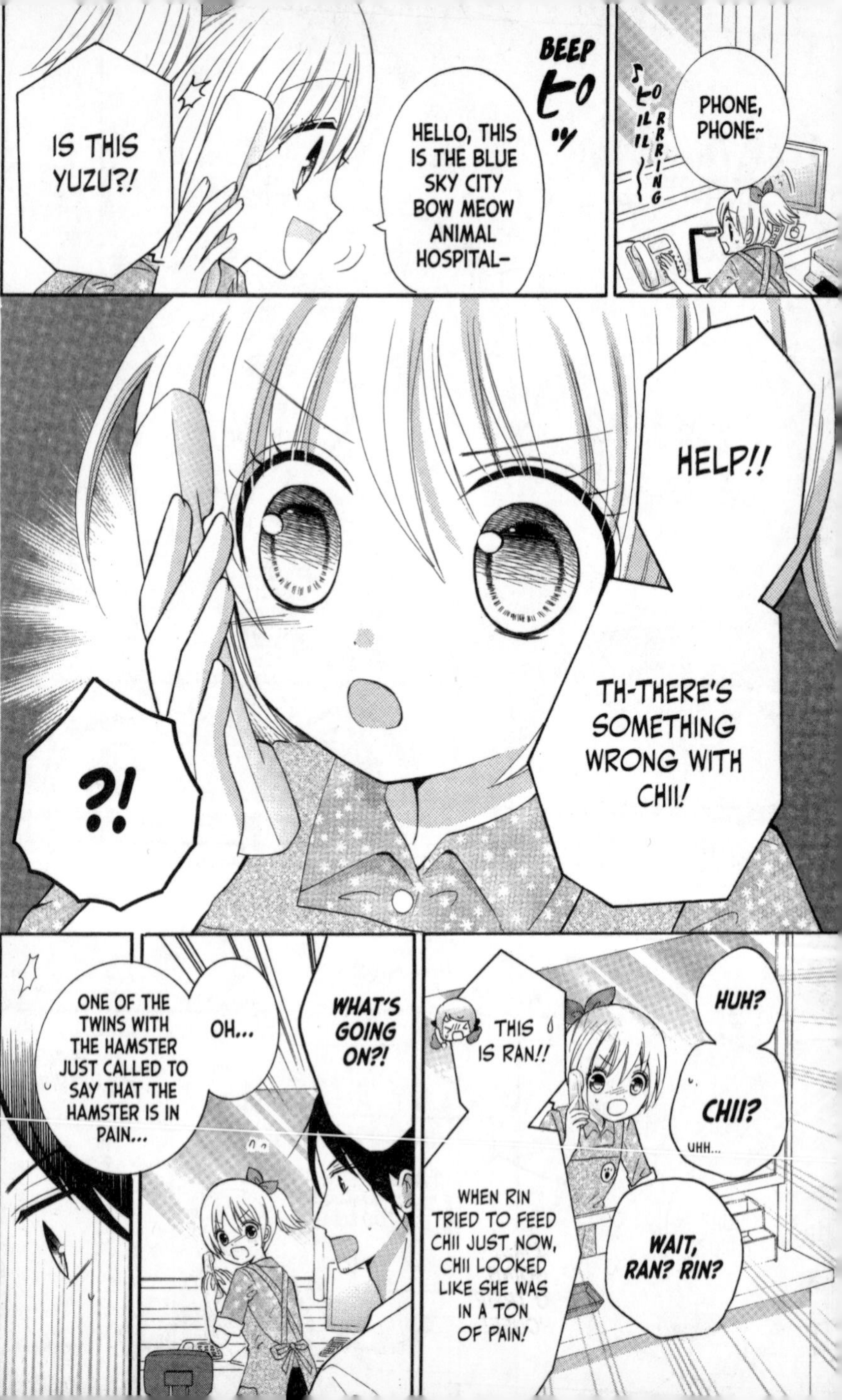
RRRING
PHONE, PHONE~
BEEP
HELLO, THIS IS THE BLUE SKY CITY BOW MEOW ANIMAL HOSPITAL–
IS THIS YUZU?!
HELP!!
TH-THERE'S SOMETHING WRONG WITH CHII!
?!
HUH?
CHII?
UHH...
THIS IS RAN!!
WAIT, RAN? RIN?
WHEN RIN TRIED TO FEED CHII JUST NOW, CHII LOOKED LIKE SHE WAS IN A TON OF PAIN!
WHAT'S GOING ON?!
OH...
ONE OF THE TWINS WITH THE HAMSTER JUST CALLED TO SAY THAT THE HAMSTER IS IN PAIN...

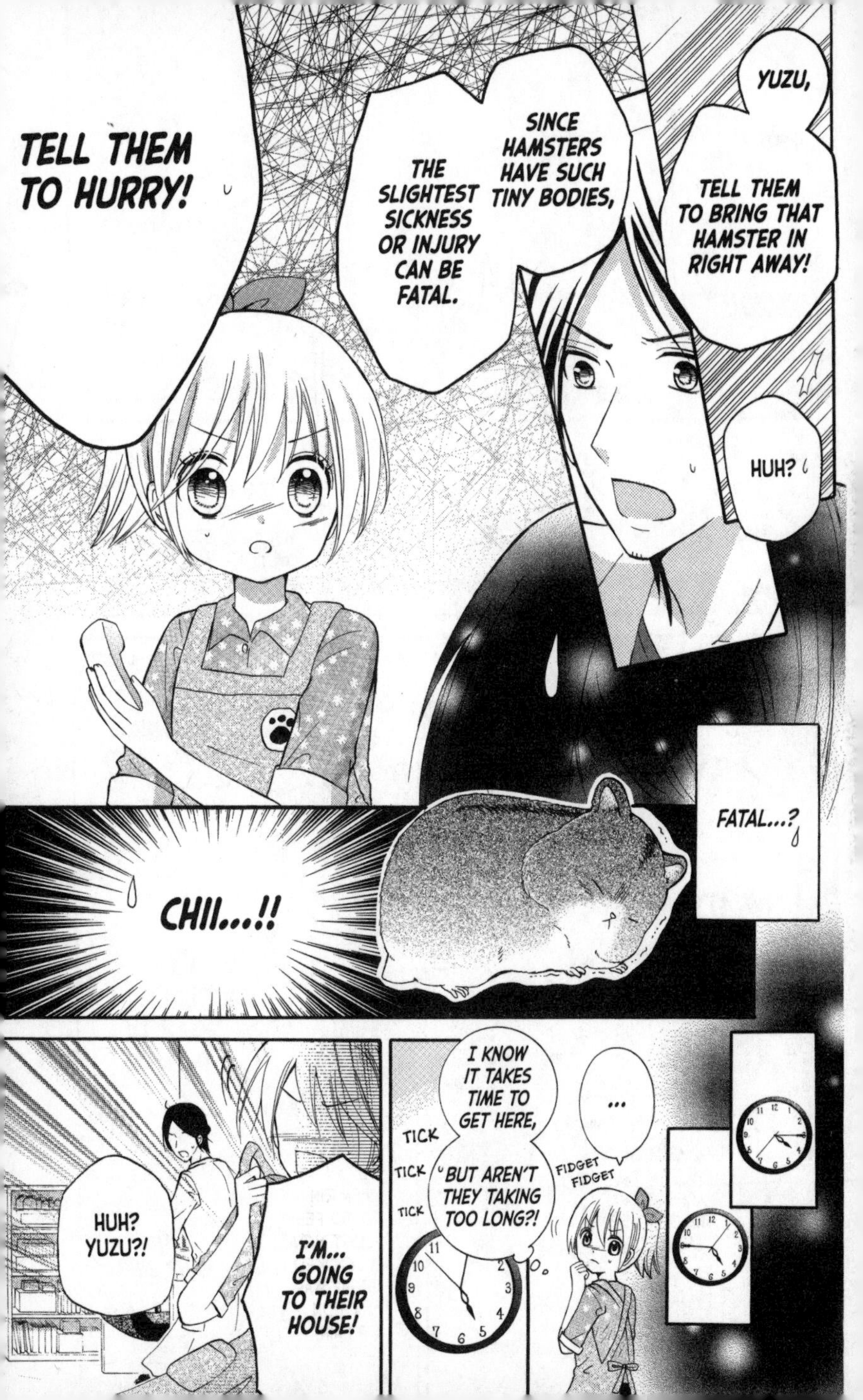
YUZU, TELL THEM TO BRING THAT HAMSTER IN RIGHT AWAY!
SINCE HAMSTERS HAVE SUCH TINY BODIES,
THE SLIGHTEST SICKNESS OR INJURY CAN BE FATAL.
TELL THEM TO HURRY!
HUH?
FATAL...?
CHII...!!
...
FIDGET FIDGET
I KNOW IT TAKES TIME TO GET HERE,
BUT AREN'T THEY TAKING TOO LONG?!
TICK
TICK
TICK
I'M... GOING TO THEIR HOUSE!
HUH? YUZU?!

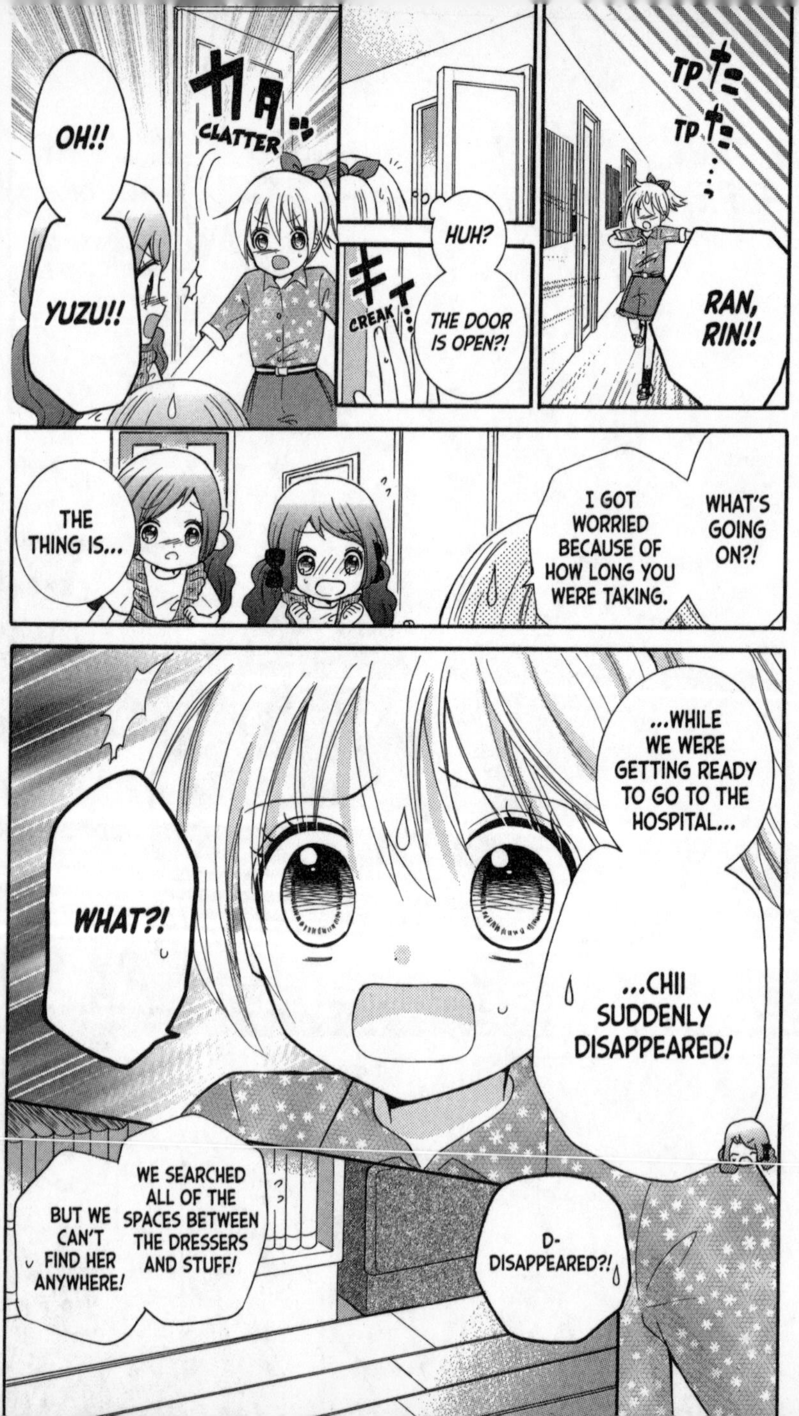
TP
TP
RAN, RIN!!
CREAK
HUH?
THE DOOR IS OPEN?!
CLATTER
OH!!
YUZU!!
WHAT'S GOING ON?!
I GOT WORRIED BECAUSE OF HOW LONG YOU WERE TAKING.
THE THING IS...
...WHILE WE WERE GETTING READY TO GO TO THE HOSPITAL...
...CHII SUDDENLY DISAPPEARED!
WHAT?!
D-DISAPPEARED?!
WE SEARCHED ALL OF THE SPACES BETWEEN THE DRESSERS AND STUFF!
BUT WE CAN'T FIND HER ANYWHERE!

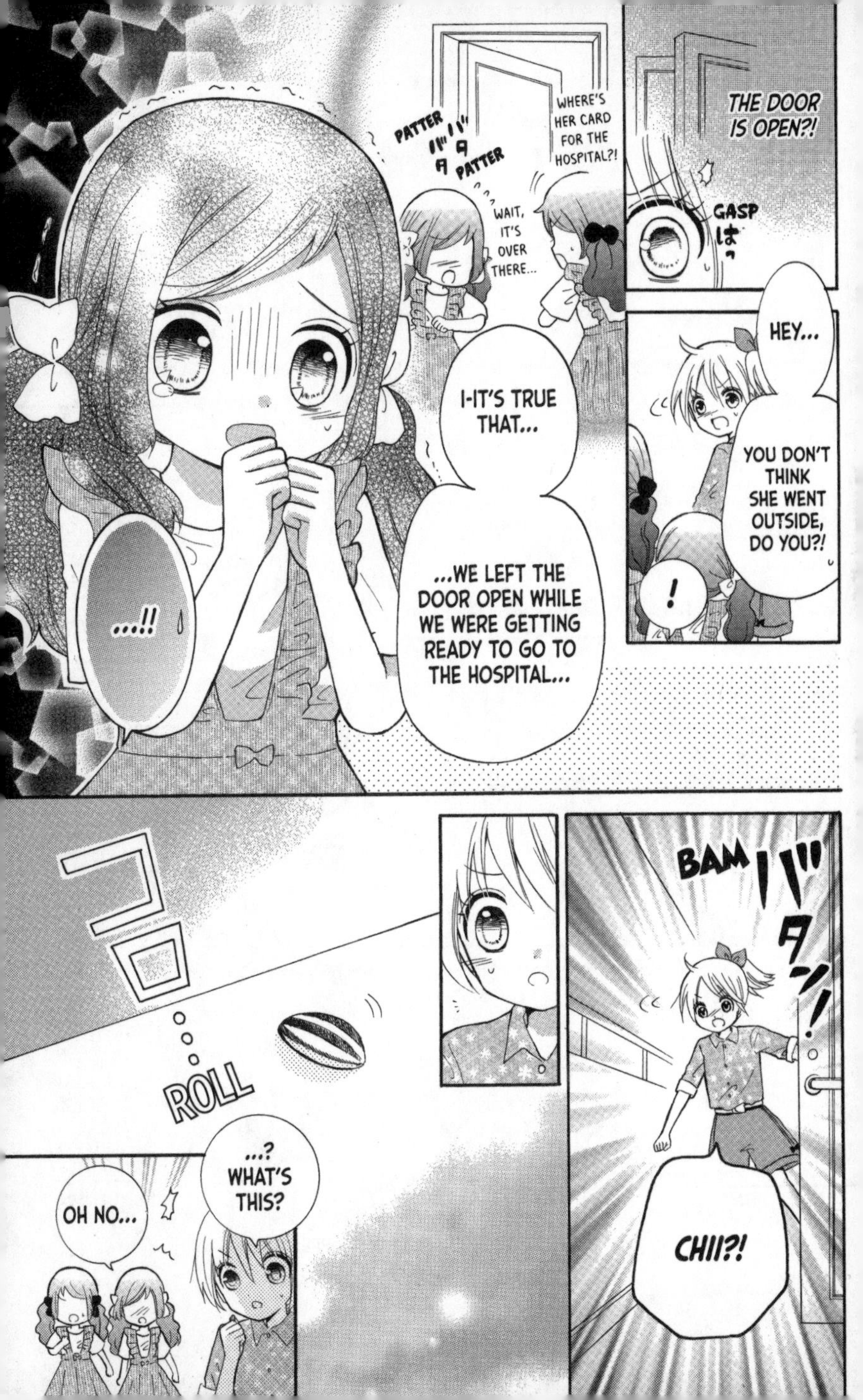
THE DOOR IS OPEN?!
GASP
HEY...
YOU DON'T THINK SHE WENT OUTSIDE, DO YOU?!
!
WHERE'S HER CARD FOR THE HOSPITAL?!
PATTER PATTER
WAIT, IT'S OVER THERE...
I-IT'S TRUE THAT...
...WE LEFT THE DOOR OPEN WHILE WE WERE GETTING READY TO GO TO THE HOSPITAL...
...!!
BAM
CHII?!
ROLL
...? WHAT'S THIS?
OH NO...

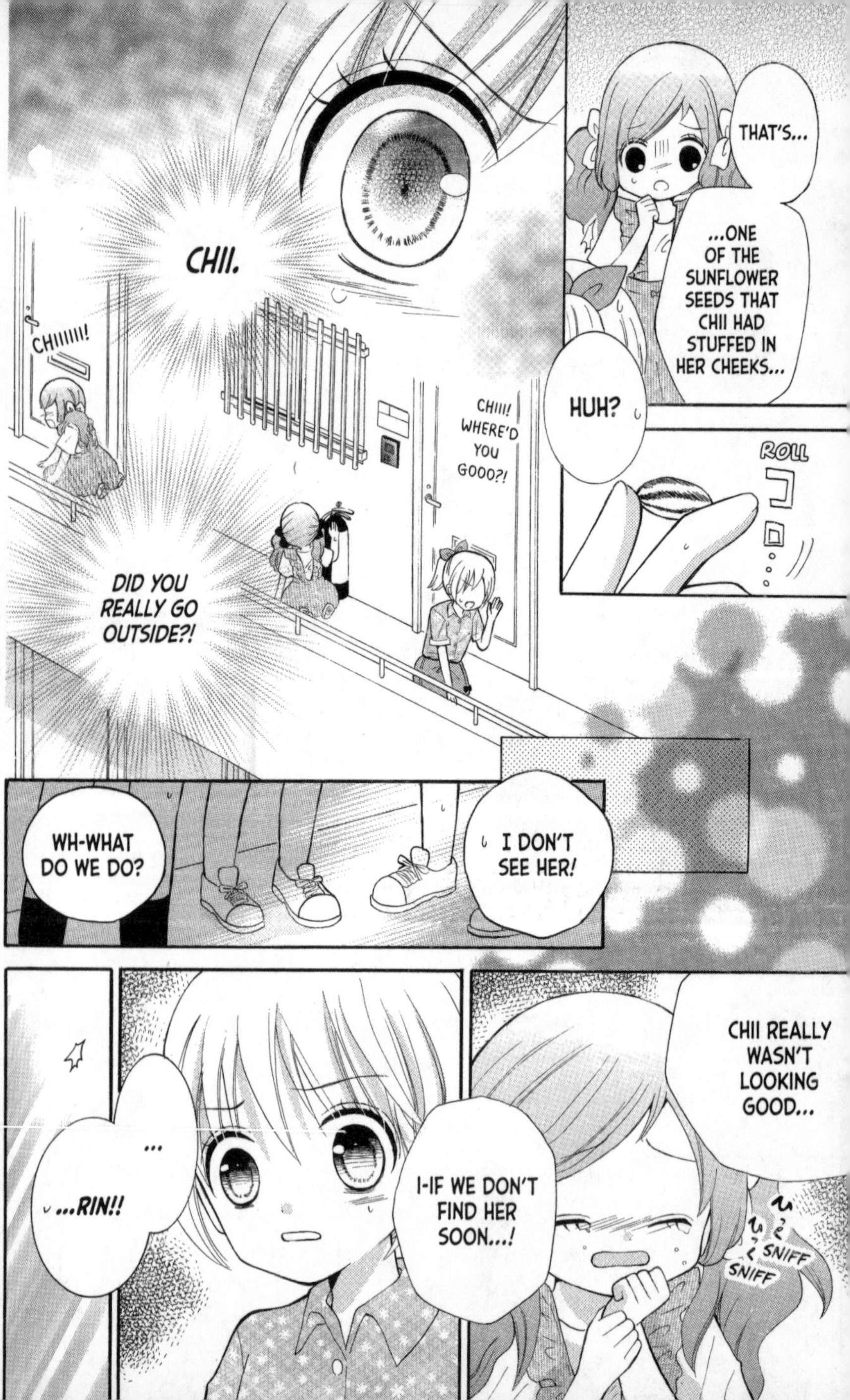
THAT'S...
...ONE OF THE SUNFLOWER SEEDS THAT CHII HAD STUFFED IN HER CHEEKS...
HUH?
ROLL
CHII.
CHIII! WHERE'D YOU GOOO?!
CHIIIIII!
DID YOU REALLY GO OUTSIDE?!
I DON'T SEE HER!
WH-WHAT DO WE DO?
CHII REALLY WASN'T LOOKING GOOD...
SNIFF
SNIFF
I-IF WE DON'T FIND HER SOON...!
...
...RIN!!

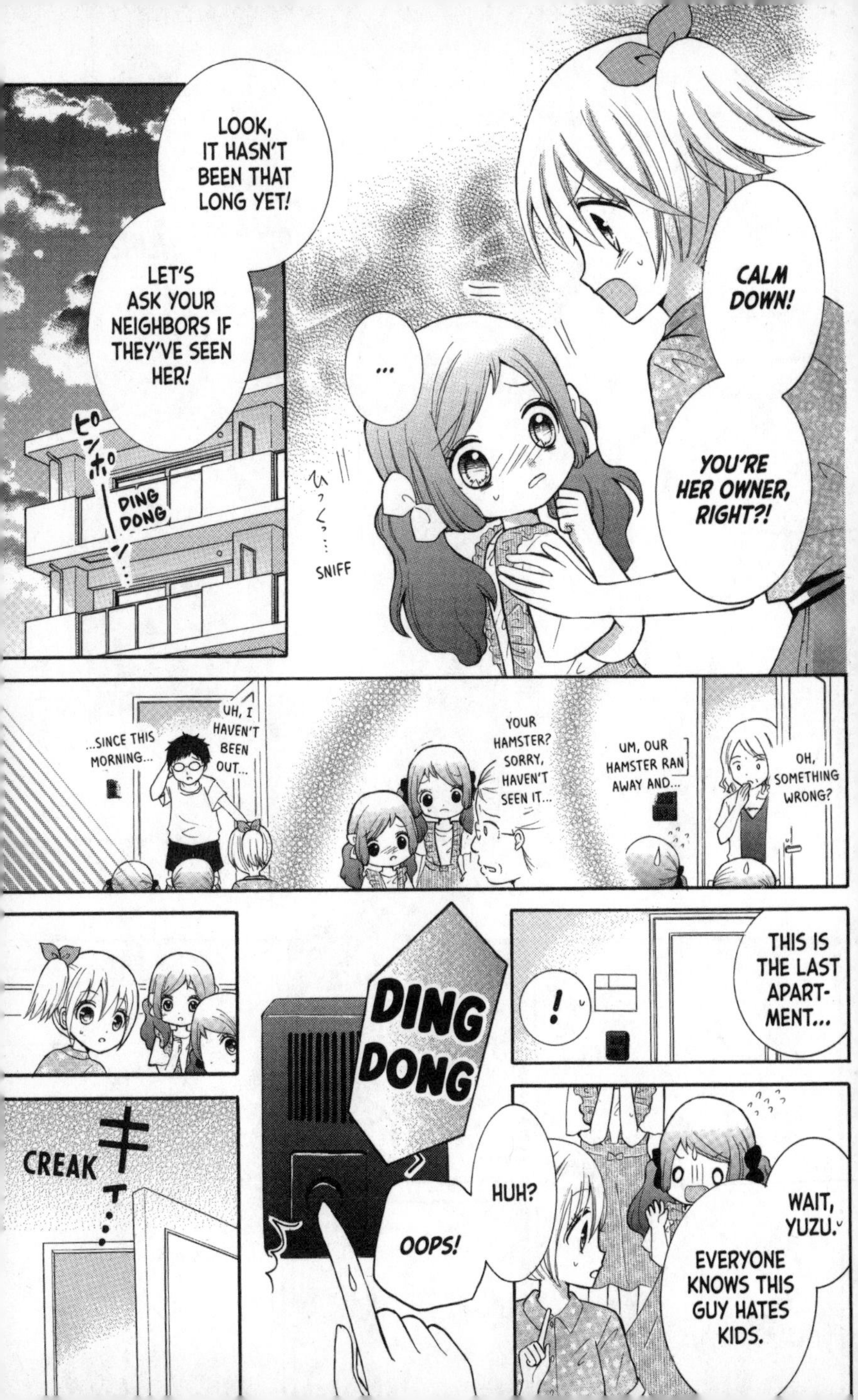
CALM DOWN!
YOU'RE HER OWNER, RIGHT?!
...
SNIFF
LOOK, IT HASN'T BEEN THAT LONG YET!
LET'S ASK YOUR NEIGHBORS IF THEY'VE SEEN HER!
DING DONG
OH, SOMETHING WRONG?
UM, OUR HAMSTER RAN AWAY AND...
YOUR HAMSTER? SORRY, HAVEN'T SEEN IT...
UH, I HAVEN'T BEEN OUT...
...SINCE THIS MORNING...
THIS IS THE LAST APARTMENT...
!
WAIT, YUZU.
EVERYONE KNOWS THIS GUY HATES KIDS.
HUH?
OOPS!
DING DONG
CREAK

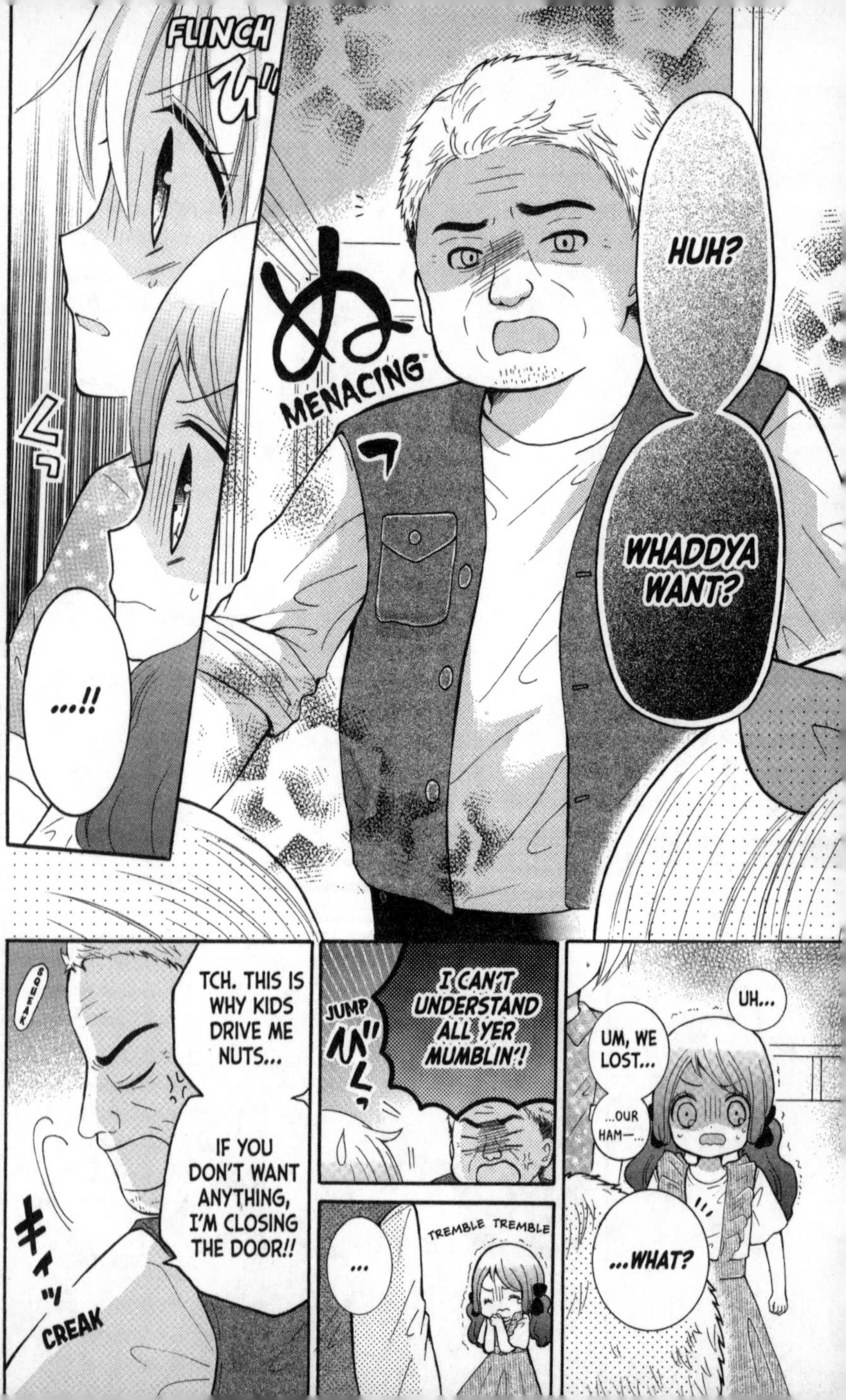
HUH?
WHADDYA WANT?
FLINCH
MENACING
...!!
UH...
UM, WE LOST...
...OUR HAM—...
...WHAT?
I CAN'T UNDERSTAND ALL YER MUMBLIN'!
JUMP
TREMBLE TREMBLE
...
TCH. THIS IS WHY KIDS DRIVE ME NUTS...
IF YOU DON'T WANT ANYTHING, I'M CLOSING THE DOOR!!
CREAK

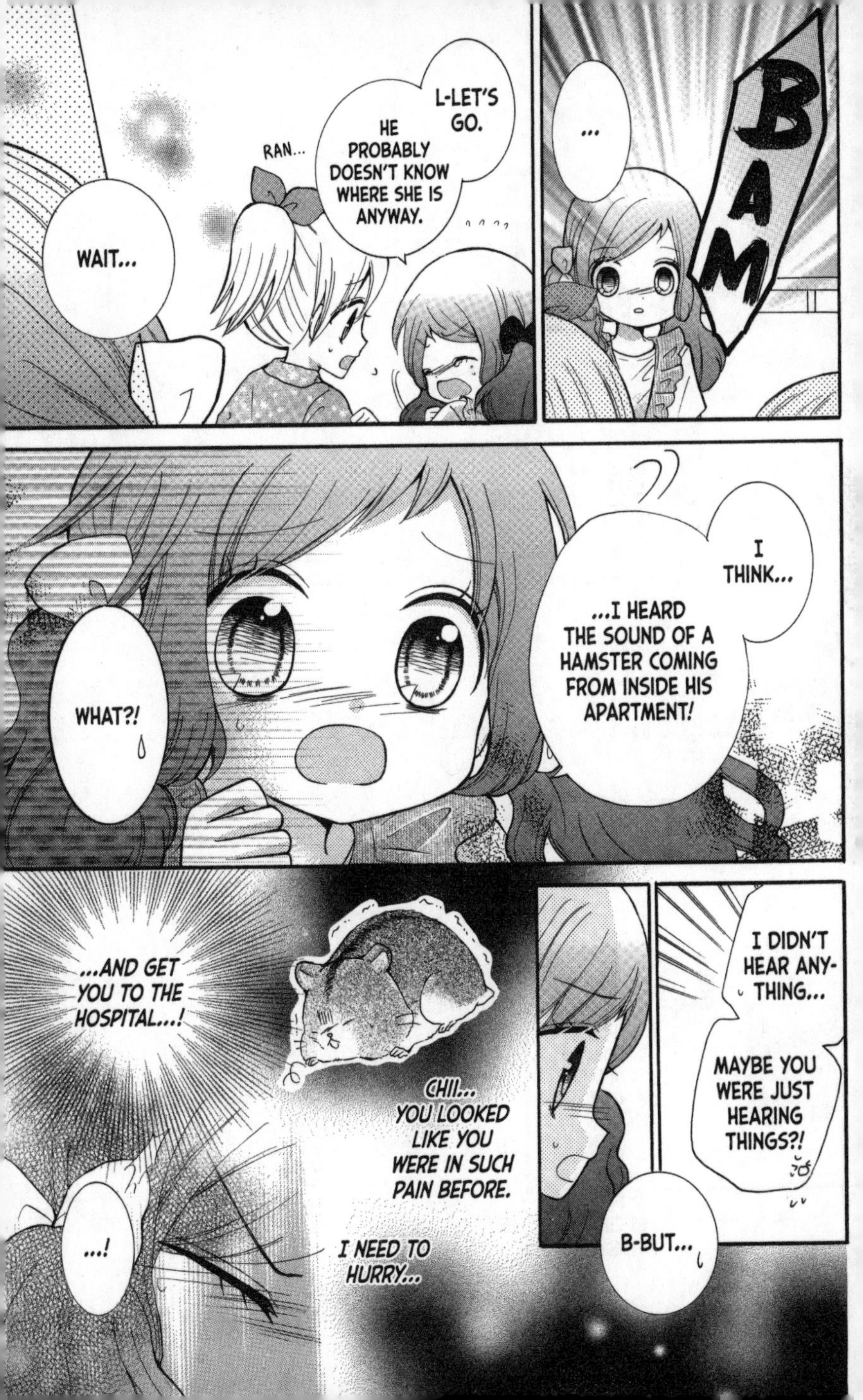
BAM
...
L-LET'S GO.
HE PROBABLY DOESN'T KNOW WHERE SHE IS ANYWAY.
RAN...
WAIT...
I THINK...
...I HEARD THE SOUND OF A HAMSTER COMING FROM INSIDE HIS APARTMENT!
WHAT?!
I DIDN'T HEAR ANY-THING...
MAYBE YOU WERE JUST HEARING THINGS?!
B-BUT...
CHII... YOU LOOKED LIKE YOU WERE IN SUCH PAIN BEFORE.
I NEED TO HURRY...
...AND GET YOU TO THE HOSPITAL...!
...!

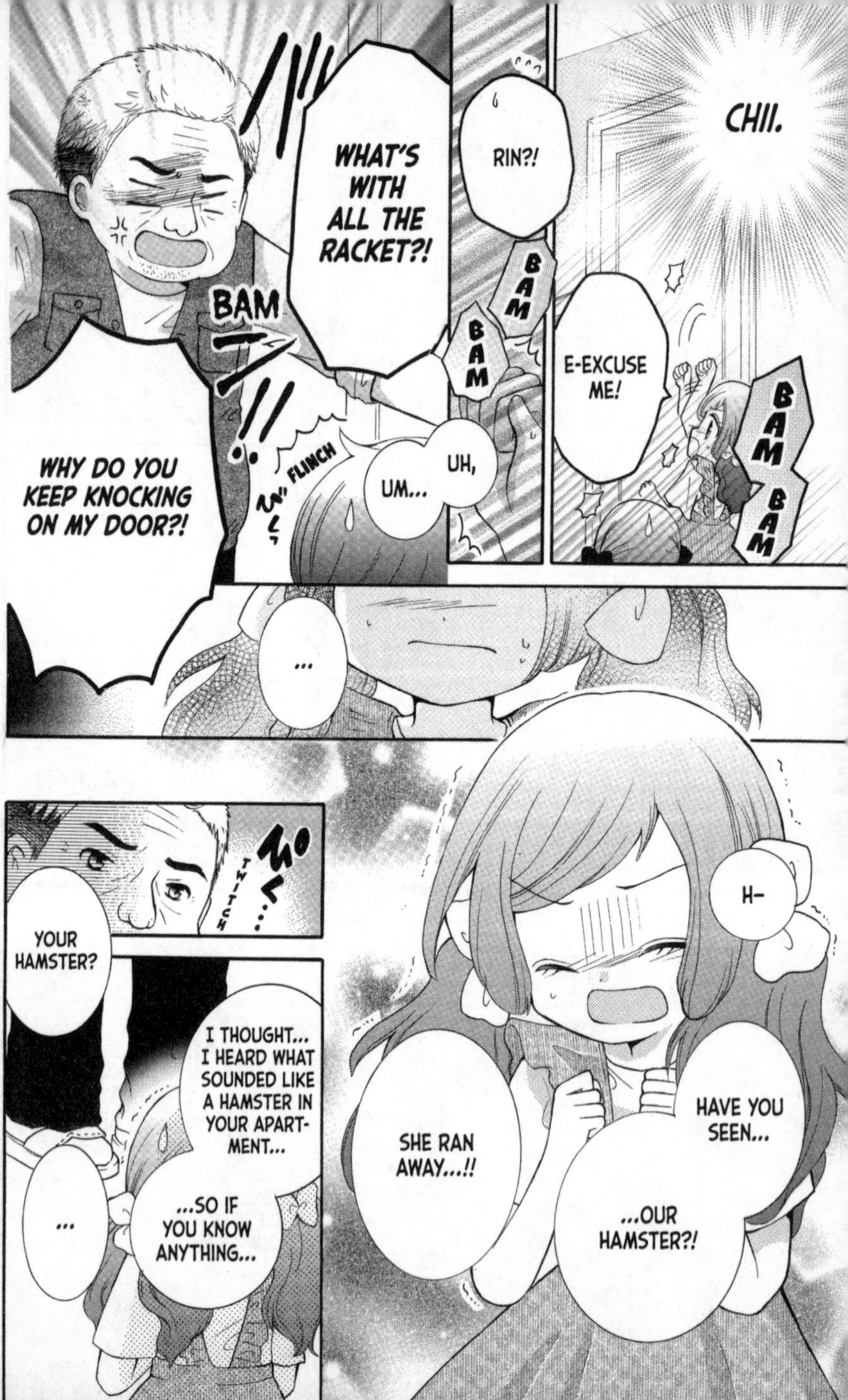
CHII.
E-EXCUSE ME!
BAM BAM BAM BAM
RIN?!
BAM BAM
BAM BAM
WHAT'S WITH ALL THE RACKET?!
BAM
UH, UM...
FLINCH
WHY DO YOU KEEP KNOCKING ON MY DOOR?!
...
H-
HAVE YOU SEEN... ...OUR HAMSTER?!
SHE RAN AWAY...!!
TWITCH
YOUR HAMSTER?
I THOUGHT... I HEARD WHAT SOUNDED LIKE A HAMSTER IN YOUR APART-MENT...
...SO IF YOU KNOW ANYTHING...
...

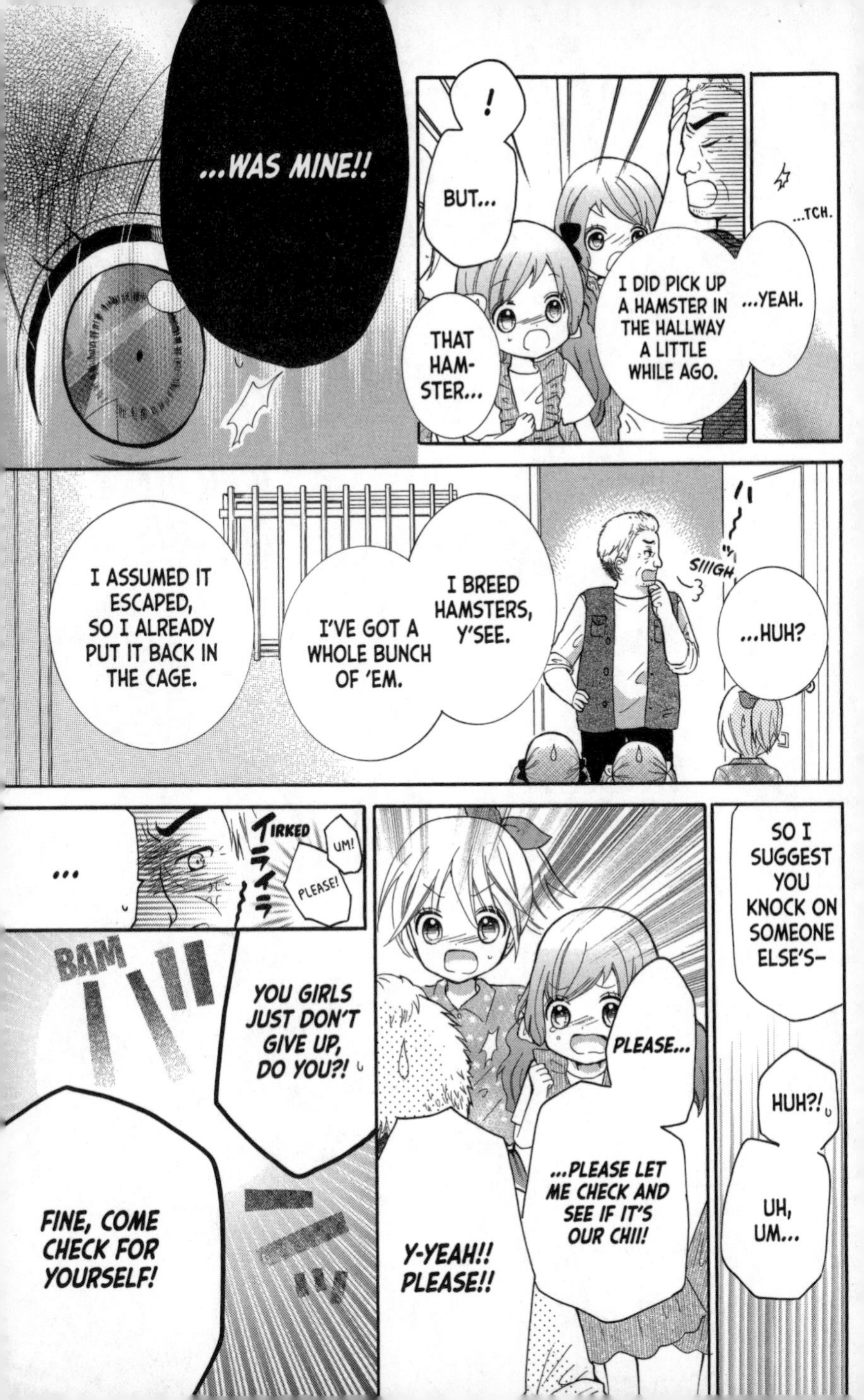

...TCH.
...YEAH.
I DID PICK UP A HAMSTER IN THE HALLWAY A LITTLE WHILE AGO.
!
BUT...
THAT HAM-STER...
...WAS MINE!!
...HUH?
SIIIGH
I BREED HAMSTERS, Y'SEE.
I'VE GOT A WHOLE BUNCH OF 'EM.
I ASSUMED IT ESCAPED, SO I ALREADY PUT IT BACK IN THE CAGE.
SO I SUGGEST YOU KNOCK ON SOMEONE ELSE'S–
HUH?!
UH, UM...
PLEASE...
...PLEASE LET ME CHECK AND SEE IF IT'S OUR CHII!
Y-YEAH!! PLEASE!!
UM!
PLEASE!
IRKED
...
YOU GIRLS JUST DON'T GIVE UP, DO YOU?!
BAM
FINE, COME CHECK FOR YOURSELF!

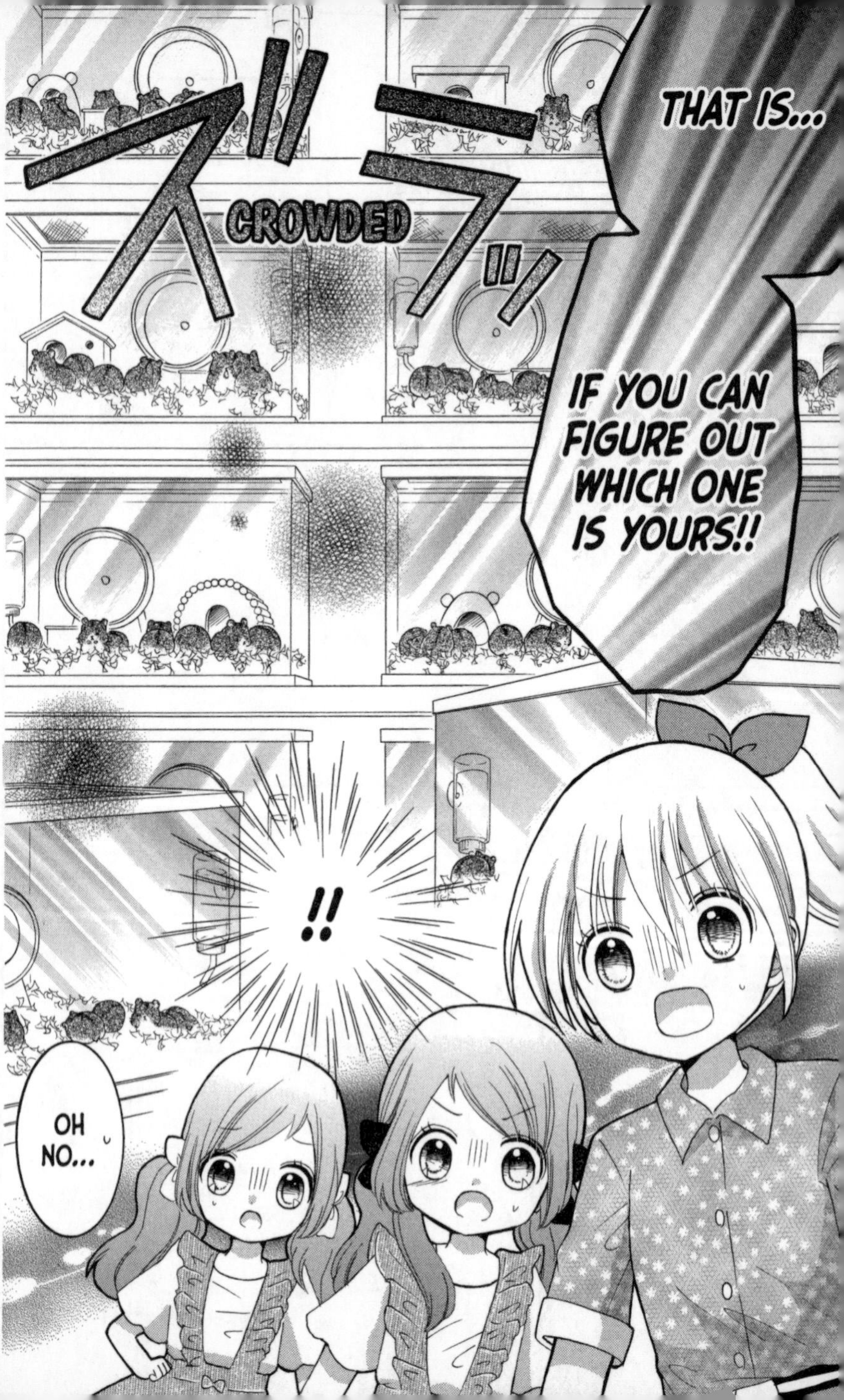
THAT IS...
IF YOU CAN FIGURE OUT WHICH ONE IS YOURS!!
CROWDED
!!
OH NO...

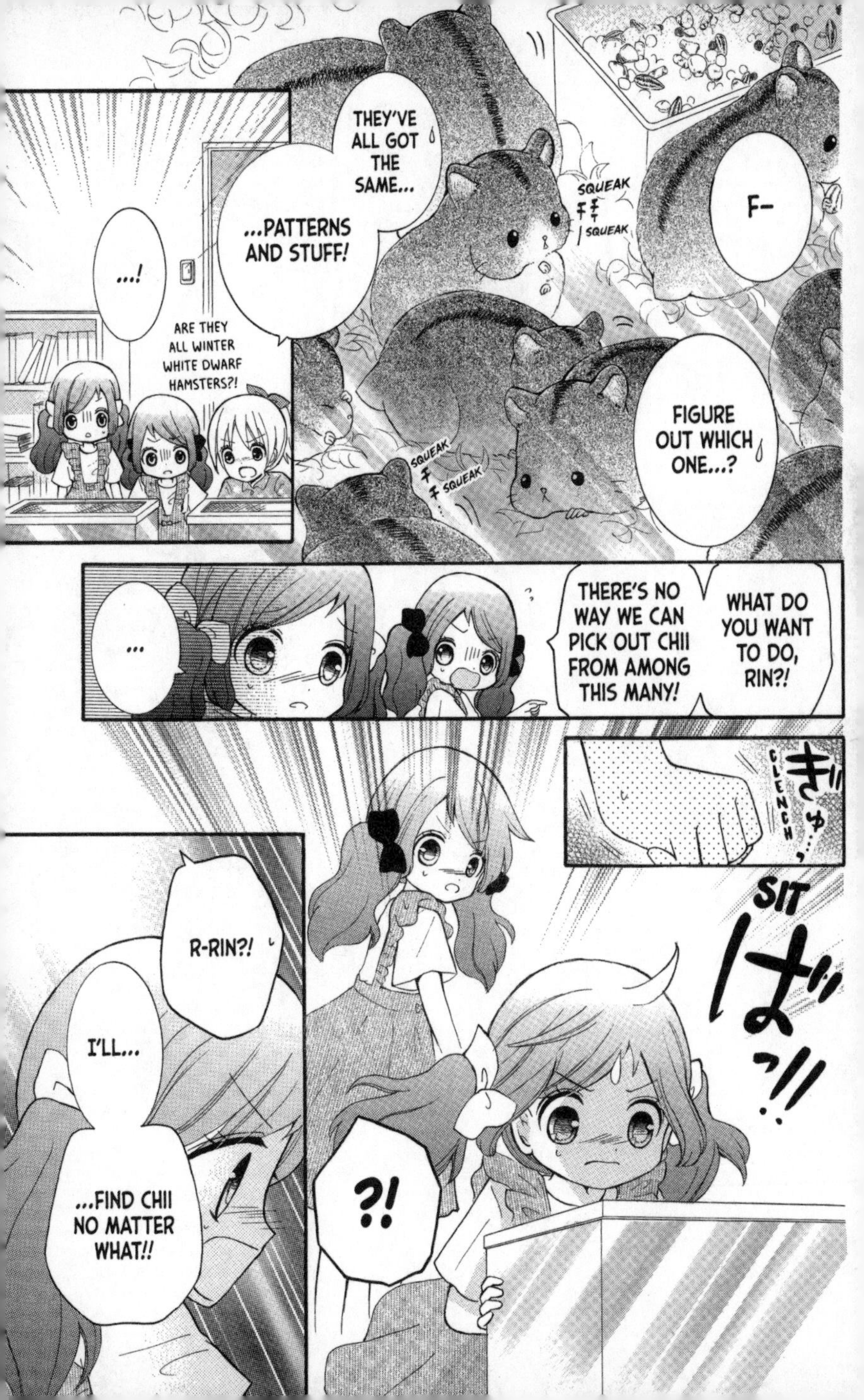
F–
SQUEAK SQUEAK
THEY'VE ALL GOT THE SAME...
...PATTERNS AND STUFF!
FIGURE OUT WHICH ONE...?
SQUEAK SQUEAK
...!
ARE THEY ALL WINTER WHITE DWARF HAMSTERS?!
WHAT DO YOU WANT TO DO, RIN?!
THERE'S NO WAY WE CAN PICK OUT CHII FROM AMONG THIS MANY!
...
ぎゅ…
CLENCH
SIT
ばっ?!!
?!
R-RIN?!
I'LL...
...FIND CHII NO MATTER WHAT!!

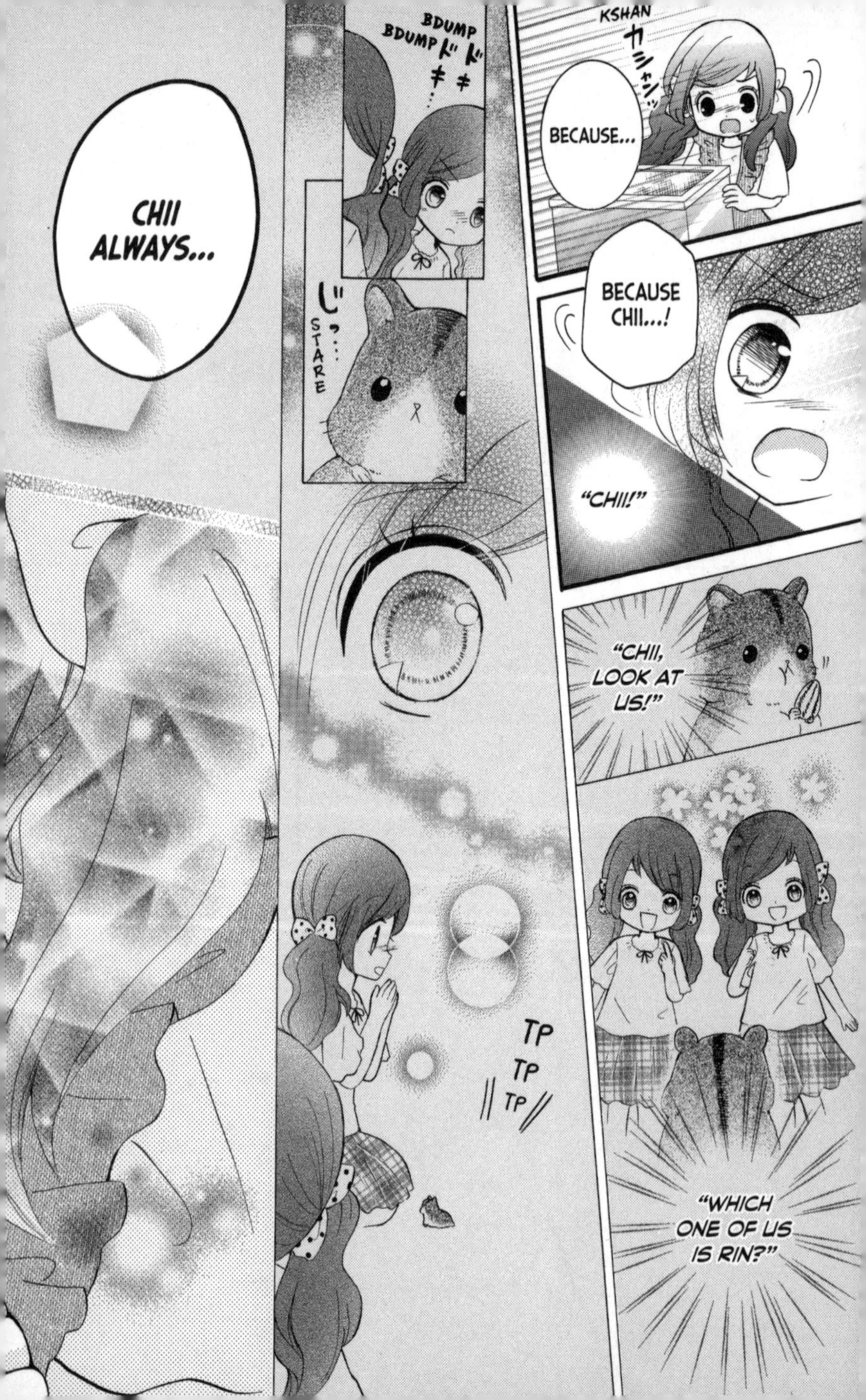
KSHAN カシャン
BECAUSE...
BECAUSE CHII...!
"CHII!"
"CHII, LOOK AT US!"
"WHICH ONE OF US IS RIN?"
BDUMP BDUMP ドキドキ...
じっ... STARE
TP TP TP
CHII ALWAYS...

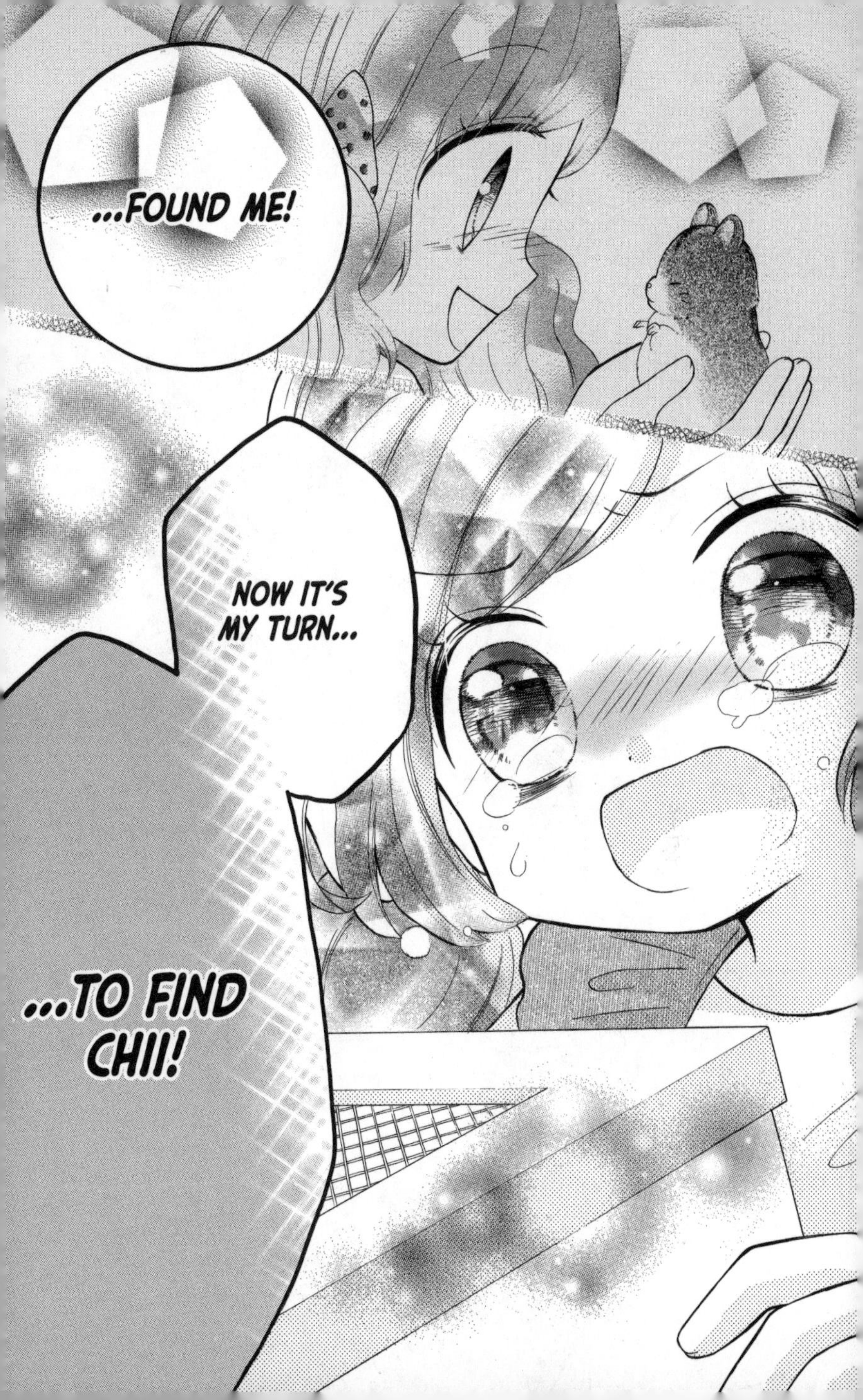
...FOUND ME!
NOW IT'S MY TURN...
...TO FIND CHII!

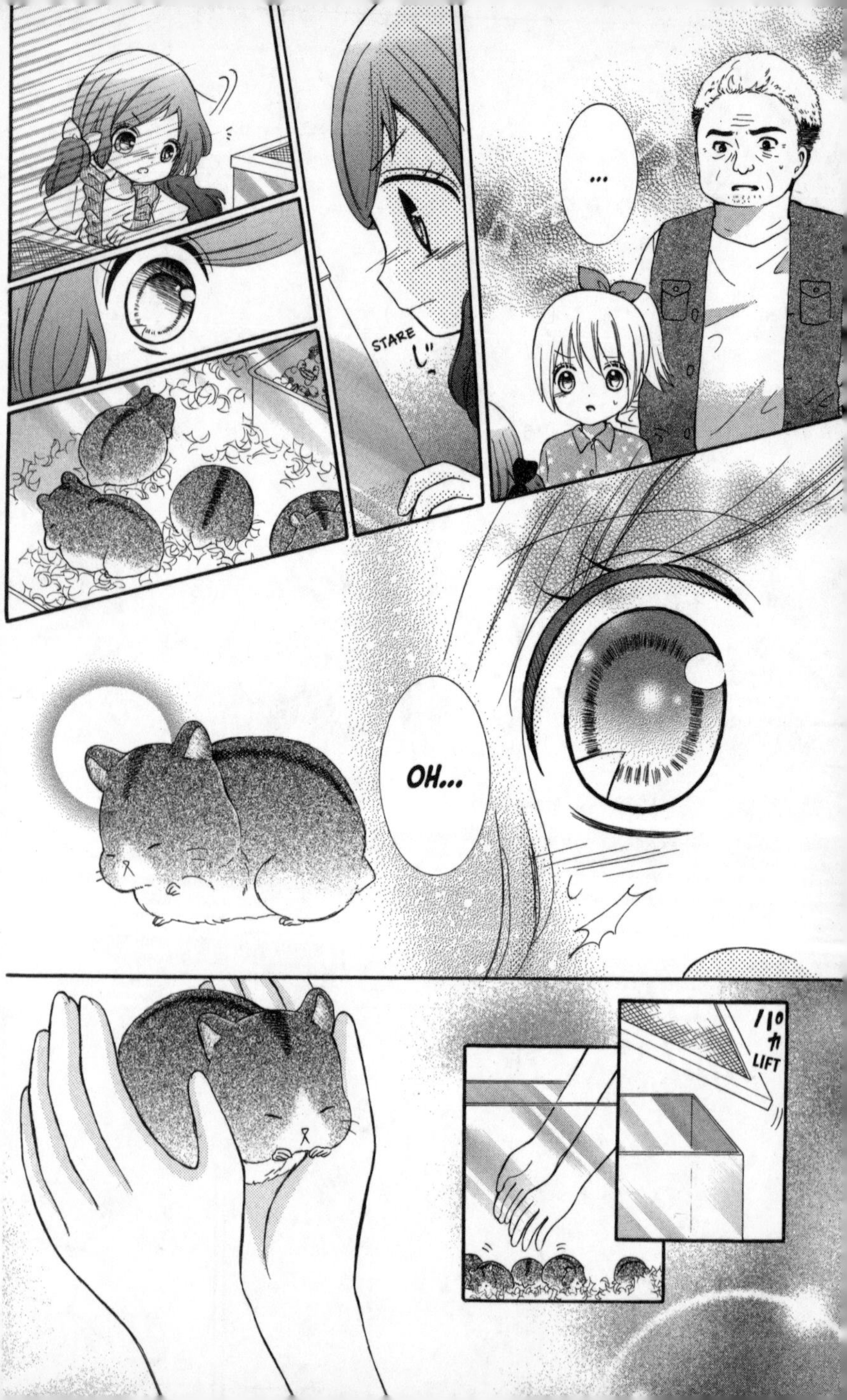
...
STARE
じ
OH...
パカ
LIFT

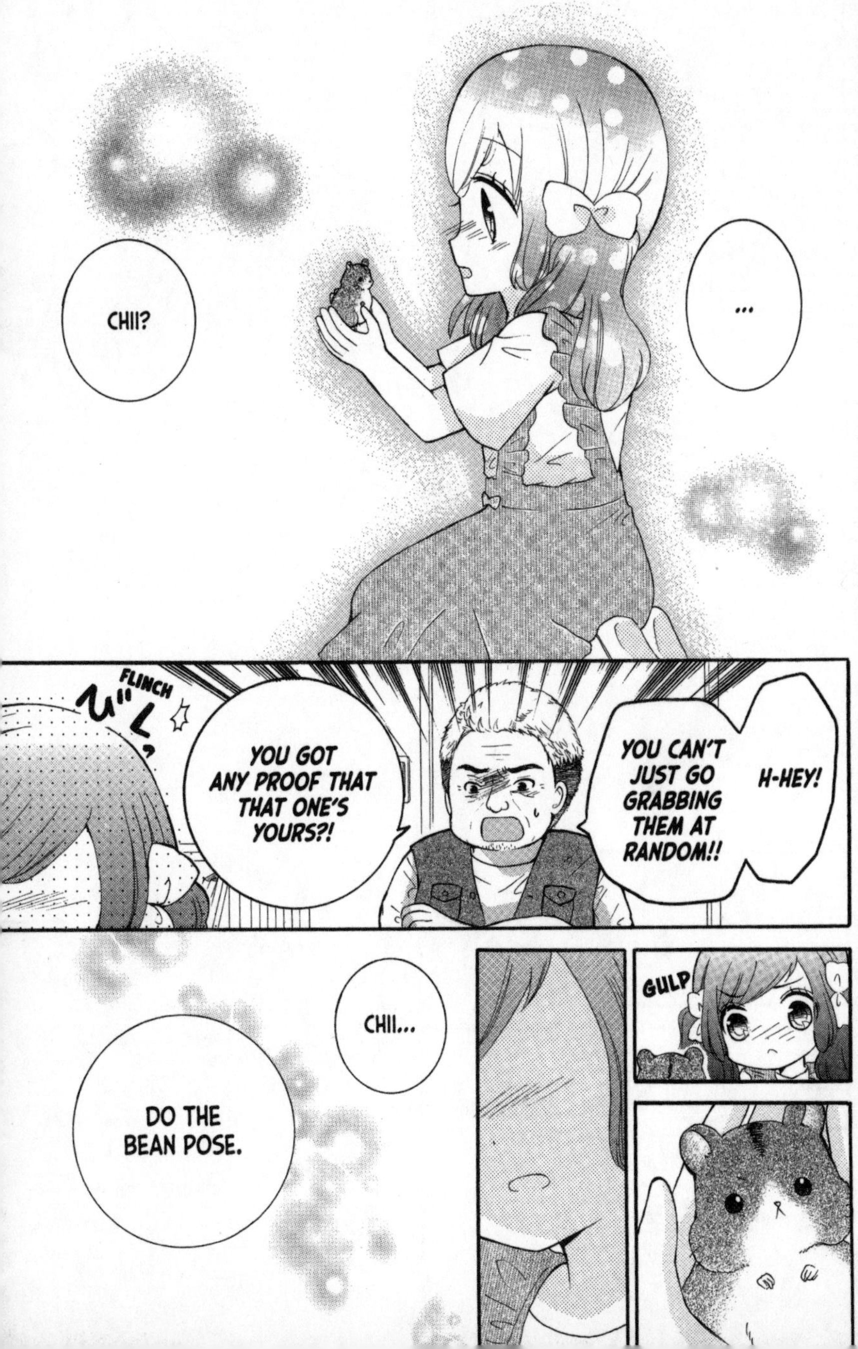
...
CHII?
H-HEY!
YOU CAN'T JUST GO GRABBING THEM AT RANDOM!!
YOU GOT ANY PROOF THAT THAT ONE'S YOURS?!
FLINCH
GULP
CHII...
DO THE BEAN POSE.

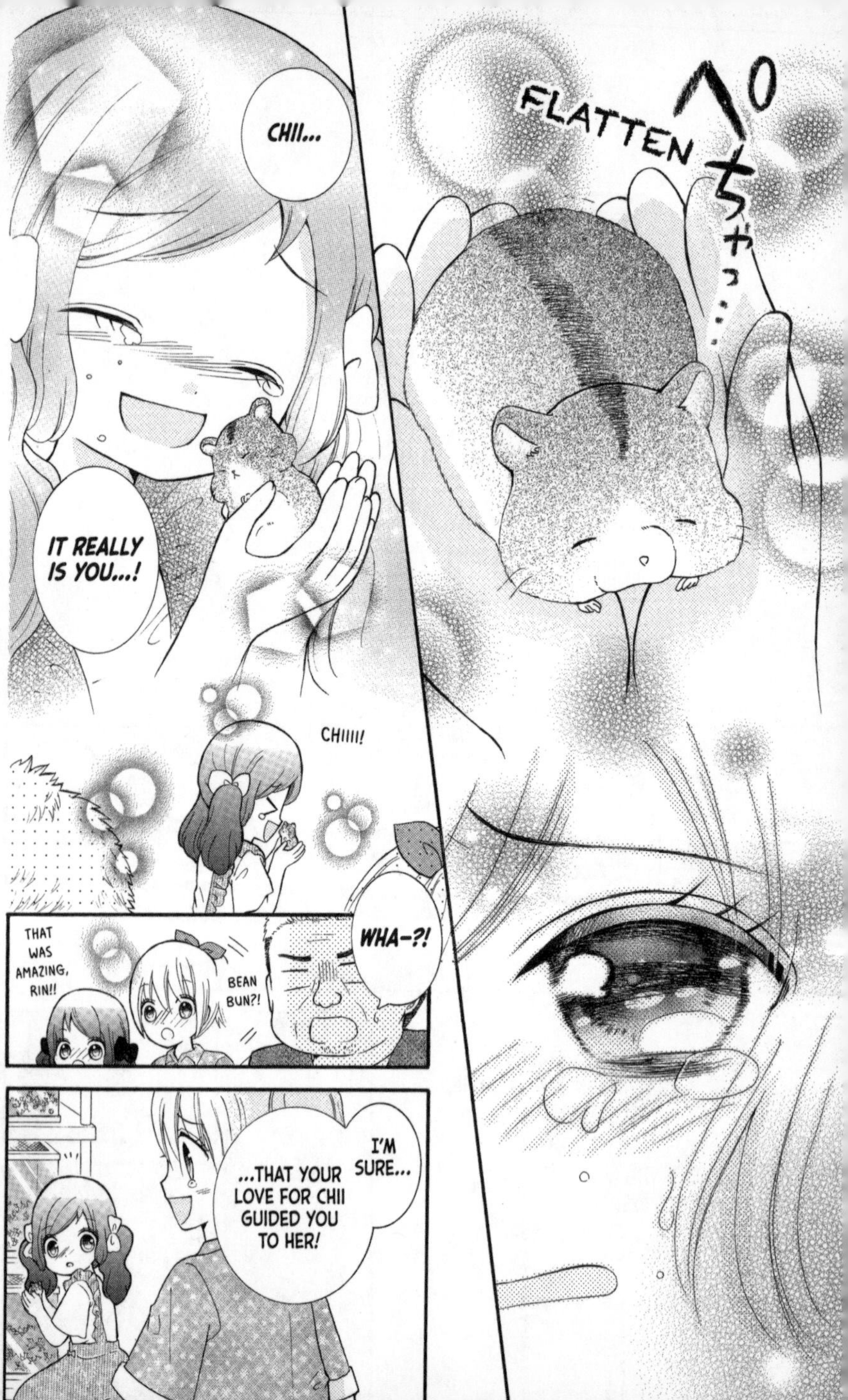
FLATTEN
ぺちゃっ…
CHII...
IT REALLY IS YOU...!
CHIIII!
WHA-?!
BEAN BUN?!
THAT WAS AMAZING, RIN!!
I'M SURE...
...THAT YOUR LOVE FOR CHII GUIDED YOU TO HER!

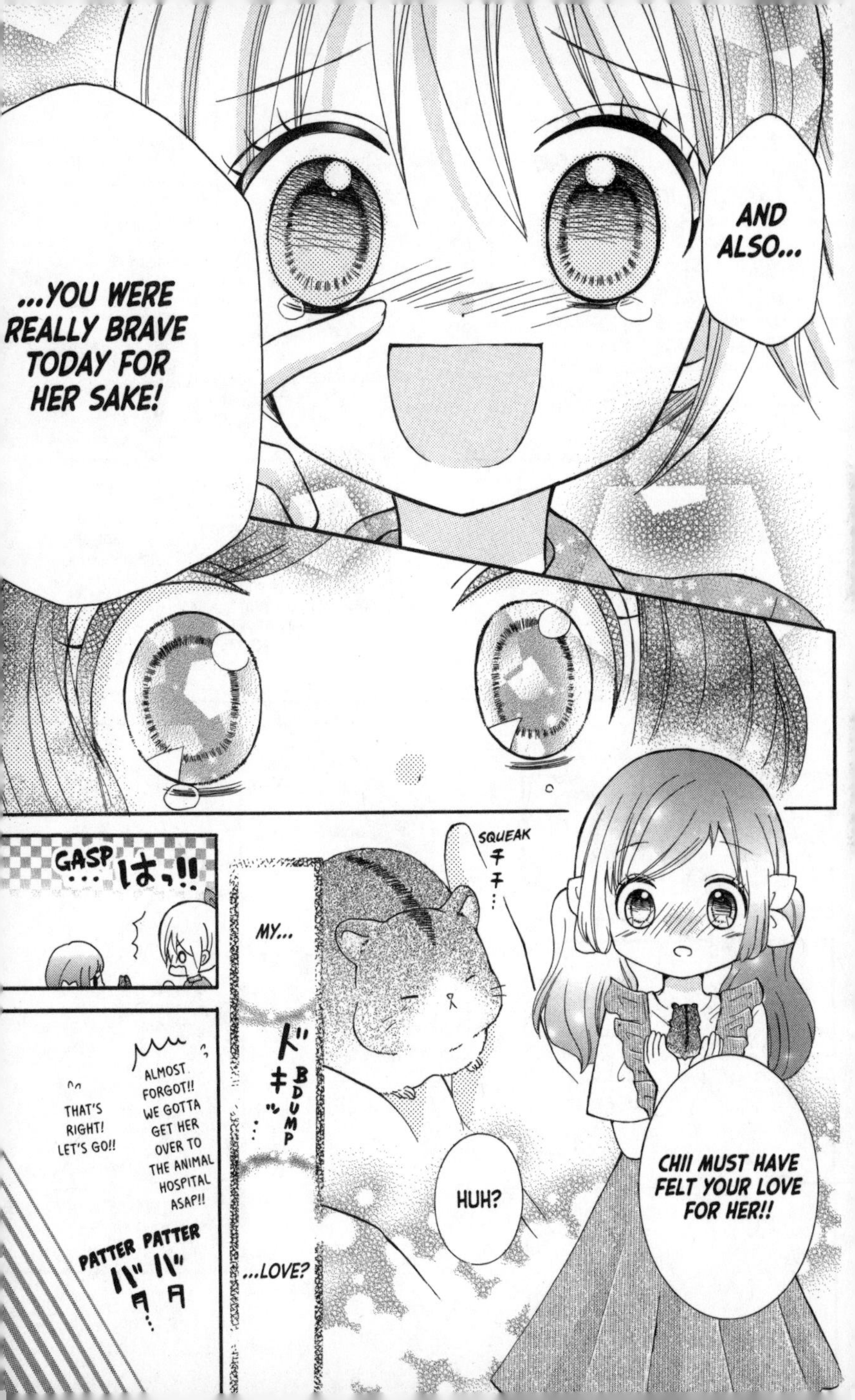
AND ALSO...
...YOU WERE REALLY BRAVE TODAY FOR HER SAKE!
SQUEAK
チチ...
CHII MUST HAVE FELT YOUR LOVE FOR HER!!
HUH?
MY...
BDUMP
ドキッ...
...LOVE?
GASP
はっ!!
...
ALMOST FORGOT!! WE GOTTA GET HER OVER TO THE ANIMAL HOSPITAL ASAP!!
THAT'S RIGHT! LET'S GO!!
PATTER PATTER
バタバタ...

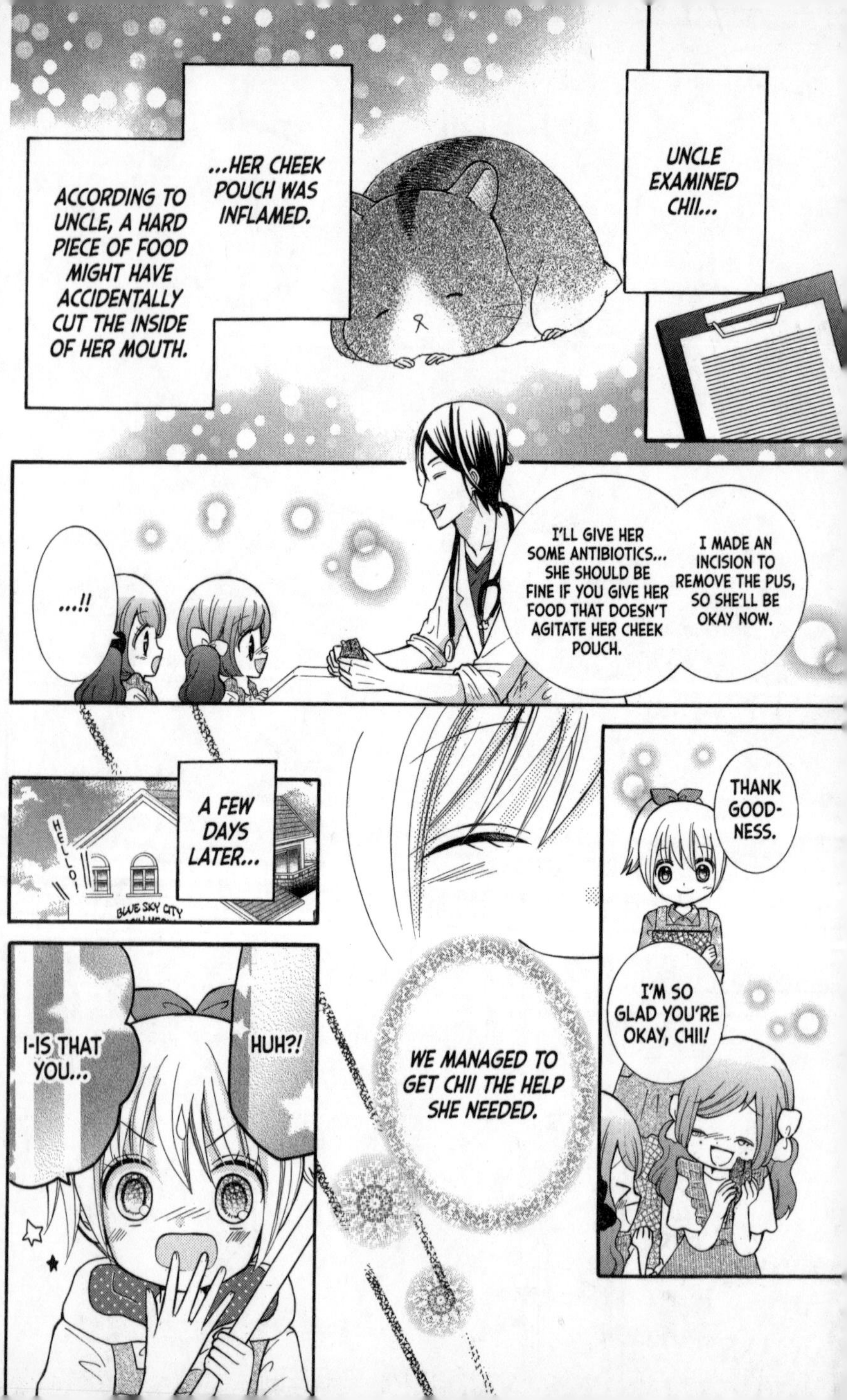
UNCLE EXAMINED CHII...
...HER CHEEK POUCH WAS INFLAMED.
ACCORDING TO UNCLE, A HARD PIECE OF FOOD MIGHT HAVE ACCIDENTALLY CUT THE INSIDE OF HER MOUTH.
I MADE AN INCISION TO REMOVE THE PUS, SO SHE'LL BE OKAY NOW.
I'LL GIVE HER SOME ANTIBIOTICS... SHE SHOULD BE FINE IF YOU GIVE HER FOOD THAT DOESN'T AGITATE HER CHEEK POUCH.
...!!
THANK GOOD-NESS.
I'M SO GLAD YOU'RE OKAY, CHII!
WE MANAGED TO GET CHII THE HELP SHE NEEDED.
A FEW DAYS LATER...
HELLO!
BLUE SKY CITY
HUH?!
I-IS THAT YOU...

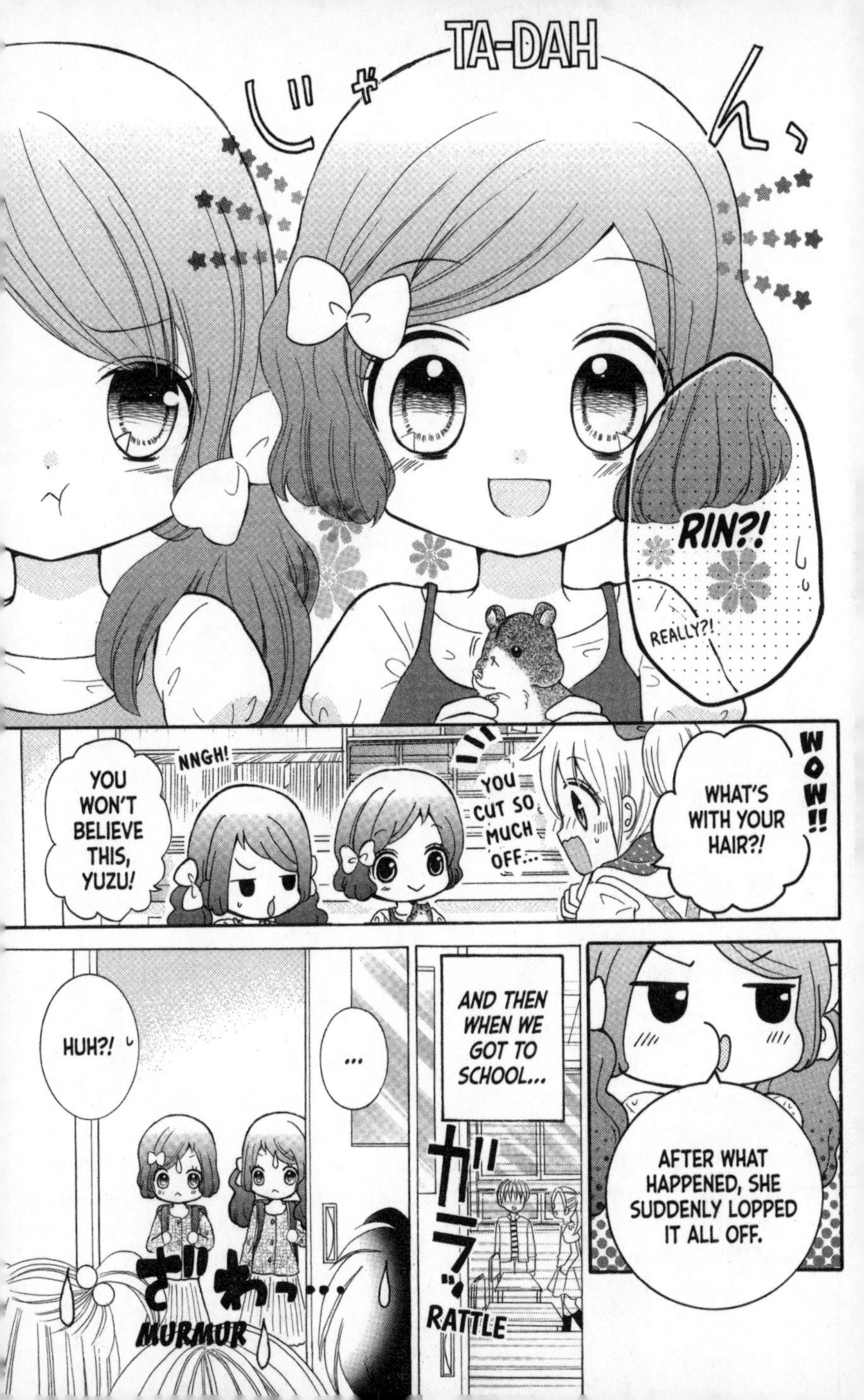
TA-DAH
RIN?!
REALLY?!
WOW!!
WHAT'S WITH YOUR HAIR?!
YOU CUT SO MUCH OFF...
NNGH!
YOU WON'T BELIEVE THIS, YUZU!
AFTER WHAT HAPPENED, SHE SUDDENLY LOPPED IT ALL OFF.
AND THEN WHEN WE GOT TO SCHOOL...
RATTLE
...
HUH?!
MURMUR

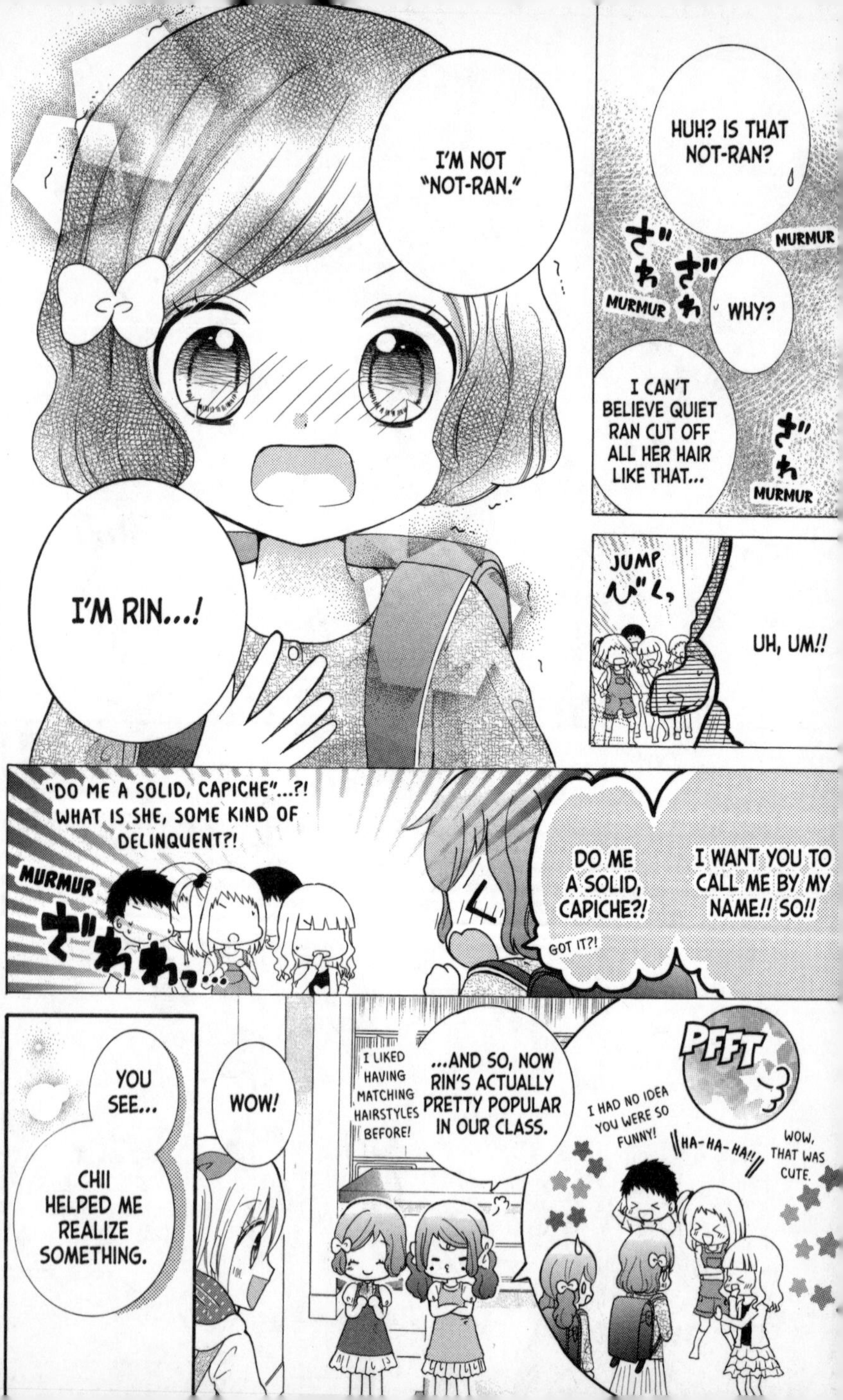

HUH? IS THAT NOT-RAN?
MURMUR
ざわ ざわ
MURMUR
WHY?
I CAN'T BELIEVE QUIET RAN CUT OFF ALL HER HAIR LIKE THAT...
ざわ
MURMUR
JUMP
びくっ
UH, UM!!
I'M NOT "NOT-RAN."
I'M RIN...!
I WANT YOU TO CALL ME BY MY NAME!! SO!!
DO ME A SOLID, CAPICHE?!
GOT IT?!
"DO ME A SOLID, CAPICHE"...?! WHAT IS SHE, SOME KIND OF DELINQUENT?!
MURMUR
ざわわっ...
PFFT
WOW, THAT WAS CUTE.
HA-HA-HA!!
I HAD NO IDEA YOU WERE SO FUNNY!
...AND SO, NOW RIN'S ACTUALLY PRETTY POPULAR IN OUR CLASS.
I LIKED HAVING MATCHING HAIRSTYLES BEFORE!
WOW!
YOU SEE...
CHII HELPED ME REALIZE SOMETHING.

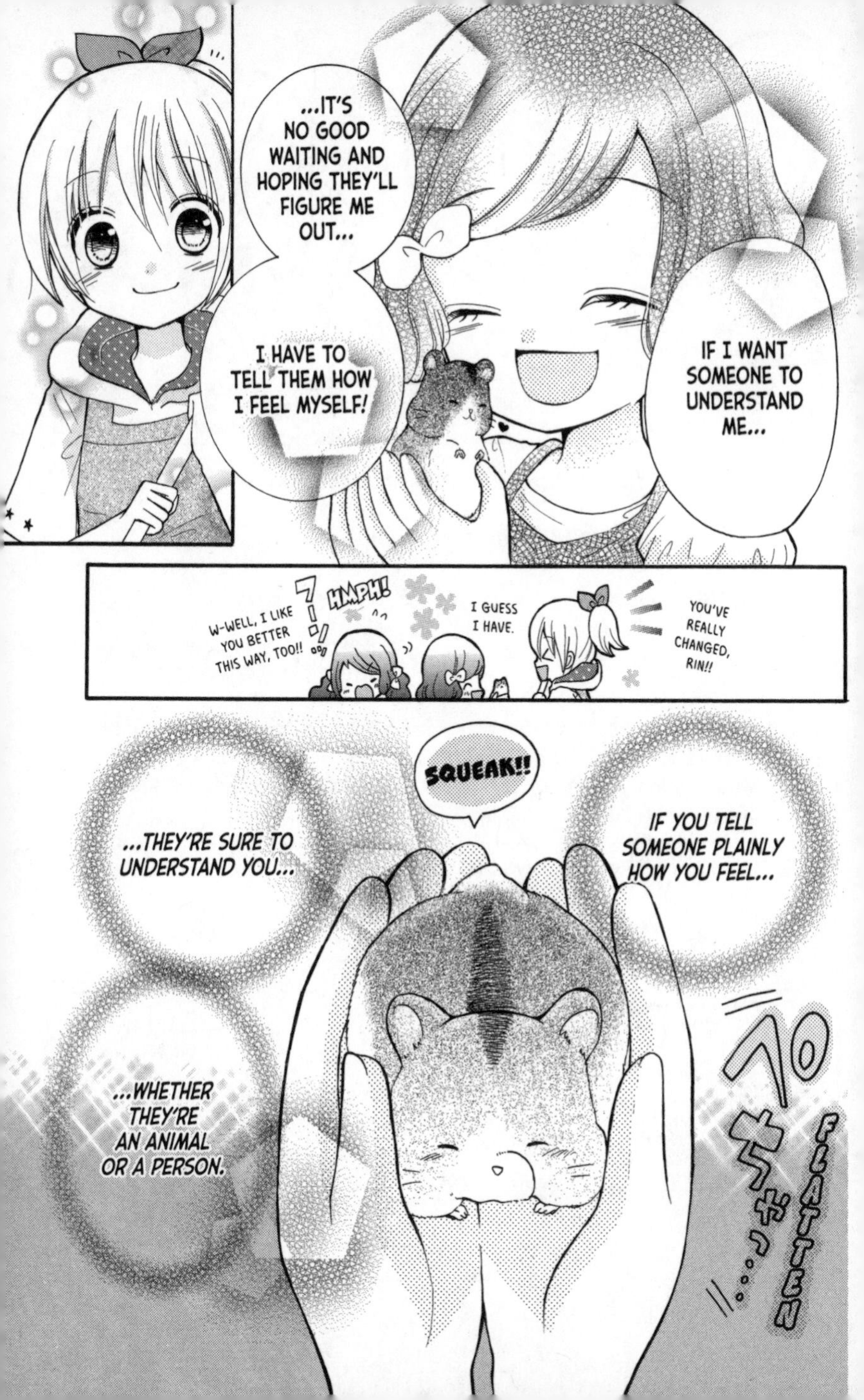
IF I WANT SOMEONE TO UNDERSTAND ME...
...IT'S NO GOOD WAITING AND HOPING THEY'LL FIGURE ME OUT...
I HAVE TO TELL THEM HOW I FEEL MYSELF!
YOU'VE REALLY CHANGED, RIN!!
I GUESS I HAVE.
HMPH!
W-WELL, I LIKE YOU BETTER THIS WAY, TOO!!
IF YOU TELL SOMEONE PLAINLY HOW YOU FEEL...
SQUEAK!!
...THEY'RE SURE TO UNDERSTAND YOU...
...WHETHER THEY'RE AN ANIMAL OR A PERSON.
FLATTEN

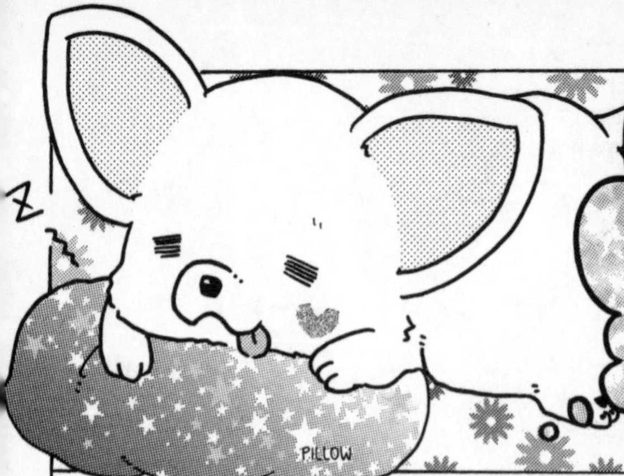
Z
PILLOW

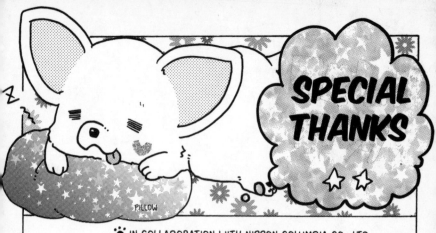

SPECIAL THANKS

- IN COLLABORATION WITH NIPPON COLUMBIA CO., LTD.
- SUPERVISOR: TAISEI HOSOIDO

- EDITORS: NAKAZATO, NAGANO, SHINOHARA
- DESIGNER: KOBAYASHI
- EVERYONE FROM NAKAYOSHI'S EDITING DEPARTMENT

- INTERVIEW THANKS: EVERYONE FROM THE DAIRY FARMING TOCHIGI AGRICULTURAL COOPERATIVE EVERYONE FROM THE ISHIKAWA FARM DOCTOR HONJOU, VETERINARIAN

- MANUSCRIPT ASSISTANTS: ANCHAN, NAOCHAN, MEIRA ISHIZAKA, KOUTEI PENGUIN DX, BONCHI

PLEASE SEND YOUR OPINIONS ABOUT THE MANGA AND WHATEVER ELSE YOU WANT TO WRITE TO THIS ADDRESS!!

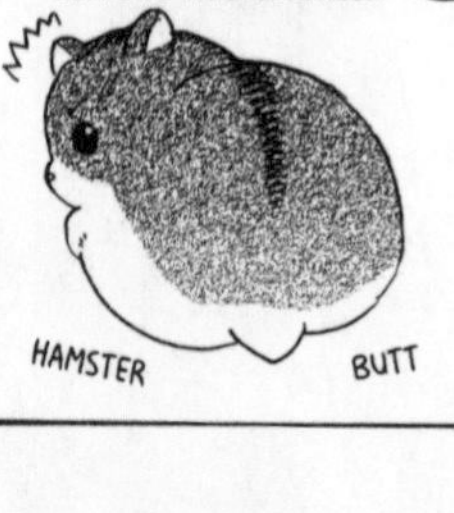
HAMSTER
BUTT

MINGO ITO
KODANSHA COMICS
451 PARK AVE. SOUTH,
7TH FLOOR
NEW YORK, NY 10016

BLOG
MINGOROKU
http://ameblo.jp/itoumingo/

twitter
@itoumingo

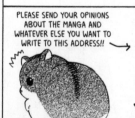

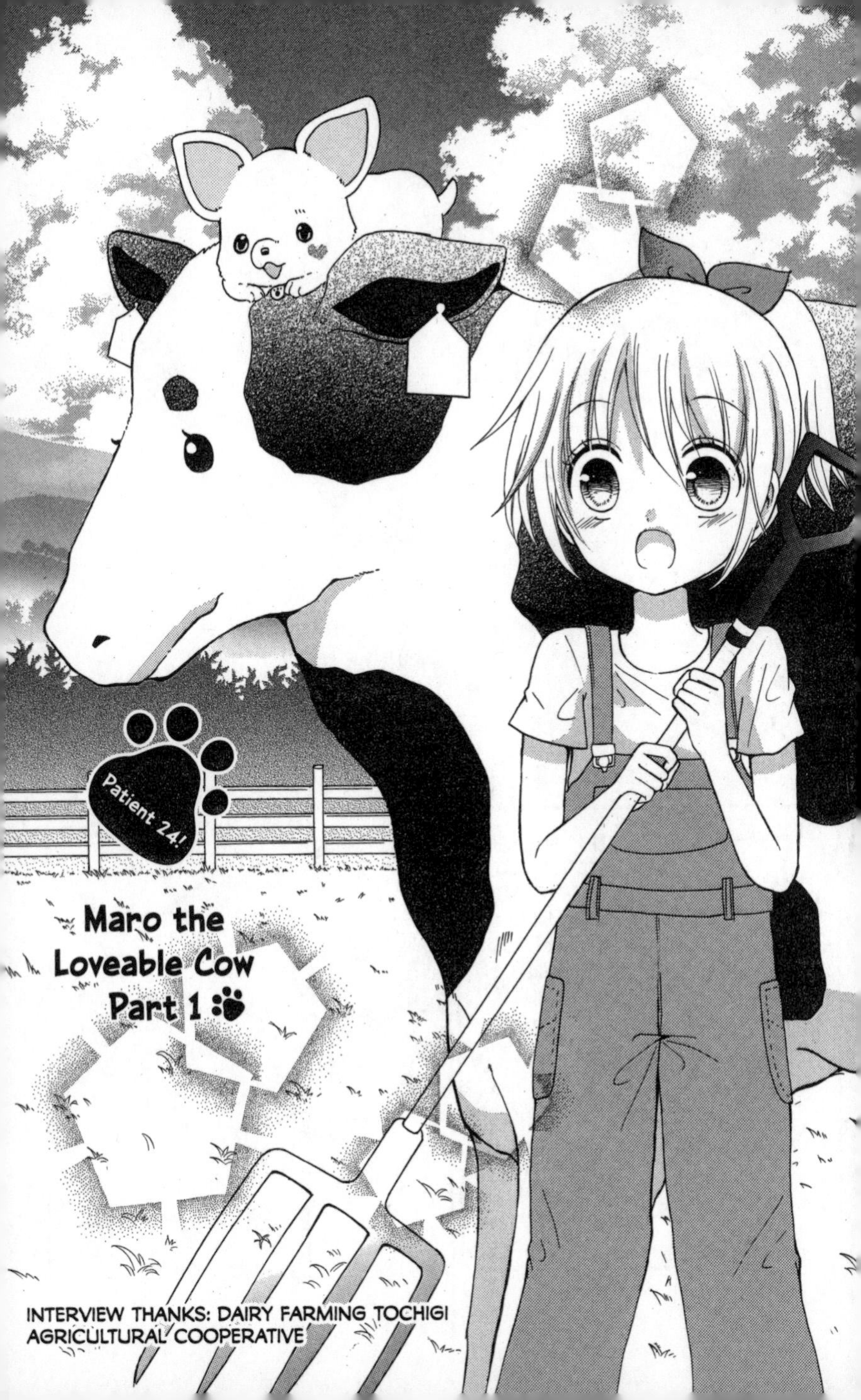
Patient 24!
Maro the Loveable Cow Part 1
INTERVIEW THANKS: DAIRY FARMING TOCHIGI AGRICULTURAL COOPERATIVE

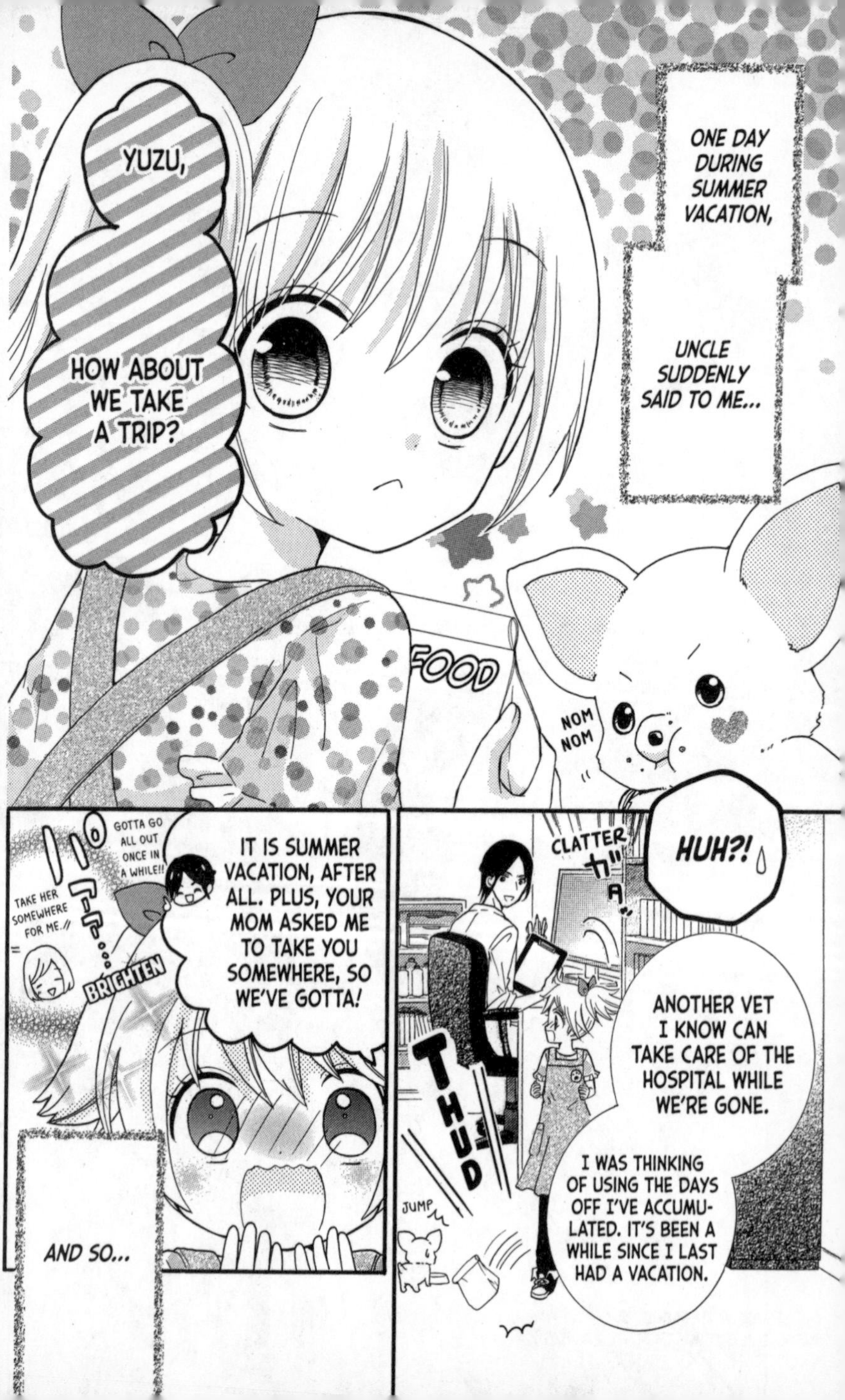
ONE DAY DURING SUMMER VACATION,
UNCLE SUDDENLY SAID TO ME...
YUZU,
HOW ABOUT WE TAKE A TRIP?
FOOD
NOM NOM
HUH?!
CLATTER
ANOTHER VET I KNOW CAN TAKE CARE OF THE HOSPITAL WHILE WE'RE GONE.
I WAS THINKING OF USING THE DAYS OFF I'VE ACCUMULATED. IT'S BEEN A WHILE SINCE I LAST HAD A VACATION.
THUD
JUMP
IT IS SUMMER VACATION, AFTER ALL. PLUS, YOUR MOM ASKED ME TO TAKE YOU SOMEWHERE, SO WE'VE GOTTA!
GOTTA GO ALL OUT ONCE IN A WHILE!!
TAKE HER SOMEWHERE FOR ME.//
BRIGHTEN
AND SO...

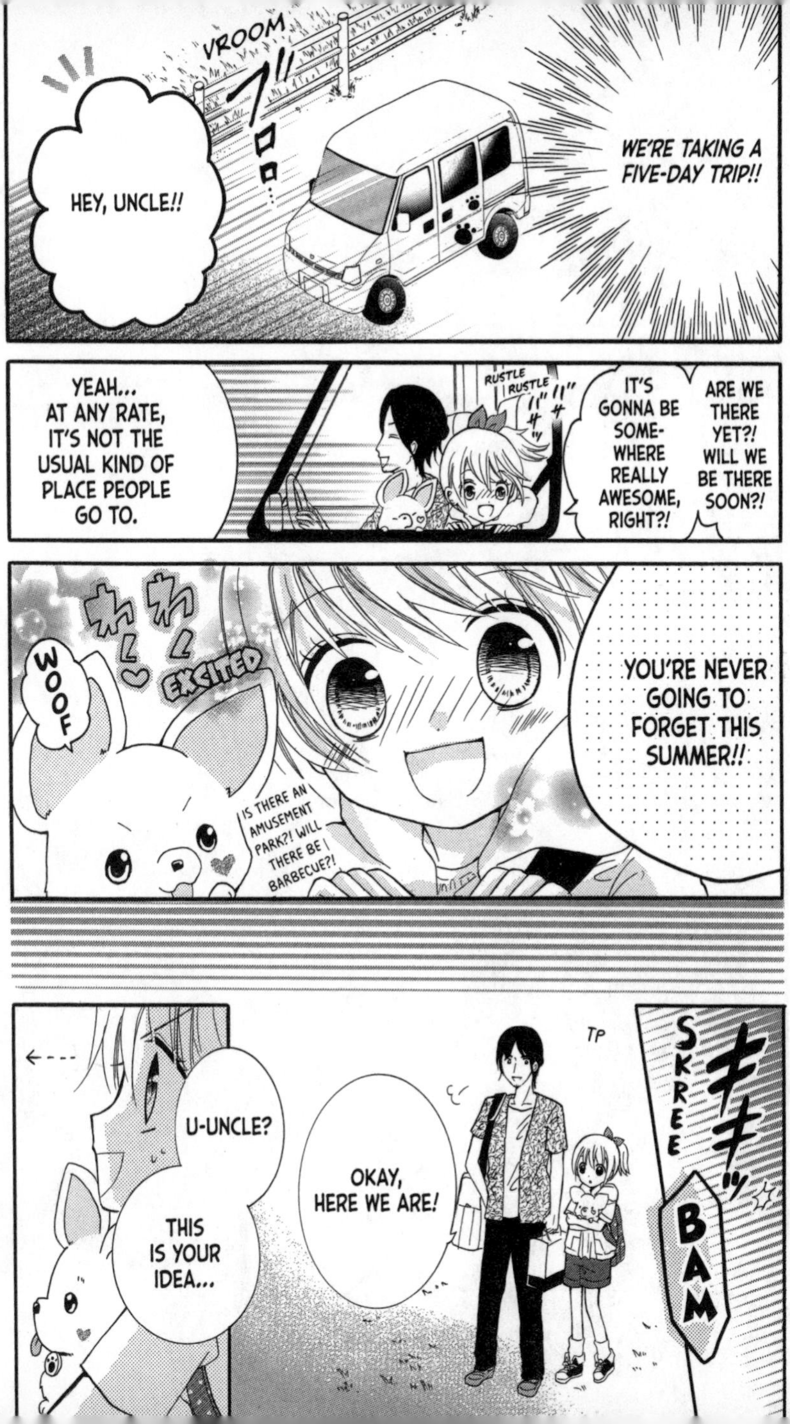
VROOM
WE'RE TAKING A FIVE-DAY TRIP!!
HEY, UNCLE!!
ARE WE THERE YET?! WILL WE BE THERE SOON?!
IT'S GONNA BE SOME-WHERE REALLY AWESOME, RIGHT?!
RUSTLE RUSTLE
YEAH... AT ANY RATE, IT'S NOT THE USUAL KIND OF PLACE PEOPLE GO TO.
YOU'RE NEVER GOING TO FORGET THIS SUMMER!!
EXCITED
IS THERE AN AMUSEMENT PARK?! WILL THERE BE BARBECUE?!
WOOF
SKREE
BAM
TP
OKAY, HERE WE ARE!
U-UNCLE?
THIS IS YOUR IDEA...

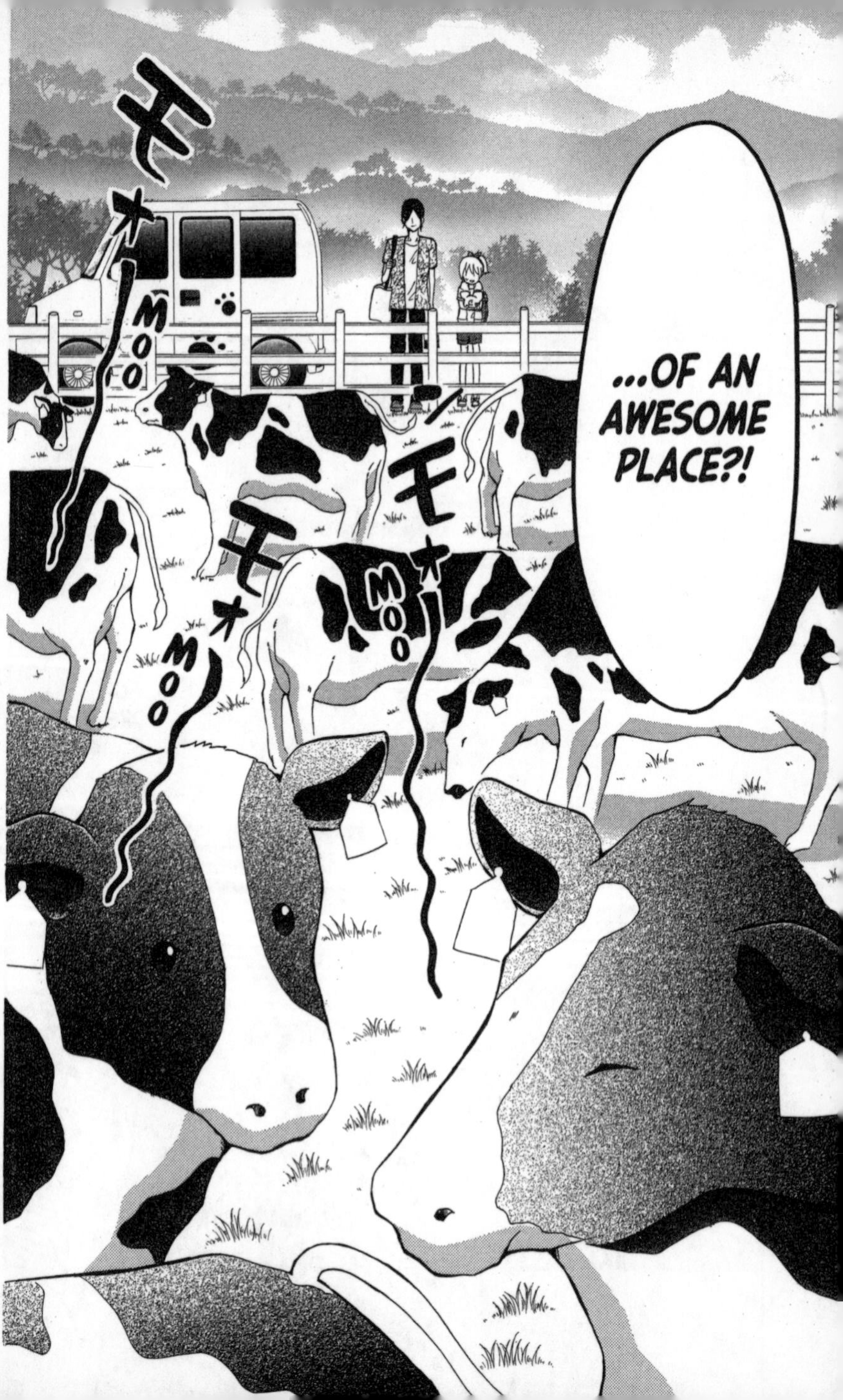
...OF AN AWESOME PLACE?!
MOO
MOO
MOO

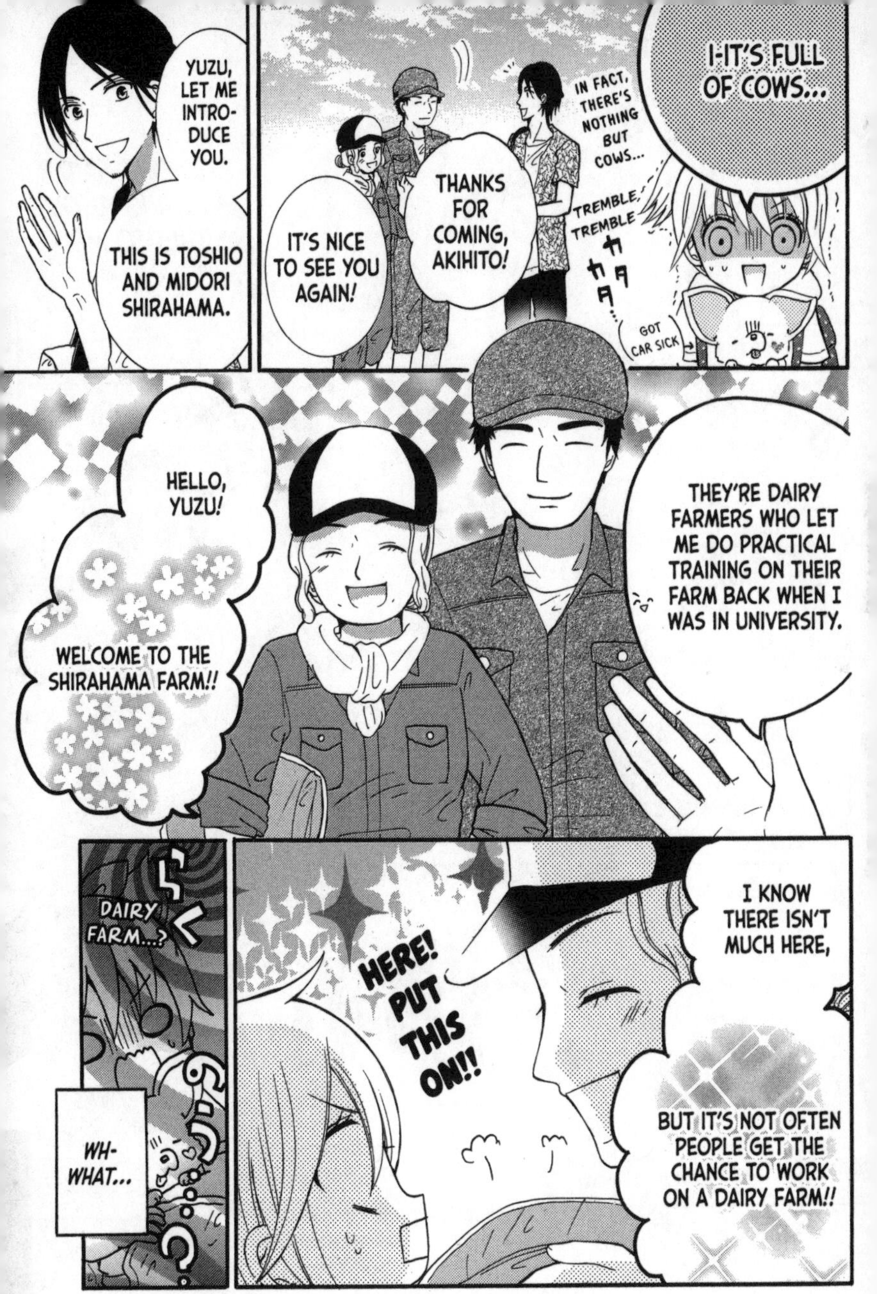
I-IT'S FULL OF COWS...
IN FACT, THERE'S NOTHING BUT COWS...
TREMBLE, TREMBLE
カタカタ
GOT CAR SICK
THANKS FOR COMING, AKIHITO!
IT'S NICE TO SEE YOU AGAIN!
YUZU, LET ME INTRO-DUCE YOU.
THIS IS TOSHIO AND MIDORI SHIRAHAMA.
THEY'RE DAIRY FARMERS WHO LET ME DO PRACTICAL TRAINING ON THEIR FARM BACK WHEN I WAS IN UNIVERSITY.
HELLO, YUZU!
WELCOME TO THE SHIRAHAMA FARM!!
I KNOW THERE ISN'T MUCH HERE,
BUT IT'S NOT OFTEN PEOPLE GET THE CHANCE TO WORK ON A DAIRY FARM!!
HERE! PUT THIS ON!!
DAIRY FARM...?
WH-WHAT...

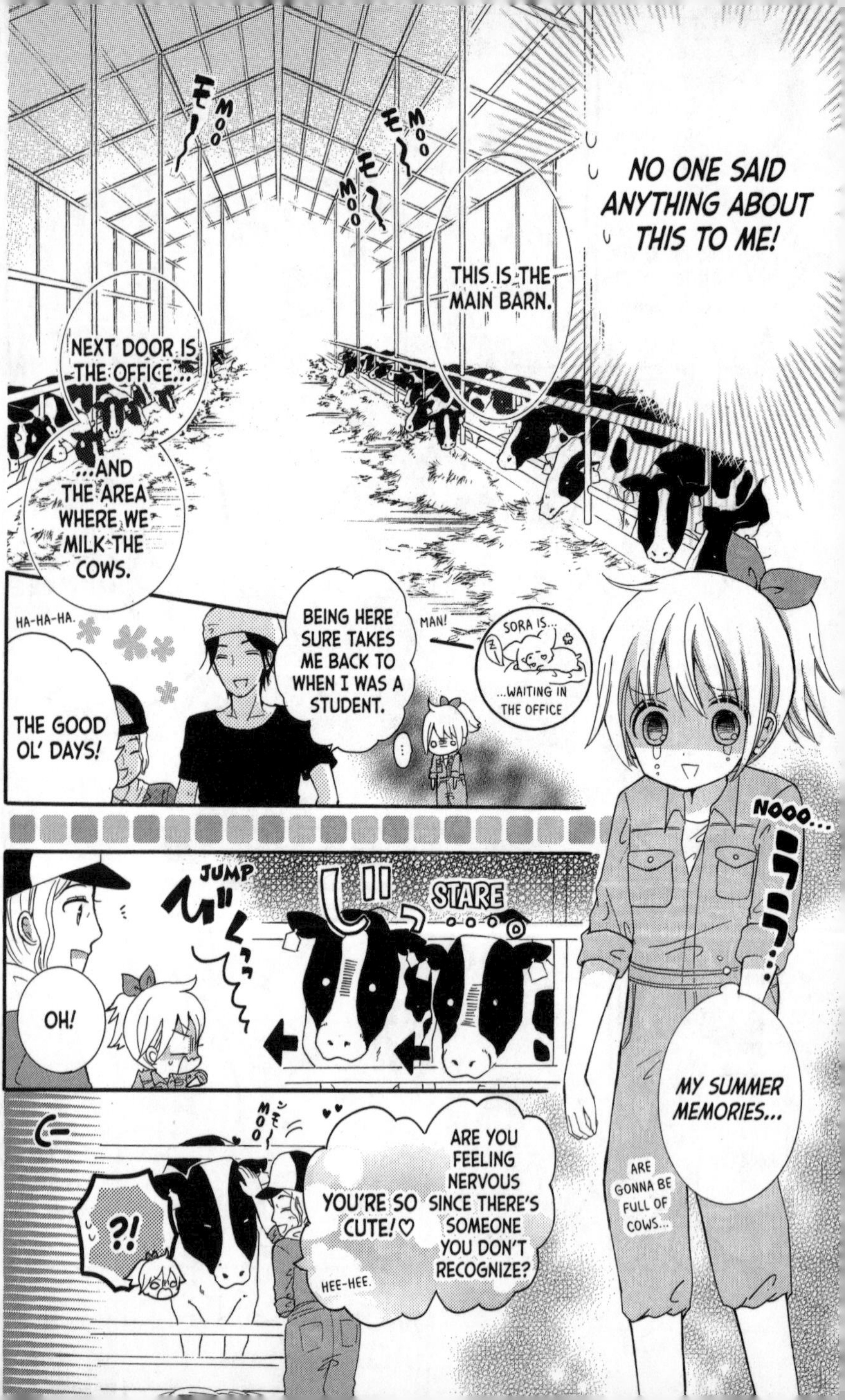
NO ONE SAID ANYTHING ABOUT THIS TO ME!
MOO
MOO
MOO
THIS IS THE MAIN BARN.
NEXT DOOR IS THE OFFICE...
...AND THE AREA WHERE WE MILK THE COWS.
NOOO...
MY SUMMER MEMORIES...
ARE GONNA BE FULL OF COWS...
SORA IS...
...WAITING IN THE OFFICE
MAN!
BEING HERE SURE TAKES ME BACK TO WHEN I WAS A STUDENT.
HA-HA-HA.
THE GOOD OL' DAYS!
...
STARE
JUMP
OH!
MOO
ARE YOU FEELING NERVOUS SINCE THERE'S SOMEONE YOU DON'T RECOGNIZE?
YOU'RE SO CUTE!♡
HEE-HEE.
?!

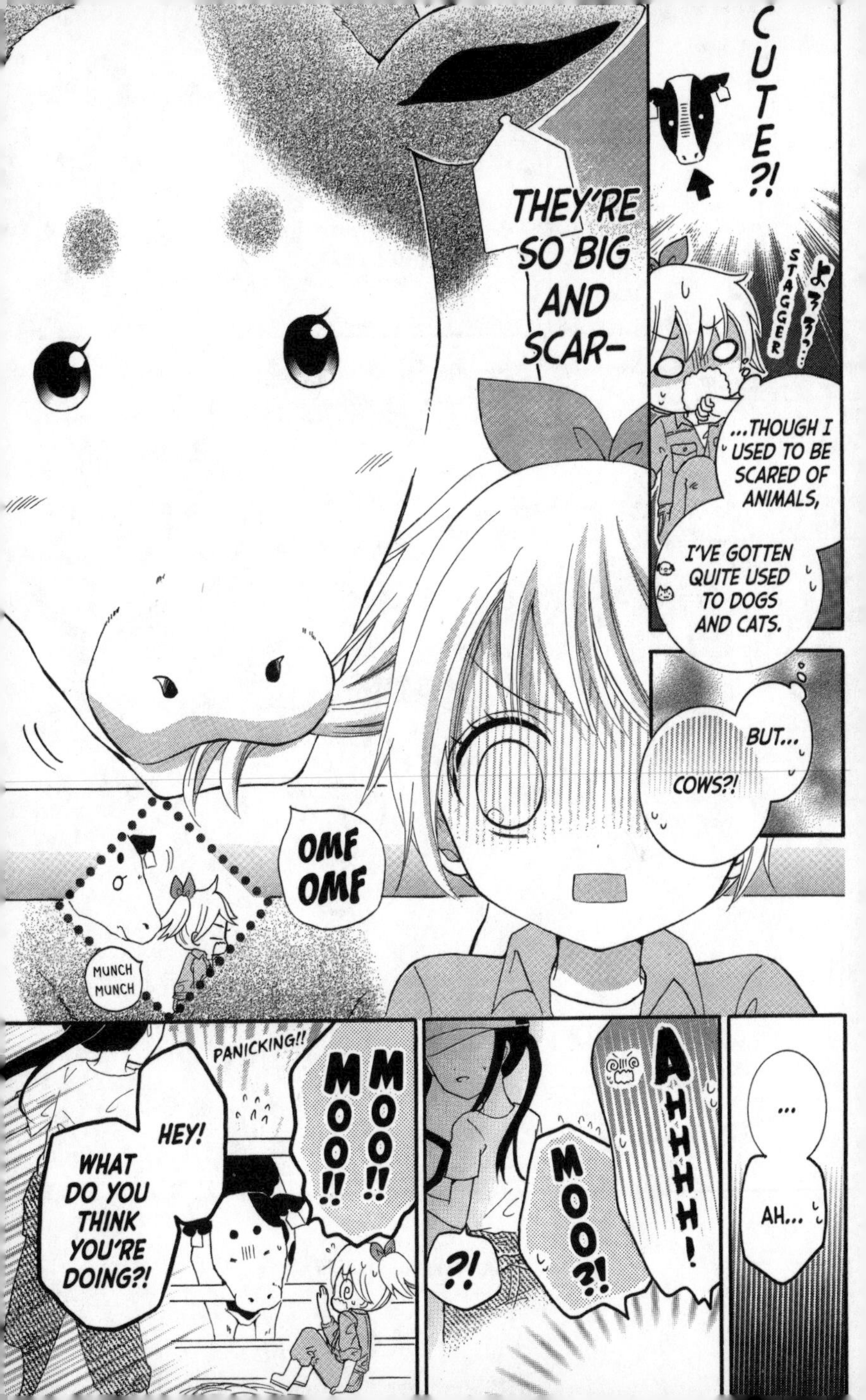
CUTE?!
STAGGER
...THOUGH I USED TO BE SCARED OF ANIMALS,
I'VE GOTTEN QUITE USED TO DOGS AND CATS.
BUT... COWS?!
THEY'RE SO BIG AND SCAR-
OMF OMF
MUNCH MUNCH
...
AH...
AHHHH!
MOO?!
?!
MOOO!!
MMOOO!!
PANICKING!!
HEY!
WHAT DO YOU THINK YOU'RE DOING?!

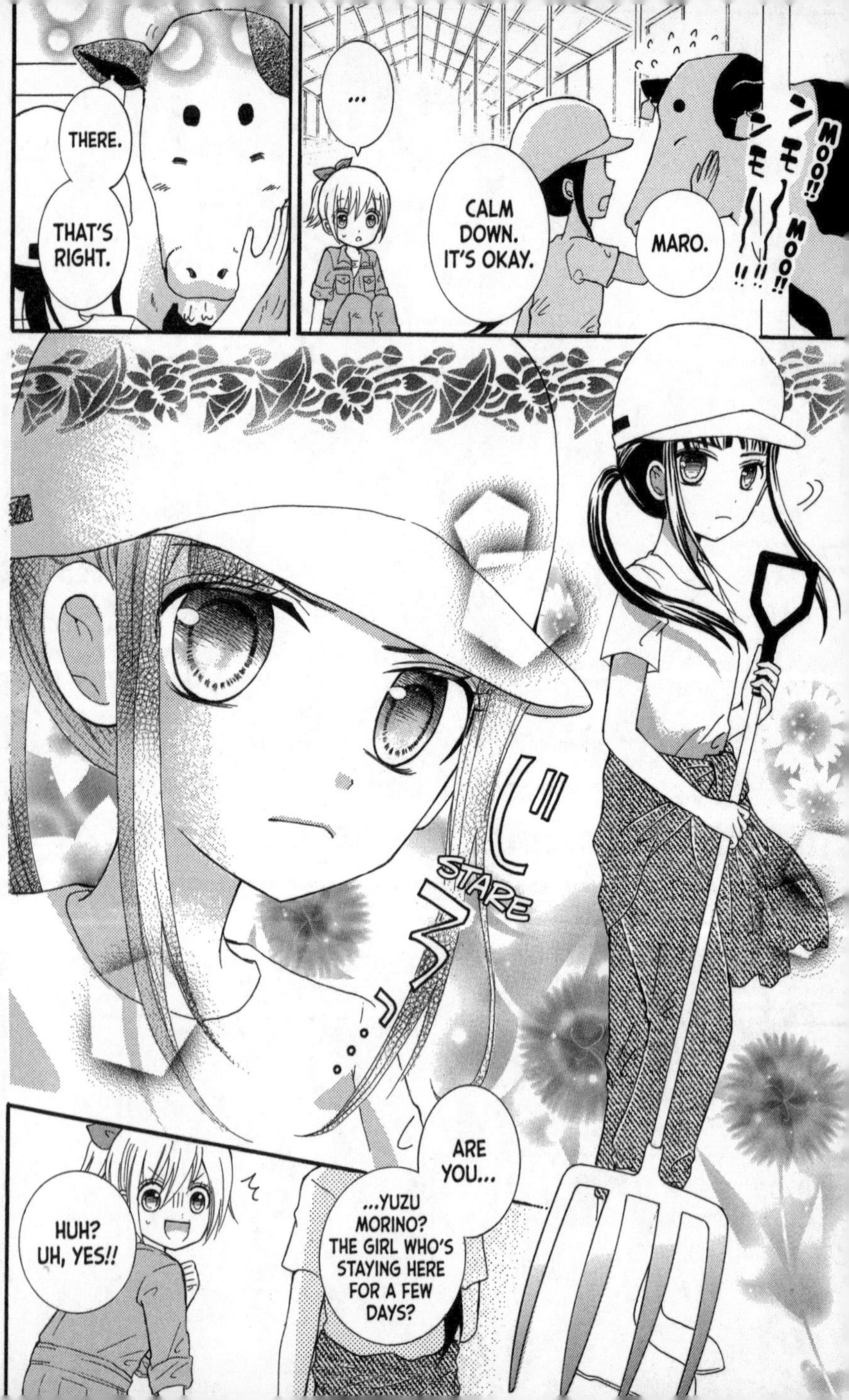
MOO!!
MOOO!!
MARO.
CALM DOWN. IT'S OKAY.
...
THERE.
THAT'S RIGHT.
STARE
ARE YOU...
...YUZU MORINO? THE GIRL WHO'S STAYING HERE FOR A FEW DAYS?
HUH? UH, YES!!

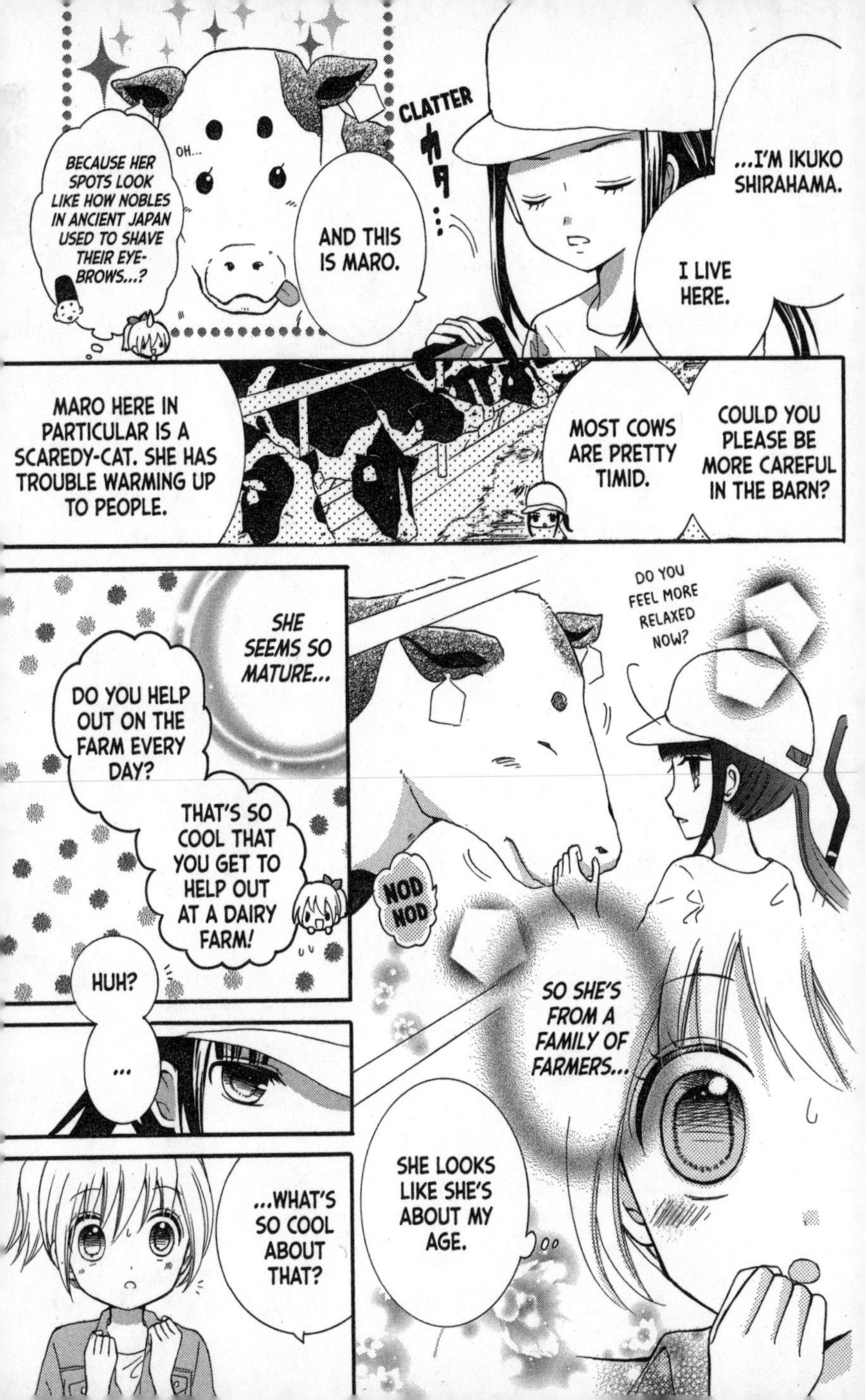
...I'M IKUKO SHIRAHAMA.
I LIVE HERE.
CLATTER
カタ
AND THIS IS MARO.
OH...
BECAUSE HER SPOTS LOOK LIKE HOW NOBLES IN ANCIENT JAPAN USED TO SHAVE THEIR EYE-BROWS...?
COULD YOU PLEASE BE MORE CAREFUL IN THE BARN?
MOST COWS ARE PRETTY TIMID.
MARO HERE IN PARTICULAR IS A SCAREDY-CAT. SHE HAS TROUBLE WARMING UP TO PEOPLE.
DO YOU FEEL MORE RELAXED NOW?
NOD NOD
SO SHE'S FROM A FAMILY OF FARMERS...
SHE LOOKS LIKE SHE'S ABOUT MY AGE.
SHE SEEMS SO MATURE...
DO YOU HELP OUT ON THE FARM EVERY DAY?
THAT'S SO COOL THAT YOU GET TO HELP OUT AT A DAIRY FARM!
HUH?
...
...WHAT'S SO COOL ABOUT THAT?

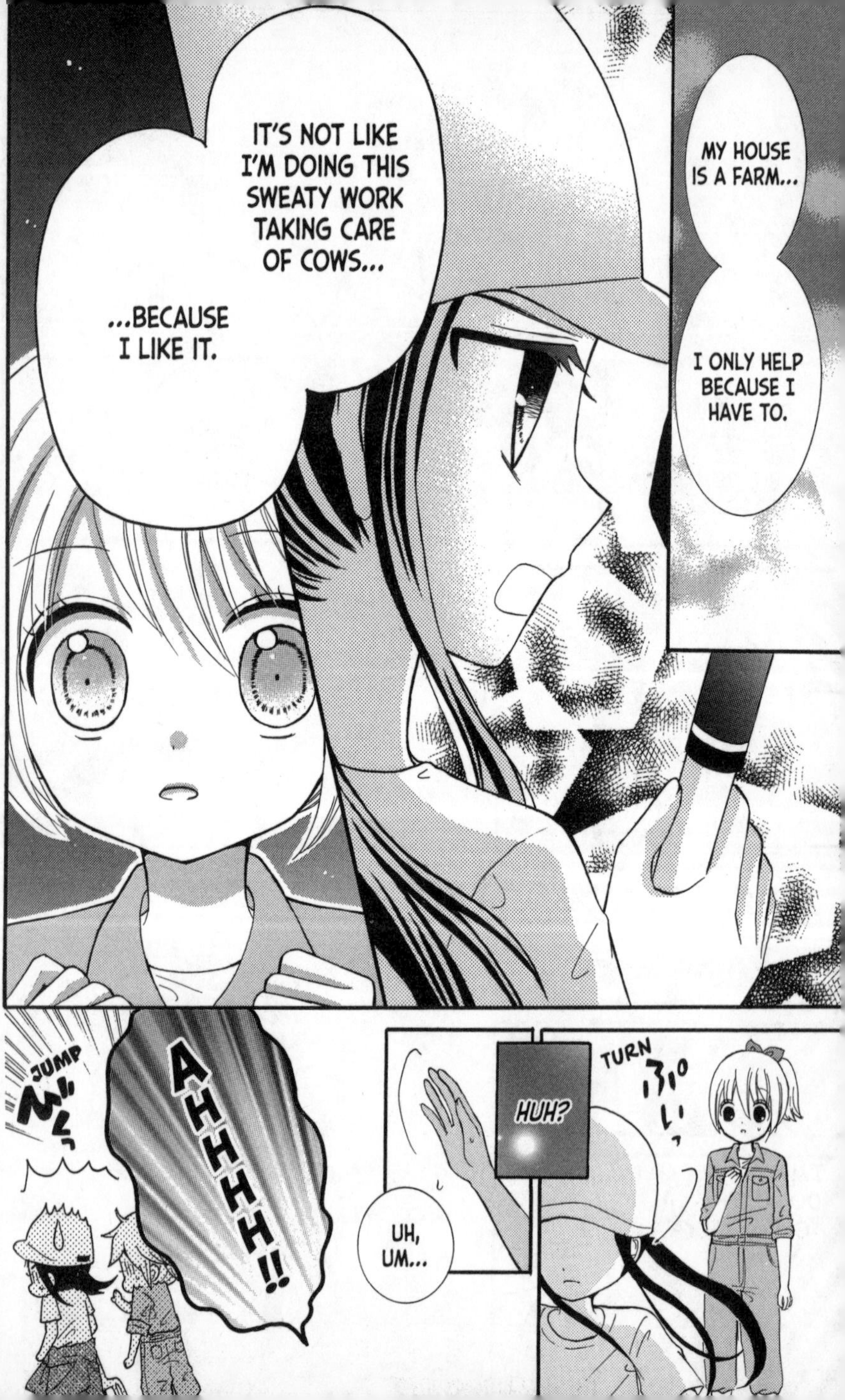
MY HOUSE IS A FARM...
I ONLY HELP BECAUSE I HAVE TO.
IT'S NOT LIKE I'M DOING THIS SWEATY WORK TAKING CARE OF COWS...
...BECAUSE I LIKE IT.
TURN
HUH?
UH, UM...
AHHHHH!!
JUMP

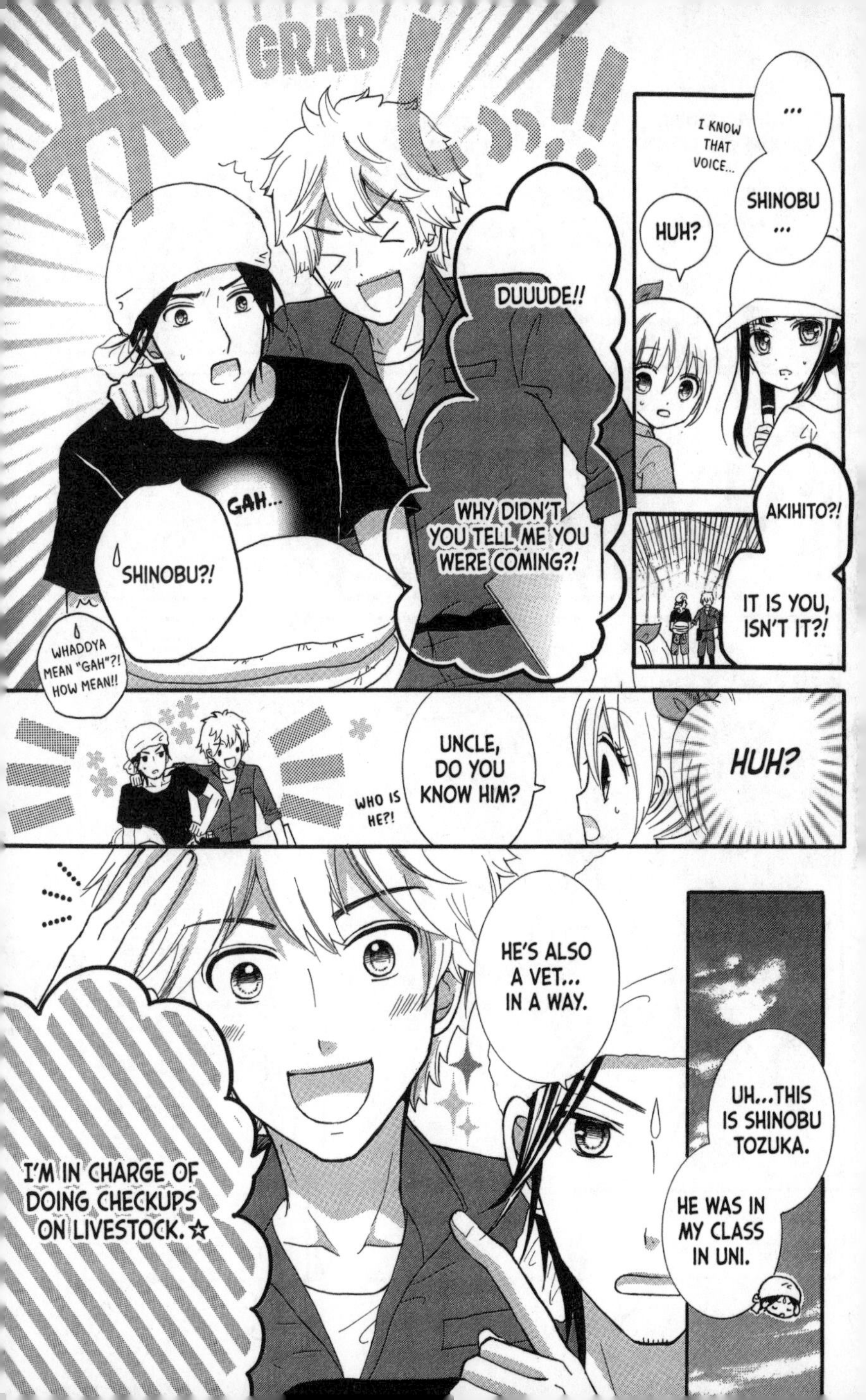
...
SHINOBU ...
I KNOW THAT VOICE...
HUH?
AKIHITO?!
IT IS YOU, ISN'T IT?!
GRAB
DUUUDE!!
WHY DIDN'T YOU TELL ME YOU WERE COMING?!
GAH...
SHINOBU?!
WHADDYA MEAN "GAH"?! HOW MEAN!!
HUH?
UNCLE, DO YOU KNOW HIM?
WHO IS HE?!
UH...THIS IS SHINOBU TOZUKA.
HE WAS IN MY CLASS IN UNI.
HE'S ALSO A VET... IN A WAY.
I'M IN CHARGE OF DOING CHECKUPS ON LIVESTOCK.☆

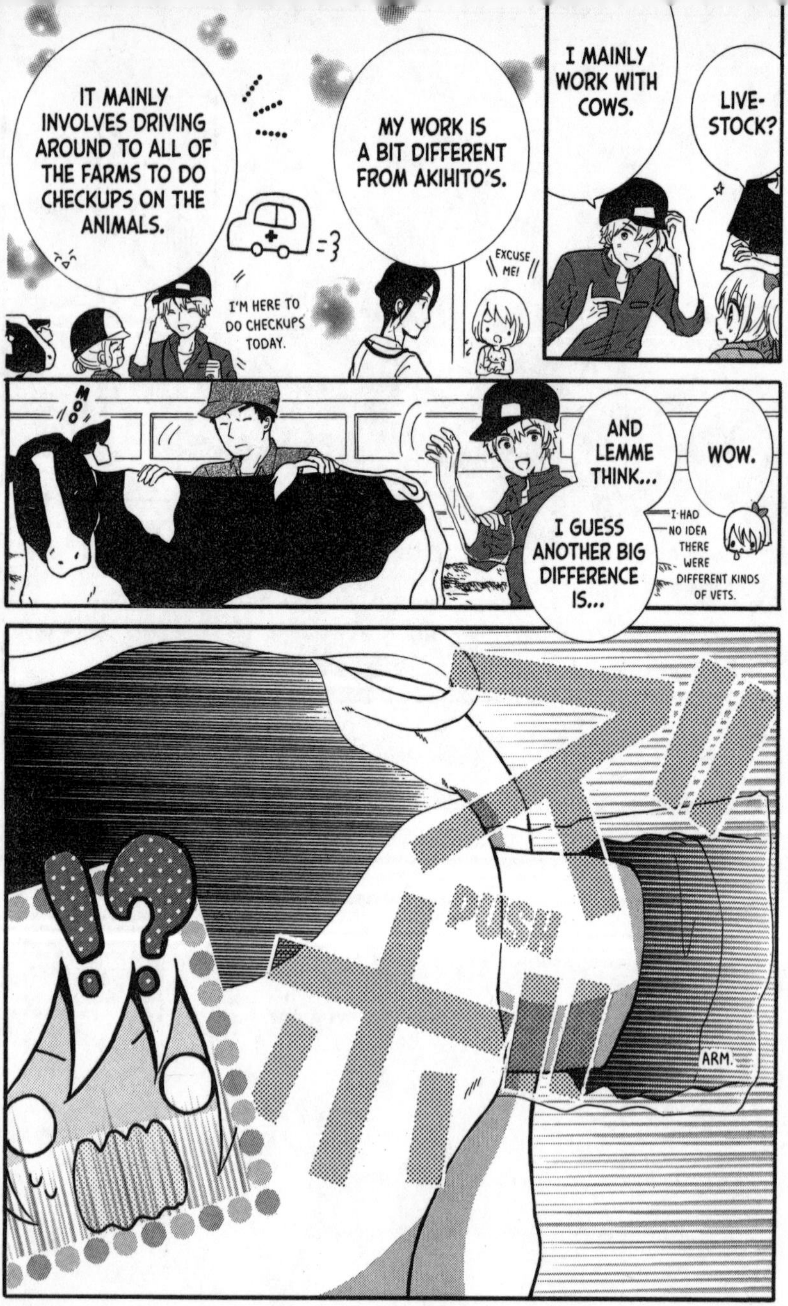
LIVE-STOCK?
I MAINLY WORK WITH COWS.
MY WORK IS A BIT DIFFERENT FROM AKIHITO'S.
EXCUSE ME!
IT MAINLY INVOLVES DRIVING AROUND TO ALL OF THE FARMS TO DO CHECKUPS ON THE ANIMALS.
I'M HERE TO DO CHECKUPS TODAY.
WOW.
I HAD NO IDEA THERE WERE DIFFERENT KINDS OF VETS.
AND LEMME THINK...
I GUESS ANOTHER BIG DIFFERENCE IS...
MOO
PUSH
ARM.

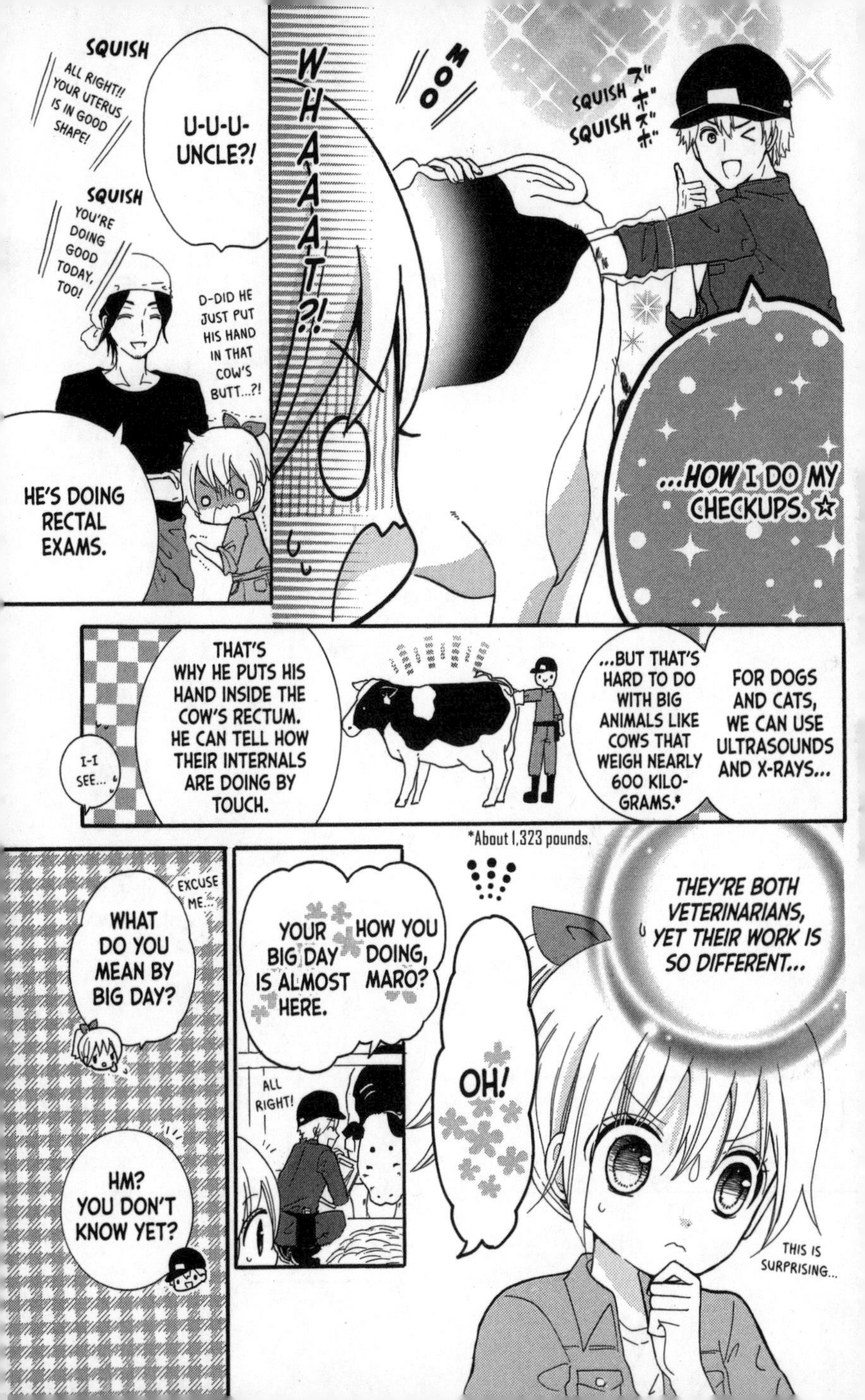
MOO
SQUISH ズボ SQUISH ズボ
WHAAAAT?!
...HOW I DO MY CHECKUPS. ☆
U-U-U-UNCLE?!
SQUISH
ALL RIGHT!! YOUR UTERUS IS IN GOOD SHAPE!
SQUISH
YOU'RE DOING GOOD TODAY, TOO!
D-DID HE JUST PUT HIS HAND IN THAT COW'S BUTT...?!
HE'S DOING RECTAL EXAMS.
FOR DOGS AND CATS, WE CAN USE ULTRASOUNDS AND X-RAYS...
...BUT THAT'S HARD TO DO WITH BIG ANIMALS LIKE COWS THAT WEIGH NEARLY 600 KILOGRAMS.*
THAT'S WHY HE PUTS HIS HAND INSIDE THE COW'S RECTUM. HE CAN TELL HOW THEIR INTERNALS ARE DOING BY TOUCH.
I-I SEE...
THEY'RE BOTH VETERINARIANS, YET THEIR WORK IS SO DIFFERENT...
THIS IS SURPRISING...
OH!
HOW YOU DOING, MARO?
YOUR BIG DAY IS ALMOST HERE.
ALL RIGHT!
EXCUSE ME...
WHAT DO YOU MEAN BY BIG DAY?
HM? YOU DON'T KNOW YET?

*About 1,323 pounds.

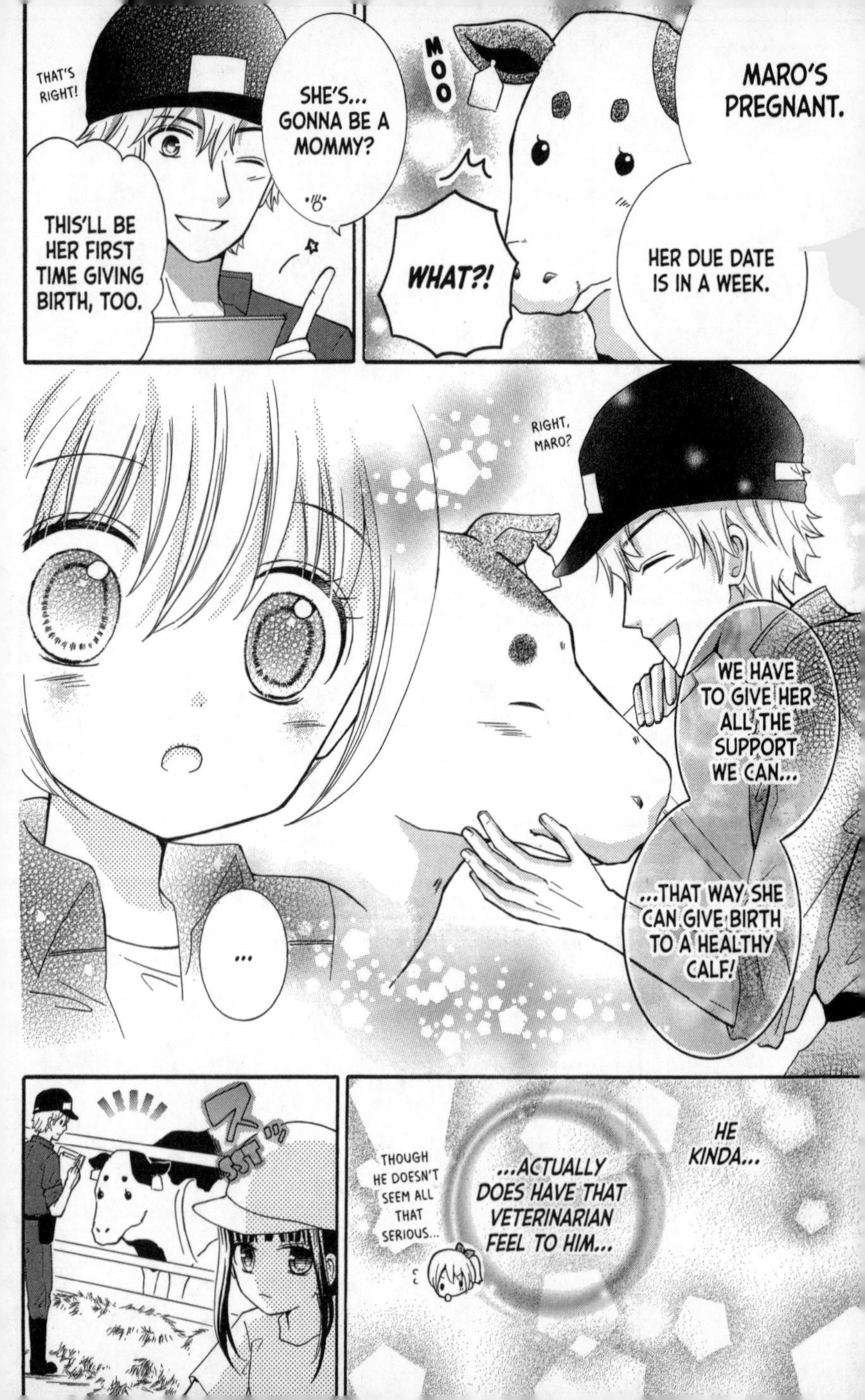
MARO'S PREGNANT.
MOO
HER DUE DATE IS IN A WEEK.
WHAT?!
SHE'S... GONNA BE A MOMMY?
THAT'S RIGHT!
THIS'LL BE HER FIRST TIME GIVING BIRTH, TOO.
RIGHT, MARO?
WE HAVE TO GIVE HER ALL THE SUPPORT WE CAN...
...THAT WAY SHE CAN GIVE BIRTH TO A HEALTHY CALF!
...
HE KINDA...
...ACTUALLY DOES HAVE THAT VETERINARIAN FEEL TO HIM...
THOUGH HE DOESN'T SEEM ALL THAT SERIOUS...
SST

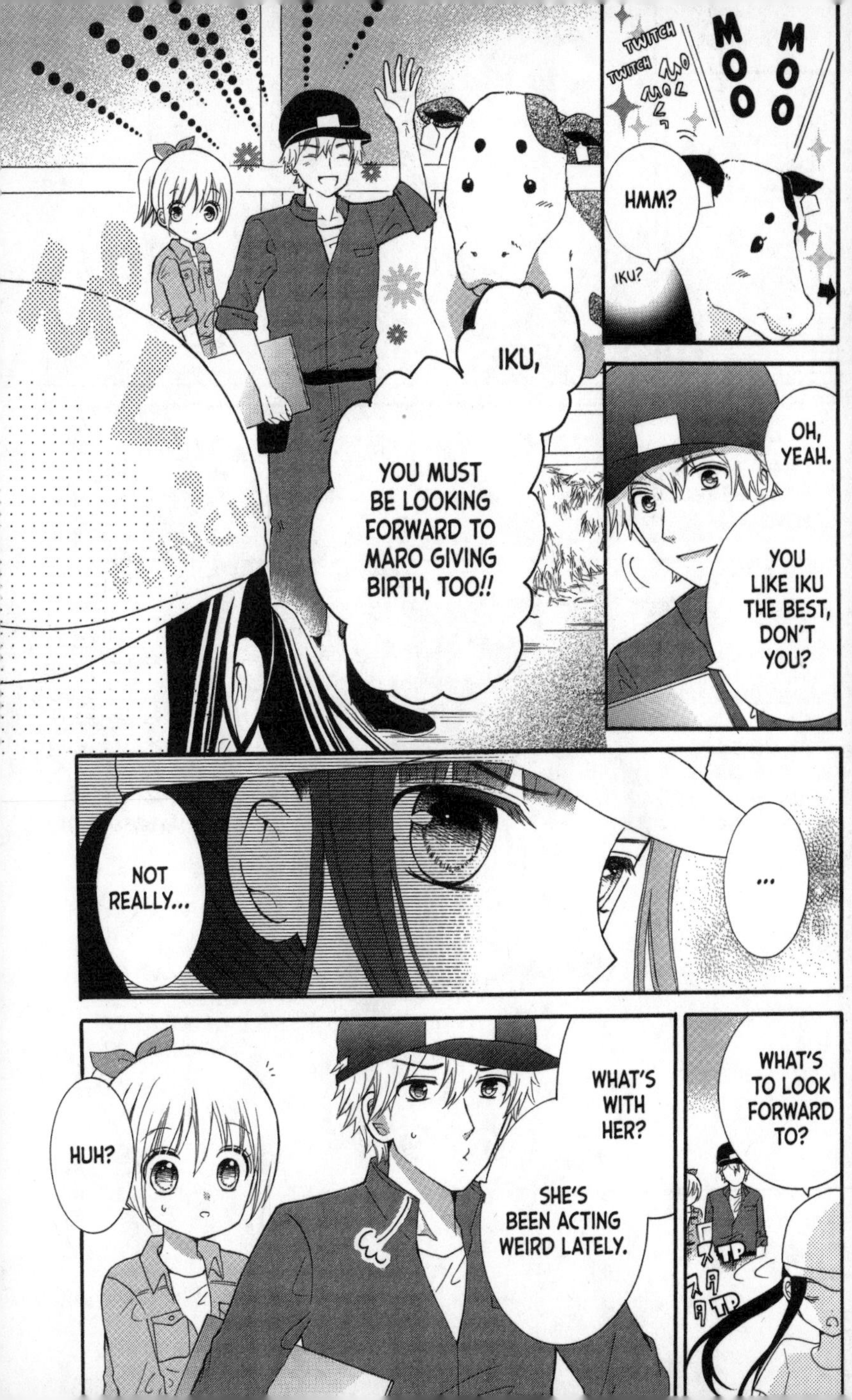
MOO
MOO
TWITCH
TWITCH
HMM?
IKU?
OH, YEAH.
YOU LIKE IKU THE BEST, DON'T YOU?
IKU,
YOU MUST BE LOOKING FORWARD TO MARO GIVING BIRTH, TOO!!
FLINCH
...
NOT REALLY...
WHAT'S TO LOOK FORWARD TO?
TP
TP
WHAT'S WITH HER?
SHE'S BEEN ACTING WEIRD LATELY.
HUH?

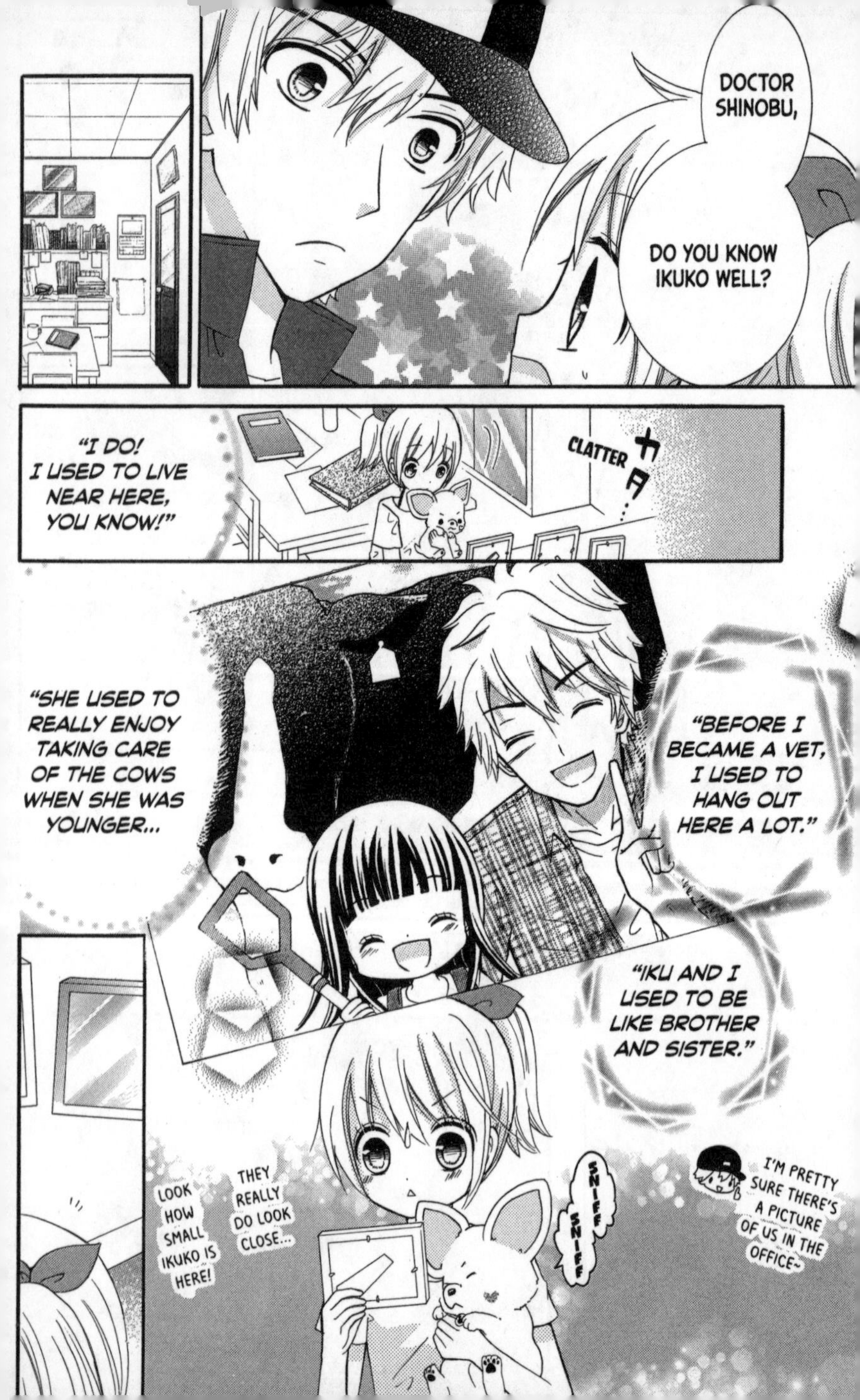
DOCTOR SHINOBU,
DO YOU KNOW IKUKO WELL?
CLATTER
カタ…
"I DO! I USED TO LIVE NEAR HERE, YOU KNOW!"
"BEFORE I BECAME A VET, I USED TO HANG OUT HERE A LOT."
"SHE USED TO REALLY ENJOY TAKING CARE OF THE COWS WHEN SHE WAS YOUNGER...
"IKU AND I USED TO BE LIKE BROTHER AND SISTER."
I'M PRETTY SURE THERE'S A PICTURE OF US IN THE OFFICE~
SNIFF SNIFF
THEY REALLY DO LOOK CLOSE...
LOOK HOW SMALL IKUKO IS HERE!

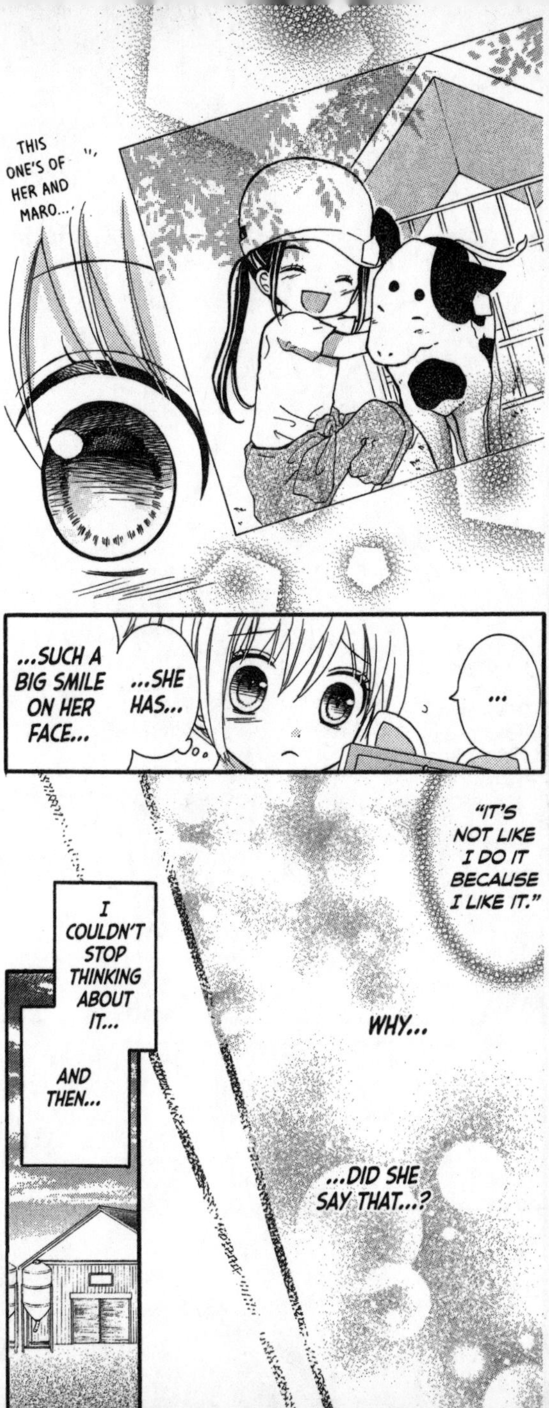
THIS ONE'S OF HER AND MARO...
...
...SHE HAS...
...SUCH A BIG SMILE ON HER FACE...
"IT'S NOT LIKE I DO IT BECAUSE I LIKE IT."
WHY...
...DID SHE SAY THAT...?
I COULDN'T STOP THINKING ABOUT IT...
AND THEN...

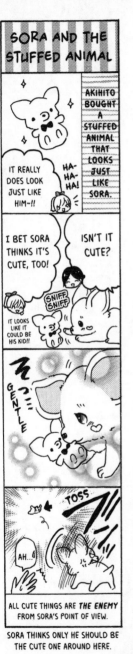

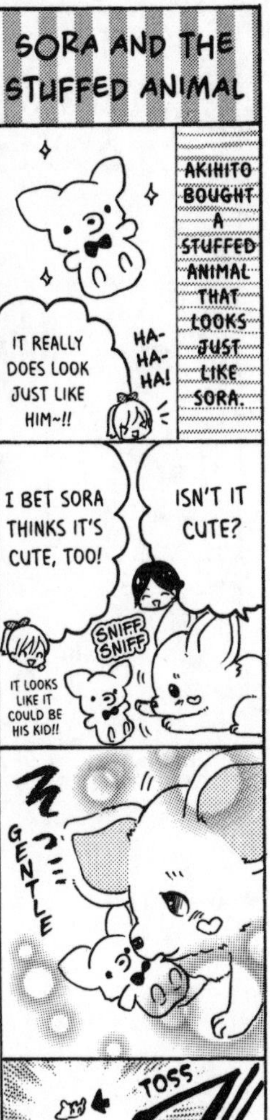
SORA AND THE STUFFED ANIMAL
AKIHITO BOUGHT A STUFFED ANIMAL THAT LOOKS JUST LIKE SORA.
HA-HA-HA!
IT REALLY DOES LOOK JUST LIKE HIM~!!
ISN'T IT CUTE?
I BET SORA THINKS IT'S CUTE, TOO!
SNIFF SNIFF
IT LOOKS LIKE IT COULD BE HIS KID!!
GENTLE
TOSS
AH...
ALL CUTE THINGS ARE *THE ENEMY* FROM SORA'S POINT OF VIEW.

SORA THINKS ONLY HE SHOULD BE THE CUTE ONE AROUND HERE.

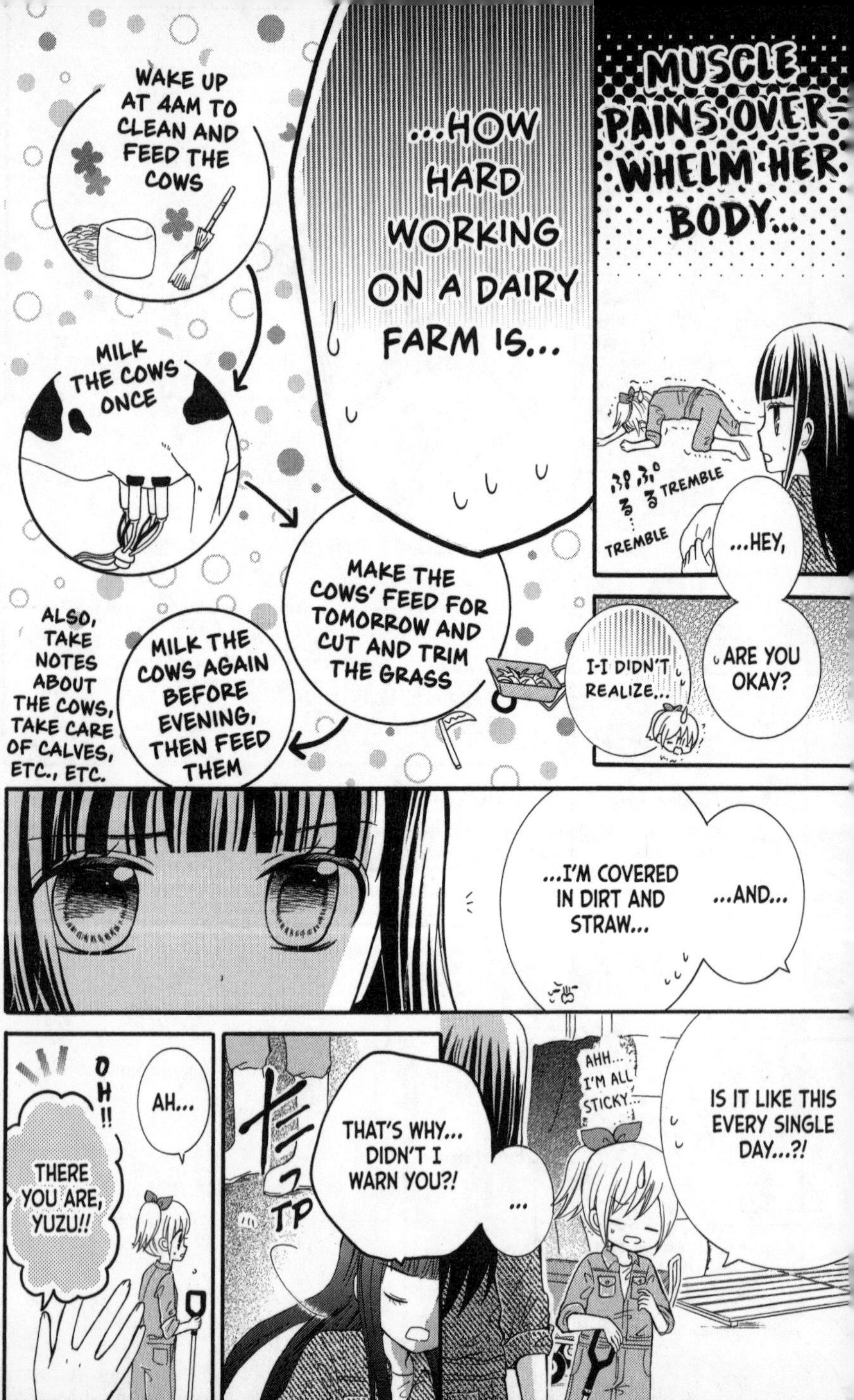
MUSCLE PAINS OVERWHELM HER BODY...
TREMBLE
TREMBLE
...HEY,
ARE YOU OKAY?
I-I DIDN'T REALIZE...
...HOW HARD WORKING ON A DAIRY FARM IS...
WAKE UP AT 4AM TO CLEAN AND FEED THE COWS
MILK THE COWS ONCE
MAKE THE COWS' FEED FOR TOMORROW AND CUT AND TRIM THE GRASS
MILK THE COWS AGAIN BEFORE EVENING, THEN FEED THEM
ALSO, TAKE NOTES ABOUT THE COWS, TAKE CARE OF CALVES, ETC., ETC.
...I'M COVERED IN DIRT AND STRAW...
...AND...
IS IT LIKE THIS EVERY SINGLE DAY...?!
AHH... I'M ALL STICKY...
...
THAT'S WHY... DIDN'T I WARN YOU?!
TP
OH!!
AH...
THERE YOU ARE, YUZU!!

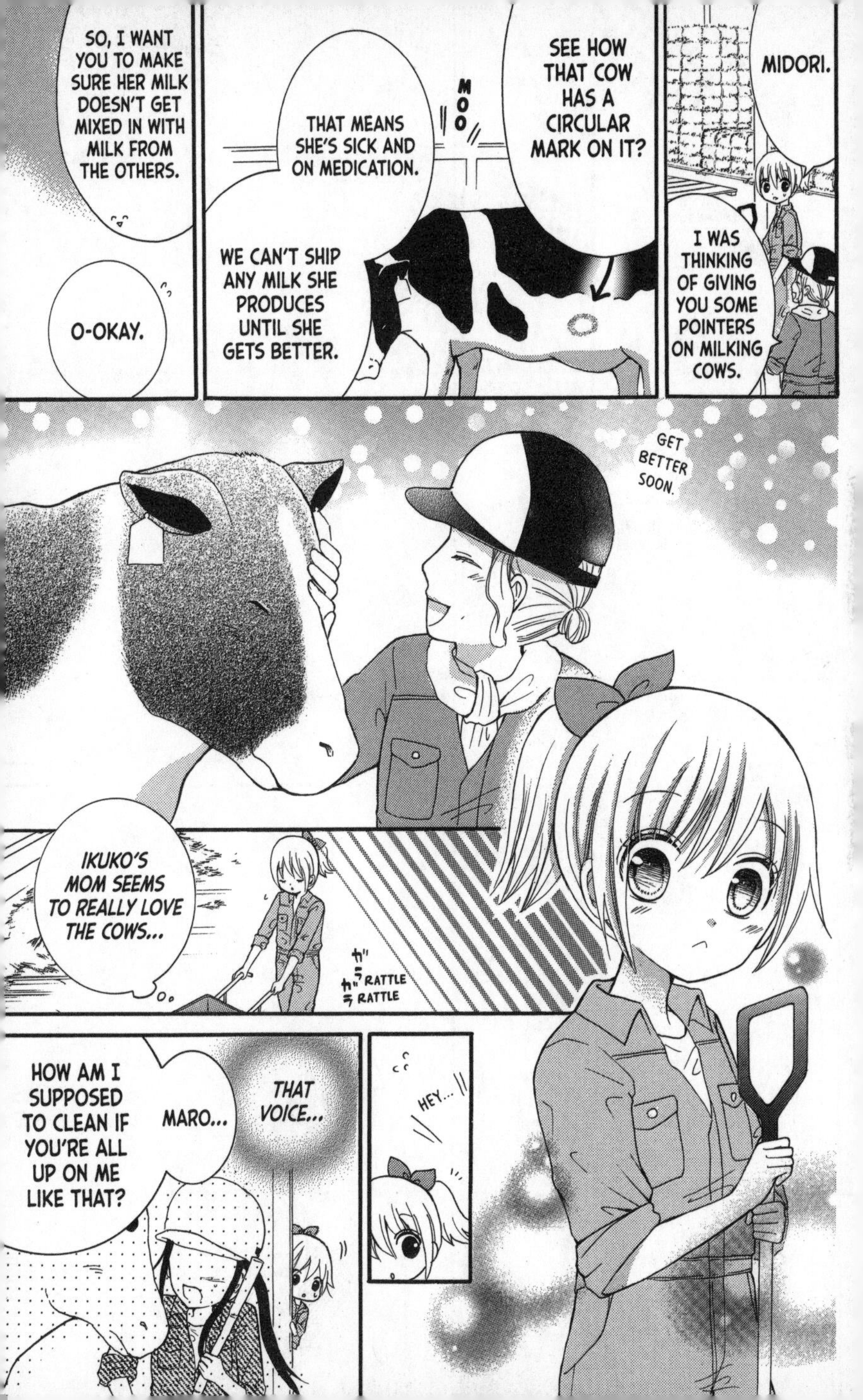
MIDORI.
I WAS THINKING OF GIVING YOU SOME POINTERS ON MILKING COWS.
SEE HOW THAT COW HAS A CIRCULAR MARK ON IT?
MOO
THAT MEANS SHE'S SICK AND ON MEDICATION.
WE CAN'T SHIP ANY MILK SHE PRODUCES UNTIL SHE GETS BETTER.
SO, I WANT YOU TO MAKE SURE HER MILK DOESN'T GET MIXED IN WITH MILK FROM THE OTHERS.
O-OKAY.
GET BETTER SOON.
IKUKO'S MOM SEEMS TO REALLY LOVE THE COWS...
ガラ RATTLE
ガラ RATTLE
HEY...
THAT VOICE...
MARO...
HOW AM I SUPPOSED TO CLEAN IF YOU'RE ALL UP ON ME LIKE THAT?

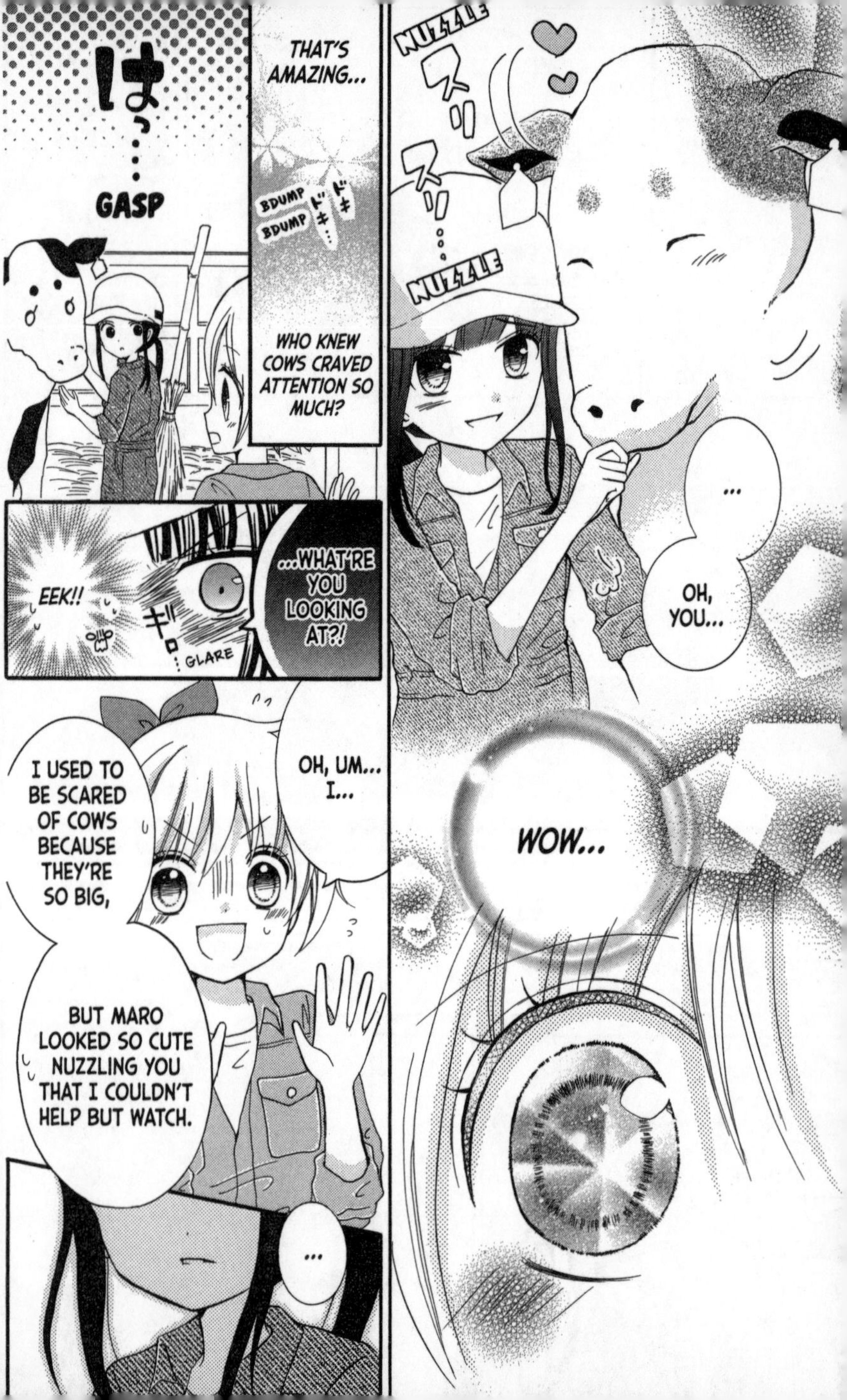
NUZZLE
スリ
スリ…
NUZZLE
…
OH, YOU…
WOW…
THAT'S AMAZING…
BDUMP BDUMP
ドキドキ…
WHO KNEW COWS CRAVED ATTENTION SO MUCH?
はっ…
GASP
…WHAT'RE YOU LOOKING AT?!
ギロ
GLARE
EEK!!
OH, UM… I…
I USED TO BE SCARED OF COWS BECAUSE THEY'RE SO BIG,
BUT MARO LOOKED SO CUTE NUZZLING YOU THAT I COULDN'T HELP BUT WATCH.
…

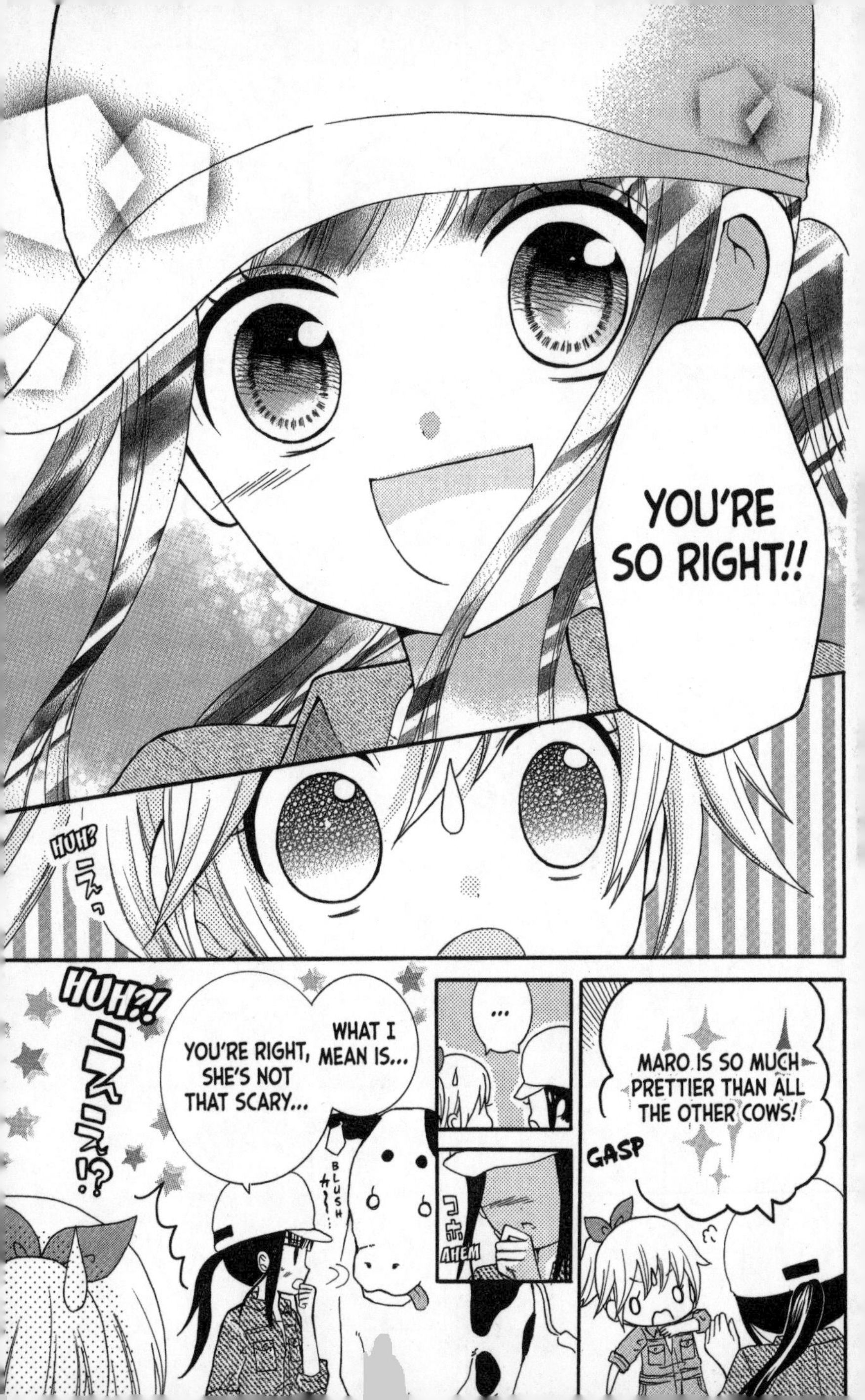
YOU'RE SO RIGHT!!
HUH?
え、
MARO IS SO MUCH PRETTIER THAN ALL THE OTHER COWS!
GASP
...
AHEM
WHAT I MEAN IS... YOU'RE RIGHT, SHE'S NOT THAT SCARY...
BLUSH
HUH?!

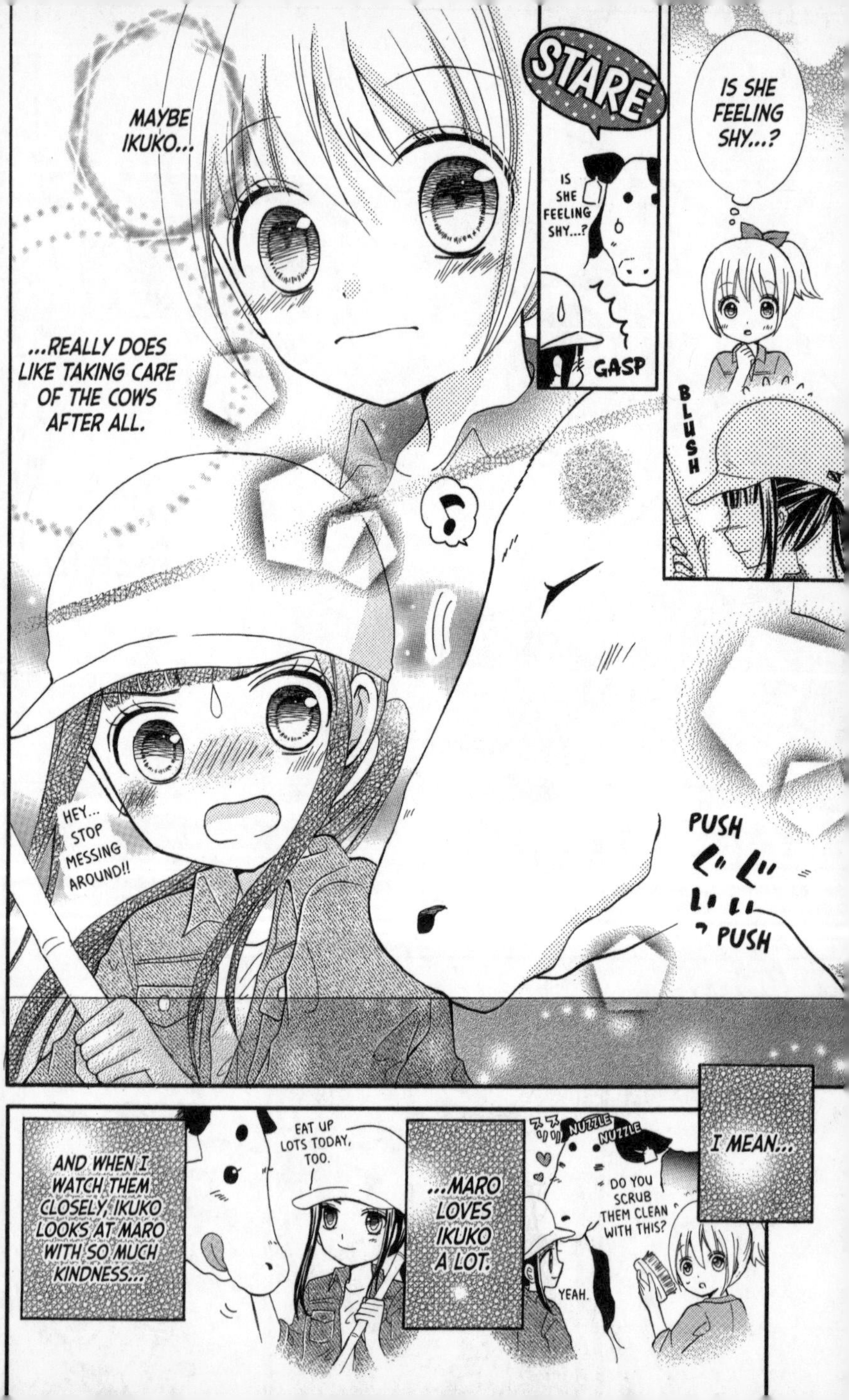
IS SHE FEELING SHY...?
BLUSH
STARE
IS SHE FEELING SHY...?
GASP
MAYBE IKUKO...
...REALLY DOES LIKE TAKING CARE OF THE COWS AFTER ALL.
PUSH
PUSH
HEY... STOP MESSING AROUND!!
I MEAN...
NUZZLE NUZZLE
DO YOU SCRUB THEM CLEAN WITH THIS?
YEAH.
...MARO LOVES IKUKO A LOT.
EAT UP LOTS TODAY, TOO.
AND WHEN I WATCH THEM CLOSELY, IKUKO LOOKS AT MARO WITH SO MUCH KINDNESS...

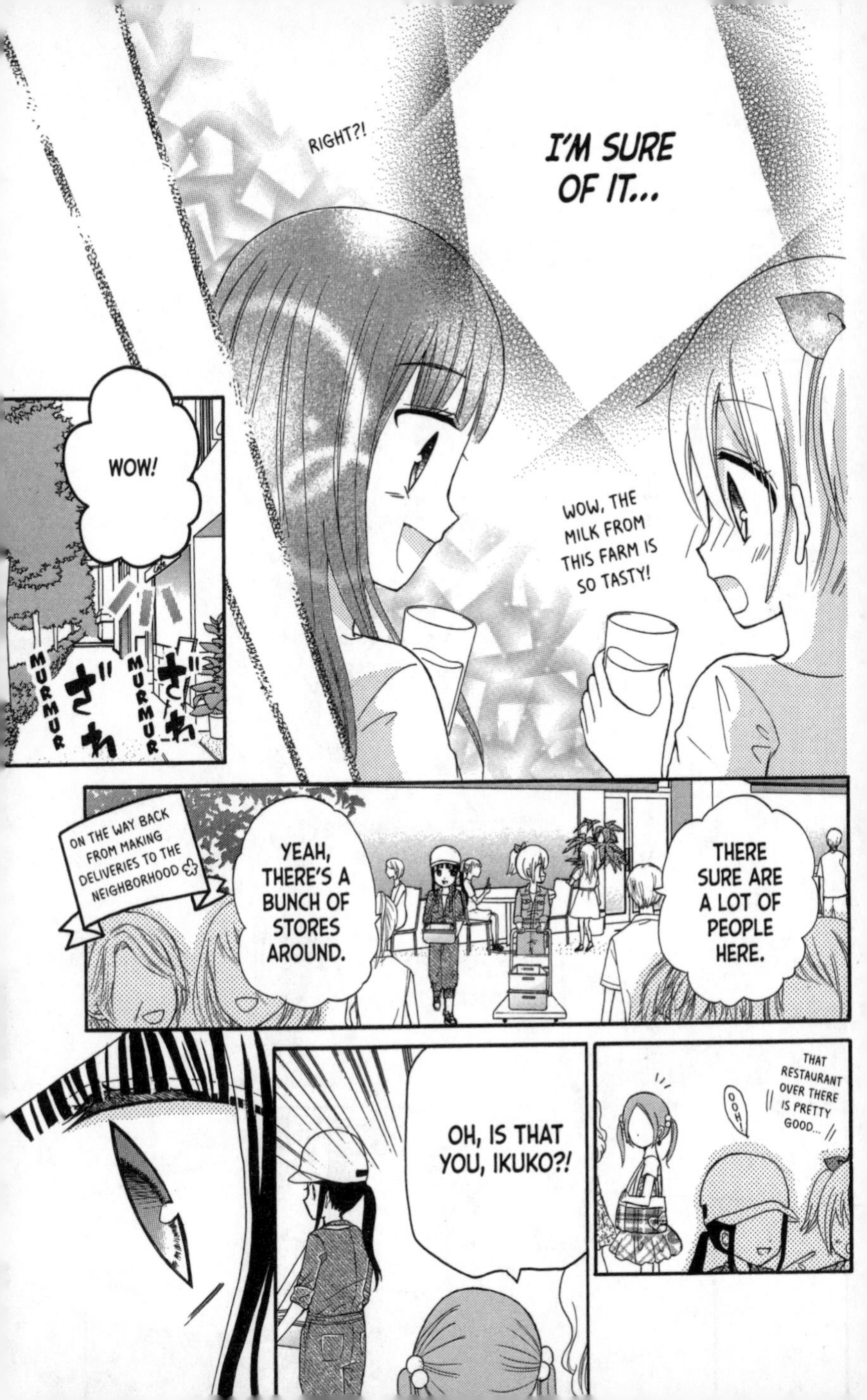
I'M SURE OF IT...
RIGHT?!
WOW, THE MILK FROM THIS FARM IS SO TASTY!
WOW!
ざわ MURMUR
ざわ MURMUR
THERE SURE ARE A LOT OF PEOPLE HERE.
YEAH, THERE'S A BUNCH OF STORES AROUND.
ON THE WAY BACK FROM MAKING DELIVERIES TO THE NEIGHBORHOOD
THAT RESTAURANT OVER THERE IS PRETTY GOOD...
OOH!
OH, IS THAT YOU, IKUKO?!

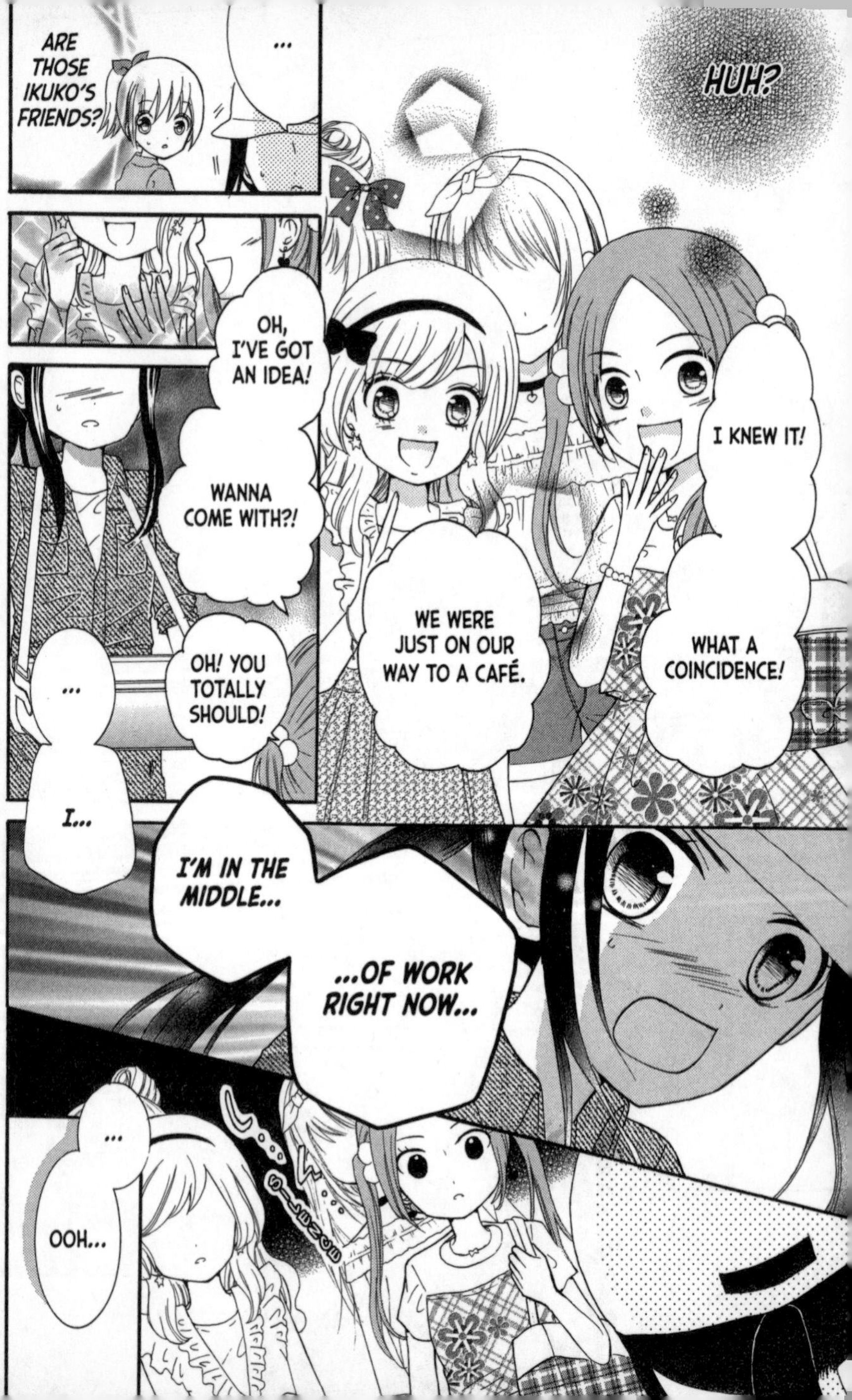
HUH?
I KNEW IT!
WHAT A COINCIDENCE!
WE WERE JUST ON OUR WAY TO A CAFÉ.
ARE THOSE IKUKO'S FRIENDS?
...
OH, I'VE GOT AN IDEA!
WANNA COME WITH?!
OH! YOU TOTALLY SHOULD!
...
I...
I'M IN THE MIDDLE...
...OF WORK RIGHT NOW...
...
OOH...

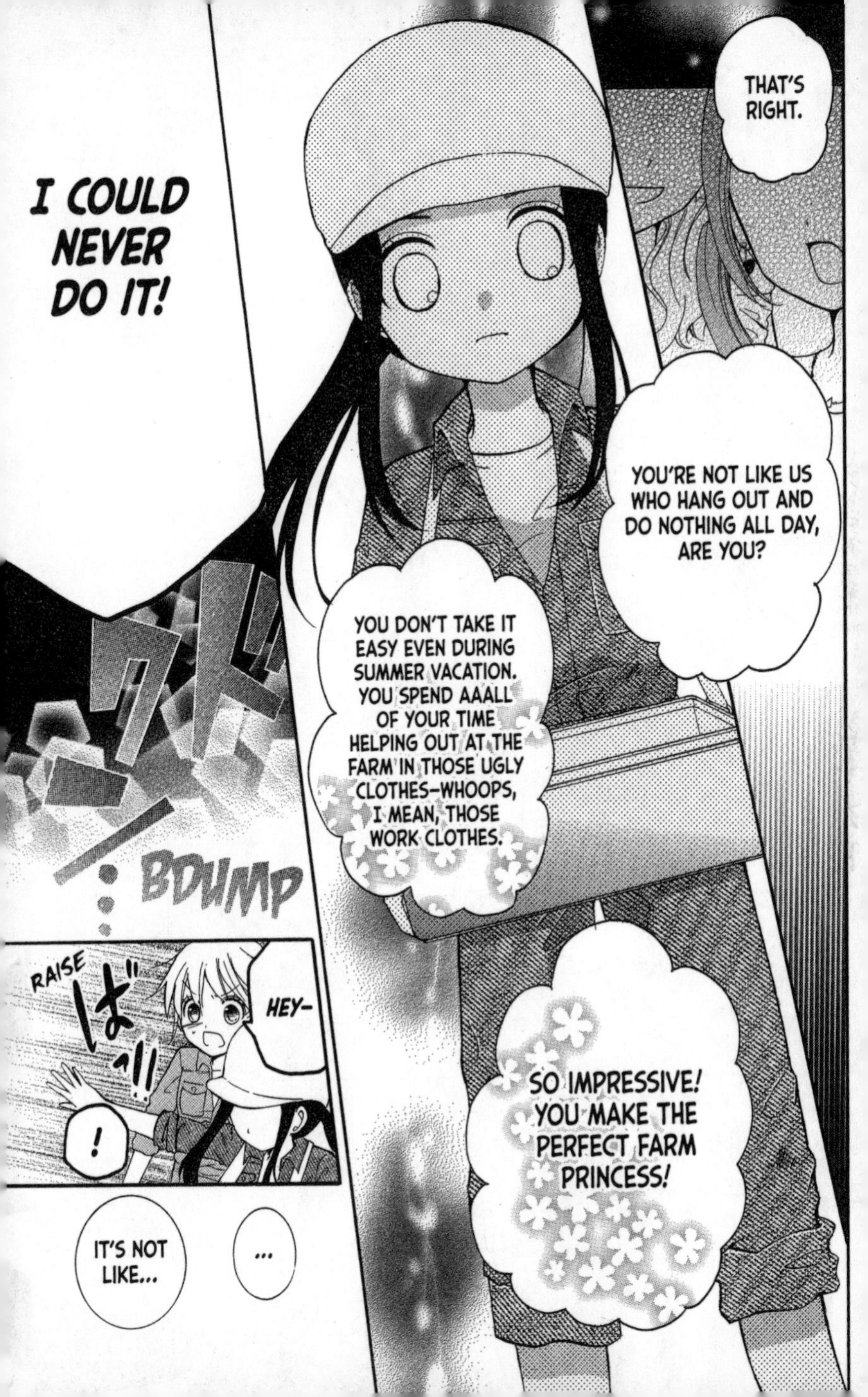
THAT'S RIGHT.
YOU'RE NOT LIKE US WHO HANG OUT AND DO NOTHING ALL DAY, ARE YOU?
YOU DON'T TAKE IT EASY EVEN DURING SUMMER VACATION. YOU SPEND AAALL OF YOUR TIME HELPING OUT AT THE FARM IN THOSE UGLY CLOTHES–WHOOPS, I MEAN, THOSE WORK CLOTHES.
SO IMPRESSIVE! YOU MAKE THE PERFECT FARM PRINCESS!
I COULD NEVER DO IT!
BDUMP
HEY–
RAISE
!
...
IT'S NOT LIKE...

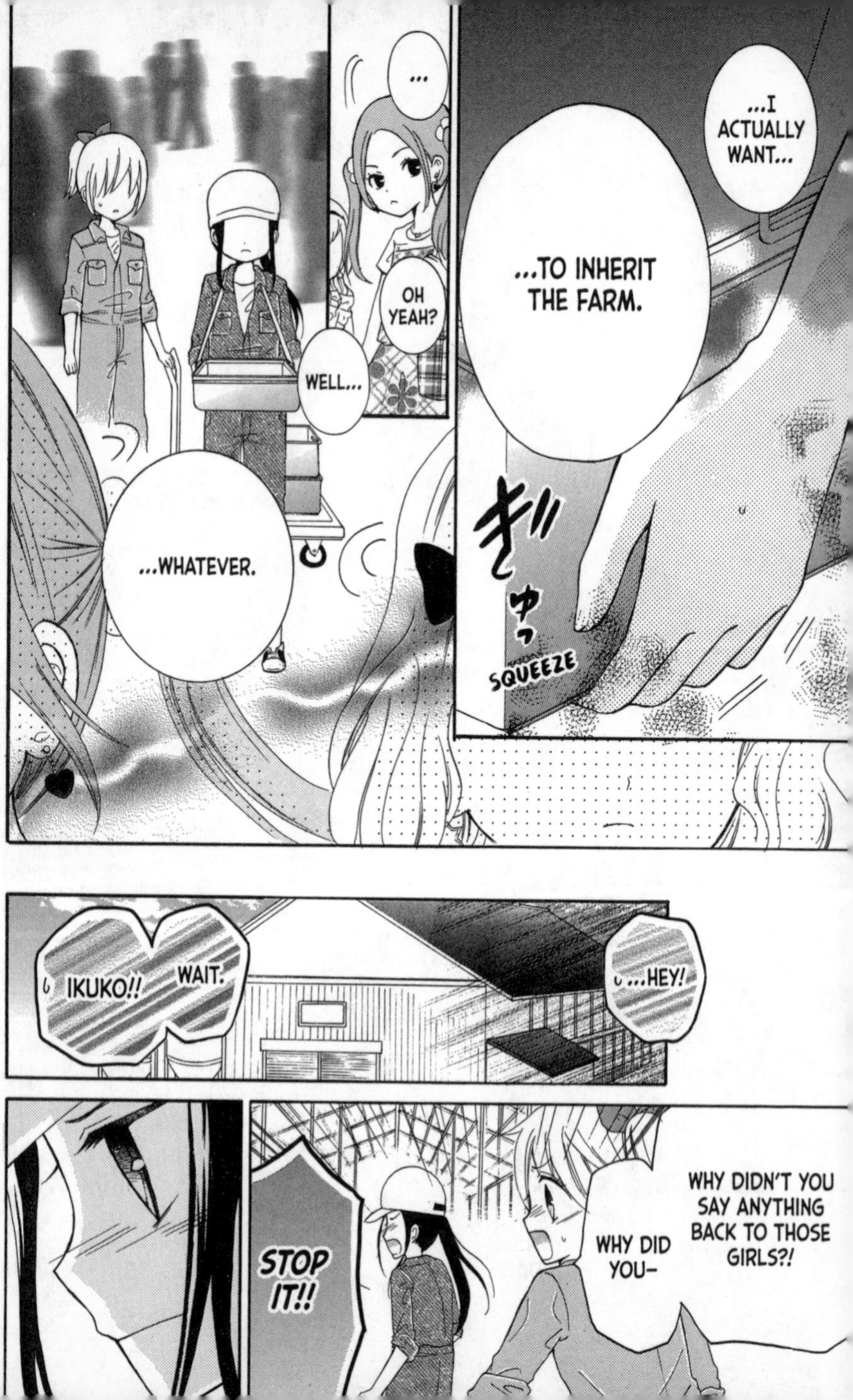
...I ACTUALLY WANT...
...TO INHERIT THE FARM.
SQUEEZE
...
OH YEAH?
WELL...
...WHATEVER.
...HEY!
IKUKO!! WAIT.
WHY DIDN'T YOU SAY ANYTHING BACK TO THOSE GIRLS?!
WHY DID YOU–
STOP IT!!

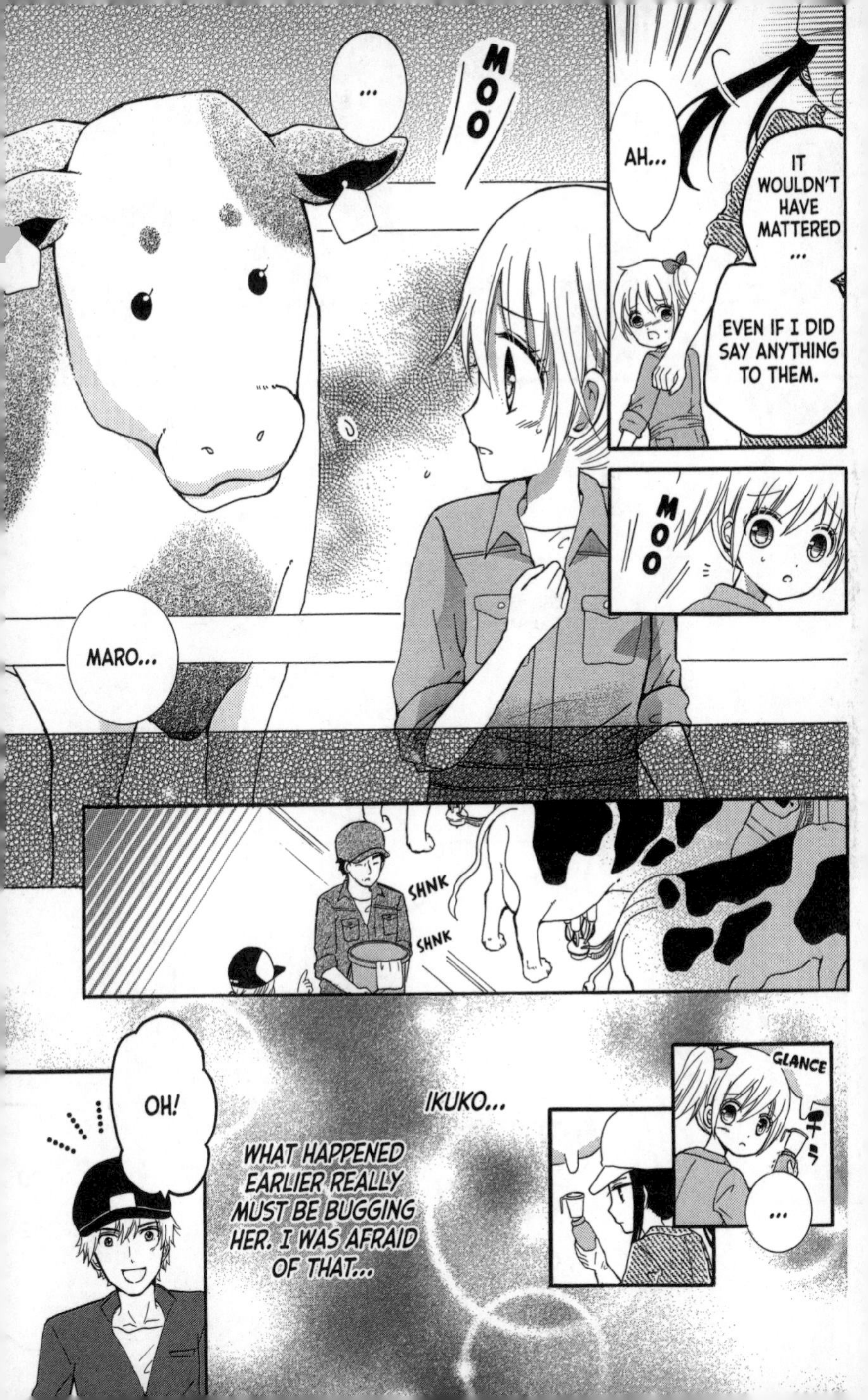
IT WOULDN'T HAVE MATTERED...
EVEN IF I DID SAY ANYTHING TO THEM.
AH...
MOO
MOO
...
MARO...
SHNK
SHNK
GLANCE
...
IKUKO...
WHAT HAPPENED EARLIER REALLY MUST BE BUGGING HER. I WAS AFRAID OF THAT...
OH!

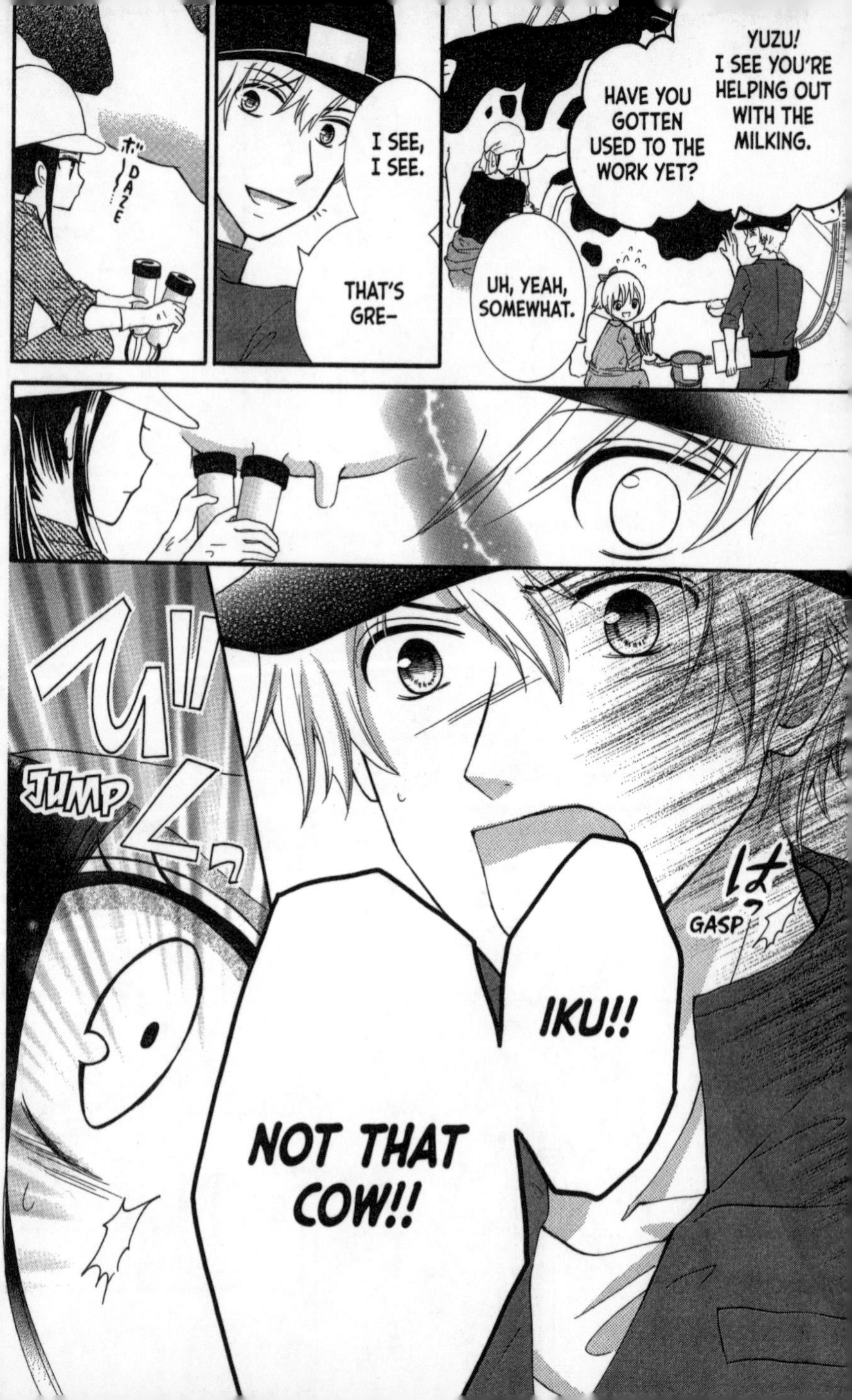
YUZU! I SEE YOU'RE HELPING OUT WITH THE MILKING.
HAVE YOU GOTTEN USED TO THE WORK YET?
UH, YEAH, SOMEWHAT.
I SEE, I SEE.
THAT'S GRE–
DAZE
JUMP
はっ
GASP
IKU!!
NOT THAT COW!!

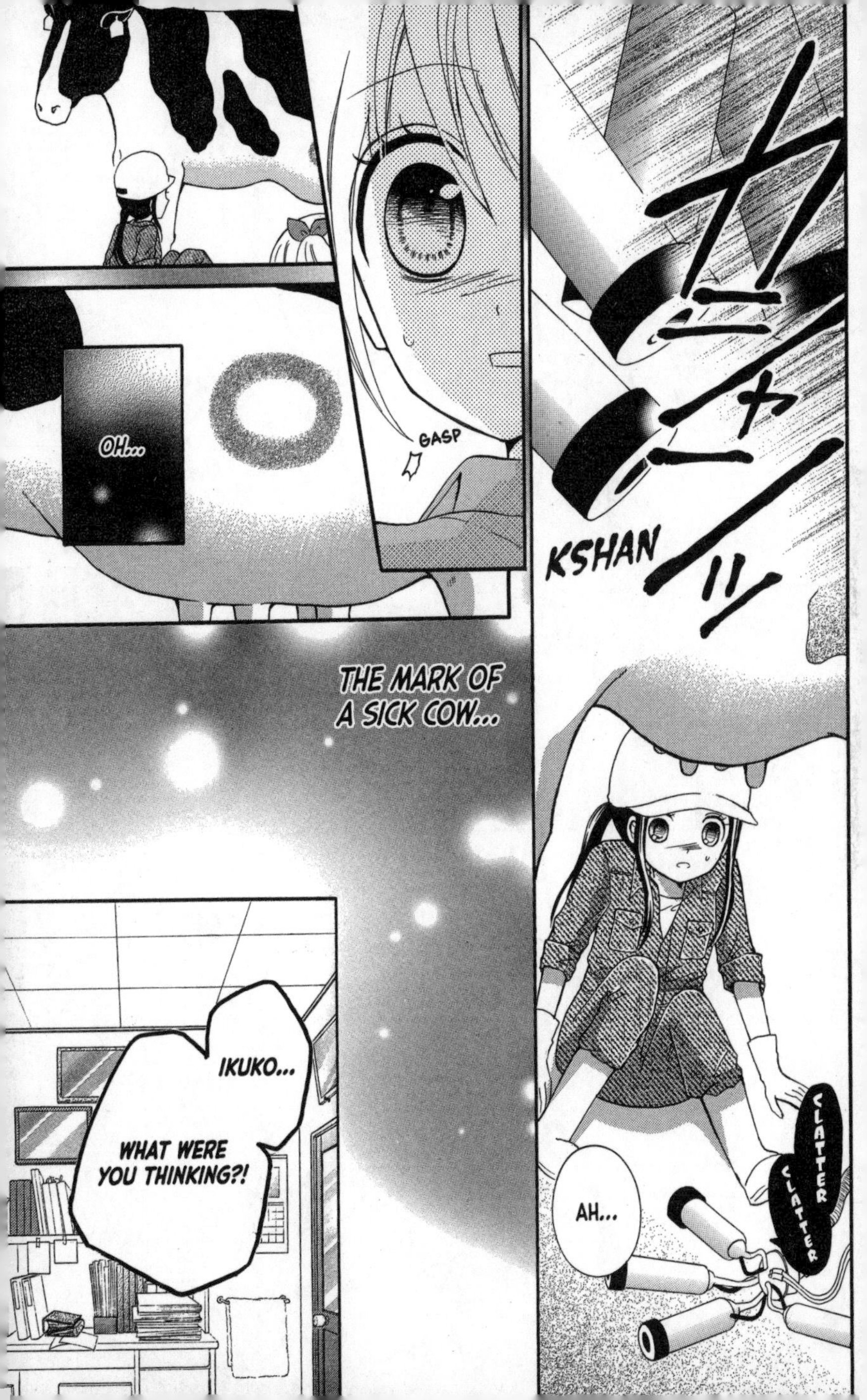
KSHAN
CLATTER CLATTER
AH...
GASP
OH...
THE MARK OF A SICK COW...
IKUKO...
WHAT WERE YOU THINKING?!

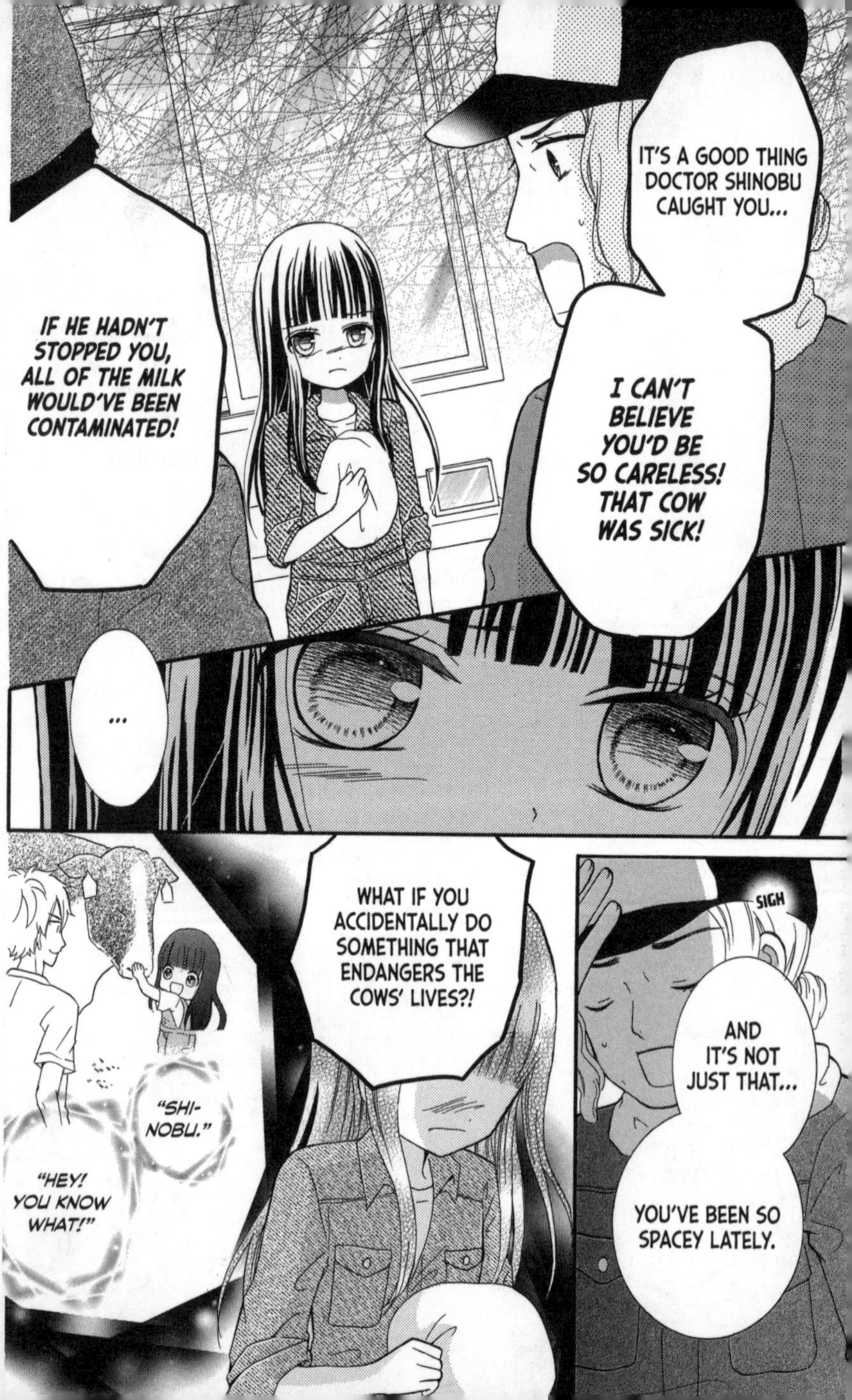
IT'S A GOOD THING DOCTOR SHINOBU CAUGHT YOU...
IF HE HADN'T STOPPED YOU, ALL OF THE MILK WOULD'VE BEEN CONTAMINATED!
I CAN'T BELIEVE YOU'D BE SO CARELESS! THAT COW WAS SICK!
...
SIGH
AND IT'S NOT JUST THAT...
YOU'VE BEEN SO SPACEY LATELY.
WHAT IF YOU ACCIDENTALLY DO SOMETHING THAT ENDANGERS THE COWS' LIVES?!
"SHI-NOBU."
"HEY! YOU KNOW WHAT!"

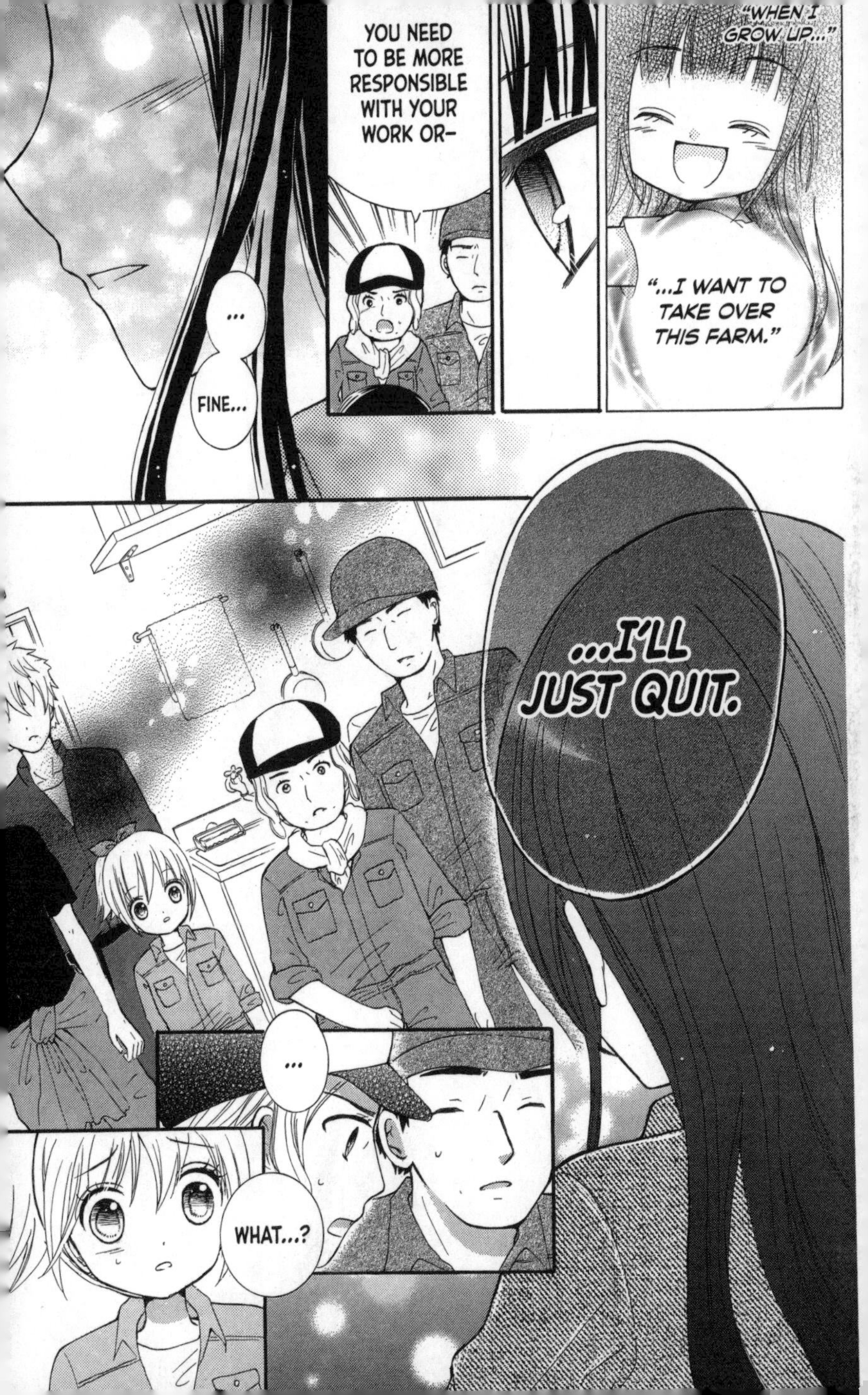
"WHEN I GROW UP..."
"...I WANT TO TAKE OVER THIS FARM."
YOU NEED TO BE MORE RESPONSIBLE WITH YOUR WORK OR–
...
FINE...
...I'LL JUST QUIT.
...
WHAT...?

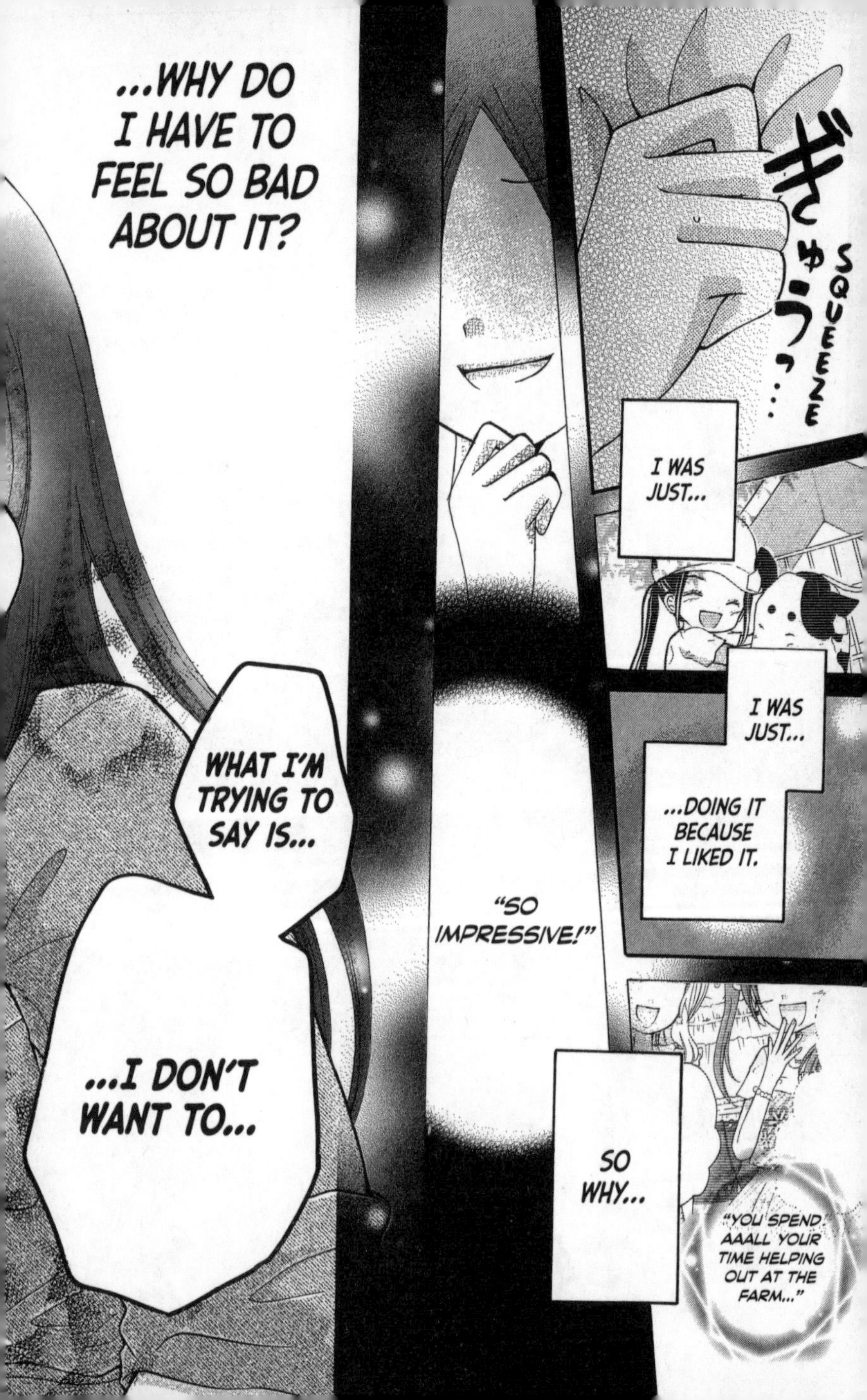ぎゅうっ…
SQUEEZE
I WAS JUST...
I WAS JUST...
...DOING IT BECAUSE I LIKED IT.
"YOU SPEND AAALL YOUR TIME HELPING OUT AT THE FARM..."
SO WHY...
"SO IMPRESSIVE!"
...WHY DO I HAVE TO FEEL SO BAD ABOUT IT?
WHAT I'M TRYING TO SAY IS...
...I DON'T WANT TO...

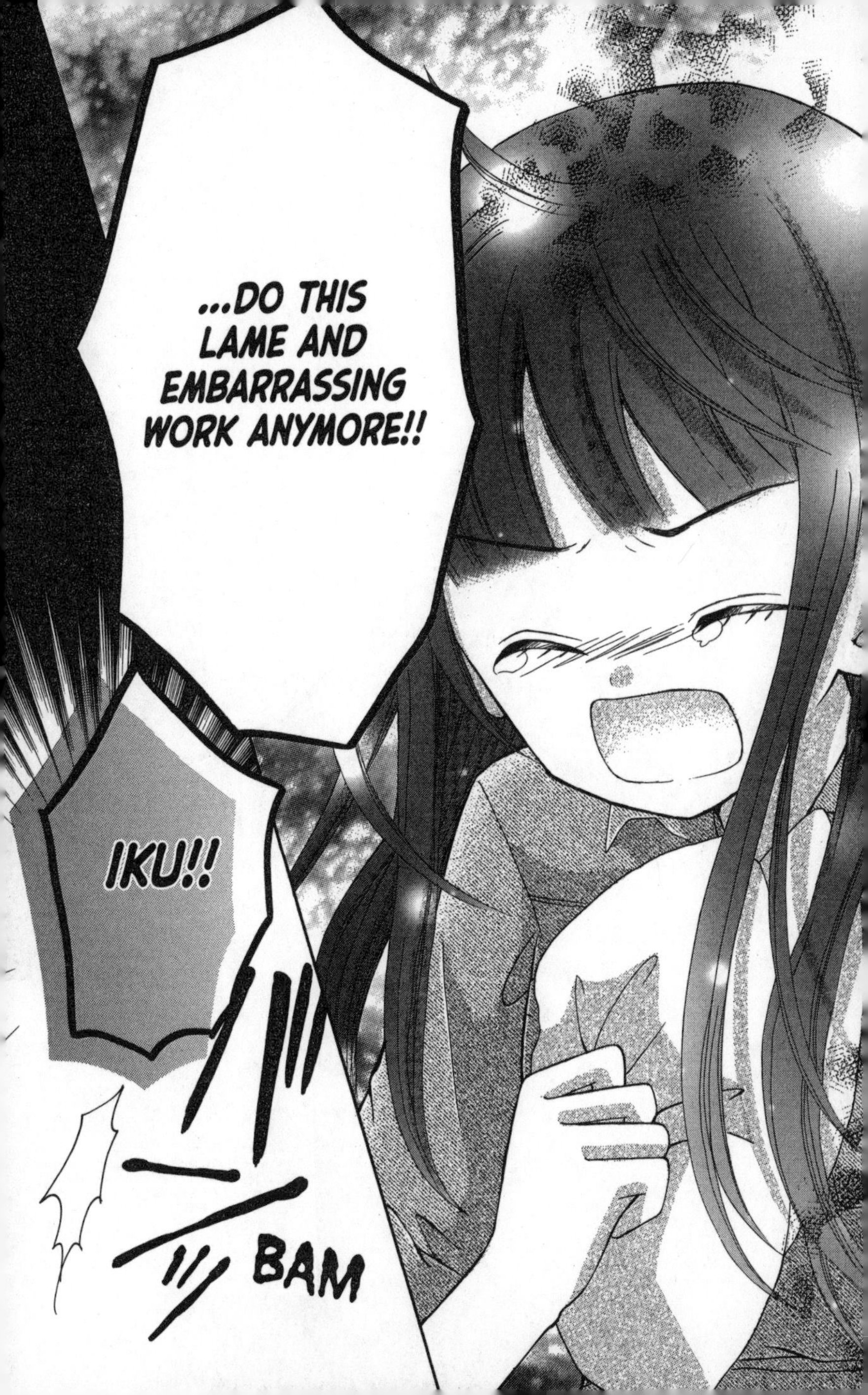
...DO THIS LAME AND EMBARRASSING WORK ANYMORE!!
IKU!!
BAM

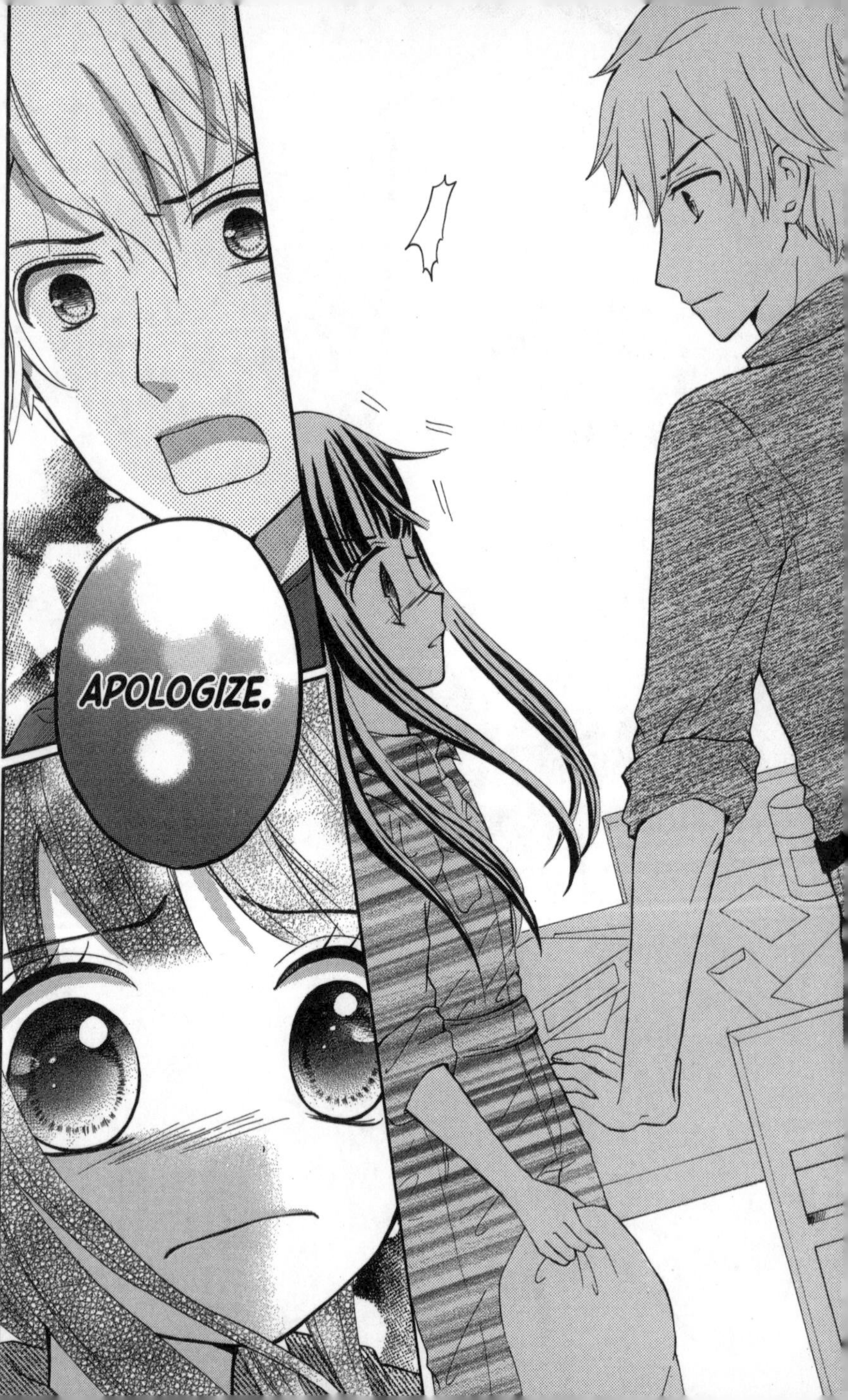
APOLOGIZE.

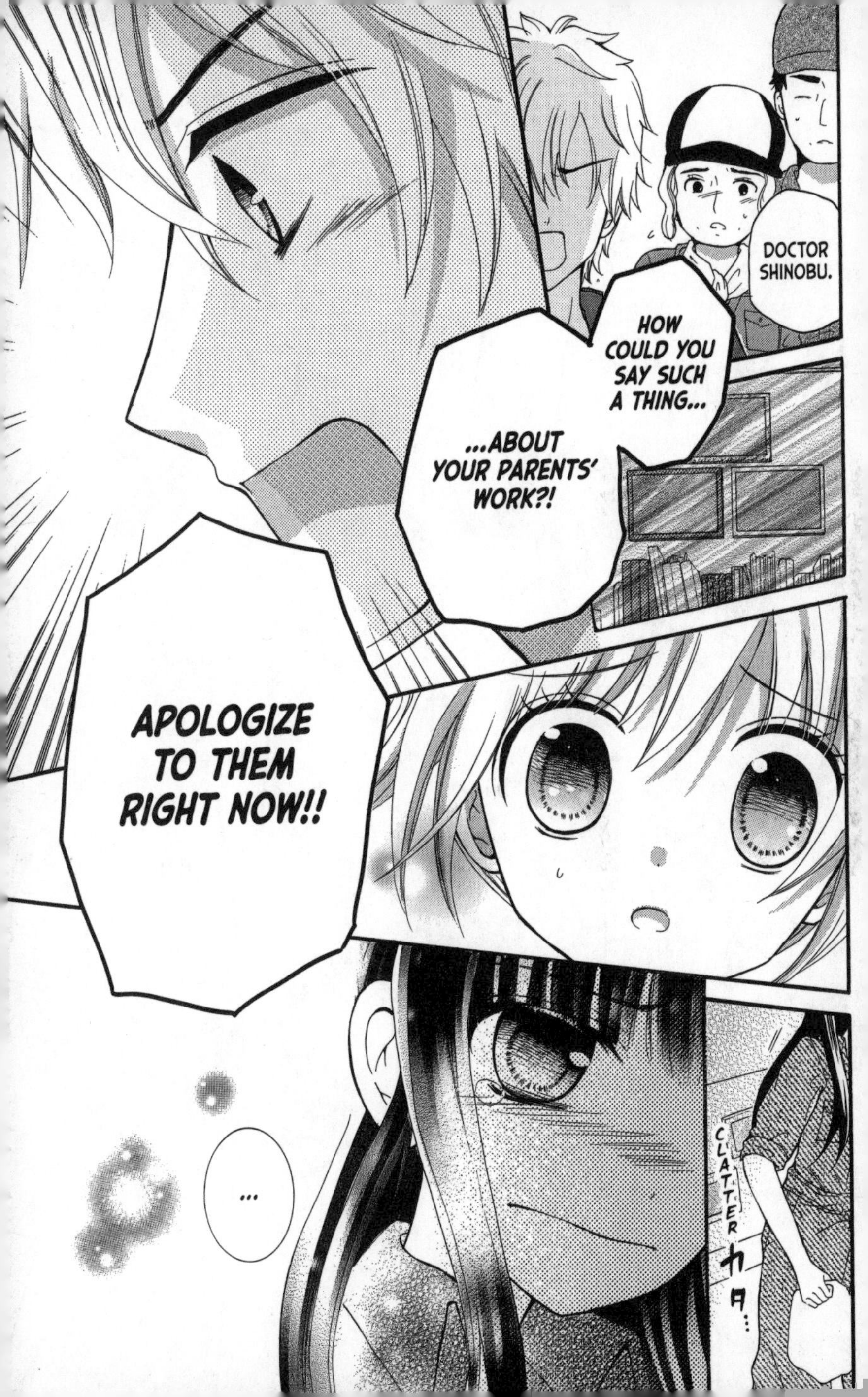
DOCTOR SHINOBU.
HOW COULD YOU SAY SUCH A THING...
...ABOUT YOUR PARENTS' WORK?!
APOLOGIZE TO THEM RIGHT NOW!!
CLATTER カタ...
...

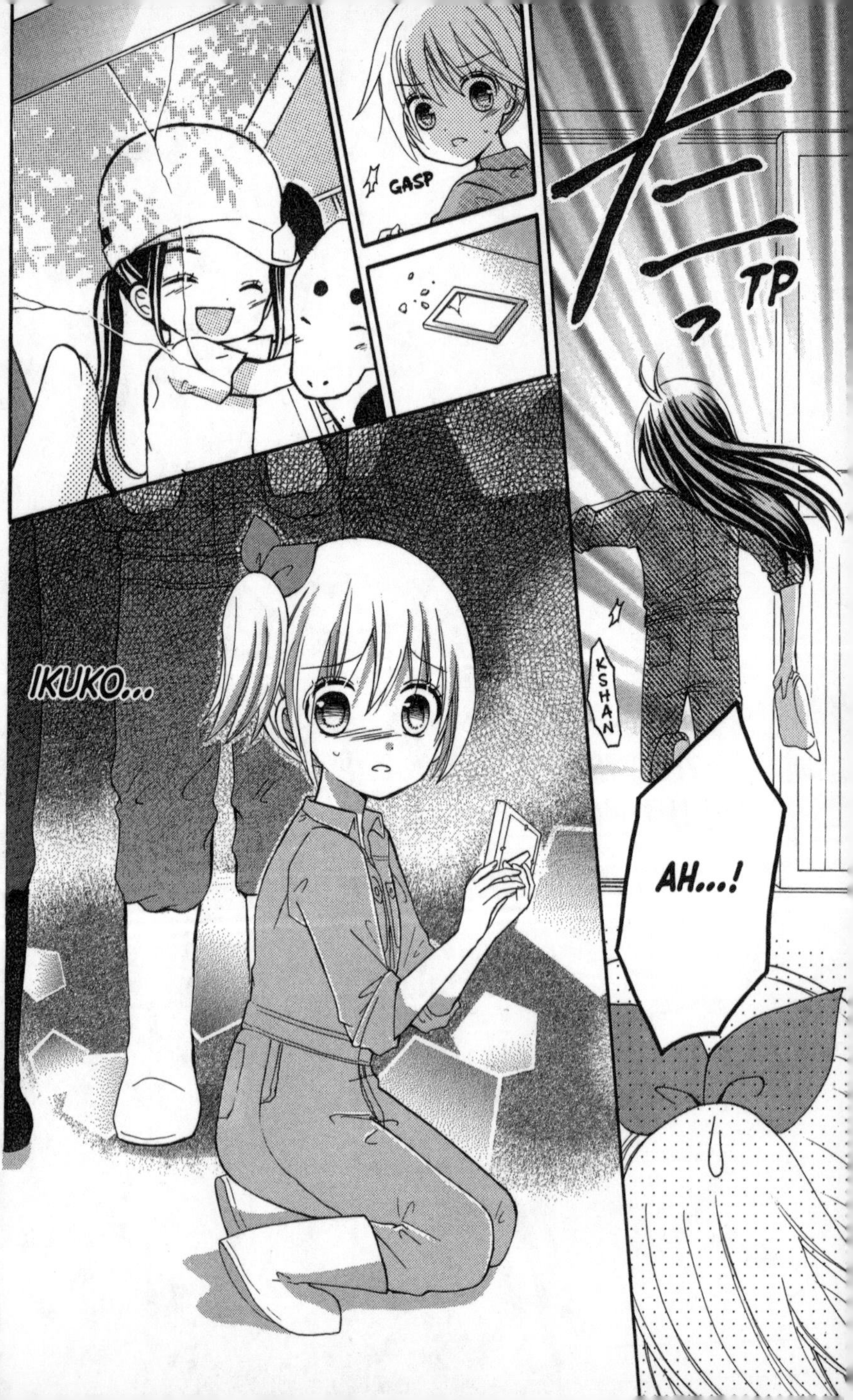
TP
KSHAN
AH...!
GASP
IKUKO...

To be
continued in
volume 7.

WOOF *

BEHIND THE SCENES

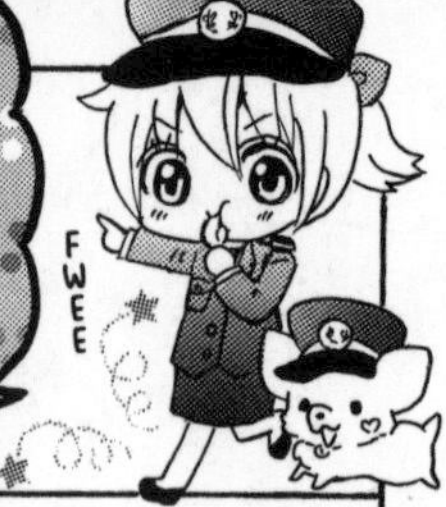
FWEE

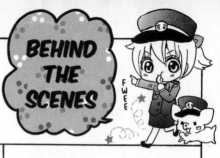

THANK YOU FOR READING TO THE END!! I DREW A BONUS MANGA THAT STARTS ON THE NEXT PAGE, SO PLEASE READ IT! ←

CHAPTER 21

<ALAN THE DOG WHO WON'T BOND PART 2>

EVER SINCE I WROTE THE STORY ABOUT PET LOSS IN VOLUME 1, I'VE WANTED TO DRAW A STORY ABOUT WHAT IT WAS LIKE WHEN PETS LOSE THEIR BELOVED OWNERS. WITH THIS STORY, THAT FINALLY CAME TRUE. I REALLY LIKE THE CHAPTER TITLE PAGE WITH THE BEACH.

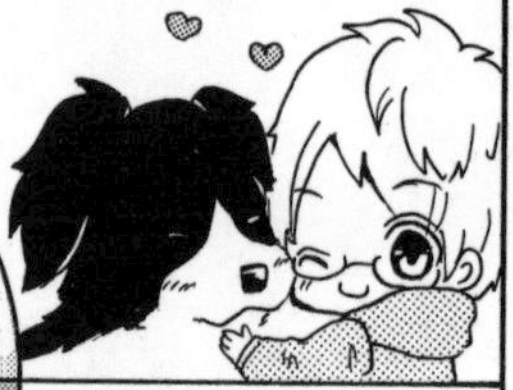

CHAPTER 22

<HOKUTO THE DOG WHO WANTS TO BE A POLICE DOG>

I USED TO HAVE THIS IMAGE OF POLICE DOGS BEING RIGID AND STERN LIKE DOBERMANS. THEN ONE DAY ON TV, I HAPPENED TO CATCH A SEGMENT ABOUT HOW SMALL, CUTE BREEDS ARE BECOMING POLICE DOGS IN JAPAN, TOO. I MENTIONED IT TO MY EDITOR, AND THUS THE TINY DUO OF WAKABA AND HOKUTO WERE BORN.

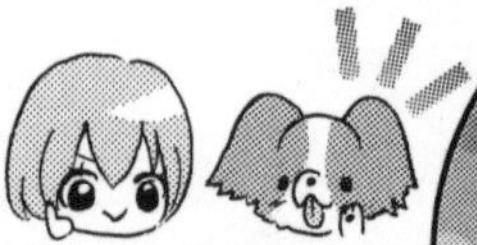

CHAPTER 23

<CHII THE HAMSTER WHO CAN TELL TWINS APART>

I'VE HAD THE IDEA FOR PET OWNERS WHO WERE TWINS SINCE I FIRST STARTED DRAWING THIS MANGA. ORIGINALLY, I WAS THINKING OF THEIR PET AS A DOG OR A CAT, BUT SOMETHING DIDN'T FEEL RIGHT. THEN, WHEN A FRIEND WHO WAS HELPING ME WITH MY DRAWING MENTIONED THAT SHE ONCE FOUND A STRAY HAMSTER IN HER APARTMENT BUILDING, A LIGHTBULB WENT OFF IN MY HEAD. THAT WOUND UP BEING THE INSPIRATION BEHIND THIS STORY.

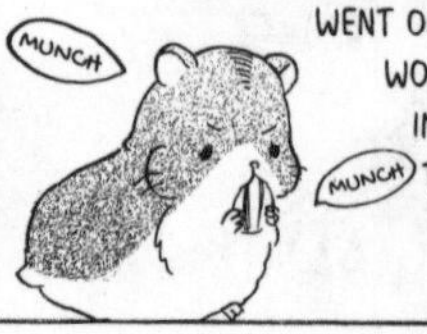
MUNCH
MUNCH

CHAPTER 24

<MARO THE LOVEABLE COW PART 1>

THIS MANGA USUALLY TAKES PLACE AT THE BOW MEOW ANIMAL HOSPITAL, BUT THIS TIME, THE STORY IS SET AT A FARM, OF ALL PLACES!!

IT'S YUZU'S FIRST TIME SEEING COWS UP CLOSE. AS THIS WAS ALSO THE FIRST TIME I HAD TO DRAW COWS, MY DESK WAS BURIED IN REFERENCE PHOTOGRAPHS OF THEM. (LOL) THIS STORY WILL CONTINUE IN VOLUME 7, SO I HOPE TO SEE YOU THERE!!

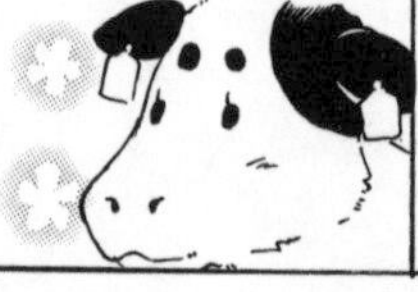

• YUZU'S MOM'S THOUGHTS •

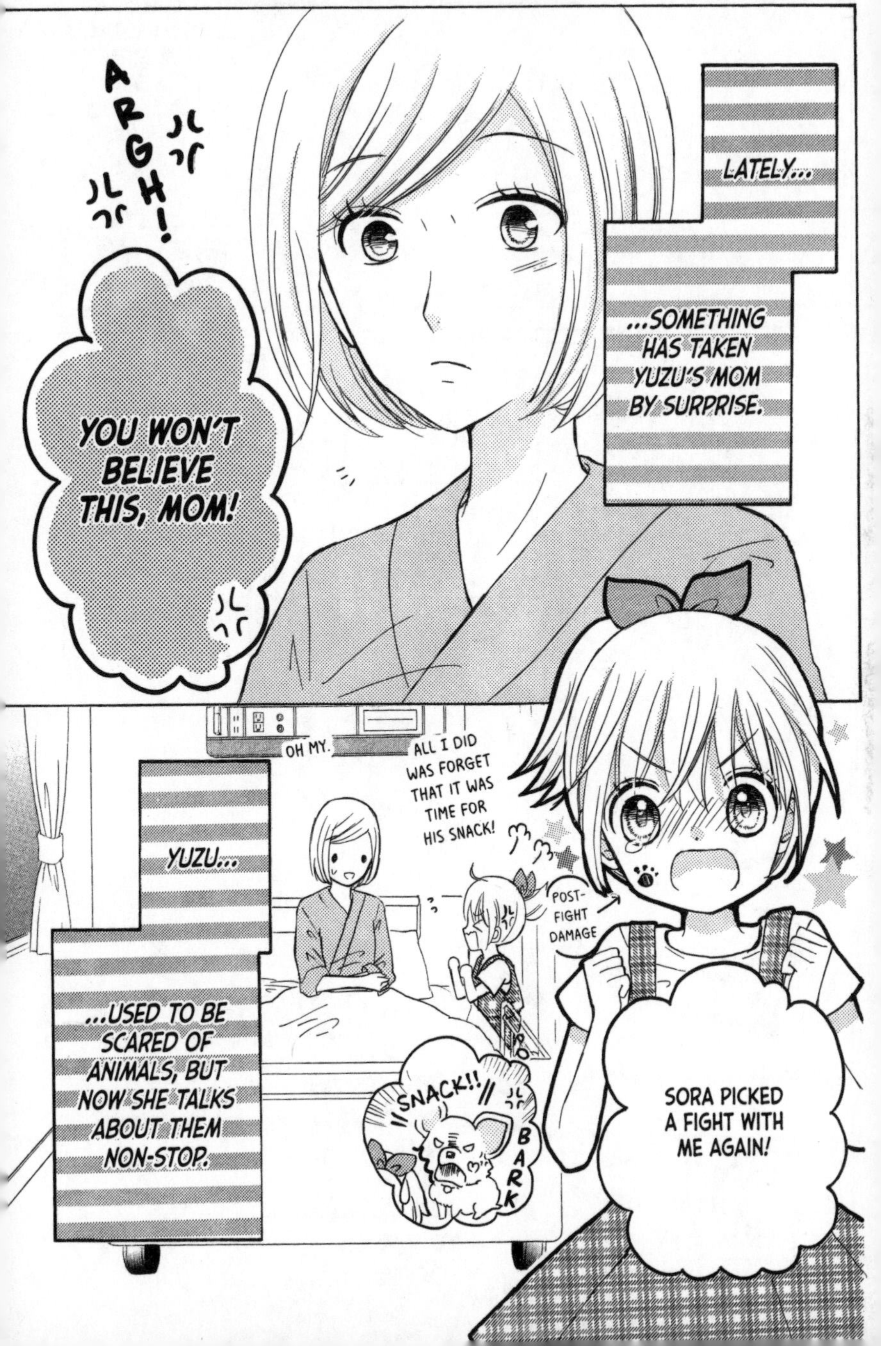

LATELY...
...SOMETHING HAS TAKEN YUZU'S MOM BY SURPRISE.
ARGH!
YOU WON'T BELIEVE THIS, MOM!
SORA PICKED A FIGHT WITH ME AGAIN!
POST-FIGHT DAMAGE
ALL I DID WAS FORGET THAT IT WAS TIME FOR HIS SNACK!
OH MY.
SNACK!!
BARK
YUZU...
...USED TO BE SCARED OF ANIMALS, BUT NOW SHE TALKS ABOUT THEM NON-STOP.

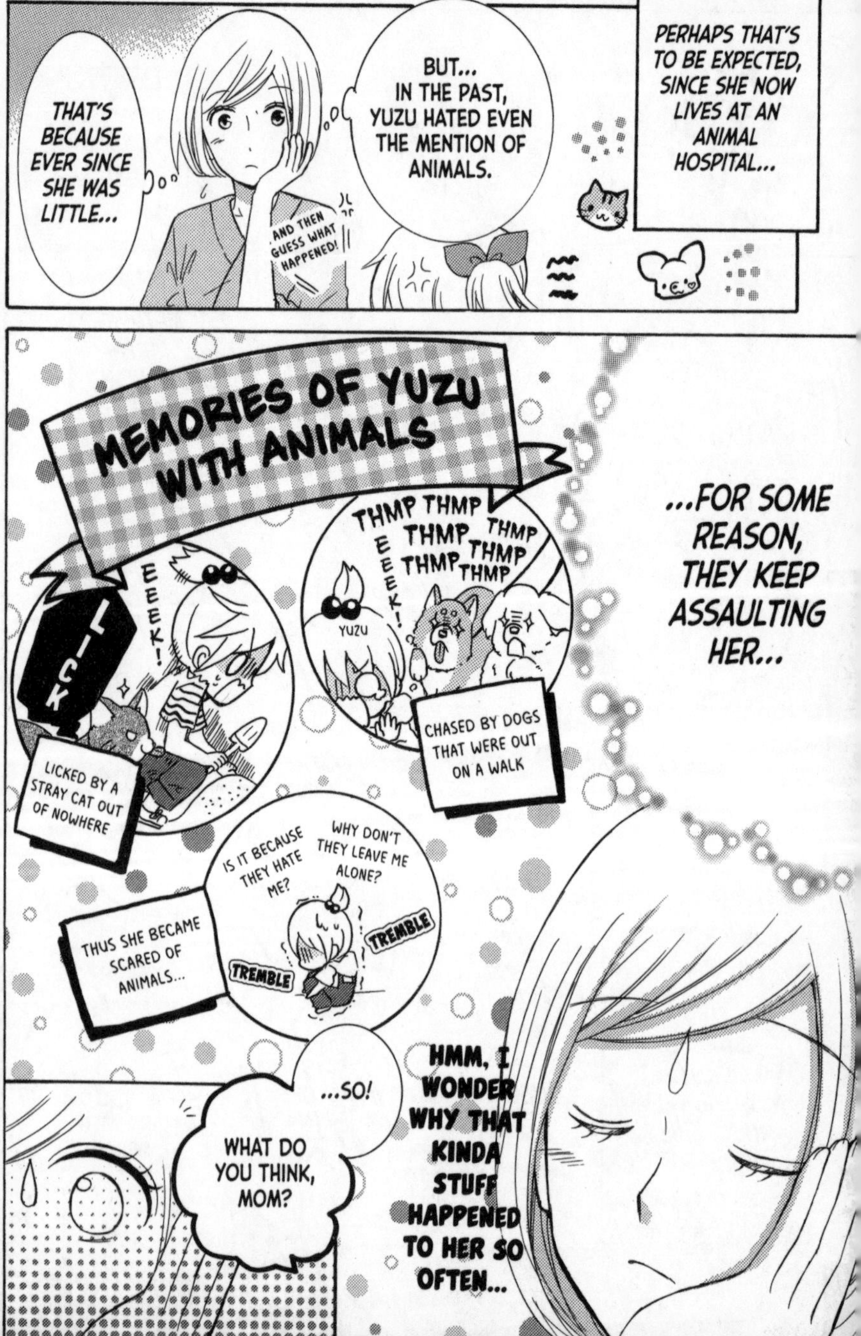
PERHAPS THAT'S TO BE EXPECTED, SINCE SHE NOW LIVES AT AN ANIMAL HOSPITAL...
BUT... IN THE PAST, YUZU HATED EVEN THE MENTION OF ANIMALS.
AND THEN GUESS WHAT HAPPENED!
THAT'S BECAUSE EVER SINCE SHE WAS LITTLE...
...FOR SOME REASON, THEY KEEP ASSAULTING HER...
MEMORIES OF YUZU WITH ANIMALS
THMP THMP THMP THMP THMP THMP THMP THMP
EEEEK!
YUZU
CHASED BY DOGS THAT WERE OUT ON A WALK
EEEK!
LICK
LICKED BY A STRAY CAT OUT OF NOWHERE
WHY DON'T THEY LEAVE ME ALONE?
IS IT BECAUSE THEY HATE ME?
TREMBLE
TREMBLE
THUS SHE BECAME SCARED OF ANIMALS...
HMM, I WONDER WHY THAT KINDA STUFF HAPPENED TO HER SO OFTEN...
...SO!
WHAT DO YOU THINK, MOM?

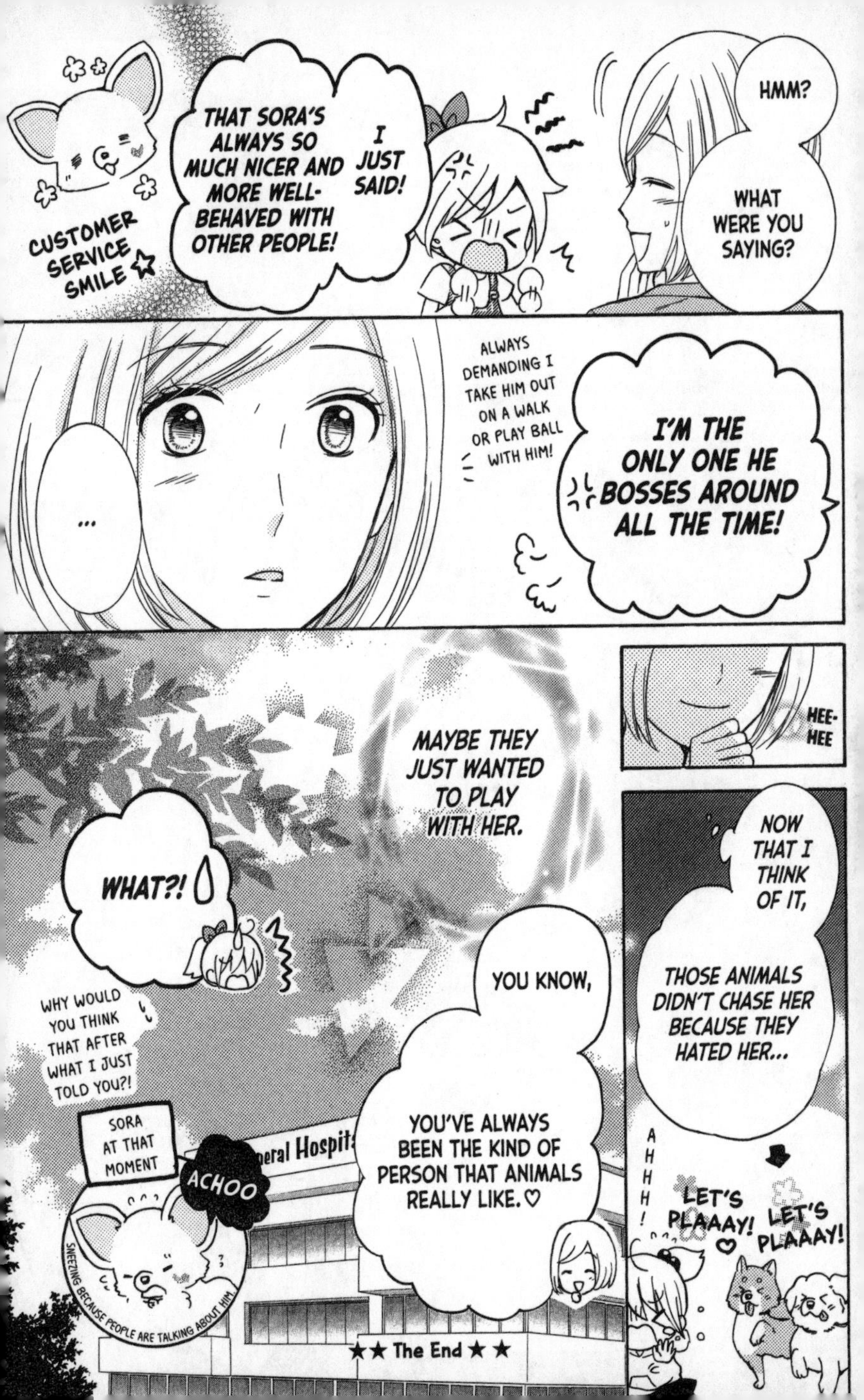

HMM?
WHAT WERE YOU SAYING?
I JUST SAID!
THAT SORA'S ALWAYS SO MUCH NICER AND MORE WELL-BEHAVED WITH OTHER PEOPLE!
CUSTOMER SERVICE SMILE ☆
I'M THE ONLY ONE HE BOSSES AROUND ALL THE TIME!
ALWAYS DEMANDING I TAKE HIM OUT ON A WALK OR PLAY BALL WITH HIM!
...
HEE-HEE
NOW THAT I THINK OF IT,
THOSE ANIMALS DIDN'T CHASE HER BECAUSE THEY HATED HER...
AHHHH!
LET'S PLAAAY!
LET'S PLAAAY!
MAYBE THEY JUST WANTED TO PLAY WITH HER.
YOU KNOW,
YOU'VE ALWAYS BEEN THE KIND OF PERSON THAT ANIMALS REALLY LIKE. ♡
WHAT?!
WHY WOULD YOU THINK THAT AFTER WHAT I JUST TOLD YOU?!
SORA AT THAT MOMENT
ACHOO
SNEEZING BECAUSE PEOPLE ARE TALKING ABOUT HIM.
★★ The End ★★

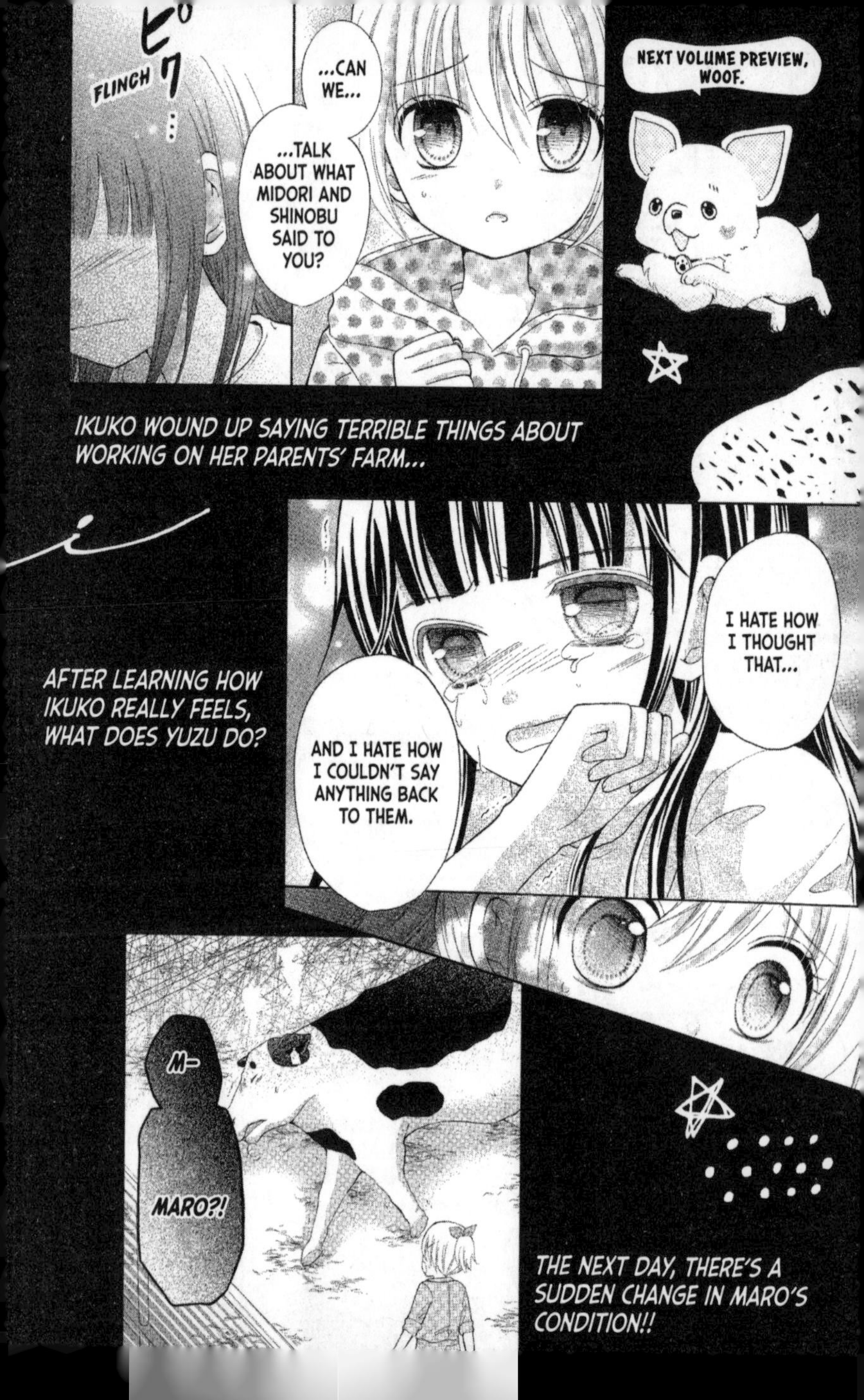
NEXT VOLUME PREVIEW, WOOF.
FLINCH
...CAN WE...
...TALK ABOUT WHAT MIDORI AND SHINOBU SAID TO YOU?
IKUKO WOUND UP SAYING TERRIBLE THINGS ABOUT WORKING ON HER PARENTS' FARM...
I HATE HOW I THOUGHT THAT...
AND I HATE HOW I COULDN'T SAY ANYTHING BACK TO THEM.
AFTER LEARNING HOW IKUKO REALLY FEELS, WHAT DOES YUZU DO?
THE NEXT DAY, THERE'S A SUDDEN CHANGE IN MARO'S CONDITION!!
M–
MARO?!

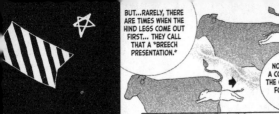

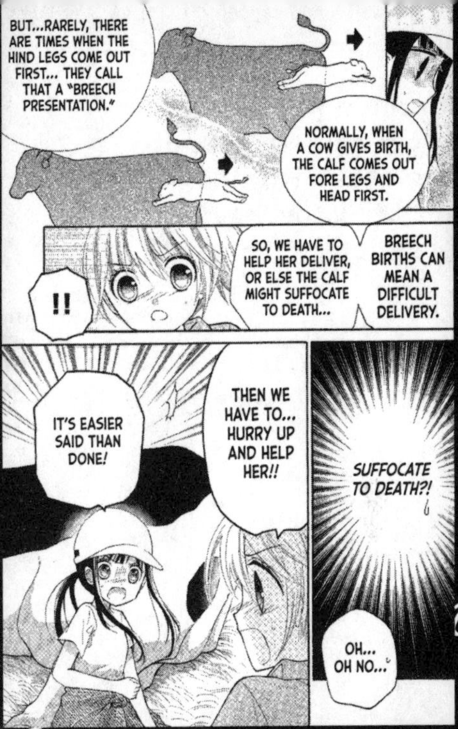

NORMALLY, WHEN A COW GIVES BIRTH, THE CALF COMES OUT FORE LEGS AND HEAD FIRST.
BUT...RARELY, THERE ARE TIMES WHEN THE HIND LEGS COME OUT FIRST... THEY CALL THAT A "BREECH PRESENTATION."
BREECH BIRTHS CAN MEAN A DIFFICULT DELIVERY.
SO, WE HAVE TO HELP HER DELIVER, OR ELSE THE CALF MIGHT SUFFOCATE TO DEATH...
!!
SUFFOCATE TO DEATH?!
OH... OH NO...
THEN WE HAVE TO... HURRY UP AND HELP HER!!
IT'S EASIER SAID THAN DONE!

THOUGH THE SITUATION HAS GOTTEN DIRE, YUZU AND IKUKO ARE THE ONLY ONES ON THE FARM...!

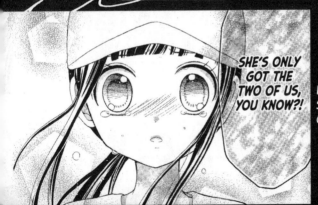

SHE'S ONLY GOT THE TWO OF US, YOU KNOW?!

WILL THEY BE ABLE TO SAVE MARO AND HER CALF?!

YUZU THE PET VET 7

COMING SOON!!

A Kodansha Comics Trade Paperback Original
Yuzu the Pet Vet 6 copyright © 2018 Mingo Ito © 2018 NIPPON COLUMBIA CO., LTD. English translation copyright © 2021 Mingo Ito © NIPPON COLUMBIA CO., LTD.

Published in the United States by Kodansha Comics, an imprint of Kodansha USA Publishing, LLC, New York.

Publication rights for this English edition arranged through Kodansha Ltd., Tokyo.

First published in Japan in 2018 by Kodansha Ltd., Tokyo as Yuzu no Doubutsu Karute ~Kochira Wan Nyan Doubutsu Byouin~, volume 6.

ISBN 978-1-64651-082-5

Original cover design by Tomoko Kobayashi

Printed in the United States of America.

www.kodansha.us

9 8 7 6 5 4 3 2 1
Translation: Julie Goniwich
Lettering: David Yoo
Editing: Ryan Holmberg
Kodansha Comics edition cover design by Matthew Akuginow

Publisher: Kiichiro Sugawara

Director of publishing services: Ben Applegate
Associate director of operations: Stephen Pakula
Publishing services associated managing editor: Madison Salters
Production managers: Emi Lotto, Angela Zurlo
Logo and character art ©Kodansha USA Publishing, LLC

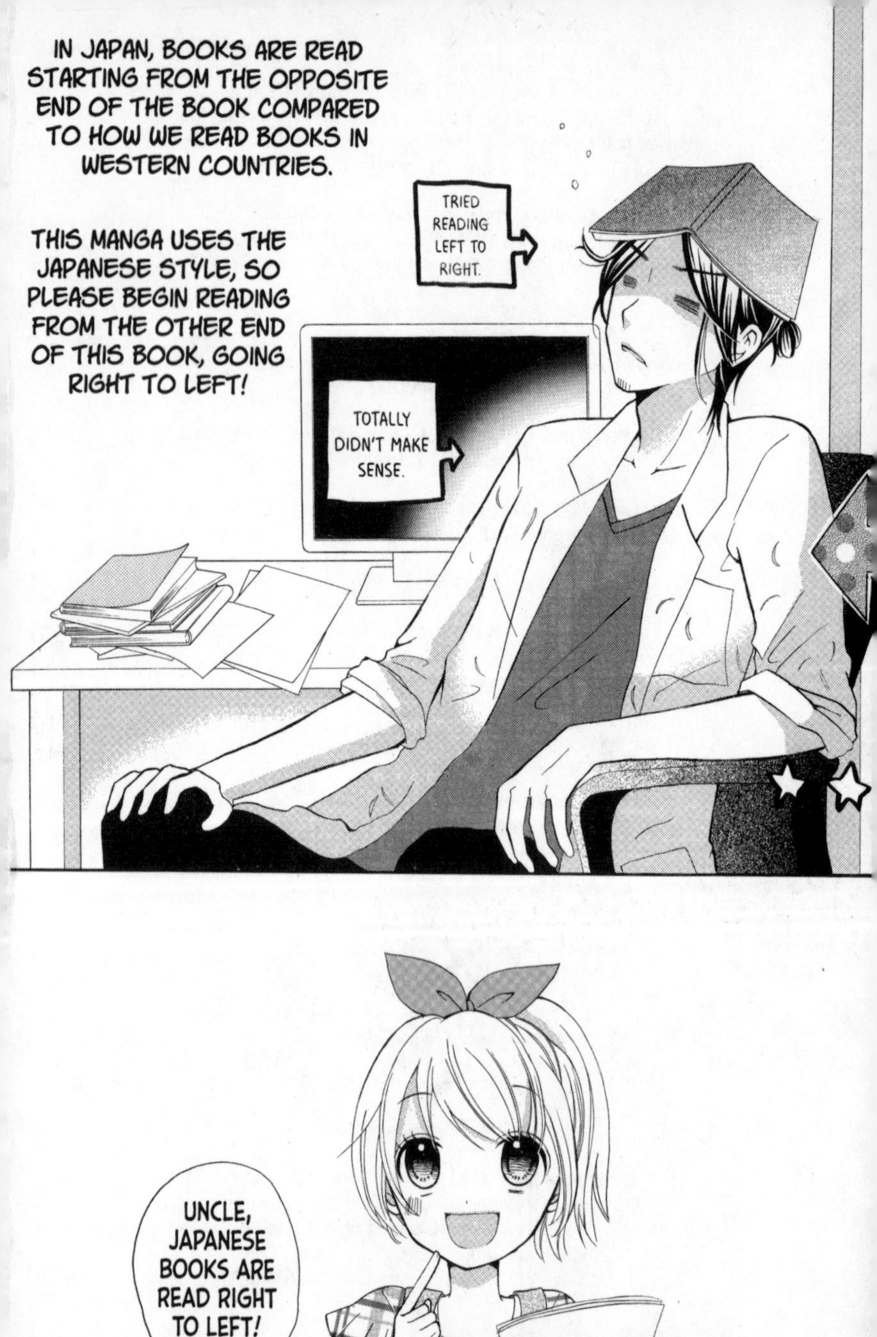
IN JAPAN, BOOKS ARE READ STARTING FROM THE OPPOSITE END OF THE BOOK COMPARED TO HOW WE READ BOOKS IN WESTERN COUNTRIES.
THIS MANGA USES THE JAPANESE STYLE, SO PLEASE BEGIN READING FROM THE OTHER END OF THIS BOOK, GOING RIGHT TO LEFT!
TRIED READING LEFT TO RIGHT.
TOTALLY DIDN'T MAKE SENSE.
UNCLE, JAPANESE BOOKS ARE READ RIGHT TO LEFT!